WOMEN, WORK, AND LIFE CYCLE IN
A MEDIEVAL ECONOMY

Women, Work, and Life Cycle in a Medieval Economy

Women in York and Yorkshire
c.1300–1520

P. J. P. GOLDBERG

CLARENDON PRESS · OXFORD

Oxford University Press, Great Clarendon Street, Oxford OX2 6DP

Oxford New York
Athens Auckland Bangkok Bogota Bombay
Buenos Aires Calcutta Cape Town Dar es Salaam
Delhi Florence Hong Kong Istanbul Karachi
Kuala Lumpur Madras Madrid Melbourne
Mexico City Nairobi Paris Singapore
Taipei Tokyo Toronto
and associated companies in
Berlin Ibadan

Oxford is a trade mark of Oxford University Press

First published by Oxford University Press 1992
Special edition for Sandpiper Books Ltd, 1996

British Library Cataloguing in Publication Data
Goldberg, P. J. P., 1958-
Women, work, and life cycle in a medieval economy : women in York
and Yorkshire c.1300-1520 / P. J. P. Goldberg.
p. cm.
Includes bibliographical references and index.
1. Women—England—York—Economic conditions. 2. Women—England-
-Yorkshire—Economic conditions. 3. Marriage—England—York-
-History. 4. Marriage—England—Yorkshire—History. 5. Women-
-History—Middle Ages. 500-1500. 6. England—Economic conditions-
-Medieval period, 1066-1485. 7. England—Social conditions-
-Medieval period, 1066-1485. I. Title.
HQ1600.Y67G65 1992
305.42'094281'0902—dc20 92-12228

ISBN 0-19-820154-0

Printed in Great Britain by
Bookcraft Ltd.,
Midsomer Norton, Somerset

For Patricia

Acknowledgements

I am very grateful for the interest a number of people have shown in my work, for their often valuable advice and comments, and their hospitality. I wish to mention a few by name. Richard Smith, who supervised much of the thesis from which this book derives, has always encouraged me and I have benefited greatly from his guidance and advice. Barrie Dobson has been most supportive and I have greatly valued his help since he supervised my MA dissertation. Sandra Raban, my undergraduate Director of Studies, has shown me like kindness during my time in Cambridge, and I wish to thank her for the excellence of her teaching and the wisdom of her advice. Peter Biller has been a good friend and I value his understanding and discussion of a variety of issues.

I am grateful to the Cambridge Group for the History of Population and Social Structure, and to the Trustees of the Ellen McArthur Fund for helping to fund my time as a research student. I am especially grateful to the Department of History at the University of Keele for appointing me as a lecturer during the first part of 1985–6 and making me so welcome there. I wish to thank the Master and Fellows of Clare College for supporting me in a research fellowship for two years. Lastly, I owe a debt to my present colleagues in the Department of History at the University of York for giving me the opportunity to come and work in this most wonderful of cities. Without this support it is doubtful if my thesis or this book could have been achieved.

I wish to note my sincere gratitude to Judith Bennett, Claire Cross, John Henderson, Rosemary Horrox, Maryanne Kowaleski, Peter Laslett, Marjorie McIntosh, Richard Helmholz, Dorothy Owen, Sarah Rees Jones, Zvi Razi, Felicity Riddy, Peter Rycraft, and Roger Schofield for their interest and advice. I wish to thank my friends from York and Cambridge who have shown me kindness and hospitality, and have helped keep me cheerful through the past few years of research and writing. I wish finally to thank my parents for their encouragement and support at all time. For all errors and inaccuracies I am solely responsible.

P.J.P.G.

Department of History, University of York
Feast of St Sytha, 1990

Contents

List of Figures

List of Maps

List of Tables

List of Abbreviations

Annales: ESC	*Annales: Économies, Sociétés, Civilisations*
BIHR	Borthwick Institute of Historical Research, York
EETS	Early English Text Society
LJRO	Lichfield Joint Record Office, Lichfield
NRO, NCR	Norfolk Record Office, Norwich City Records
VCH	*Victoria History of the Counties of England*
YCA	York City Archives
YML	York Minster Library

1

Introduction

How far was marriage an economic necessity for medieval women? This was the question that first inspired this book. To such a simple question there is, of course, no simple answer. It is not an issue hitherto much explored by secondary writers, nor is it directly addressed in any of the surviving source material. The period is almost devoid of letters written by women and autobiographical material scarcely exists. Comparatively few records allow women to be heard even at second hand. The historian is thus confronted by many problems both of sources and of methodology. She or he must address several major debates, ranging from the nature of late medieval social structure to the changing economic status of women. This study attempts to meet these difficulties by focusing on one community and its immediate rural hinterland over a relatively limited period of time, namely York and the county of Yorkshire from the early fourteenth to the early sixteenth century. The experience of this region is compared and contrasted with that of other regions of later medieval Europe, notably early fifteenth-century Tuscany. Comparison is also made with England in the post-medieval era and some patterns of continuity and change are suggested.

The choice of York and its region in the later medieval era to form this particular case study was not difficult. The wealth and range of contemporary sources available in that city is rare by English standards. York was both a provincial capital, on occasion even the seat of royal government, and, since the seventh century, the centre of an ecclesiastical province.[1] In addition to civic and gild ordinances contained in the city's Memorandum Book, the records of the urban franchise, the financial records of the city chamberlains, and various rental material, there survive for the wider region two major probate collections and the refreshingly

[1] The most useful introduction to the city and its history is P. M. Tillot (ed.), *VCH, City of York* (Oxford, 1961).

lively deposition material associated with litigation in the Church court.[2] These sources all commence at some date in the fourteenth century. There survive unusually full returns for the city from both the 1377 and 1381 poll taxes, and for Howdenshire (East Riding) and the entire West Riding from the 1379 tax within the Public Record Office.[3] The only major source conspicuously lacking for York is the records of the borough court, but this can to some degree be compensated for by drawing upon similar sources surviving from other urban communities.

The problem thus becomes not so much one of lack of evidence, for all these sources have to a greater or lesser degree a bearing on the history of women, but of how to use and interpret a variety of sometimes rather indirect sources to attempt an answer to the original question. The methodology pursued during the course of this study was to consider separately each of the three main sources, that is wills, poll taxes, and depositions.[4] Each was explored to obtain the maximum of information whilst, in principle, doing the minimum of violence through imposing over-specific questions on otherwise unyielding source material. In practice it was found that the evidence often suggested more interesting questions and lines of analysis than were initially conceived. The patterns that emerged were all the more suggestive because they were derived independently from more than one source. The chronological span of the sources used, moreover, was designed to be sufficiently wide as to allow real secular trends to be distinguished. By reading sources over a long time period, it was further possible to generate samples that, if at times small, were at least statistically significant in most cases. Much of the analysis is essentially prosopographical in approach since insufficient evidence survives for women as individuals outside the aristocracy, though occasionally nominal linkages could be made between sources and individual women emerged from obscurity.

It is the development of a hypothesis consistent with this variety of evidence that is the concern of this book. Each source has its own problems, its own imperfections. As Gold found in her

---

[2] For a fuller discussion of the sources used in this study see 'A Note on Sources' below and Appendices I–III.

[3] 'Assessment Roll of the Poll-Tax for Howdenshire . . . 1379', *Yorkshire Archaeological Journal*, 9 (1886), 129–62.

[4] See Appendices I–III.

valuable study of women in twelfth-century French society, to draw dogmatic conclusions from any one source would be rash indeed.[5] But it is the hope here that by suggesting a coherent thesis on the basis of the range of source material, some credence may be placed in the thesis itself, at least to the extent of challenging other scholars to try to demonstrate it or deny it from their own exploration of other communities and regions.

WRITING ABOUT MEDIEVAL WOMEN: SOME HISTORIOGRAPHICAL OBSERVATIONS

Much earlier work on women's history has tended to focus on their economic role, an emphasis pursued again here. This interest in economic matters follows from an increasing concern about working conditions for women in the decades before the First World War, a period which also saw the growth of a women's trades union movement, the women's suffrage movement, but also the opening of universities to female students. The war itself created, if only temporarily, many new openings to women workers, and may also have helped prompt questions about the wider historical context of women's work. Annie Abram, whose pioneering article 'Women Traders in Medieval London' appeared in 1916, had, for example, earlier contributed a chapter on Newcastle to the report of the Women's Industrial Council entitled *Married Women's Work*.[6] Several noted researchers were associated with the London School of Economics and were colleagues or pupils of Lilian Knowles, herself a student in the 1890s of William Cunningham in Cambridge.[7] Three names in particular stand out, namely those of Eileen Power, who was appointed Professor of Economic History at the London School of Economics from 1931, Alice Clark, and Ivy Pinchbeck. All three

[5] P. S. Gold, *The Lady and the Virgin: Image, Attitude, and Experience in Twelfth-Century France* (Chicago, 1985), pp. xvi–xvii.

[6] A. Abram, 'Women Traders in Medieval London', *Economic Journal*, 26 (1916), 276–85.

[7] M. Chaytor and J. Lewis, 'Introduction', in A. Clark, *Working Life of Women in the Seventeenth Century* (2nd edn., London, 1982), pp. x, xv; C. K. Webster, 'Obituary: Eileen Power', *Economic Journal*, 50 (1940), 561-72. Webster observes that Power was dissuaded from a more general study of women by Coulton.

Introduction

benefited from a scholarship endowed by Mrs G. B. Shaw specifically for women to pursue research at 'first hand'. Pinchbeck researched her book under the supervision of Power, a testimony to the range of Power's own interests. Both Clark in her *Working Life of Women in the Seventeenth Century* and Pinchbeck in *Women Workers and the Industrial Revolution, 1750–1850* were concerned, as their titles suggest, with women in economic life.[8] These classic works rightly remain influential. Their conclusions respecting the social consequences of industrialization differ, but their field of debate was essentially the same. Neither, however, attempted substantial analysis of statistical evidence despite a very full use of contemporary sources.

This last observation applies also to the writings of Power. These make instead particularly sensitive use of literary material. Sadly, Power's own work on women in the medieval era was never completed and, apart from her major study of the English nunneries, few of her writings on the subject have been published.[9] The third chapter of her posthumous *Medieval Women* was, according to Michael Postan's introduction, an essentially collaborative piece, but, whether the authorship is purely Power's or partially Postan's, this does not detract from the lucidity of this brief account of the economic role of women in both urban and rural society. Power's concern was to stress the range of economic functions associated with women. In this respect she was one of the first writers to realize the potential of the published 1379 West Riding poll tax returns. She observed that, although wives regularly assisted their husbands, women tended not to enjoy a single craft identity as was often true of men, but frequently engaged in more than one by-employment. This pattern, she argued, 'militated against the organisation of women in gilds'.[10] With regard to the attitude of craft gilds to women, a problem also explored by Marion K. Dale in her 1928 London MA thesis, she produced

---

[8] Clark, *Working Life*; I. Pinchbeck, *Women Workers and the Industrial Revolution, 1750–1850* (2nd edn., London, 1981).

[9] E. E. Power, *Medieval English Nunneries* (Cambridge, 1922); ead., 'The Position of Women', in C. G. Crump and E. F. Jacobs (eds.), *The Legacy of the Middle Ages* (Oxford, 1926). Some essays were published posthumously under the editorship of her husband M. M. Postan as *Medieval Women* (Cambridge, 1975).

[10] Power, *Medieval Women*, 62.

conflicting evidence.[11] Unlike some later writers, however, she was clearly aware that women were sometimes gild members in their own right. Her analysis of women's work, and especially the position of the unmarried woman in the labour market, was still rooted in the notion that, whereas most women aspired to marriage, not all women were able to marry. This view derived from the work of Karl Bücher, who observed that a variety of late medieval German urban sources suggest that women outnumbered men, but it may also derive from the notion, current at the time Power was researching the position of women in later medieval society, that many young women would not have been able to marry because their potential spouses had been killed in the 'Great War'.[12] Paid employment was thus seen not as a liberating experience, but as an economic necessity imposed upon women by the supposedly peculiar demographic circumstances of the later Middle Ages.

Abram, Clark, Dale, Pinchbeck, and Power all made a most distinguished and still influential contribution to women's history in terms of research, writing, and teaching. The generation that followed was not so productive, despite growing interest in the fields of economic and social history. It is only comparatively recently, with the growth in the contemporary Women's Movement, that interest in this area has been revived. At the time of writing, the study of the history of women in the Middle Ages has the appearance of a fast growing field, especially in the United States, where scholarship is supported both by academic institutions and by publishers. Yet within the context of Women's History generally, the medieval period is still of minority interest and the pre-industrial period as a whole is not much better served. The reason must be in part that the longer historical perspective does not fit any simple linear model, though such has been described for the modern era. Thus a new historiography has emerged that maps the Women's Movement from the metaphorical 'Dark Ages' of the Victorian era to the present. The Married Women's Property Acts, the repeal of the Contagious Diseases Acts, the extension of the franchise, the advent of birth control

---

[11] This formed the basis of her article 'The London Silkwomen of the Fifteenth Century', *Economic History Review*, 4 (1933), 324–35.

[12] K. Bücher, *Die Frauenfrage in Mittelalter* (Tübingen, 1910); Power, *Medieval Women*, 53–5.

clinics, and the Equal Pay and Sex Discrimination Acts can all be viewed as landmarks in an essentially progressive development.

This subjective view is not intended to detract from the very real value and quality of much historical scholarship of recent years. Indeed some writings using, for example, the techniques of oral history capture a past society in a way the medievalist can only envy. Perhaps it is the very range of more immediate, personal evidence in the form of letters, diaries, memoirs, and oral record that renders the more recent past accessible and the distant past uninviting. It is, moreover, some of the particular aspects of social history rightly taken up by feminist historians as legitimate matters for investigation, namely women's attitudes to and experience of sex and sexuality, matrimony, and childbirth, that are least well documented for earlier periods. The medievalist must often use less tractable sources to obtain answers to seemingly more mundane questions which may nevertheless provide a framework by which these other questions may be approached.

These mundane questions cannot, however, be dismissed as historical sidelights. An exploration of the economic status of women and of the role of women in decisions relating to marriage is crucial to any understanding of the way the economy worked and of the interrelationship between economic and demographic movements. It is a veritable failing of so many earlier commentators on the pre-industrial economy and society that no proper consideration has been given to these. Any exploration of the evidence, moreover, indicates that the economic or social status of women in the pre-industrial era was not one that appears either uniform and unchanging or subject to a simple linear development. It is not a 'bon vieux temps' or some kind of renaissance for women that is looked for, but an understanding of the way the prevailing social structure accommodated and responded to economic and demographic fluctuations, and how these affected women.

The thesis that will be outlined is an essentially simple one. In presenting it briefly now, the concern is to assist the reader to evaluate the arguments as they unfold. But in presenting it in advance of the evidence upon which it is grounded, it should not be thought that the hypothesis anticipated the reading of the evidence. Rather it was that some previous writings in the broader field, notably the Wrigley and Schofield thesis relating movements in nuptiality to wider economic trends with its heavy emphasis on aggregative statistics, were thought unconvincing, but that only empiric study of a body of source materials would allow new hypotheses to be developed.[13] The broad outlines of the thesis presented here lay particular stress on the impact of demographic recession in the decades following the Black Death. A substantial fall in population in 1348–9 created an acute temporary shortage of labour and a consequent surge in wages paid to wage labourers. The growth in the spending power of labour stimulated demand for goods and services, and thus demand for labour to create those goods and services. Within the context of a 'liberal', late marriage regime, women were increasingly drawn into the labour force in response to a growing labour shortage, further stimulating the economy. In some arable regions, however, the twin consequences of rising labour costs and falling cash returns saw a contraction or even an abandonment of labour-intensive arable farming and the shedding of labour, notably of the young and mobile, and perhaps especially of women. This labour would readily have been absorbed into the correspondingly buoyant urban economy.

As women, from an economic perspective newly enfranchised, chose to delay marriage, even not to marry at all, the birth-rate drifted downwards. This only served to prolong demographic recession in an era of endemic disease. By about the middle of the fifteenth century, however, the population had shrunk to a point where economic growth could not be sustained and the model just outlined started to go into reverse. Men sought to preserve their own position in a period of recession by excluding competition from female labour. Women were thus forced back into positions of dependency within marriage. From a demographic perspective, they married earlier and more often. The resultant upward trend in birth rates, possibly coinciding with a downward trend in mortality, only aggravated competition in the labour market to the disadvantage of women. The exclusion of female labour in one generation served to harden gender perceptions in the next. This has implications that extend far beyond the later Middle Ages, but to demonstrate such a thesis an understanding of late medieval marriage regimes and social structures, and the relative

[13] E. A. Wrigley and R. S. Schofield, *The Population History of England, 1541–1871: A Reconstruction* (London, 1981).

fortunes of the rural and urban economies is required. Any survey of the recent literature reveals, however, that these are all intellectual minefields.

SOCIAL STRUCTURE AND ECONOMIC CHANGE IN PRE-INDUSTRIAL SOCIETY: A BIBLIOGRAPHICAL SURVEY

The question of continuity or change in respect of marriage regimes seems to be an issue that has attracted especially intense debate. Hajnal's pioneering study set up the debate by producing evidence to suggest that the marriage regime prevailing in the West, characterized by late companionate marriage, was essentially post-medieval in date.[14] This hypothesis was, and still is, attractive because it coincided with the notion of wider cultural change associated with a supposed transition from feudal to capitalist modes of production and the implicit assumption that a Western marriage regime is an essentially modern phenomenon. The analysis of parish register evidence conducted by Wrigley and Schofield has been widely accepted to demonstrate that a Western marriage regime prevailed in England from at least the mid-sixteenth century, thus narrowing the area for debate. On the other hand, Razi has argued from family reconstitutions derived from the court rolls of the manor of Halesowen between 1270 and 1400 that for villein families with access to land, marriage was early, males in their early twenties marrying females perhaps 'three or four years' younger.[15] Razi further postulates that marriage ages fell in the half-century after the Black Death as land became more plentiful.[16]

The most substantive medieval evidence, however, is that provided by the Florentine *catasto* of 1427. Herlihy and Klapisch-Zuber have calculated a mean age at first marriage for females in

---

[14] J. Hajnal, 'European Marriage Patterns in Perspective', in D. V. Glass and D. E. V. Eversley (eds.), *Population in History: Essays in Historical Demography* (London, 1965), 101–43.

[15] Z. Razi, *Life, Marriage and Death in a Medieval Parish* (Cambridge, 1980), 60–3.

[16] Ibid. 136–8.

their late teens.[17] Yet the differences between the 'medieval' marriage regime observed in later medieval Tuscany and that described for rural Worcestershire in the fourteenth century are more marked than their similarities. Male age at marriage in Tuscany is calculated to have been some ten years later than that for females, and new household formation appears not to have been so regular a feature of matrimony. Smith has drawn attention to the distinctiveness of this Tuscan regime, which he places within a 'Mediterranean' rather than a 'medieval' framework in his review of the *catasto* study.[18] But he has also questioned Hajnal's evidence for a non-Western regime prevailing in England after the Black Death. Smith further presents a range of material suggestive of a marriage structure more in line with that found for the early modern period, noting evidence for proportions married and single, exogamous marriage, and proportions of servants inconsistent with a non-Western regime.[19] Bennett has likewise suggested a degree of individualism in marriage formation within peasant society, drawing attention both to the frequency with which villein daughters were responsible for their own merchet payments and to a pattern of marital exogamy.[20]

The problem of marriage formation in medieval England has also been examined from the record of litigation in the Church courts. Some writers have been rather more interested in the legal and administrative aspects of the evidence than its social and demographic implications. This is perhaps true of Helmholz's substantial and authoritative study of marriage litigation.[21] Helmholz suggests a change in social conventions to explain an observed

---

[17] D. Herlihy and C. Klapisch-Zuber, *Tuscans and Their Families: A Study of the Florentine Catasto of 1427* (New Haven, Conn., 1985), 87, 210–11, 215. This is an abridged translation of their *Les Toscans et leurs familles: Une étude du Catasto Florentin de 1427* (Paris, 1978).

[18] R. M. Smith, 'The People of Tuscany and their Families in the Fifteenth Century: Medieval or Mediterranean?', *Journal of Family History*, 6 (1981), 107–28.

[19] R. M. Smith, 'Some Reflections on the Evidence for the Origins of the "European Marriage Pattern" in England', in C. C. Harris (ed.), *The Sociology of the Family: New Directions for Britain* (Sociological Review Monograph, 28; Keele, 1979), 74–112; id., 'Hypothèses sur la nuptialité en Angleterre aux XIIIe–XIVe siècles', *Annales: ESC*, 38 (1983), 107–36.

[20] J. M. Bennett, 'Medieval Peasant Marriage: An Examination of Marriage License Fines in the *Liber Gersumarum*', in J. A. Raftis (ed.), *Pathways to Medieval Peasants* (Toronto, 1981), 193–246.

[21] R. H. Helmholz, *Marriage Litigation in Medieval England* (Cambridge, 1974).

decline in matrimonial litigation, especially multi-party actions, during the fifteenth century. He argues that the formal solemnization of matrimony *in facie ecclesie*, i.e. at the church door, tended to displace purely private contracts with their scope for subsequent repudiation, hence that there was a growth in matrimonial stability.[22] Another review of marriage litigation over the period *c.*1350–1640, also notes an increasing acceptance of Church solemnization as a reason for a decline in contract disputes, but suggests a growing reluctance by the courts to confirm such contracts.[23] Neither approach considers in any depth how the circumstances of individuals contracting marriage may have changed with time such that the likelihood of dispute arising, especially in respect of alleged pre-contracts, may have diminished. Sheehan, by considering only the evidence of an Ely court book for the period 1374–82, is unable to comment on such secular trends, but he argues for a real degree of matrimonial stability even at this early date.[24] Sheehan, unlike some of those who have used his work, is most careful to distinguish private contracts 'not intended to create a marriage bond' from other more formal unions, whether technically 'clandestine' or otherwise. He concludes that the 'court was primarily a body for the proof and defence of marriage rather than an instrument of easy annulment'.[25]

More recently Donahue has drawn attention to some striking differences between later medieval English matrimonial litigation and equivalent North French material.[26] The relative absence of 'clandestine' *de presenti* contracts from French sources he attri-

---

[22] Helmholz, *Marriage Litigation in Medieval England*, 57–9, 166–8. The concept that medieval marriages were inherently unstable is common to much of the literature.

[23] M. Ingram, 'Spousals Litigation in the English Ecclesiastical Courts *c.*1350–*c.*1640', in R. B. Outhwaite (ed.), *Marriage and Society: Studies in the Social History of Marriage* (London, 1981), 35–57.

[24] M. M. Sheehan, 'The Formation and Stability of Marriage in Fourteenth-Century England: Evidence of an Ely Register', *Medieval Studies,* 33 (1971), 228–63.

[25] Ibid. 256, 263. Hilton consistently uses Sheehan's evidence to argue for informality and thus instability of peasant medieval marriages: see his 'Small Town Society in England Before the Black Death', *Past and Present,* 105 (1984), 72; id., 'Women in the Village', in id., *The English Peasantry in the Later Middle Ages* (Oxford, 1975), 107–8.

[26] C. Donahue, 'The Canon Law on the Formation of Marriage and Social Practice in the Later Middle Ages', *Journal of Family History,* 8 (1983), 144–58.

butes to a greater degree of parental authority over their children in respect of choice of marriage partners.[27] Finch, working from a comparative analysis of matrimonial data from Cerisy in Normandy, Hereford, and Rochester, has criticized this thesis as oversimplistic.[28] The typicality of this French evidence, particularly in the case of the Paris Register, where many litigants are of high social status, must certainly be open to question, but the contrast with the English evidence still appears striking. As Sheehan has observed, much later medieval English marriage litigation concerned disputed 'clandestine' contracts of marriage. The persistence in England of marriages contracted outside church by way of trothplight or handfasting beyond the medieval period, even if intended to be followed by formal solemnization at church, is well illustrated by a survey of litigation from Durham dated 1560–1630.[29] The implications of this evidence are far from clear, but it is again tempting to suggest a rather greater degree of continuity from later medieval times than has generally been allowed to date.[30]

Some older notions that canon law was a 'seducer's charter' and that medieval marriage was inherently unstable seem no longer to command respect. Little, however, has been done hitherto to consider the demographic and social implications of observed patterns of litigation in town and country. This undoubtedly follows from the nature of the sources explored. Act books offer valuable evidence for the types of litigation entertained within the Church courts and the ways in which canon law was deployed and enforced, but generally little evidence for the circumstances out of which litigation arose. This is only possible where actual depositions survive as at York or in the diocese of Armagh, studied by Cosgrove, but these are only rarely recorded in Act

[27] Ibid. 156.
[28] A. J. Finch, 'Crime and Marriage in Three Late Medieval Ecclesiastical Jurisdictions: Cerisy, Rochester and Hereford', D.Phil. thesis (York, 1988), 260–76.
[29] P. Rushton, 'The Broken Marriage in Early Modern England: Matrimonial Cases from the Durham Church Courts, 1560–1630', *Archaeologia Aeliana*, 5th ser. 13 (1985), 187–96.
[30] Cf. R. M. Smith, 'Marriage Processes in the English Past: Some Continuities', in L. Bonfield, R. M. Smith, and K. Wrightson (eds.), *The World We Have Gained: Histories of Population and Social Structure* (Oxford, 1986), 43–99.

books.[31] By focusing on deposition material, this present study is able to distinguish different types of 'clandestine' contract and to reconstruct something of the particular background to individual marriage cases.

The changing rural economy and the position of women in that economy has recently been the subject of a number of important studies, but no clear picture has yet emerged. Roberts has suggested from pictorial evidence that women were more active at least at harvest time in the post-plague rural economy, and has linked this to labour shortage. It is also implicit in his analysis that women were paid at the same rate as men when engaged in identical work, an observation made a number of years before by Beveridge in his analysis of wages derived from manorial account rolls of the abbey of Westminster and earlier still by Thorold Rogers.[32] In a more narrowly focused study, Penn has used presentments under the Statute of Labourers to explore the role of women in the rural labour force in the decades following the Black Death. He finds that 'the evidence by and large reveals the women to be involved in traditional female activities', but is justifiably cautious about concluding whether women were more active at this date than was true of the pre-plague era in view of the absence of comparative statistical data.[33] He also raises a major problem of interpretation. The numbers of women presented may have been determined both by the numbers of women liable to be presented as being in breach of the Statute and by the willingness or otherwise of those enforcing the Statute to present women. If, for example, the jurors wanted to enforce 'traditional' wage differentials, then women workers paid at the same rate as males would have been presented disproportionately to their actual numbers.[34] The evidence may still reflect absolute trends since women seem to have been most conspicuous within pastoral regions, where they might find paid work as spinsters or weavers,

[31] A. Cosgrove, 'Marriage in Medieval Ireland', in id. (ed.), *Marriage in Ireland* (Dublin, 1985), 25–50; Helmholz, *Marriage Litigation*, 8–11.

[32] M. Roberts, 'Sickles and Scythes: Women's Work and Men's Work at Harvest Time', *History Workshop*, 7 (1979), 3–28; W. Beveridge, 'Westminster Wages in the Manorial Era', *Economic History Review*, 2nd ser. 8 (1955), 30–5; Hilton, 'Women in the Village', 102.

[33] S. A. C. Penn, 'Female Wage-Earners in Late Fourteenth-Century England', *Agricultural History Review*, 35 (1987), 1–3, 5–6.

[34] Ibid. 4–5, 9–10.

and the existence of 'traditional' wage differentials is, as just observed, open to question. The evidence is silent, however, as to the unpaid labour of countrywomen.[35]

The most substantial recent analysis of women in the medieval countryside is that contained in Bennett's monograph on the women of three Midland England manors before the Black Death. This is based upon a reading of court roll evidence, a source limited by the nature of its legal jurisdiction both in terms of the type of material recorded and the range of people who appear before the court. Male villein tenants are relatively conspicuous. Women, in contrast, are not very conspicuous since only a minority held land in their own right. Her principal manor, Brigstock, was, moreover, ancient demesne and women were there exempt from merchet, so Bennett has little to say on the subject of marriage. Fines for breach of the Assizes of Bread and Ale are, however, recorded and the most substantial and important part of her analysis is concerned with the participation of women in these two industries.[36] McIntosh also has valuable information on female brewsters in her study of the manor of Havering before 1500, but perhaps her most interesting evidence relates to patterns of landholding among women.[37] Here she finds that the number of women tenants appears to have declined sharply over a period of a hundred years from a possible peak immediately following the Black Death. This startling observation she suggests may be related to the influx of migrants experienced by the manor in the post-plague decades, but it would be interesting to test this finding for other manors experiencing rather different patterns of migration.

Two other studies of women in late medieval rural society may briefly be noted. Hilton devoted one of his Ford lectures to women in the village and, more recently, Hanawalt has written about rural women's contribution to the domestic economy.[38]

---

[35] Ibid. 14.

[36] J. M. Bennett, *Women in the Medieval English Countryside: Gender and Household in Brigstock before the Plague* (New York, 1987). Marriage is discussed in her 'The Tie that Binds: Peasant Marriages and Families in Late Medieval England', *Journal of Interdisciplinary History*, 15 (1984), 111–29.

[37] M. K. McIntosh, *Autonomy and Community: The Royal Manor of Havering, 1200–1500* (Cambridge, 1986), 171–5.

[38] Hilton, 'Women in the Village'; B. A. Hanawalt, 'Peasant Women's Contribution to the Home Economy in Late Medieval England', in ead. (ed.), *Women*

Both are concerned primarily with the range of tasks women engaged in, but Hilton argues that 'peasant women's gains went in step with the gains of the whole of their class', whereas Hanawalt is keen to demonstrate a sexual division of labour with separate spheres of activity, that of the woman revolving around the home and home-making. This last is heavily influenced by her reading of coroners' rolls which tend to show that accidental deaths involving women were more likely to occur around the home than was true of male deaths. A more critical interpretation of the same evidence would serve to modify this conclusion since two gender-specific tasks, namely fetching water (female) and carting (male), appear to have been especially hazardous and may thus have unduly distorted the overall pattern. The analysis is further limited by its slightly timeless quality; it is less than clear how the patterns she describes may have changed over the period of the Black Death or between differing agrarian economies.[39]

The economy of later medieval English towns has been rather more extensively explored over a longer period of time. The case of York has featured prominently in this literature since the evidence here is so voluminous. The story of later medieval York will be explored shortly, but it is worth noting immediately that Bartlett's classic essay on the economic fortunes of York in the fourteenth and fifteenth centuries constitutes a landmark in the debate over the fortunes of urban communities after the Black Death.[40] Bartlett's analysis depends on the assumption that economic fortunes followed demographic trends, a position independently echoed by Miller.[41] Bartlett's treatment of the franchise data has, however, been implicitly criticized by Dobson in his important study of the York material.[42] More recently Rees Jones has

and *Work in Preindustrial Europe* (Bloomington, Ind., 1986), 3–20, also printed as ch. 9 of her *The Ties that Bound: Peasant Families in Medieval England* (New York, 1986).

[39] For a more substantial critique of Hanawalt see P. J. P. Goldberg, 'The Public and the Private: Women in the Pre-Plague Economy', in P. R. Coss and S. Lloyd (eds.), *Thirteenth-Century England III* (Woodbridge, 1991), 75–89.

[40] J. N. Bartlett, 'The Expansion and Decline of York in the Later Middle Ages', *Economic History Review*, 2nd ser. 12 (1959), 17–33.

[41] E. Miller, 'Medieval York', in P. M. Tillot (ed.), *VCH, City of York* (Oxford, 1961), 25–116.

[42] R. B. Dobson, 'Admissions to the Freedom of the City of York in the Late Middle Ages', *Economic History Review*, 2nd ser. 23 (1973), 1–22.

questioned Bartlett's use of rental evidence by arguing that rent movements were responsive to a range of factors, notably fluctuations in demand for particular kinds of housing stock from particular social groups, other than just simple demographic trends.[43] Kermode, attacking another plank in the 'urban decline' thesis, uses the case of York to show that there was no widespread 'flight from office' in the face of recession.[44]

That the fifteenth century saw a general downturn in the nation's economy which was reflected in the urban sector does, however, appear still to command considerable support.[45] This is very much the theme of a survey by Dobson that draws heavily on York evidence.[46] Phythian-Adams argues for an initial contraction of smaller urban communities and markets under pressure from larger, more vital urban centres that themselves experienced crisis by the early sixteenth century.[47] His thesis is much influenced by the case of Coventry, which itself may not be entirely representative. The reverse may indeed have been true of York in respect of competition from the nascent urban communities of the West Riding. Another dissenting view is that developed by Bridbury, who warns against confusing civic overspending and consequent pleas of poverty for evidence of wider communal impoverishment.[48] Certainly there are reasons to believe that traditional sources of civic revenue, notably from tolls and rents, would have declined as a consequence of the proliferation of chartered privileges, the expansion of the franchise, and continued demographic recession. It may be that historians need to look elsewhere to justify and explain the apparently failing fortunes of many English towns at the close of the Middle Ages.

[43] S. R. Rees Jones, 'Property, Tenure and Rents: Some Aspects of the Topography and Economy of Medieval York', D.Phil. thesis (York, 1987).

[44] J. I. Kermode, 'Urban Decline? The Flight from Office in Late Medieval York', *Economic History Review*, 2nd ser. 35 (1982), 179–98.

[45] Cf. J. Hatcher, *Plague, Population and the English Economy, 1348–1530* (London, 1977); C. Platt, *The English Medieval Town* (London, 1979); S. Reynolds, *An Introduction to the History of English Medieval Towns* (Oxford, 1977).

[46] R. B. Dobson, 'Urban Decline in Late Medieval England', *Transactions of the Royal Historical Society*, 5th ser. 27 (1977), 1–22.

[47] C. Phythian-Adams, 'Urban Decay in Late Medieval England', in P. Abrams and E. A. Wrigley (eds.), *Towns in Society* (Cambridge, 1978), 1–32.

[48] A. R. Bridbury, 'English Provincial Towns in the Later Middle Ages', *Economic History Review*, 2nd ser. 39 (1981), 1–24.

No writer has attempted to consider the changing role of women in urban society as a measure of economic vitality. Few individual town studies seriously explore beyond the mercantile élite, and describe, contrary to the evidence, an apparently masculine society. Kowaleski's important and meticulous study of women in Exeter from the later fourteenth-century borough court rolls or the more general surveys of women in later medieval London by Lacey and, most recently, Barron are still rare exceptions to this rule.[49] We also need to know more about individual towns and cities in order to assess the possibility of regional variation in long-term economic trends. Some progress has already been made in this area. One of the more important regional studies is Britnell's work on Colchester in the later Middle Ages. This makes full use of the town's fine series of court rolls to present a well-argued and generally convincing account of the town's changing economic fortunes in terms of expansion after the Black Death and subsequent contraction. Sadly the court roll evidence has not been much explored in respect of the economic contribution of women.[50] Phythian-Adams's exemplary study of Coventry is concerned primarily with the early sixteenth century, but suggests a process of profound recession experienced by that date.[51] It is, however, still too early to distinguish regional patterns in economic development between towns. Such comparatively well-documented Midlands towns as Nottingham and Shrewsbury, which both possess remarkably full series of court rolls, or Northampton and Leicester still lack modern histories. We need to know more about the wider impact of the sustained economic expansion of the capital. The changing patterns of wealth distribution observed by Schofield from the lay subsidies of 1334 and 1515, suggest a shift of wealth in favour of *inter alia* the South-

[49] M. Kowaleski, 'Women's Work in a Market Town: Exeter in the Late Fourteenth Century', in Hanawalt (ed.), *Women and Work,* 145–64; K. E. Lacey, 'Women and Work in Fourteenth and Fifteenth Century London', in L. Charles and L. Duffin (eds.), *Women and Work in Pre-Industrial England* (London, 1985), 24–82; Barron, C. M., 'The "Golden Age" of Women in Medieval London', *Reading Medieval Studies,* 15 (1990), 35–58.

[50] R. H. Britnell, *Growth and Decline in Colchester, 1300–1525* (Cambridge, 1986).

[51] C. Phythian-Adams, *Desolation of a City: Coventry and the Urban Crisis of the Late Middle Ages* (Cambridge, 1979).

East, the Thames Valley, and the South-West.[52] This may also
have been reflected in the urban sector, but until more local
studies have been completed it will remain difficult to assess how
far the experience of York followed or diverged from that of other
English towns.

Turning to continental Europe, a recent study by Howell has
tried to explain the changing economic profile of women, measured in terms of 'labour status', through the later fifteenth and
early sixteenth centuries. This influential work rests on a highly
selective study of primary records from Leiden and of printed and
secondary material for Cologne. Its lengthy theoretical analysis is
thus insufficiently rooted in empiric study.[53] She argues that
women's access to high-status occupations was traditionally
through the family. As trade gilds became more closely identified
with civic government, in her own words, as 'the growing political
organisation of work weakened the bond between work and
family', so gild membership came to be restricted to male individuals since women were traditionally debarred from participation in government.[54] By the later fifteenth century, therefore,
gilds tended to undermine the family unit and thus the ability of
women to participate within those crafts regulated by the gilds.
This is an attractive thesis, but it does little to explain the observed
chronology of gild regulation against women and the evidence for
the erosion of economic opportunities for women generally from
the middle of the century. There was, after all, nothing new about
the regulatory or governmental role played by gilds in the late
fifteenth century. This is implicit in, for example, Swanson's
stimulating and controversial analysis of the relationship between civic government and the gilds.[55] Howell may thus have
identified the symptoms, but not the actual causes of change.
Perhaps more rewarding because less tied by purely theoretical
propositions is Wiesner's study of women's work in early modern

---

[52] R. S. Schofield, 'The Geographical Distribution of Wealth in England,
1334–1649', *Economic History Review,* 2nd ser. 18 (1965), 145–64.
[53] M. C. Howell, *Women, Production and Patriarchy in Late Medieval Cities*
(Chicago, 1986).
[54] Ibid. 90.
[55] H. C. Swanson, 'The Illusion of Economic Structure: Craft Guilds in Late
Medieval English Towns', *Past and Present,* 121 (1988), 29–48.

Germany.[56] Besides providing an unusually detailed account of a range of female economic activities in towns over a wide time period, she is able to show that the decline in working opportunities is to be seen as part of a broader social response to economic recession.

The social structure of specifically urban communities has been explored from census-type material, notably by Goose for early Stuart Cambridge, McIntosh for Elizabethan Romford, and, with admirable clarity, by Clark and Clark for a suburb of Canterbury at about the same time.[57] For Coventry in 1523 Phythian-Adams is able to reconstruct in addition the occupational structure of the entire community and to relate this to aspects of the city's social and demographic structure.[58] It must be an open question how patterns observed in Coventry at a time of deep recession are to be interpreted, but Phythian-Adams's work does serve to draw attention to the position of women within the social fabric of a major town at the end of the Middle Ages. This last is pursued by Souden from a demographic perspective for the end of the seventeenth century using ecclesiastical court depositions and data drawn from the Marriage Duty Act enumerations. He explores gender-specific migration patterns in a period characterized by urban growth, but more general demographic stagnation.[59] A rare and thought-provoking study of female group solidarity and collective action is presented in a paper by Houlbrooke.[60] This last primarily focuses on the early modern period and it is difficult to know if there is simply more evidence by this later date or, because society was more clearly divided along lines of gender, women were thus more likely to act as a group apart from men.

[56] M. E. Wiesner, *Working Women in Renaissance Germany* (New Brunswick, NJ, 1986).

[57] N. Goose, 'Household Size and Structure in Early-Stuart Cambridge', *Social History*, 5 (1980), 347–85; M. K. McIntosh, 'Servants and the Household Unit in an Elizabethan English Community', *Journal of Family History*, 9 (1984), 3–23; P. and J. Clark, 'The Social Economy of the Canterbury Suburbs: The Evidence of the Census of 1563', in A. Detsicas and N. Yates (eds.), *Studies in Modern Kentish History* (Kent Archaeological Society, 1983), 65–86.

[58] Phythian-Adams, *Desolation of a City*.

[59] D. Souden, 'Migrants and the Population Structure of Later Seventeenth-Century Provincial Cities and Market Towns', in P. Clark (ed.), *The Transformation of English Towns, 1600–1800* (London, 1984), 133–68.

[60] R. A. Houlbrooke, 'Women's Social Life and Common Action in England from the Fifteenth Century to the Eve of the Civil War', *Continuity and Change*, 1 (1986), 171–89.

The impediments, legal, material, and domestic, placed upon women that served effectively to frustrate their participation on a more equitable basis in the economic life of the later medieval or pre-industrial town are indeed a regular theme of much recent literature. The limitations of such literature lie in its shallowness of focus, though this is in part a product of a lack of source material and a scarcity of critical studies of other communities for comparative purposes. Too often writers appear to have approached their material on the presumption that the social organization of the medieval (or even the pre-industrial) town was relatively uniform across time and even space, and that this must have differed materially from that subsequently prevailing. This is harsh criticism and it is unlikely that this wider perspective was always a conscious element in each writer's understanding of the evidence. Some recent, and highly influential writing on the medieval social structure has, moreover, lent weight to this long-standing view of cultural uniformity.[61] But too much work has been done on too few sources. Gold's study, admittedly concerned with different social groups for an earlier period, is unusual in the range of source material employed.[62] It is salutary that she is consequently sceptical of what conclusions can be drawn from each source because of her increased awareness of the problems inherent in reading the evidence. Davis likewise demonstrates how much more satisfying can be the results of a more critical methodology applied to a much wider range of sources.[63] It is the contention here that the study of women's economic activity in the past must take proper notice of the wider economic, demographic, cultural, and secular context, and at the same time be alert to secular variation within these interdependent parameters. So long as the subject remains in its infancy, this is more valuable than trying to force limited data into predetermined and over-simplistic models.

This does not pretend to be an exhaustive survey of the recent writings and debate. Our purpose is to demonstrate that, despite

[61] Cf. D. Herlihy, *Medieval Households* (Cambridge, Mass., 1985); S. Shahar, *The Fourth Estate: A History of Women in the Middle Ages* (London, 1983); Razi, *Life, Marriage and Death*; J. Bossy, *Christianity in the West* (Oxford, 1985).

[62] Gold, *The Lady and the Virgin*.

[63] N. Z. Davis, 'Women in the Crafts in Sixteenth-Century Lyon', *Feminist Studies*, 8 (1982), 47–80, repr. in Hanawalt (ed.), *Women and Work*, 167–97.

the proliferation of literature on medieval women over the past decade, there remain a number of serious lacunae in the broad research field addressed here. This present study cannot claim to be more than a small contribution. Its purpose is twofold. First, the major chapters on the themes of marriage, servanthood, and women's work are designed to present the findings of research involving primary source material principally from York in the period from the Black Death until c.1520. Secondly, by suggesting certain secular relationships between the prevailing social structure, wider economic and demographic trends, urbanization, and the status of women within the public economy, it is hoped that others will be tempted to engage in similar research either to test or to challenge our conclusions. Our intention is thus to stimulate scholarship and not to lay down dogmatic conclusions.

Implicit in this framework is a critical re-examination of the Wrigley and Schofield thesis, which links trends in nuptiality to movements in real wages. Drawing on our knowledge of the particular circumstances of acute labour shortage following the Black Death, our analysis places a new emphasis on the earning capacity of women liable to marry. From this follows our stress on female agency. Our model further suggests a more complex relationship between demographic movements and the urban economy than has hitherto been usually allowed by medievalists. Finally, our interpretation endorses the view suggested by Smith that English society of the later fourteenth and fifteenth centuries was characterized by a demographic regime of life-cycle servanthood, late, companionate marriage, and high proportions never marrying. Such a regime distinguishes England culturally from other more southerly regions of medieval Europe and brings English society of the later Middle Ages much closer to that of the early modern era. It remains to introduce the reader first to a brief review of the economy of York and the wider region in the later medieval period by way of setting the specific context of this study, and secondly to the range of sources upon which this analysis depends.

YORK IN THE LATER MIDDLE AGES

York is sited on low marshy ground at the junction of the Rivers Ouse and Foss in the heart of the Vale of York. Much of the surrounding region was originally wooded and still in the medieval era the Forest of Galtres stood immediately north of the city. The Forest of Ouse and Derwent lying to the south-east of the city likewise was part of the royal forest until 1234.[64] The Vale itself is bounded to the west by the Pennines, to the north by the Hambleton and Howardian Hills, and to the east by the chalk uplands of the Yorkshire Wolds. The marshlands of the Humber-head levels lie to the south. The River Ouse is tidal as far as York. Upstream from York the river is formed by the confluence of the Rivers Swale, Ure, and Nidd. Downstream to the south the Rivers Wharfe, Derwent, Aire, and Don feed the Ouse before its junction with the Trent to form the Humber Estuary. The city thus enjoyed access by water to both the Pennine Dales and, via the Trent, the north Midlands. The Humber provided passage to the sea and overseas trade, though from the late thirteenth century goods were regularly transhipped at the port of Hull.[65] A number of important roadways, several based on old Roman routes, also linked York to the wider region. Roads led north-east to Malton, Pickering, and Scarborough, south-east to Pocklington, Market Weighton, and Beverley, to Howden, and, to the south, Selby. The old Roman road to Tadcaster, west of York, there branched south to Pontefract and the Great North Road, south-west to Leeds, and west to Ilkley. Another Roman road also ran west to Knaresborough and then across to Ribblesdale and Lancashire. Major roads likewise ran north of York to Boroughbridge, Ripon, Richmond, Northallerton, Darlington, and beyond.[66] York was thus well situated in terms of the wider economic region, but sufficiently far south to be relatively immune from attack by the Scots. These factors help explain the re-emergence of the Roman *Eboracum* in Saxon times as *Eoforwiceastor* and later, under Viking rule, as *Jorvic* from which the modern name of York ultimately derives.[67]

York was founded *c.* AD 71–4 as a legionary fortress and grew

---

[64] R. B. Pugh (ed.), *VCH, York, East Riding,* iii (Oxford, 1976), 1.

[65] K. J. Allison (ed.), *VCH, York, East Riding,* i. *City of Kingston-Upon-Hull* (Oxford, 1969), 11–15, 69.

[66] B. Harrison, 'Evidence for Main Roads in the Vale of York during the Medieval Period', *Sciant Presentes,* 13 (Yorkshire Archaeological Society, Medieval Section: 1984), 3–8.

[67] *An Inventory of the Historical Monuments in the City of York,* i. *Eburacum; Roman York* (Royal Commission on Historical Monuments, 1962), pp. xxix–xxx.

to become the major Roman settlement and river-port.[68] It had been recolonized by the early seventh century and became a royal and ecclesiastical centre following the conversion and baptism of Edwin of Northumbria by Paulinus in 632. As a trading community York seems to have enjoyed considerable expansion under Danish rule from the later ninth century. Despite the damage sustained in 1069, and still evident by the time of the Domesday survey of 1086, it appears to have continued as a major trading community and, in taxation terms, ranked only behind London under Henry II.[69] An integral factor in York's importance throughout the medieval era was that it was the seat of an archbishop. As an ecclesiastical centre York thus ranked second only to Canterbury. The city was full of churches and religious houses. There were nearly fifty parish churches. The great hospital of St Leonard's may have been of pre-Conquest foundation.[70] The wealthy Benedictine Abbey of St Mary's was founded soon after the Conquest and stood adjacent to the city walls between Bootham and the Ouse.[71] During the thirteenth century York also attracted houses of all four of the major mendicant orders.[72] But it served also as a major manufacturing and market centre. The city drew a wide range of crafts and trades, some no doubt attracted to serve the Minster and other religious houses, but its regional market function appears to have been much enhanced by the Scottish wars early in the fourteenth century. Miller has argued that the presence of the court in York and the strategic value of the city as a military base proved of particular importance to the local textile industry, which, he suggests, had previously been in decline due to pressure from rural manufacture.[73] The

[68] *An Inventory of the Historical Monuments in the City of York*, i, p. xxix.
[69] H. C. Darby (ed.), *A New Historical Geography of England* (Cambridge, 1973), 132–4.
[70] P. H. Cullum, 'Hospitals and Charitable Provision in Medieval Yorkshire, 936–1547', D.Phil. thesis (York, 1989), 68–77.
[71] J. Burton, 'St Mary's Abbey and the City of York', *Annual Report for the Year 1988* (Yorkshire Philosophical Society, 1989), 62–5.
[72] R. B. Dobson, 'Mendicant Ideal and Practice in Late Medieval York', in P. V. Addyman and V. E. Black (eds.), *Archaeological Papers from York presented to M. W. Barley* (York, 1984), 109–22.
[73] Miller, 'Medieval York', 87; id., 'The Fortunes of the English Textile Industry during the Thirteenth Century', *Economic History Review*, 2nd ser. 18 (1965), 70–1, 80; H. Heaton, *The Yorkshire Woollen and Worsted Industries* (Oxford, 1920), 28–9.

expansion of the city's cloth industry was accompanied by an increase in York mercantile activity through the nascent port and royal borough of Hull. This economic vitality is reflected in the high tax assessment imposed upon the city in 1334 which placed York behind only London and Bristol in rank.[74]

The vicissitudes of the city's cloth manufacture over the four-teenth and fifteenth centuries are central to Bartlett's now classic account of York's changing economic fortunes.[75] Certainly the cloth industry was an important part of the city's economy and a key element in the city's overseas trade. The secular fortunes of this external trade may, moreover, be readily analysed from the enrolled customs accounts. Childs's edition of Hull's customs accounts for the period 1453–90 is especially valuable in this respect.[76] But York also served a local and regional market function based upon a much wider range of economic activities. Analysis of the poll tax and franchise data demonstrates this.[77] Unlike Wakefield, Rotherham, or Northampton, it is apparent from the poll tax evidence that cloth manufacture was not the main source of employment at York. It may be that spinsters, carders, and other low status, predominantly female, piece-rate workers are poorly represented in this category and that the true proportions should consequently be higher, but there is little reason to believe that this is substantially more true of York than elsewhere. The economic structure at York as suggested from the poll tax is indeed remarkably diversified. The relative numbers employed in mercantile trades are also apparent from franchise and probate evidence. It is again likely that the cloth trade was important to this sector, but not exclusively so. Stock listed in the surviving probate inventory of a York chapman dating to 1446 includes leather goods, caps, gloves, purses, paper-books, girdles, knives made in Doncaster, and spices in addition to cloth.[78] Such a range of goods, together with the relative strength of mercantile trades, is compatible with the view that York was a major regional market centre.

[74] Darby (ed.), *A New Historical Geography of England*, 184.
[75] Bartlett, 'Expansion and Decline'.
[76] W. R. Childs (ed.), *The Customs Accounts of Hull, 1453–1490* (Yorkshire Archaeological Society Record Ser. 144; 1986).
[77] See Ch. 2 below.
[78] YML, L 1/17 (Gryssop).

This may be further suggested from the comparatively small size of victualling trades when set against other larger towns. Again it is likely that female hucksters and other petty food retailers (besides rural traders who were not part of the city's population) are not well represented, and here one may regret the loss of court records, but it seems reasonable to argue that the market in foodstuffs primarily supplied the needs of the resident populace, whereas the market for a range of manufactured goods and services not readily available in the rural hinterland was more extensive. This is also indicated by the relative importance of both the leather and metal-working trades. These may be related to the resources of the wider region. The agricultural economy of much of north and west Yorkshire and the Wolds of east Yorkshire after the Black Death, if not so markedly before, was essentially pastoral.[79] The grazing of both cattle and sheep resulted in the production not only of wool to supply the regional textile industry, but skins for parchment, and hides for leather. Lead was mined in the Dales and the High Peak district of north Derbyshire. Iron ore was extracted at a variety of regional sites, mostly in the southern part of the West Riding, and this last is reflected in the importance of metal-working to a number of communities including Rotherham and, more especially, Sheffield. Whereas smiths characterize industry in these places according to the 1379 poll tax evidence, a much wider range of specialist metal-workers is specified at York in 1381, notably cutlers, girdlers, lorimers, spurriers, pinners, and nailers. York's bell-founding industry was probably in the hands of another specialist group known as potters.[80]

It is to this range of specialist and general crafts, trades, and services that York as a regional capital owed its economic vitality. The 1381 tax returns list 126 different occupations, whereas only 51 are distinguished at Pontefract, the largest of the West Riding towns recorded in the 1379 returns. Unlike Wakefield, Sheffield, or Rotherham, York was not dependent on only one or two main industries. It did, moreover, serve as a market and distribution centre for goods manufactured elsewhere in the region. The city

---

[79] C. Dyer, 'Documentary Evidence: Problems and Enquiries', in G. Astill and A. Grant (eds.), *The Countryside of Medieval England* (Oxford, 1988), 16–19.

[80] H. Swanson, *Medieval Artisans; An Urban Class in Late Medieval England* (Oxford, 1989), 75.

also supplied the demand for luxury goods within the wider region as, for example, the products of the York bell-founders, glaziers, goldsmiths, embroiderers, and spicers. It was a sufficiently important centre for gold and silver work as to have had its own assay mark from at least as early as 1412.[81] Imported goods were distributed through York via the port of Hull. Wine, timber including bowstaves to supply the York armaments industry, furs, copper, Spanish iron and Swedish osmunds, potash, and a range of dyestuffs were regularly shipped this way.[82] It was, nevertheless, quality cloth manufactured within the city for the export market that York merchants most frequently used from the later fourteenth century to trade in exchange for these imports. Swanson notes that cloth was the only product manufactured specifically for export.[83] This trade provided employment additionally for porters and mariners.

A number of hostillers are recorded in the 1381 returns and these may have catered for the many visitors York attracted by reason of its trade, administrative, and ecclesiastical functions. Other visitors may have provided employment for the cooks and saucers who sold 'fast food' in the form of ready-cooked pies and meats. Although the city appears not to have benefited greatly from the cult of St William, whose shrine was housed in the Minster, there can be little doubt that the annual festival of Corpus Christi with its associated pageants brought in numerous visitors and additional trade.[84] The construction and maintenance of houses within the city generated demand for builders, masons, tilers, carpenters, and other unspecified labourers, but this demand must have been greatly augmented by the need to maintain the two miles of wall that surrounded the city, the Minster, the numerous other churches, the Ouse Bridge, and the

---

[81] This is prior to the assay Act of 1423: C. G. E. Bunt, *Chaffer's Handbook to Hallmarks on Gold and Silver Plate* (London, 1961), 108; Bartlett, 'Expansion and Decline', 19.

[82] Allison (ed.), *VCH, York, East Riding*, i. 59–70.

[83] Swanson, *Medieval Artisans*, 44, 141, 145.

[84] C. Wilson, *The Shrines of St William of York* (York, 1977). The unofficial cult of Richard Scrope enjoyed some popularity in the early 15th cent.: J. W. McKenna, 'Popular Canonization as Political Propaganda: The Cult of Archbishop Scrope', *Speculum*, 45 (1970), 608–23. The pageants associated with Corpus Christi regularly attracted visitors from outside the city including, in 1397, Richard II.

various gild halls and hospitals.[85] York thus differed from its regional neighbours in both scale and function. As a regional 'capital' it necessarily enjoyed a diversified economy and it is this that is reflected in the range of employment that may be demonstrated from the analysis of the occupational data contained in the 1381 poll tax returns.

A NOTE ON SOURCES

Women are not invisible in medieval sources, but equally they are often inconspicuous. Women rarely speak for themselves through surviving records, but when they do it is filtered through male hands and according to formal conventions. Married women are regularly hidden behind their husbands' names. Often there are legal and economic constraints that make it less likely that women will appear in certain sources than men. But these are not causes for despair; the medievalist is used to making a little evidence work very hard. Nor is it the case that all records are equally unhelpful. For later medieval Yorkshire there survive considerable numbers of registered wills associated with female testators. Indeed for York alone there are well over six hundred women's wills extant for the period before 1500. Wills tend only to be made by the relatively well-to-do, but women also feature in wills more generally as kith and kin, and as servants and employees. From this evidence much can be reconstructed even about individuals otherwise unlikely to make wills in their own right. Indeed wills prove a most rewarding source for the study of servants of either sex, but they also permit questions relating to widows continuing their late husbands' trades to be pursued from the evidence of bequests of tools and terms of apprenticeship.[86]

Wills are a well-known and much valued source, albeit they have more often been used to study aspects of piety and not hitherto such matters as servanthood.[87] Poll taxes are perhaps less

---

[85] H. Swanson, *Building Craftsmen in Late Medieval York* (Borthwick Paper, 63; 1983).

[86] For a fuller discussion of wills see Appendix I.

[87] Cf. P. W. Fleming, 'Charity, Faith, and the Gentry of Kent, 1422–1529', in A. J. Pollard (ed.), *Property and Politics; Essays in Later Medieval English History* (Gloucester, 1984), 36–58; P. Heath, 'Urban Piety in the Later Middle Ages: The Evidence of Hull Wills', in R. B. Dobson (ed.), *The Church, Politics and Patronage*

known, certainly as other than a crude guide to population totals at one specific date. As a tax on heads, female and male alike, they do have much to offer the historian of social structure. The nominative listings that survive from the 1377 returns in particular allow for some analysis of sex ratios, proportions married or in service, and size and structure of households. The later returns for 1379 and 1380–1 frequently provide occupational designations. These permit some insight into occupational structure and the composition of trade and craft-related households.[88] Perhaps the most valuable source for the student of later medieval social history is, however, the least known. This is the deposition evidence contained in ecclesiastical causes relating to such matters as debt, defamation, testamentary disputes, and marriage litigation.[89] This is an especially rewarding source for the study of women since women feature prominently both as parties to litigation and as deponents. For example, the depositions of some 230 women survive from matrimonial causes from the consistory and capitular courts of York prior to 1500. The depositions often contain a range of basic biographical data that permit some sort of prosopographical analysis in respect of age at marriage, patterns of migration, or servanthood. The matrimonial litigation further allows some insight into the nature and circumstances of marriage formation from both the male and the female perspective. Because cause papers survive from the early years of the fourteenth century, they, like wills, also permit some sort of secular analysis which may be set alongside the essentially static picture derived from poll tax evidence.[90]

These three principal sources, wills, poll tax returns, and cause papers, are considered at greater length in subsequent chapters. The variety of other sources used may be more briefly described.

---

in the Fifteenth Century (Gloucester, 1984), 209–34; N. P. Tanner, *The Church in Late Medieval Norwich, 1370–1532* (Toronto, 1984); J. A. F. Thomson, 'Piety and Charity in Late Medieval London', *Journal of Ecclesiastical History*, 16 (1965), 178–95.

[88] For a fuller discussion of the poll tax evidence see P. J. P. Goldberg, 'Urban Identity and the Poll Taxes of 1377, 1379, and 1380–1', *Economic History Review*, 2nd ser. 43 (1990), 194–216. See also Appendix II.

[89] The most useful introduction to marriage litigation is Helmholz, *Marriage Litigation*.

[90] For a fuller discussion of the York cause papers and a full list of those used in this study see Appendix III.

As just observed, the historian of medieval women cannot be over-selective of the available source material. Apparently unpromising lists of names, of which the poll taxes, rentals, and records of fines under the Assizes of Bread and Ale are but three examples, must be sympathetically analysed. Individual sources have their own particular problems and may act to an alarming degree as distorting lenses. Only by considering a number of such sources can a more coherent pattern emerge. At all times this study has attempted to explore the possibilities of each of a variety of sources rather than impose specific demands on a few more attractive sources. Patterns observed have been interpreted in the light of the broader socio-economic and demographic context. Where possible, moreover, sources have been examined over their entire period of survival before the early sixteenth century, since conclusions based on the examination of a particular source over but a few decades may well not be borne out over a lengthier time period.

In confronting nominative listings the investigator has to over-come certain serious problems of interpretation. Before the late fourteenth century surnames are notoriously unstable and the same individual may be known by several names even within the same source. The difficulty of identifying individuals over time and between sources is thus self-evident.[91] But the problem is compounded in the case of females. A woman changed her name on marriage, but unless the researcher has knowledge of that marriage and of the change of name, there is no way of tracing that woman over the period of her marriage. Even where married women are distinguished by reference to their spouses, it is not always possible to separate widows from currently married women. The surnames of servants often cannot be known since they are frequently described solely with reference to their employers. In law a married woman was not normally responsible for any debts she might incur. For this reason, therefore, lists of individuals fined are not always a reliable guide to the identity of the individuals whose activities are actually subject to the fine. The list of brewing fines contained in the Norwich leet rolls record

---

[91] For a recent discussion of the problem of nominal linkage between medieval records see J. M. Bennett, 'Spouses, Siblings and Surnames: Reconstructing Families from Medieval Village Court Rolls', *Journal of British Studies,* 23 (1983), 26–46.

variously husband and wife partnerships, wives only, and males only. Since there is no reason to believe that the sexual composition of Norwich brewers dramatically fluctuated from year to year, it must be concluded that many married women were active in this industry, but that they are sometimes represented by their husbands alone for record purposes. The observation is not limited to the leet rolls of the city of Norwich. This is a worrying matter and such evidence must needs be approached with due circumspection.

Similar problems are encountered when confronting the evidence of manor court rolls as is apparent in respect of Bennett's scholarly study of pre-plague Brigstock. She has described very different gender-specific patterns of brewing fines over three contrasting manors which she relates to the gender-specific demand for labour between differing agricultural economies.[92] This may be a real consideration, but it seems equally probable that these differences reflect alternative recording conventions between the three manors and that the record is often an indifferent guide to who actually brewed. Razi's pioneering demographic analysis based on the very extensive series of court rolls for the large manor of Halesowen is no less uncontroversial.[93] Though his findings regarding age at first marriage may be valid in many instances, it is unclear how representative his sample is. Manor court rolls record individuals selectively. The landless and the free did not owe suit of court; children, women, and labourers of either sex are as a consequence only observed by chance. This present work has made very limited use, confined to the published court rolls of the manor of Wakefield, of this well-known and much used source.[94] This is for two reasons. On the one hand, an analysis of a substantial body of court roll material is a task not lightly to be undertaken, but, on the other hand, some less known sources, notably the West Riding and Howdenshire poll tax returns for 1379 and the depositions contained within the York cause papers, offered to throw new light on the condition of rural women and to illuminate aspects of the rural economy not readily visible from court rolls.

[92] Bennett, *Women in the Medieval English Countryside*, 125–6.
[93] Razi, *Life, Marriage and Death*.
[94] The Wakefield court rolls are in the possession of the Yorkshire Archaeological Society in Leeds. Several rolls were published in translation early this century in the Society's record series and this task has recently been revived by the Society.

Two further sources that have been considered by historians of medieval rural society deserve brief consideration. Penn has demonstrated the value of peace sessions' rolls to study gender-specific patterns of wage labour from the evidence of presentments under the Statute of Labourers, though such presentments are but a small part of the material contained within the surviving rolls and the detail given in individual cases is never very substantial.[95] The relationship between those small numbers of individuals presented and the labouring population as a whole is also highly problematic. Penn suggests that women may sometimes be presented disproportionately to their involvement in the labour force by jurors seeking to enforce wage differentials.[96] The higher proportions of women presented in pastoral regions associated with a rural cloth industry accords, however, with poll tax evidence and probably represents a real phenomenon. Some Yorkshire evidence edited by Putnam dating from 1361–4 has been used in this present study, but it is apparent that this source deserves fuller analysis.[97] In an urban context, Statute of Labourers' court material dated 1390–2 is printed in Salter's edition of the medieval archives of the University of Oxford together with the Assizes of Bread and Ale between 1309 and 1351.[98] Coroners' rolls have been extensively used by Hanawalt, but both the validity of the surviving evidence and the relationship between accidental deaths and everyday activity is open to question. Consequently, though coroners' rolls survive for Yorkshire, they do not form part of this present work, although Sharpe's calendar of coroners' rolls for the City of London in the period 1300–78 has been consulted in respect of town life.[99]

Turning more specifically to urban society, borough court rolls, like manor court rolls, constitute an invaluable, but problematic source. Unfortunately virtually no such records survive for York

[95] Penn, 'Female Wage-Earners'.

[96] Ibid. 4–5, 9.

[97] B. H. Putnam (ed.), *Yorkshire Sessions of the Peace, 1361–4* (Yorkshire Archaeological Society Record ser. 100; 1939). See also L. R. Poos, 'The Social Context of Statute of Labourers Enforcement', *Law and History Review*, 1 (1983), 27–52.

[98] H. E. Salter (ed.), *Medieval Archives of the University of Oxford* (Oxford Historical Society, 73; 1921).

[99] R. R. Sharpe (ed.), *Calendar of Coroners Rolls of the City of London, 1300–1378* (London, 1913).

other than some rather fragmentary material from the wardmote courts for 1491, the sheriff's court for 1478–9 and 1497–8, and the Dean and Chapter's court for the Liberty of St Peter dating to 1445–6.[100] There survive also several valuable lists of brewsters' fines contained in the two surviving medieval chamberlains' books of account dating to the period 1446–54.[101] These are especially useful as fines are arranged by parish for the entire city. More substantial use has been made here of court records for a small number of towns outside the region. The Norwich leet rolls which survive, more or less complete, for a handful of years between 1288–9 and 1390–1 are especially informative.[102] No rolls survive for the sixty-year period 1313–74, however, and the last two surviving rolls (for 1374–5 and 1390–1) are much less detailed than those for the pre-plague years. The rolls record persons fined within different parts of the city for a variety of petty offences, many concerning trade. Numbers of women are listed here for forestalling grain, fish, and woollen yarn, for regrating cheese, and for trading outside the city's franchise, although the most names are recorded under the Assize of Ale. This then is a useful source for female trade activity from a comparatively early date. Certainly the original rolls are far fuller than Hudson's edition for the Selden Society would suggest.[103]

Some published borough court evidence, notably Stevenson's selections from the Nottingham court rolls, can throw much light on women's trading activities, though it must be remembered that they only become visible when they fall the wrong side of borough law.[104] The calendars of Plea and Memoranda Rolls for the City of London for the period 1323–1482 likewise provide evidence for female traders, apprenticeship, and prostitution.[105] Borough court

[100] YCA, chamberlains' account book CC 1A, fos. 135–9; sheriff's court books E 25, 25A; YML, Liberty of St Peter court roll F 1/3/1. In addition some fair court material survives for the earlier 15th cent.: Leeds Archive Office, CC/M3/34, 41, 42.

[101] YCA, chamberlains' account books CC 1, 1A.

[102] NRO, NCR Case 5, shelf b.

[103] W. Hudson (ed.), *Leet Jurisdiction in the City of Norwich During the Thirteenth and Fourteenth Century* (Selden Society, 5; 1892).

[104] W. H. Stevenson (ed.), *Records of the Borough of Nottingham* (3 vols.; Nottingham, 1882–5).

[105] A. H. Thomas and P. E. Jones (eds.), *Calendar of Plea and Memoranda Rolls of the City of London* (6 vols.; Cambridge, 1926–61). Some additional court material is contained in Bateson's edition of the medieval records of Leicester, in

evidence could further be used to study gender-specific patterns of indebtedness. This is an exercise that has yielded valuable results for Kowaleski in her study of the Exeter court rolls, but to repeat this for other periods and other towns with adequate surviving court records would be a massive undertaking.[106] The Chetham Society has, however, produced an edition of selected court rolls for Chester and these show on a more anecdotal basis debt cases involving women pledging various personal goods as security.[107] The full series of Chester court rolls, as those for Nottingham, Shrewsbury, and Tamworth, await more detailed analysis.

Whereas the records of the borough courts give some indication of the activities, albeit unlawful, of townsmen and women, and thus one particular angle on borough society, the records of borough ordinances can provide an insight into the civic concerns that shaped them and it was these the borough courts helped enforce. Some York material is entered in the city's Memorandum Book, and Prestwich has produced a useful edition of the York civic ordinances of 1301.[108] For fifteenth-century Coventry a unique source survives in the Leet Book published by the Early English Text Society.[109] For London the city's Letter-Books have been edited by Sharpe, although these were used only selectively for this study.[110] Some Oxford ordinances are contained in Salter's *Munimenta*, and some Leicester material in Bateson's edition of the borough records.[111] For Beverley, Leach's edition of borough

Owen's collection of Lynn material, and in Anderson's edition of the Assize of Bread Book for 1437–1517: M. Bateson (ed.), *Records of the Borough of Leicester*, ii. *1327–1509* (London, 1901); D. M. Owen (ed.), *The Making of King's Lynn* (Records of Social and Economic History, NS 9; London, 1984); R. C. Anderson (ed.), *The Assize of Bread Book, 1437–1517* (Southampton Record Society, 23; 1923).

[106] Kowaleski, 'Women's Work in a Market Town'.

[107] A. Hopkins (ed.), *Selected Rolls of the Chester City Courts* (Chetham Society, 3rd ser. 2; 1950).

[108] M. Prestwich (ed.), *York Civic Ordinances, 1301* (Borthwick Paper, 49; 1976).

[109] M. D. Harris (ed.), *The Coventry Leet Book* (EETS 134–5, 138, 146; 1907–13).

[110] R. R. Sharpe (ed.), *Calendar of Letter-Books . . . of the City of London* (11 vols.; London, 1899–1912).

[111] H. E. Salter (ed.), *Munimenta Civitatis Oxonie* (Oxford Historical Society, 71; 1920); Bateson (ed.), *Records of the Borough of Leicester*, ii.

records contains a number of ordinances and the Black Book of Winchester, edited by Bird, provides like material.[112]

Rentals are lists of individuals responsible for renting property and the sums they accounted for. Unlike the poll taxes, therefore, they provide no information on the family or household group the tenant may represent. They can be used, however, to study the distribution of female-headed households and, using consecutive series of rentals, how this pattern may have changed with time, and how great was the degree of turnover among tenants within properties of different values. The long, but somewhat patchy, rental series for the properties of the York Vicars Choral, dating back to *c.*1309, and selected fifteenth-century rentals of property used to maintain the Ouse Bridge have been analysed for this study.[113] The York material, and especially the long rental series of the Vicars Choral, is of especial value as it is possible to be fairly sure that those paying the rent were indeed the actual tenants. Very few names are repeated through the rentals and there is a high turnover of names between rentals, especially in the instance of cheaper properties. Where names and locations can be confirmed from alternative sources they coincide. The rentals may also, with certain major qualifications, be used to study patterns of demand for property over time and thus indirectly levels of population. Like use has been made of the stall rentals for Norwich market, recorded in the city chamberlains' account books from 1378, and these too have been noted where they have survived into the sixteenth century.[114] These rentals provide some indication of female activity, notably within the fish market, but there are problems inasmuch as the rental names only the official lessee, who may not have been personally responsible for the day-to-day management of an individual stall.

Gild ordinances can provide useful evidence for female employment and the regulation of female workers. There are several problems in interpreting the role of craft gilds. That ordinances usually only survive in official civic collections, as at York, has persuaded historians to argue that they reflect the interests of the

---

[112] A. F. Leach (ed.), *Beverley Town Documents* (Selden Society, 14; 1900); W. H. B. Bird (ed.), *The Black Book of Winchester* (Winchester, 1925).

[113] YML, VC 4/1/1–16; VC 6/2/1–78; YCA, C 82: 3–5, 10; C 83: 5; C 84: 2; C 85: 1; C 86: 1.

[114] NRO, NCR Case 18, shelf a.

mercantile oligarchy rather than those of the craft masters.[115]
There has been a tendency, moreover, to see a simple development over time in the provision of ordinances relating to a
particular craft.[116] This interpretation is difficult to sustain in the
light of the evidence of the ordinances themselves. These are
regularly presented as having been agreed first among the craft
masters and only subsequently presented for civic approval. There
is little cause to believe this to be a fiction since ordinances treated
matters of specific concern to gild members; gilds were employers'
organizations and ordinances regulating wages or hours of work
do not ultimately appear to be in the interests of other than the
craft masters, though there is no reason that their own interests
did not often coincide with the wider interests of the civic
authorities likewise concerned to maintain trading standards and
limit wages. Indeed it is this community of interest, and the need
for gilds to draw upon the support of civic authorities to exercise
discipline over even those who were outside the gild, that helps
explain the frequency with which gilds came to have those
ordinances concerned with craft regulation registered with the
civic authorities.

The revision of existing ordinances and the addition of new
ordinances do seem regularly to reflect the particular circumstances prevailing at the time of framing the ordinances as they
affected gild members. Thus increased regulation about the
employment of unskilled labour or excessive numbers of apprentices by the later fifteenth century coincides with a period of
recession and represents an attempt to divide work available
between craft masters and prevent 'unfair' competition. The
exclusion of female weavers from a number of towns at the end of
the period is but an extension of this pattern, rather than a
definition of earlier custom. This is not to deny that the crafts
were not subject to some degree of civic supervision, though, as
suggested, in terms of trade regulation their interests may often
have coincided. It was in the interests of the gilds, moreover, to
involve the civic authorities as an additional policing organization

---

[115] The general absence of socio-religious ordinances from civic collections has
likewise been used as evidence that councils were interested only in the regulation
of the craft as opposed to the fraternity. See esp. Swanson, 'The Illusion of
Economic Structure'; ead., *Medieval Artisans*, 111–20.

[116] Cf. Miller, 'Medieval York', 92–7.

so that sanctions against those within and outside the craft could be effectively prosecuted for breach of the gild ordinances. It is perhaps for this reason that fines levied were often divided between the gild and the city or borough. It is further apparent from the York evidence that the civic authorities played a key role in resolving disputes between individual crafts, possibly at the request of the crafts concerned. Thus in a dispute between the masons and the tilers of York early in the fifteenth century, it was ruled that the tilers should contribute to the masons' gild if they built a wall of stone or stone foundations to a brick building.[117]

No systematic survey of gild regulations has been attempted here, although the ordinances contained in the York Memoranda Books and other printed sources elsewhere have been analysed. A full collection of Beverley gild ordinances has been edited by Leach for the Selden Society.[118] A number of returns made in response to the 1389 survey of religious gilds or confraternities additional to those printed in Toulmin Smith's excellent collection were also consulted.[119] The concern here was the degree of provision or otherwise for female gild members and the wider welfare provision such gilds maintained. It is unfortunate that almost no medieval records of the York craft or trade gilds, besides their registered ordinances, have survived for other than the mercers' gild.[120] Little survives for the many religious confraternities outside the élite Corpus Christi Gild, although an apparently detailed account roll of the Paternoster Gild dated 1399 has been lost only this century.[121] It is consequently hardly possible, in the absence of records of membership in most instances, to say very much about the nature of the female membership of the craft and religious gilds in York.

It may sometimes be possible to use the occupational data

[117] M. Sellers (ed.), *York Memorandum Book* (Surtees Society, 120, 125; 1912–15) i. 148.
[118] Sellers (ed.), *York Memorandum Book,* i, ii; J. W. Percy (ed.), *York Memorandum Book,* iii (Surtees Society, 186; 1973); Leach (ed.), *Beverley Town Documents.*
[119] J. T. Smith (ed.), *English Gilds; Original Ordinances of the Fourteenth and Fifteenth Centuries* (EETS 40; 1870); PRO, C 47/42, 45, 46 various.
[120] M. Sellers (ed.), *The York Mercers and Merchant Adventurers, 1356–1917* (Surtees Society, 129; 1918).
[121] R. H. Skaife (ed.), *The Register of the Guild of Corpus Christi in the City of York* (Surtees Society, 57; 1872); A. Raine, *Mediaeval York* (London, 1955), 91–2.

derived from the records of admissions to the urban franchise to reconstruct the secular movement in the occupational structures of urban communities in order to relate this to possible trends in the employment of female labour. The patterns observed, however, can only be understood in the context of a more detailed analysis of the economic fortunes of individual communities, and such an analysis was only attempted for York. Printed editions of franchise material for a number of communities, namely York, Exeter, Lynn, London, Nottingham, Leicester, Norwich, Wells, Chester, and Great Yarmouth, were employed and the pattern of female admissions, themselves rare outside York, was noted.[122] Although women appear from these to have played little part in the franchise system and the associated right to trade retail, and thus to set up shop and employ labour independently, several towns operated an alternative licensing system or else imposed fines for breach of franchise with sufficient regularity to constitute such a system. An analysis of the records of those so licensed or fined reveals that women are better represented here and that these patterns can tell something of the structure of female employment. In this respect the record of the Canterbury *intrantes* from 1392, and the much more fragmentary records of the licences to traffic at Nottingham are especially valuable.[123] For York a small number of stallage payments are recorded among the surviving chamberlains' account rolls and books of account.[124] Similarly at Norwich persons fined for trading outside the franchise are listed in the city's leet rolls, but with such sufficient regularity as to constitute an informal system of licensing.[125]

[122] F. Collins (ed.), *Register of the Freemen of the City of York*, i. *1272–1588* (Surtees Society, 96; 1896); M. M. Rowe and A. M. Jackson (eds.), *Exeter Freemen, 1266–1972* (Devon and Cornwall Record Society, extra ser. 1; 1973); *A Calendar of the Freemen of Lynn, 1292–1836* (Norfolk and Norwich Archaeological Society, 1913); H. Hartopp (ed.), *Register of the Freemen of Leicester, 1196–1770* (Leicester, 1927); NRO, NCR Case 17, shelf c, 1 (Old Free Book); D. O. Shilton and R. Holworthy (eds.), *Wells City Charters* (Somerset Record Society, 46; 1932); J. H. E. Bennett (ed.), *The Rolls of the Freemen of the City of Chester*, i. *1392–1700* (Lancashire and Cheshire Record Ser. 51; 1906).

[123] J. M. Cowper (ed.), *Intrantes: A List of Persons Admitted to Live and Trade in Canterbury, 1392–1592* (Canterbury, 1904); Stevenson (ed.), *Records of the Borough of Nottingham*.

[124] R. B. Dobson (ed.), *The York Chamberlains' Account Rolls, 1396–1500* (Surtees Society, 192; 1980); YCA, C 5: 1–3; CC 1, 1A.

[125] NRO, NCR Case 5, shelf b.

One additional source for female economic activity are the aulnage accounts relating to the merchandising (rather than the manufacture) of cloth. A very full account survives from York for 1394–5 and this lists a large number of female traders. It seems that this account at least is free from the sort of criticisms made of the source generally by Carus-Wilson, although some fifteenth-century accounts do appear unsatisfactory.[126] The York roll, together with a number of other Yorkshire rolls, is published in Lister's edition of documents relating to the regional woollen industry.[127] Not only is it possible to identify some individuals against other sources, but some indication of the sexual composition of the trade at a given date may be derived.

Many of the sources discussed above must appear superficially unattractive to the social historian, especially when set alongside such literary sources as the poetry of Langland or Chaucer, or even the gild pageants associated with the Corpus Christi Play. Yet perhaps too much has been written about medieval society based solely on literary sources without a fuller awareness of their appropriate literary and historical context.[128] Used carefully, however, literary material can add to an understanding of the society in which such material was created, provided we recognize the dangers of associating such literary fictions as the Wife of Bath, Rose the Regrator, or even Noah's Wife, the products of a long-established misogynist literary genre, too closely with real models. This last is not a problem in the case of Margery Kempe's autobiographical account, though her life story, focused as it is on her spiritual development, is an indifferent source for the economic historian.[129] Of perhaps greater value here, though to be treated with no less circumspection, are writings designed to instruct women in what was regarded to be 'correct' behaviour. Power's translation of *Le Ménagier de Paris* (1392–4) and Law-

[126] E. M. Carus-Wilson, 'The Aulnage Accounts: A Criticism', *Economic History Review*, 2 (1929), 114–23.

[127] J. Lister (ed.), *The Early Yorkshire Woollen Trade* (Yorkshire Archaeological Society Record Ser. 64; 1928).

[128] Cf. A. M. Lucas, *Women in the Middle Ages; Religion, Marriage and Letters* (Brighton, 1983); M. M. Sheehan, 'The Wife of Bath and Her Four Sisters: Reflections on a Woman's Life in the Age of Chaucer', *Medievalia et Humanistica*, NS 13 (1985), 23–42.

[129] S. B. Meech and H. E. Allen (eds.), *The Book of Margery Kempe* (EETS 212; 1940).

son's translation of Christine de Pisan's *Le Livre du trésor de la cité des dames* (1405) make available in English two more substantial works of considerable importance. Both, it must be recognized, are designed primarily for the edification of a French audience drawn from the upper levels of society and are thus of strictly limited value in an English urban context.[130] In this respect 'How the Good Wijf tauȝte Hir Douȝtir', composed in English in the mid-fourteenth century, is of especial interest.[131] Such didactic literature addressed to women deserves special study. It may not say much directly about how women actually behaved, though it may say something about the normative concerns of the society out of which this literature derives. Clearly there was a perceived need for such writings, but this is not to say that they were in themselves very influential. Such questions are beyond the scope of this present study, which uses literary evidence merely to amplify findings from more conventional historical records.

[130] E. E. Power, trans., *The Goodman of Paris* (London, 1928); C. de Pisan, *The Treasure of the City of Ladies,* trans. S. Lawson (Harmondsworth, 1985).

[131] 'How the Good Wijf tauȝte Hir Dauȝtir', in F. J. Furnivall (ed.), *The Babees Book* (EETS 32; 1868), 36–47.

2

York and the Regional Economy in the Later Middle Ages

The impact of plague on the nation's economy and the fortunes of both urban and rural communities following the Black Death are, and will probably long continue, matters for keen debate among historians.[1] The older notion that the period following the Black Death was characterized by general *malaise* has been much refined, but there is as yet no general consensus as to how far either towns or rural communities prospered or failed in this period, or how this pattern may be related to wider economic trends.[2] Since the employment of women in the town must be related to trends in the demand for labour in both town and country, itself a product of wider economic and demographic considerations, it is necessary to review here the evidence for a number of urban economies and in particular that of York, and to attempt to place this in a wider regional economic context. This chapter will attempt to reconstruct the occupational structure of the community from poll tax and franchise evidence and consider how this may have changed from the fourteenth to the early sixteenth century. Parallel changes in the occupational topography of York itself may be identified by comparing poll tax and testamentary sources. These observations will be interpreted in the light of more general evidence relating to the economy of both the city and the region. It is possible by this method to propose some sort of chronology of economic change. The one feature that seems to be of especial significance is the pattern of prolonged

---

[1] See for example Hatcher, *Plague, Population and the English Economy*; C. Dyer, *Standards of Living in the Later Middle Ages: Social Change in England c.1200–1520* (Cambridge, 1989).

[2] For a recent survey of the debate in respect of towns see D. M. Palliser, 'Urban Decay Revisited', in J. A. F. Thomson (ed.), *Towns and Townspeople in the Fifteenth Century* (Gloucester, 1988), 1–21. There is increasing interest in medieval agriculture in the later Middle Ages, but rural industry and the economic fortunes of rural communities after the Black Death have received less attention.

demographic recession following the Black Death. This last has implications for the supply of labour, the demand for goods and services, and the structure of both urban and rural economies. The latter part of this chapter will more briefly review the evidence for other urban communities and for the pattern of economic development nationally. The purpose is to establish a general framework against which the detailed evidence relating specifically to women in both town and country may be understood.

URBAN OCCUPATIONAL STRUCTURE: THE POLL TAX EVIDENCE

A rare insight into the structure of the urban economy of the late fourteenth century exists in the surviving returns for the poll tax or subsidy levied on heads. Three successive poll taxes were raised in the space of four years (1377, 1379, and 1380–1) as novel means to meet the financial burden of the Hundred Years War. The basis for assessment differed in each case.[3] That for the first was a simple flat-rate levy of a groat (4*d.*) for every lay person aged 14 or more. Only the clergy, taxed separately, and the indigent were exempt. Because the same rate of tax was to be paid by all, comparatively few nominative listings (those recording individual taxpayers by name) appear to have been kept. The assessment of 1379 was levied on adults and adolescents over 16 years, but on a differential basis according to status. Servants and labourers were assessed at a minimum rate of 4*d.*, but artisans at 6*d.*, 1*s.* or more, and the upper ranks of society at still higher rates. Married couples, however, were assessed together as if a single person at the individual rate. It follows that some returns record the names of married men, but not their wives since no extra tax was due in respect of a married woman. The final, and most controversial, assessment of 1380–1 was an unhappy compromise between the flat rate and the graduated assessments. Lay persons over 15 were taxed at differing rates above a minimum of 4*d.* such that the mean assessment within any given vill or parish was exactly a

---

[3] *Rotuli Parliamentorum* (6 vols., London, 1783), ii. 363–4; iii. 57–8, 90; M. W. Beresford, *Lay Subsidies and Poll Taxes* (Canterbury, 1963).

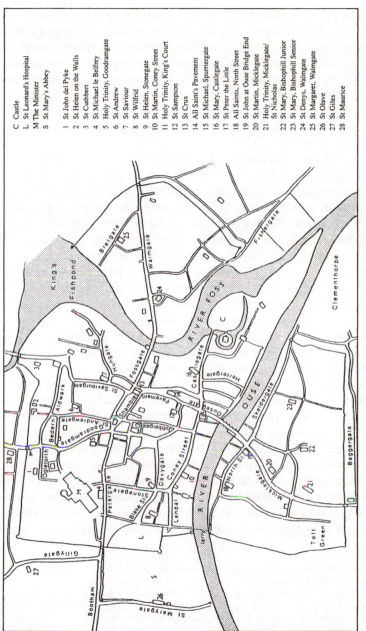

C Castle
L St Leonard's Hospital
M The Minster
S St Mary's Abbey

1   St John del Pyke
2   St Helen on the Walls
3   St Cuthbert
4   St Michael le Belfrey
5   Holy Trinity, Goodramgate
6   St Andrew
7   St Saviour
8   St Wilfrid
9   St Helen, Stonegate
10 St Martin, Coney Street
11 Holy Trinity, King's Court
12 St Sampson
13 St Crux
14 All Saint's Pavement
15 St Michael, Spurriergate
16 St Mary, Castlegate
17 St Peter the Little
18 All Saints, North Street
19 St John at Ouse Bridge End
20 St Martin, Micklegate
21 Holy Trinity, Micklegate/
    St Nicholas
22 St Mary, Bishophill Junior
23 St Mary, Bishophill Senior
24 St Denys, Walmgate
25 St Margaret, Walmgate
26 St Olave
27 St Giles
28 St Maurice

Map 2.1. York in the Fifteenth Century

shilling (12*d.*) a head.[4] Each county, excluding the palatinates of Durham and Cheshire, was assessed by individuals appointed to each hundred or wapentake working from vill to vill and parish to parish. Many major towns, however, were assessed separately, usually by parish, ward, or street. The method of compiling the returns, which were then forwarded to the Exchequer, varied consequently from one assessment to another and it is possible to observe considerable differences between returns relating even to the same year.

The poll tax evidence may be analysed in a variety of ways. It is the returns for 1379 and 1380–1 that provide much useful evidence for employment and economic structure at one specific date, and some more detailed returns, as for example those for Howdenshire, the West Riding, Oxford, and Southwark, are especially valuable sources for the employment of women. The quality of the returns nevertheless varies considerably. Most criticism has been directed at the returns for 1380–1. A pattern of underenumeration, especially among females and female servants, was first described by Oman and has been reiterated more recently by Hilton.[5] This defect must be acknowledged, but to some extent any skewed pattern may be a product of migration from rural districts into the towns, since urban communities are characterized by low sex ratios according to the same poll tax evidence. Bartlett, writing about the York returns for 1381, concludes that the tax there was modelled not on actual heads, but rather on the earlier subsidy of 1374. The 'evidence of deliberate fraud' is again real enough, but it does not invalidate the source since the effects of the 'fraud' can be understood. Bartlett's analysis also suggests that the problem of underenumeration was the product not of evasion, but of exclusion. The level of underenumeration at York was in fact much more marked than was true of a number of other towns. Indeed it would appear that the urban poll tax returns for 1380–1 are generally more comprehensive than those surviving for larger

---

[4] Servants are sometimes separately listed at the end of the return in both the 1379 and 1380–1 listings.

[5] C. Oman, *The Great Revolt of 1381* (2nd edn., Oxford, 1969), 28; Hilton, *The English Peasantry*, 27–8. A list of published poll tax returns is contained in the note to Table II.1 below. A list of original poll tax material consulted (PRO, E 179 various) is contained in the bibliography of primary sources. All subsequent references are to these sources.

village communities due to the thoroughness of the survey at the street, ward, or parish level.[6]

The survival of poll tax listings from the 1379 West Riding survey is especially fortunate both because it allows York to be compared against a number of other manufacturing towns within the Yorkshire region, and because, together with the surviving Howdenshire returns, it provides evidence for a major part of the rural economy of the region. The chief value of the 1379 and 1380–1 returns lies in the designation of occupations to individual taxpayers. The bias in the composition of the tax population is probably that more substantial artisans and traders are recorded at the expense of those more marginally employed and, in some instances, single female workers. The Oxford and, more especially, the Southwark returns for 1381 list independent female traders, namely spinsters, shepsters, washerwomen, and, in the case of Southwark, hucksters in some quantity. But at York (1381) and Shrewsbury single women tend to be noted only as labourers, an imprecise term denoting employees or workers of low status. The Lichfield returns list a number of female 'cottars', whereas the fragmentary Northampton (1381) returns fail singularly to record female householders of any description, despite the inclusion of a large and miscellaneous group of male labourers. Only the York, Lichfield, Lynn (1379), and Sheffield (1379) assessments distinguish widows with any consistency. Despite these limitations, the later poll tax returns do constitute a unique source by which the occupational structure of towns in the later fourteenth century may be analysed.

The recording of trades is much more consistent for the 1381 returns than those for 1379, where only persons formally designated as artisans, and thus liable to pay tax at a higher rate, were described in occupational terms. Where recorded surnames coincide with trade names, however, it is often implicit that these alone were thought sufficient to identify individual taxpayers. This is true of the York returns, where trade designations are only given where the occupational surname is inappropriate.[7] Given

---

[6] J. N. Bartlett (ed.), *The Lay Poll Tax Returns for the City of York in 1381* (Hull, 1953), 7. An analysis of rural returns for the East Riding in 1381 against the equivalent returns for 1377 suggests that the larger the community, the more defective the 1381 total is likely to be.

[7] Ibid. 1.

the probable degree of instability demonstrated by surnames at this period, especially in the North, it has been thought reasonable here to use occupational surnames as evidence of trade or craft allegiance, even for individuals otherwise loosely designated as labourers or artisans. This does serve to increase the population identifiable by craft, particularly in respect of the 1379 returns, without introducing an unnecessary degree of error. The number of persons for whom occupations can be so identified constitutes some 44 per cent of the total recorded population of Lynn, some 52 per cent of Pontefract, and 58 per cent of Wakefield in 1379 together with some 78 per cent of Oxford and 83 per cent of Southwark in 1381.[8] The sex ratios (calculated as the numbers of males to females) of these populations tend to be only a little higher than for the total tax populations due to the exclusion of widows and other single females enjoying no recorded craft or trade status. There is little reason to believe that this population constitutes other than a statistically impressive sample of the true population and, but for some specific female traders, is not unduly biased against any sectors of the urban economy.

For comparative purposes, the poll tax data have been analysed not by individual trades, but by grouping related occupations under twelve separate heads. The twelve occupational categories adopted are modelled upon those used by Phythian-Adams to analyse the Coventry enumeration of 1523.[9] The purpose of such broad classifications of economic activity is twofold. It allows for ready comparison between communities and, where compatible data are available, over time within communities. It further obviates some of the difficulties inherent in single trade analyses. As Swanson has demonstrated, craft terminology tended not to be entirely stable and the work performed within different gilds tended to overlap.[10] At the expense of sacrificing knowledge of individual commercial activities, the use of trade categories does still permit some sort of measure to be used. The choice of categories, however, must necessarily be somewhat arbitrary as is also the allocation of craft or trade activities to specific categories.

---

[8] Persons designated as agriculturalists and certain other non-productive groups i.e. yeomen, gentlemen, and civic officials, are not included within this economic population.

[9] Phythian-Adams, *Desolation of a City*, 311–17.

[10] Swanson, *Medieval Artisans*, 117–18.

TABLE 2.1. *Occupational categories adopted*

Category	Occupations included	Occupations excluded
1. Victuals	hucksters, millers, grocers	chapmen
2. Leather	cordwainers, sutors, etc.	cappers, glovers
3. Textiles	spinsters	
4. Clothing	shepsters, cappers, glovers, pointers	mercers, drapers
5. Mercantile	mercers, drapers, chapmen	grocers
6. Metal	grinders, armourers, potters	
7. Building	glaziers, painters, stainers	wrights, sawyers
8. Wood	wrights, sawyers	
9. Transport	mariners, carters, porters, boatmen	
10. Armaments	bowyers, stringers, fletchers	armourers
11. Chandlers	soap-makers	
12. Others	barbers, clerks, doctors, gardeners	yeomen, gentlemen

Note: The classifications used have been based upon those adopted by Phythian-Adams for Coventry in 1523 and only more marginal cases are indicated. The categories of 'official' and 'professional' have been dropped, although some occupations are included under 'others': Phythian-Adams, *Desolation of a City*, table 38, pp. 311–15. Grocers and spicers appear as victualling traders, and glovers, pursers, and pouch-makers are classified as clothing traders. These are comparatively minor changes in terms of their effect on the structure derived. Some labourers are listed under 'building' where the term appears not to be used indiscriminately. Potters, as opposed to earth potters, are counted as metalworkers: Swanson, *Medieval Artisans*, 75.

The present analysis is limited to manufacturing, mercantile, and service occupations. Agriculture has been entirely omitted with the marginal exception of gardeners. Only for the small market town of Howden does this serve to exclude a significant element within the urban tax population. The groupings adopted, together with some indication of the distribution of marginal cases, are tabulated in Table 2.1. The results achieved for individual towns are set out in Table 2.2.

Because of the limitations of the source material, the individual statistics should be regarded as only approximate. The data for Worcester and Northampton are particularly fragile being based upon very fragmentary returns, but there is little reason to doubt the broad patterns that emerge in respect of most other communities. The evidence suggests that certain structural features of occupational categories may be identified as characteristically

TABLE 2.2.   *Urban occupational structure from the poll tax by trade*
category (%)

	N	Category											
		1	2	3	4	5	6	7	8	9	10	11	12
1377													
York†*	958	14.5	10.4	14.9	11.8	12.6	14.5	5.0	5.3	1.4	2.8	0.8	5.8
1379													
Doncaster	296	20.6	15.9	12.2	8.4	8.8	10.1	5.1	6.4	4.4	3.4	—	4.7
Howden	225	40.9	12.4	8.0	12.4	5.3	7.6	6.7	2.7	—	—	0.4	3.6
Lynn†	510	12.2	11.0	15.1	10.4	19.4	8.4	3.5	2.5	10.6	1.0	2.4	3.5
Pontefract	476	24.8	14.1	14.1	11.3	10.9	10.7	1.7	4.0	1.3	4.8	—	2.3
Ripon	277	19.1	17.0	12.3	13.0	10.4	7.6	4.0	7.9	2.9	0.7	—	5.0
Rotherham	184	22.8	12.0	21.2	9.2	10.3	13.0	2.7	4.3	2.2	—	0.5	1.6
Sheffield	124	16.9	13.7	7.2	16.1	2.4	25.0	1.6	8.9	1.6	2.4	—	4.0
Wakefield	180	11.1	10.6	21.1	15.6	15.6	12.2	2.8	6.7	—	—	—	4.4
1381													
Lichfield	365	17.5	15.9	10.4	11.5	4.1	8.8	8.8	12.1	1.4	1.9	—	7.6
Northampton†	262	20.2	11.1	23.3	8.8	3.1	6.5	16.0	1.5	0.8	—	2.7	6.1
Oxford	1535	27.2	14.7	13.5	11.9	4.7	6.2	7.0	3.2	2.7	1.6	2.0	5.3
Southwark	865	27.2	13.5	5.9	13.2	0.2	5.8	9.0	6.2	7.7	0.7	0.8	9.8
Worcester†	164	21.3	19.5	17.7	11.6	5.5	5.5	5.5	3.7	3.0	—	3.7	3.0
York	2193	15.8	15.0	11.6	8.4	15.5	12.8	3.6	5.7	2.6	2.1	0.4	6.4

† Partial return only. Structure may not be representative.
* Occupations identified by comparison with freemen's register and 1381 returns
following J. I. Leggett (ed.), 'The 1377 Poll Tax Returns for the City of York',
Yorkshire Archaeological Journal, 43 (1971), 128–46.
Sources: See Table II.1 below.

urban. Local variation may be identified within this broader
structure. In the majority of towns the victualling trades form the
largest single group, though the port of Lynn and the textile town
of Wakefield enjoy only relatively low proportions. The Howden
figure is atypically high, but this may partly be explained by the
large proportion of female brewsters identifiable from this
unusually comprehensive return and also from the effect of
excluding agricultural workers. Proportions engaged in the
leather, textiles, clothing, and metal trades appear surprisingly
uniform. All these trades seem to have been major employers.
This was true not least of York. The importance here of other

manufacturing industries besides textiles may be noted, an observation that warns that the economic fortunes of a relatively mature urban economy cannot be explained solely in terms of fluctuations in a single industry.[11] The strikingly large numbers of persons engaged in tailoring and allied trades in Wakefield is demonstrative of the way the manufacture and merchandising of textiles and clothing dominated the town. The importance of textiles to Rotherham and likewise to Northampton, despite the limitations of the small sample, seems also to be demonstrated.

Southwark is conspicuous for the general absence of manufacturing trades, particularly textiles, and the corresponding total absence of drapers and mercers. As at the port of Lynn, however, an appreciable proportion of persons was engaged in transport, in this instance as Thames boatmen. The dependent nature of Southwark upon London as part of a larger economic unit does much to explain this unusual structure. The importance of trade and merchandising to Lynn and likewise to York, whose merchants operated through the port of Hull, is similarly demonstrated. The proximity of Lichfield to Cannock Chase and the Forest of Arden is reflected in the numbers of craftsmen in wood recorded there. The trends observed do thus appear to accord sufficiently well with expectation to inspire confidence in most instances.

A similar exercise may be conducted in respect of the rural West Riding returns for 1379. Given that the largest proportion of this population was engaged primarily in agriculture and there was thus less certainty that the rather limited range of trade name surnames identified actual occupations, it was decided to use only specific trade designations to calculate the structure of the population engaged in craft or trade.[12] The structure so derived is tabulated in Table 2.3. This departs radically from the pattern derived for urban society. The range of trades noted is very narrow. Many communities contained one or more smiths, carpenters, tailors, and souters or shoemakers. Weavers were also common, but more specifically concentrated. Few other crafts occur with any regularity. The occupational structure displays

[11] Cf. Bartlett, 'Expansion and Decline of York', 19.

[12] In a number of rural communities certain surnames recur several times. Since this may indicate kin relationship even where the surname is also a common trade name, to use other than specific occupational designations was thought unsafe.

TABLE 2.3.   *Rural West Riding occupational structure from the 1379 poll tax by trade category (%)*

Wapentake	N	Category											
		1	2	3	4	5	6	7	8	9	10	11	12
Strafforth	220	7.3	7.7	6.8	20.9	15.0	20.0	4.5	16.4	—	0.9	—	0.5
Tickhill	185	3.2	4.3	16.8	20.5	12.4	26.5	2.2	13.5	—	—	—	0.5
Staincross	132	8.3	26.5	9.8	16.7	9.8	24.2	3.0	0.8	—	—	—	0.8
Osgodcross	318	7.5	7.5	18.2	22.6	8.2	21.1	4.4	7.2	2.2	0.3	—	0.6
Aggbrigg	120	1.7	21.7	10.8	25.0	8.3	16.7	0.8	14.2	—	—	—	0.8
Claro	281	12.5	8.9	21.4	21.4	4.6	12.8	3.6	12.8	—	1.1	0.4	1.4
Ainsty	107	19.6	2.8	19.6	15.0	7.5	15.9	0.9	15.9	—	1.9	—	0.9
Staincliffe	192	6.3	5.7	26.6	19.3	9.9	13.0	3.6	12.5	—	1.0	—	2.1

Notes: Only those wapentakes where the numbers of designated artisans or traders were in excess of a hundred have been tabulated here. Beast merchant, i.e. trader in livestock, has been counted under mercantile.

Source: 'Rolls of the Collectors in the West Riding of the Lay-Subsidy (Poll Tax) 2 Richard II', *Yorkshire Archaeological Journal*, 5–7 (1879–84).

greater variety. With the exception of the Ainsty, York's immediate neighbour and from 1396 to be administratively dependent upon York, comparatively small proportions are found engaged in victualling trades. Even the larger proportions within Claro Wapentake and the Ainsty are due to the numbers of brewers and brewsters recorded there. The proportions engaged in clothing are uniformly high and generally in excess of equivalent urban proportions. There is, however, no obvious correlation between proportions engaged in clothing and in textiles. The proportions counted under leather, textiles, and metal vary widely and must reflect closely the pattern of resources within the local economy. Thus it is possible to identify wool, livestock, and mining regions from the distribution of weavers, souters, and smiths respectively. The distribution of workers in wood, described for the most part variously as wrights or carpenters, may likewise tend to reflect the local availability of timber. The categories of transport, chandlers, and miscellaneous are almost empty. This last is in marked contrast to the equivalent urban proportions, that reflect the diversified and specialist nature of the urban economy.

URBAN OCCUPATIONAL STRUCTURE:
THE FRANCHISE EVIDENCE

The poll tax evidence provides a coherent, but static picture of the occupational structure of a range of urban communities some three decades after the Black Death. For a dynamic picture an alternative source must be explored. The surviving records of admissions to the urban franchise, which frequently record craft affiliation, will allow the occupational structure of a community to be viewed over time and some measure of economic change to be derived. This is, however, not an easy source to handle and it is possible here to consider only some of the limitations inherent. Circumstances varied substantially from town to town over time and, in the absence of more detailed case studies such as that by Swanson for York, the autonomous value of such data must be taken on trust.[13] The observed correlation between poll tax and franchise statistics is, nevertheless, encouraging. In general, the principles of analysis adopted correspond to those applied to the poll tax occupational evidence. A number of freemen's rolls have been published, usually with the interests of the genealogist at heart, but little attempt has so far been made to reconstruct urban trade structure from this source for a period prior to the sixteenth century.[14] Such a reconstruction represents, however, a more direct use of the evidence than attempts to estimate demographic trends or fluctuations in urban prosperity.[15]

Relatively little has been written to date on how the franchise system operated or what role the enfranchised performed within the wider community.[16] On the one hand, for those admitted, the franchise bestowed real advantages, notably exemption from tolls, the right to engage apprentices, and the right to trade retail. Often it was a necessary qualification for gild mastership and, in theory

[13] H. C. Swanson, 'Craftsmen and Industry in Late Medieval York', D.Phil. thesis (York, 1980), 13; ead., *Medieval Artisans*, 5; Dobson, 'Admissions to the Freedom'.

[14] A. R. Bridbury, *Economic Growth: England in the Later Middle Ages* (London, 1962), 49–50; Bartlett, 'Expansion and Decline of York', 17–33.

[15] Cf. Reynolds, *English Medieval Towns*, 142.

[16] Exceptions are Dobson, 'Admissions to the Freedom'; Rowe and Jackson (eds.), *Exeter Freemen*, pp. xi–xxix; Thomas (ed.), *Calendar of Plea and Memoranda Rolls, 1364–81*, pp. xxv–xliv; Swanson, *Medieval Artisans*, 107–10.

at least, it allowed a voice in urban government. It can be argued that most townsfolk aspired to the franchise and it was perhaps with some pride that those who achieved it invariably described themselves as burgess or citizen in their testaments. On the other hand, it was civic policy to exercise tight control over trade, not least retail trade, as a means of social control.[17] Enfranchisement was a licence to trade retail, but it was seldom an exclusive right. A number of towns operated a system of regular fines, stallage payments, or annual licences to traffic which permitted those outside the franchise ('foreigners') to engage in trade.[18] In many towns there were ecclesiastical and other liberties apparently exempt from civic jurisdiction in respect of trade. Such was the liberty of St Peter's in York, although by the fourteenth century it appears that its residents were not actually excluded from the civic franchise.[19] The same may have been true of other urban liberties. The unfree might also trade on a carefully regulated basis within the official market.

Entry to the franchise was thus not the sine qua non for the independent trader wishing to engage in business. This may have been all the more true given the limitations of law enforcement in a medieval urban context. Not all artisans would, moreover, have had need to trade retail since some were in effect contracted employees passing their finished products on to an entrepreneur rather than offering for sale on the open market. This may have been especially true of some textile artisans who were in effect employees of drapers or merchants.[20] No less problematic in its implication for the use of franchise data as a guide to occupational structure is the observation that civic authorities appear to have exercised a real degree of control over admissions. This may, however, have been less true of the later fourteenth and fifteenth centuries. The wholesale exclusion of certain trades, notably weavers and fullers before the earlier fourteenth century, seems

---

[17] This is most forcefully argued in Swanson, 'The Illusion of Economic Structure'; ead., *Medieval Artisans*, 129–30; R. H. Hilton, 'Lords, Burgesses and Hucksters', *Past and Present*, 97 (1982), 7.

[18] As at Canterbury, Nottingham, Shrewsbury, and Hull. See also Swanson, *Medieval Artisans*, 110.

[19] Rees Jones, 'Property, Tenure and Rents', 294–5.

[20] Swanson, *Medieval Artisans*, 129.

not to have characterized the post-plague era.[21] Civic prejudice against the admission of women may have been real, though the observation that some women were enfranchised in most towns suggests that other factors may have been more important in determining their low profile.[22] The franchise material, nevertheless, can only usefully describe patterns of male employment.

These points require elaboration, for if franchise records are to be used to reconstruct the occupational structure of a community, then the trades of those admitted must be representative of the labouring and mercantile community as a whole. Comparison of the occupations of those purchasing licenses to traffic and those admitted to the freedom in Nottingham show some real differences.[23] From an analysis by occupational category, it appears that 'wood' and 'armaments' are virtually unrepresented amongst the enfranchised, whereas 'leather' and 'mercantile' are comparatively over-represented. Likewise, very few barbers or cappers are noticed, though butchers, bakers, glovers, and tanners are noted in number. This may indicate that where a fully fledged two-tier system of trade regulation operated, the franchise was weighted towards the higher-status crafts and trades whose members tended to be of more than average wealth. To conclude that Nottingham actually discriminated against lower-status crafts would, however, be unsound. Their needs were probably better suited to the payment of a small annual fine than to the considerable capital outlay required to purchase the freedom. This is perhaps the primary reason why no women are to be found among those admitted to the franchise for the limited number of years that record survives, whereas a number are recorded as purchasing licences to traffic. The occupational structure thus derived from

[21] Dobson, 'Admissions to the Freedom', 17–18; Bridbury, *Economic Growth*, 58–9; W. Hudson and J. C. Tingey (eds.), *The Records of the City of Norwich* (2 vols.; Norwich, 1906–10), vol. ii, p. xxii.

[22] Cf. Kowaleski, 'Women's Work in a Market Town', 146 and n. 5. Only four women are recorded, for example, as having been admitted to the franchise at Norwich in the later Middle Ages, but this is sufficient to show that no actual bar operated: NRO, NCR Case 17, shelf c, 1. It is probable that, following the legal notion that husband and wife were one person, widows of freemen were invariably regarded as members of the franchise. Since their husbands' names would already be registered, no record would have been kept of their changed status. Any calculation of female membership of the franchise based solely on recorded female names is thus a serious underestimate.

[23] Stevenson (ed.), *Records of the Borough of Nottingham*.

the limited number of known admissions at Nottingham does not accord well with the pattern found elsewhere. This in itself suggests that where alternatives to the franchise were not generally well developed then the franchise record may be a fairly satisfactory guide to occupational structure. The inclusion by the later fourteenth century of such previously disenfranchised low-status trades as weaver and fuller tends to add weight to this view.

That many towns including York failed to admit weavers or fullers as freemen before the early fourteenth century demonstrates that civic authorities could and did exercise control over admissions. But as towns grew in size and civic power came to be increasingly concentrated in the hands of a predominantly mercantile élite, so the influence of the enfranchised as a body can only have diminished.[24] It follows that the need to restrict admissions may also have diminished. Indeed to dilute the franchise by operating a relatively open-door policy may have served to augment the hold of the ruling oligarchy, who in any case controlled access to civic office.[25] In practice, civic authorities may have tended to respond on an ad hoc basis to changing circumstances rather than pursue a predetermined policy. This appears true of London. In 1364, at a time of acute labour shortage following the Black Death and subsequent epidemics, the fine for admission by apprenticeship was increased to the high level of 60s. (£3) on the basis that those unable to raise such a sum would better serve the city in the employ of others than by setting themselves up as independent masters. By 1366 it became necessary to modify this policy since it was found that labour, presumably skilled labour, was simply going elsewhere.[26] The demand for labour and consequent leap in admissions to replace freemen who

---

[24] Cf. Swanson, *Medieval Artisans*, 110. Cf. also M. C. Howell, 'Citizenship and Gender: Women's Political Status in Northern Medieval Cities', in M. Erler and M. Kowaleski (eds.), *Women and Power in the Middle Ages* (Athens, Ga., 1988), 37–60. Howell seems not to have considered the possibility that widows of citizens may have enjoyed equivalent status, but would not be separately registered.

[25] Such a policy operated at Exeter in the earlier 14th cent.: Rowe and Jackson (eds.), *Exeter Freemen*, pp. xvi, 6–28. For civic control of office holding see Kermode, 'Urban Decline?' The sale of the franchise brought immediate financial gain, but alienated long-term income.

[26] Thomas (ed.), *Calendar of Plea and Memoranda Rolls, 1364–81*, pp. liii–liv; Sharpe (ed.), *Calendar of Letter-Books: 'G'*, 180, 211. The Grey Death of 1361 is associated with very high rates of mortality.

had died in the plague is observable elsewhere, as at York and Exeter.[27]

It is possible to derive a rather crude measure of how restrictive or otherwise admission policy was in practice by comparing total admissions over a number of years against the recorded poll tax (1377) population. By counting admissions in the half-century following the Black Death, distortions caused by unusually high admission rates in the years immediately following plague should be obviated. It seems probable that the total number of freemen in an urban community remained broadly constant over long periods. High rates of admissions following epidemic merely represent a replenishing of numbers and are invariably followed by years of relatively few admissions. By taking a broad period the effect of such annual fluctuations should be balanced out. The 1377 poll tax population totals are probably not the ideal measure of population levels over this fifty-year period since they can give little idea of the actual numbers aspiring to admission, especially as the majority of admissions by redemption were probably of recent migrants. Nor can they make any allowance for the possibly varying rates of population turnover through migration. The poll tax totals are, however, the only figures available and, if not ideal, are equally not without value. The ratios of admissions to tax population are tabulated in Table 2.4.

Though the ratio can only represent a very crude measure, the findings are not inconsistent with expectation. It is remarkable that ratios derived for the early modern period for Exeter, Leicester, Norwich, and York are not too dissimilar.[28] Only very radical differences in circumstances between communities could alter significantly the order of ratios achieved. The Lynn ratio alone points to serious under-registration. The low Exeter ratio is indicative of the restrictive policy adopted from the 1340s and an equivalent ratio for the first half of the fourteenth century would

[27] Dobson, 'Admissions to the Freedom', 17–18; P. J. P. Goldberg, 'Mortality and Economic Change in the Diocese of York, 1390–1514', *Northern History*, 24 (1988), nn. 22, 46. High levels of admissions recorded in the fragmentary Chester rolls for 1401–2, 1408–9, and 1474–5 may likewise coincide with epidemics: Bennett (ed.), *Rolls of the Freemen of Chester*, pp. xii–xiii.

[28] Ratios of the mean annual rate of admissions to total population ($\times$ 100) at some period in the later 16th or early 17th cents. are Exeter = 0.27, Norwich = 0.24, Leicester = 0.67, York = 0.62: calculated from D. M. Woodward, 'Freemen's Rolls', *Local Historian*, 9 (1970), 91.

TABLE 2.4. *Ratio of admissions to the franchise, c.1350–1399, and poll tax population (1377) totals*

	Total admissions	Tax population	Ratio
Exeter*	393	1560	0.25
Hull**	573	1557	0.37
Leicester	457+524***	2101	0.47
Lynn	434+35***	3127	0.15
Norwich	1237+349***	3952	0.40
Wells	182+280***	901	0.51
York	4838	7248	0.67

* Exeter total includes admissions for 1349.
** Hull admissions relate to the period 1370–1419.
*** Additional figure represents an estimate for years for which the record is missing based on the mean for surviving years. For Leicester the record breaks off in 1380, but for Wells the record only commences in 1377. The ratio here may be understated due to the proportionately greater numbers normally admitted in the aftermath of the Black Death.

Sources: J. C. Russell, *British Medieval Population* (Albuquerque, N.Mex., 1948), table 6.6, pp. 142–3; Rowe and Jackson (eds.), *Exeter Freemen, 1266–1972*; Allison (ed.), *VCH, York, East Riding*, i. 55–6; Hartopp (ed.), *Register of the Freemen of Leicester*; *A Calendar of the Freemen of Lynn*; NRO, NCR Case 17, shelf c, 1 (Norwich Old Free Book); Tillot (ed.), *VCH, York, City of York*, 114–16; Shilton and Holworthy (eds.), *Wells City Charters*.

probably be rather higher.[29] For York the ratio is conspicuously high. This is suggestive of an 'open-door' policy in the absence of a well-developed two-tier system of regulating trade and is entirely in accord with the comparatively large number of female admissions to be found. This diversity of ratios tends to support Dobson's assertion of civic manipulation and detracts from attempts to utilize freemen's registers as a guide to broad demographic trends. It could be argued that only where the ratio is relatively high is the occupational composition of entrants to the freedom more likely to reflect that of the entire work-force.[30] This must in part be true, but, as will be shown, need not invalidate the data as a whole.

[29] Rowe and Jackson (eds.), *Exeter Freemen*, pp. xv–xvi.
[30] Bartlett suggests that in York 'some 22 per cent of the lay population over the age of 14 in the final quarter of the fourteenth century' were enfranchised. This would constitute a very high proportion of the adult male population: Bartlett (ed.), *The Lay Poll Tax Returns for the City of York in 1381*, 22.

There remain several difficulties in converting records of admissions into measures of occupational structure. The records themselves are seldom complete, though this is more often true of the pre-plague than the post-plague period. Sometimes this follows from simple failures in record-keeping or the loss of registers over time.[31] Another problem is the failure of some registers to record certain classes of entrant. In York admissions by patrimony are not recorded before 1397. In London similarly it was not until the later fourteenth century that a move was made to obtain a satisfactory record of such admissions. This is a further reflection of and a response to changed circumstances. Whereas in the pre-plague era the enfranchised population remained sufficiently small to be known without record, by the later medieval period, with the high level of migrant labour and population turnover, records became more normal because more necessary. Before the late Middle Ages entry by right of patrimony was invariably free. No record of payment of fine was consequently kept and thus this group is lost to posterity. In London, however, and this must have been the case elsewhere, there was concern that the oath was not regularly administered to those claiming the freedom by patrimony. In 1387, therefore, formal regulations for administering the oath, and thus for proper registration, were passed.[32]

In Exeter it appears that before the Black Death it was possible to enter the franchise in succession to a brother or uncle in addition to, as was normal elsewhere, a father.[33] It was the custom at Wells that persons marrying the widows of freemen were admitted without fine, and at Canterbury persons marrying the daughters of freemen were admitted on payment of a much reduced fine.[34] At York daughters were sometimes admitted by right of patrimony. Admissions by right of apprenticeship are less well documented. The York register does not normally distinguish

[31] The years 1380–1465 are, for example, lost from the surviving Leicester register. Cf. Rowe and Jackson (eds.), *Exeter Freemen*, p. xiv.

[32] Dobson, 'Admissions to the Freedom', 8; Thomas (ed.), *Calendar of Plea and Memoranda Rolls, 1364–81*, pp. xxviii–xxix.

[33] Rowe and Jackson (eds.), *Exeter Freemen*, p. xiv.

[34] Shilton and Holworthy (eds.), *Wells City Charters*, p. xxvi; J. M. Cowper (ed.), *The Roll of the Freemen of the City of Canterbury, 1392–1800* (Canterbury, 1903), p. x.

entries by apprenticeship.[35] A small number of apprentices are recorded as admitted to the freedom of Exeter after 1358, but this must in itself be evidence for considerable underenumeration.[36] Were apprenticeship indeed 'the normal method of entry', such omissions, if real, would tend to detract from the representativeness of the sample population.[37] But as early as 1309–12 less than 28 per cent or 253 of 909 recorded admissions in London were by apprenticeship.[38] Urban growth was dependent very largely upon immigration from the countryside. In the labour-starved climate of the decades after 1348–9 this may have translated into high proportions of admissions by redemption. As Bridbury observes, apprenticeships cannot have seemed so attractive in this period; in London some gilds were moved to adopt protective regulation regarding apprenticeship and in 1408 requested that the franchise even be restricted to apprentices. There is thus little to suggest that apprenticeship was either popular or the normal mode of entry.[39] These are somewhat patchy observations and they reflect the lack of research into this important area of urban economic organization. They do, however, tend to confirm the view that by the later fourteenth century recorded admissions are probably sufficiently complete to be regarded as fairly representative of all admissions.

Not all the records indicate consistently the trades of those admitted. This is unfortunate for present purposes. In some towns the franchise became so closely associated with membership of a craft gild that it was normal to record the entrant's occupation. In York the relationship between the franchise and gild mastership is implicit in the oath administered to those admitted, and in Norwich in 1415 it was ruled that only members of craft gilds might be enfranchised.[40] Elsewhere the information recorded

---

[35] Collins (ed.), *Register of the Freemen of the City of York*, i. 204–12. Apprentices are recorded only for the years 1482–7, but account for only 28% of all admissions as against 56% by redemption.

[36] Rowe and Jackson (eds.), *Exeter Freemen*, p. xiv.

[37] Bridbury, *Economic Growth*, 63. In London it was the custom that sons of freemen who had served as apprentices should be permitted entry only by right of apprenticeship: Thomas (ed.), *Calendar of Plea and Memoranda Rolls, 1364–81*, p. xxix.

[38] Ibid., pp. xxxii–xxxiii, xlvii.

[39] Ibid., p. xxxviii; Bridbury, *Economic Growth*, 63–4.

[40] Hudson and Tingey (eds.), *Records of the City of Norwich*, vol. ii, p. xlvi.

TABLE 2.5. *Proportions with identifiable occupations admitted to the franchise*

	Years	%
Exeter	1349–99	20.4
Leicester	1350–79	60.0
Lynn	1350–94	22.4
Norwich	1349–99	55.7
York	1350–99	88.3
Chester	1450–99	55.2

seems to have varied with the whim of the recording clerk such that in some years no indication of occupation or gild allegiance is made. In the case of Exeter trades are recorded only occasionally and, apparently, at random. Elsewhere the proportion of trades identified to total entries may be too small to generate useful statistics. The proportion of individuals known to have been admitted to the franchise whose occupations are identifiable is set out in Table 2.5. By the fifteenth century proportions everywhere tend to be substantially higher.[41] It is apparent that where samples are relatively small, the numbers of recorded entries into any particular trade vary considerably over time and sometimes within a given time period no person is recorded to certain trades. In part this is a simple product of unsatisfactory sample size, but it may also reflect underlying changes in craft associations and terminology. It is hoped that the use here of the previously adopted occupational categories will considerably reduce this potential source of error.

Further distortion might be caused by persons engaging in trades other than that under which they were registered or by individuals pursuing more than one trade simultaneously. For both of these there is some evidence, but it is again doubtful that they detract from the representativeness of the material as a whole. Males, but not females, were restricted by statute of 1363 to employment within a single occupation, although the effectiveness of such legislation must always be open to doubt. Gild ordinances do, however, seem to have tried to uphold this

[41] Swanson, *Medieval Artisans*, 4.

principle. On the other hand, such repeated regulations suggest that some persons did indeed engage in more than one trade, although only a few such persons can be identified from poll tax evidence.[42] Some 1379 Canterbury returns point to artisans combining the crafts of dyer and fuller, and to other craftworkers also engaged in brewing.[43] An analysis of the non-privileged taxpayers of Oxford in 1524 likewise indicates that only the trades of brewer, baker, tailor, and chandler were combined with any frequency.[44] It seems, therefore, that measures of occupational structure will not be much distorted on this account, especially since the use of broad categories will tend to minimize the effect. There is evidence that some traders transferred to a more prestigious trade in order to achieve civic office, and in Norwich low-status crafts were specifically excluded from civic office. The numbers, however, cannot have been large. London records indicate some abuse of the franchise by individuals entering under one craft to pursue a more remunerative trade, so avoiding a higher entry fine. Such abuse was probably mostly limited to related trades, as in the case of the haberdashers allegedly trading as mercers, so trade categorization will again tend to overcome these problems.[45]

More problematical is the relationship between the enfranchised and the economic community as a whole. It must be broadly true that the unfree worked as servants, apprentices, and journeymen for the enfranchised, though some unenfranchised women may have engaged independently in victualling, retail, and some service trades. If all trades drew equally from this dependent labour force then it would be possible to apply the occupational structure of the enfranchised to the working community as a whole. Clearly the size of the dependent labour force in relation to the enfranchised varied according to how general the franchise was. Thus in York the free constituted a greater proportion of total labour than was the case in later medieval Exeter. These differences are unlikely to have influenced the actual distribution of dependent labour. Poll tax evidence would suggest that the mercantile trades

[42] Swanson, *Medieval Artisans*, 6.

[43] PRO, E 179/123/47.

[44] A. Crossley (ed.), *VCH, Oxfordshire*, iv. *City of Oxford* (Oxford, 1979), 103.

[45] Bridbury, *Economic Growth*, 59–60; Hudson and Tingey (eds.), *Records of the City of Norwich*, ii. 1; Thomas (ed.), *Calendar of Plea and Memoranda Rolls, 1364–81*, p. lv; Sharpe (ed.), *Calendar of Letter-Books: 'H'*, 257–9.

drew disproportionately from this workforce, but there is little to indicate that there was no general correlation in terms of occupational structure between the enfranchised and the working population as a whole. Where direct comparison can be made between poll tax and franchise evidence, as at York or Lynn, a remarkably good fit is observed. Despite reservations, therefore, the franchise evidence does appear to provide valuable evidence for occupational structure from the later Middle Ages. The structure derived for a number of communities is presented in Table 2.6.

Some consistent trends are discernible within the various occupational categories. These tend to accord with the poll tax structure described earlier and confirm the notion that urban economies were characterized by the range of occupations found. Where the data seem incompatible, this can be explained in terms of the known defects of the original material. A significant proportion of freemen are invariably found in the victualling trades, though the proportions tend to be lower in the larger towns. The figures are entirely in accord with, though mostly below, the poll tax mean of 21.3 per cent. Fairly high proportions are likewise found engaged in the leather trades, whereas no more than 15 per cent, and invariably rather less, are found in the low status 'building', 'wood', 'armaments', and 'chandlers' categories taken together. This again accords with poll tax evidence and is suggestive of an underlying occupational structure common to the needs of larger urban communities regardless of any commercial or industrial specialization. Both the characteristic and the individual aspects of the structures of differing urban communities are in this way demonstrated. Thus the relative importance of the textile industry at Norwich and at Wells is evident. The apparent expansion of the industry at Wells is particularly interesting as it coincides with a more general economic shift that favoured the South-Western textiles region. The particular function of the port community of Lynn is also evident from the proportions engaged in mercantile and transport functions and from the low level of industrial activity.[46]

The observed patterns are thus compatible with expectation and accord with poll tax evidence. The somewhat unsatisfactory nature

[46] A similar pattern is suggested from franchise data for the ports of Hull and Great Yarmouth.

TABLE 2.6.   *Occupational structure as derived from franchise and related sources (%)*

	N	Category											
		1	2	3	4	5	6	7	8	9	10	11	12
Canterbury													
1400–39	413	22.8	12.8	13.8	12.3	9.2	9.9	—	4.8	—	1.2	5.6	7.5
1440–99	504	28.4	11.0	10.6	17.3	8.9	7.7	—	4.8	—	1.7	4.6	5.1
Chester													
1450–99	153	19.6	16.3	9.8	13.7	16.3	7.8	2.0	6.5	0.7	5.2	—	2.0
1500–30	212	17.5	15.1	16.5	14.6	13.2	10.8	1.4	5.2	0.5	2.4	—	2.8
Coventry													
1523	535	15.6	9.3	17.4	17.2	10.4	9.9	6.5	4.1	—	0.9	0.9	7.7
Exeter													
1300–48	222	16.2	29.3	10.8	11.7	8.6	10.8	4.1	0.9	0.5	—	3.2	4.1
1349–99	80	21.3	13.8	10.0	11.3	5.0	21.3	3.8	1.3	—	3.8	1.3	7.5
1400–49	121	26.4	27.3	7.4	6.6	4.1	14.9	4.1	2.5	—	—	—	6.6
1450–99	122	18.9	27.0	7.4	9.8	17.2	9.0	3.3	1.6	—	—	—	5.7
1500–29	219	19.6	14.2	11.4	19.2	16.0	8.2	2.3	—	—	3.2	2.3	3.7
Leicester													
1300–47	242	20.2	25.6	10.3	3.3	10.7	16.5	0.4	5.8	—	0.4	0.4	6.2
1350–79	274	21.9	21.2	8.0	7.3	7.7	12.8	6.9	5.1	1.5	0.4	0.4	6.9
1465–99	363	18.7	14.3	10.2	13.5	13.5	9.9	5.5	5.8	0.6	1.9	1.1	5.0
1500–30	246	27.2	17.1	9.3	7.3	12.2	7.3	5.7	4.1	0.8	2.4	2.0	4.5
Lynn													
1350–99	97	13.4	11.3	12.4	3.1	22.7	10.3	2.1	3.1	8.2	3.1	5.2	5.2
1400–49	313	11.8	7.3	13.4	6.4	38.7	4.8	1.6	5.4	1.6	0.3	4.8	3.8
1450–99	395	20.8	9.1	9.1	9.9	19.2	8.6	2.8	7.6	3.0	0.5	4.3	5.1
1500–30	220	30.0	9.5	4.5	10.0	24.5	3.2	2.3	3.2	4.1	1.8	2.7	4.1
Norwich													
1349–99*	259	13.1	18.9	22.0	11.2	5.4	11.2	3.5	4.2	1.5	1.5	1.9	5.4
1400–49	1430	13.2	13.4	23.1	10.4	10.8	7.8	4.5	5.9	2.7	1.0	1.1	5.9
1450–99	1448	16.0	11.5	23.0	7.5	10.0	7.0	5.0	7.3	5.4	1.0	1.0	5.5
Northampton													
1524	409	16.1	7.6	13.0	23.2	6.1	7.8	7.3	3.7	1.7	1.5	1.2	10.8
*Nottingham***													
1459–1511	232	6.0	12.5	15.9	26.3	0.9	15.9	5.2	1.7	—	5.6	0.9	9.1
1459–1511	83	20.5	21.7	8.4	21.7	13.3	8.4	3.6	—	—	—	—	2.4
Wells													
1377–99	108	26.9	11.1	19.4	12.0	—	11.1	8.3	4.6	—	0.9	0.9	4.6
1400–49	203	19.2	10.8	25.1	11.8	3.4	5.9	8.9	6.9	—	0.5	1.5	5.9
1450–99	134	20.1	11.3	31.3	11.2	0.7	10.4	4.5	5.2	0.7	—	0.7	3.7

TABLE 2.6. (*Continued*)

	N	Category											
		1	2	3	4	5	6	7	8	9	10	11	12
York													
1307–49	1945	23.0	19.7	5.3	8.4	13.2	14.6	2.1	2.7	4.4	1.0	0.4	5.2
1350–99	4269	11.3	13.1	14.0	11.2	16.5	11.3	3.8	4.8	3.3	2.2	0.2	8.5
1400–49	4193	14.2	11.4	11.8	8.5	15.1	11.4	5.0	5.5	3.6	2.2	0.3	11.1
1450–1509	3532	17.4	10.9	13.2	10.5	12.0	11.2	5.4	4.3	3.5	1.7	0.3	9.7

* Several years between 1350 and 1364 are lost from the record.
** The first line represents licences to traffic, the second admissions to the franchise.

Sources: A. F. Butcher, 'Freeman Admissions and Urban Occupations: Towards a Dynamic Analysis', TS paper (Urban History Conference, Canterbury; 1983); Bennett (ed.), *The Rolls of the Freemen of Chester*; Phythian-Adams, *Desolation of a City*, table 38, pp. 311–15; A. D. Dyer, 'Northampton in 1524', *Northamptonshire Past and Present*, 6 (1979), 77–9; as Table 2.4 above.

of the Exeter material is, nevertheless, evident from the exclusion of lesser trades and the abnormally low mercantile sector in the period before 1450. In part this must be due to the somewhat unsatisfactory nature of the small sample of identifiable trades, but may also be influenced by a failure satisfactorily to record admissions by apprenticeship and patrimony, and also by the operation of a relatively closed admissions policy. The disproportionately large merchant community found at Lynn may also reflect adversely upon the representativeness of the occupational sample. A more precise assessment of the likely limitations of the franchise material may be obtained from a direct comparison of franchise and poll tax evidence available for York and Lynn.[47] This is presented in Table 2.7. In both instances the similarity is remarkable. There is, however, no consistent pattern of variation between the two sources beyond an unsurprising tendency for the freemen's material to overstate the proportions associated with the mercantile sector. On the basis that the poll tax evidence is the more representative, it would appear that the York franchise

[47] Some additional occupations lost through damage to the surviving York 1381 returns can be supplied from the franchise register, but this was not here attempted on the grounds that loss appeared random and the inclusion of additional data from the franchise data would tend to bias the pattern observed.

TABLE 2.7.   *Occupational structure from poll tax and franchise*
sources, Lynn and York (%)

	N	Category											
		1	2	3	4	5	6	7	8	9	10	11	12
Lynn													
Poll Tax, 1379	510	12.2	11.0	15.1	10.4	19.4	8.4	3.5	2.5	10.6	1.0	2.4	3.5
Freemen, 1350–99	97	13.4	11.3	12.4	3.1	22.7	10.3	2.1	3.1	8.2	3.1	5.2	5.2
York													
Poll Tax, 1381	2193	15.8	15.0	11.6	8.4	15.5	12.8	3.6	5.7	2.6	2.1	0.4	6.4
Freemen, 1350–99	4296	11.3	13.1	14.0	11.2	16.5	11.3	3.8	4.8	3.3	2.2	0.2	8.5

Sources: Tables 2.2 and 2.6 above.

data fail to describe the victualling trades in full. Likewise the
equivalent Lynn material may understate the relative size of the
'clothing' and 'transport' categories, though the Lynn franchise
population is too small to be representative at this level. Certain
observations must, however, limit the value of the observed
correlation. The Lynn poll tax data are based upon a sample
population representing only 44 per cent of the total tax population. Those identified are biased towards the more substantial
artisans and traders. Thus both the poll tax and the franchise
evidence are liable to understate the proportions engaged in low-
status occupations. Similarly at York the 1381 returns are not as
representative of the total population liable to tax as is true of
some other towns assessed the same year. The bias of the sample
is again weighted towards the more substantial householders, who
are most likely, given the broad nature of the franchise, to
coincide with the enfranchised population. To some limited
extent, therefore, the two sources are recording the same sort of
individuals.

The franchise material has the advantage that it may be used to
consider secular changes in occupational structure, but clearly
these patterns may be distorted by changes in civic policy in
respect of admissions to the franchise. The value of the York data
for textile-workers before the Black Death is thus especially
fragile. The regulation of admissions in Exeter, as already noticed,
seems to have been particularly strict and it is difficult to know

how much weight of interpretation to put on the patterns observed there.[48] There seems, however, little reason to disregard the data derived elsewhere from the later fourteenth century if used with due caution. There is a crude apparent correlation between community size and the numbers of miscellaneous trades supported, and a similar inverse correlation between community size and proportions enfranchised within the victualling sector. The growth suggested from the franchise material of the cloth industry in Wells, a town of no more than 1500 persons in 1377, can be documented from other sources.[49] Carus-Wilson described a real growth in overseas trade through the port of Exeter during the fifteenth century and this coincides with the observed increase in the proportion of mercantile admissions.[50] A more modest growth of the mercantile sector is noticed for Norwich, but admissions of textile-workers appear remarkably stable. If the evidence for economic change in the fifteenth century is ambiguous, the real importance of cloth, and especially worsteds, to the economy of Norwich is none the less demonstrated.[51]

The York data are similarly enigmatic. Those for the period before the Black Death are untrustworthy, but those for the remainder of the period indicate a remarkably high degree of stability. Certain modest trends are, nevertheless, apparent. From 1350 there is a steady increase in the proportion of traders in food and drink enfranchised, but a modest decrease in the proportion of tanners, saddlers, and other leather-workers. The proportion of textile artisans admitted is surprisingly uniform given the volume of evidence to the effect that the cloth industry in York was in decline through the fifteenth century. Of perhaps greater economic significance, however, is the observed decline in the proportion of merchants, mercers, chapmen, and drapers admitted. This last is most marked between the first and second halves of the fifteenth century. A more thorough investigation of the York evidence may help to explain these observations.

[48] Rowe and Jackson (eds.), *Exeter Freemen*, pp. xiv–xvii.
[49] W. Page (ed.), *VCH, Somerset*, ii (London, 1911), 408, 411.
[50] E. M. Carus-Wilson, *The Expansion of Exeter at the Close of the Middle Ages* (Exeter, 1963), 7–21.
[51] B. Green and R. M. R. Young, *Norwich: The Growth of a City* (Norwich, 1981), 17–21.

THE OCCUPATIONAL TOPOGRAPHY OF
LATER MEDIEVAL YORK

Secular variation in occupational structure derived from the register of admissions to the franchise may suggest certain crude patterns, but it is not the only guide to change in the economy of York over time. Changes in urban economic structure may be reflected in parallel changes in economic topography. For York the 1381 poll tax data, which are arranged by parish, provide evidence for the spatial location of occupational groups in the later fourteenth century. Alongside this material may be set data derived from testamentary sources, which allow the occupation and parish of the testator to be identified in most cases. So as to provide some measure of secular change wills drawn from the period 1445–1500 have been chosen. The mapping of occupations in late medieval York from poll tax and testamentary sources presents a range of problems. Clearly the two sources are not compatible and the methods adopted must differ. Use has been made here of the parish as the basic unit of reference. Since parishes are numerous in medieval York, individuals may be located with some precision. The poll tax fell in theory on all the adult population and in practice on a significant proportion of the same, but there was no equivalent obligation to make and have registered a will. Thus the map derived for 1381 is based on a population of 2175 taxpaying individuals, including wives and servants, whose occupation is known, but that for the period *c*.1445–1500 upon rather less than six hundred wills from the Exchequer and Dean and Chapter courts relating to persons engaged in identifiable trade or industrial activity. Wives and servants are recorded in wills, but probably with rather less consistency than is true of the poll tax and these have thus been omitted from calculations. Independent female traders are, unsurprisingly, scarcely to be found among the testamentary population and none were in this period, yet there are a number indicated by the 1381 poll tax.

The testamentary data are biased towards individuals, particularly males, of some wealth or property, and there is a particular bias towards wealthier at the expense of less prosperous parishes. The poll tax in contrast seems to record a rather fuller range of trades and status groups, but there is evidence that the scope of the enumeration varies from one parish to another according to the prosperity and wealth distribution of individual parishes. Indeed certain poor parishes appear to be actually excluded, whereas individuals, and presumably the range of occupations, are perhaps most fully recorded in those, usually wealthier, parishes that experienced a wide distribution of wealth.[52] It follows from these considerations that the two sources must be treated differently, the emphasis with the 1381 data being on the parish and with the testamentary data on the specific occupation. It is, however, evident that for a number of less prosperous city and suburban parishes in 1381 only a part of the lay population was subjected to the tax and numbers are thus small.[53] It was decided, consequently, to group some parishes so as to reduce the degree of imbalance between the populations of each unit. Thus the suburban extra-mural parishes were grouped as also the lesser urban parishes south-west of the Ouse and some smaller central parishes. In general, only adjacent parishes demonstrating broadly similar occupational structures were so grouped. Occupations were then mapped by identifying those that represented a significant proportion of the economic population of individual parishes or parish units.[54] The same parish units were retained in order to map occupations from will data, but occupations were distinguished not by their relative proportional significance on a parish basis, but by absolute values.[55] The resultant maps (Maps 2.2, 2.3, and 2.4)

[52] See Ch. 7 below.

[53] Goldberg, 'Urban Identity and the Poll Taxes'.

[54] Where 7% or more of the economic population, excluding labourers, were associated with a given occupation then this was mapped. Where the level was 14% or more this was further distinguished. Since the population of individual units was relatively uniform, at least for most central parish units, it follows that similar-size labour forces specifically located would be identified and so mapped. In two exceptional cases, i.e. the tanners of North Street (All Saints) and the butchers of the Shambles (Holy Trinity, King's Court), a large proportion of the economic population was engaged in a single craft (76.7 and 42.2% respectively). These have been specifically indicated.

[55] Three levels of concentration have been mapped, i.e. 3 or more, 5 or more, and 8 or more in any given parish unit. Only in one instance, that of the butchers of Holy Trinity, King's Court, is this upper figure greatly exceeded, where 18 butchers are recorded from wills, and this has been specifically indicated. The choice of a relatively low minimum figure is designed to permit possible concentrations of even relatively low-status trades, under-represented among the will-making population, to be mapped. Where an occupational group is confined to one parish within a parish unit, then this has been shown within the appropriate parish.

(*a*) 1381 Poll Tax

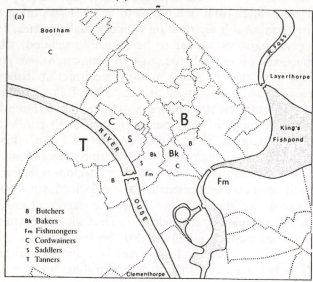

(*b*) Probate Series, *c.*1445–1500

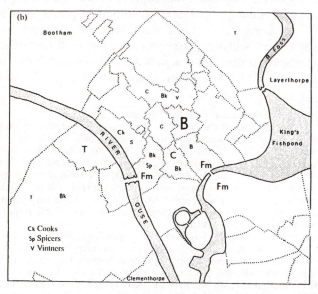

Map 2.2. Occupational Topography of York for Victuals and Leather

(*a*) 1381 Poll Tax

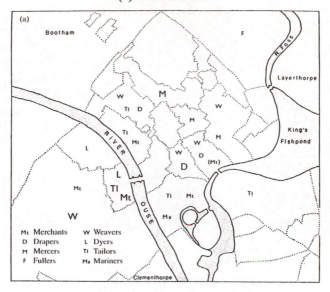

(*b*) Probate Series, *c*.1445–1500

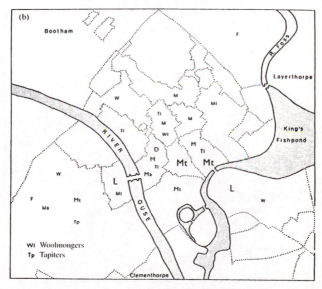

Map 2.3. Occupational Topography of York for Textiles, Clothing, Mercantile, and Transport

(*a*)　1381 Poll Tax

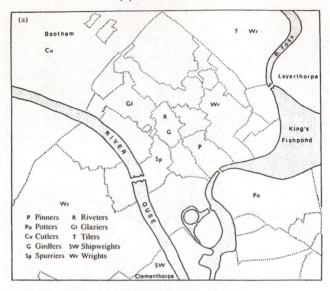

(*b*)　Probate Series, *c*.1445–1500

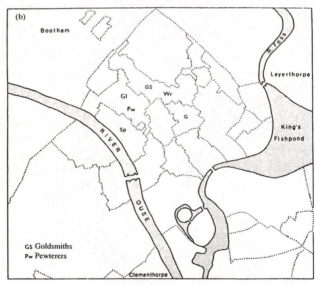

Map 2.4. Occupational Topography of York for Metal, Wood, and Building

should allow at least a general comparison between the two periods, namely the later fourteenth and the later fifteenth centuries, although not too much weight can be placed on the absolute values indicated.

Certain observed patterns are a product of the natural environment. Two trades requiring water as part of the manufacturing process were located by the Ouse, but on the opposite river bank from the commercial heart of the city located to the north and east of the Ouse. Thus the dyers appear to be concentrated in St John's and All Saints, North Street, in the earlier period and St John's and St Denys, Walmgate, by the later fifteenth century, and the tanners, most markedly in 1381, also in the parish of All Saints, North Street. The butchers remained heavily concentrated at both periods within the Shambles, largely inside the parish of Holy Trinity, King's Court, but there is little evidence for the perdurance of a smaller group of butchers across Ouse Bridge in St John's parish. The bakers remained concentrated around Ousegate in the parishes of St Michael's, Spurriergate, and All Saints, Pavement (High Ousegate). The later will evidence suggests, however, that bakers were then located additionally in less central areas outside the main grain market on Pavement. The fishmongers had their stalls at the two main bridges, freshwater fish on the north side of Ouse Bridge and saltwater fish on the east or Walmgate side of Foss Bridge. The latter had evidently spread to both sides of Foss Bridge by the later fifteenth century.[56]

Less secular continuity is suggested for a number of other trades, even allowing for error due to comparing unlike sources. Merchants, drapers, and mercers, probably overlapping trade designations, appear to have become more heavily concentrated within one commercial quarter centred on Fossgate, where the merchants had their gildhall, and the parishes of St Crux and All Saints, Pavement. In the later fifteenth century mercers and drapers are found in the region of Ousegate and Jubbergate, but no longer are mercantile traders so conspicuous in the Coney Street, Davygate, or Petergate areas or south of the Ouse as in St John's, North Street, parish. By this later period also there is less evidence for the lower-status trades of tailor or weaver within the

---

[56] For further information on the topography of the medieval city see Raine, *Mediaeval York*.

commercial quarter. Will evidence for the metal-working and construction trades is equally unsatisfactory, but the limited evidence again points to a move away from the most central area. The proliferation of building-workers in extra-mural districts, evident in 1381, cannot unfortunately be shown from will sources.

Whilst acknowledging the difficulty of combining unlike sources, it is apparent that at both periods there existed a distinct commercial quarter. This quarter appears to have shrunk and become more closely defined by the later period. There was consequently an increasing polarization between this commercial quarter and other areas where trade and industrial activities were located. The metal trades came to be concentrated within the intra-mural parishes between Petergate and Coney Street, but some extra-mural activity probably remained in Bootham. The peripheral and suburban districts are not well documented. Several parishes were apparently excluded from the 1381 assessment, probably on grounds of poverty, and the marked absence of testamentary material relating to these and other marginal parishes points towards the same conclusion. The limited data suggest a concentration here of humbler textile trades (weaving and fulling), construction trades (tilers and wrights), and some antisocial trades. This last is suggested by metal-working in Bootham, and the apparent dispersal of tanning over the period from North Street into the suburbs. This dispersal of tanners may reflect pressures on an antisocial industry, but also accords with the evidence that this was a declining industry. The concentration of the city's mercantile quarter also coincides with a real decrease in the proportion of merchants, mercers, and drapers admitted to the franchise.

No clear conclusion relating to the textile crafts is possible due to the unsatisfactory nature of the evidence. It is possible to detect a general concentration of economic activity within the walled area of the city either side of the Ouse, but away from the suburbs, the Walmgate area, and even St Saviour's parish within the main area. This would indicate a decline in the economic vitality of those parishes associated with cloth manufacture. Both weavers and fullers were often employed on a piece-rate basis and were not necessarily liable to take up the freedom.[57] Although the

---

[57] Swanson, *Medieval artisans*, 34–5, 40.

franchise data must thus be used with circumspection, these data do tend to confirm that the cloth industry was in decline by the second half of the fifteenth century. The numbers of fullers and shearmen nevertheless remained relatively stable and this last may indicate that the city continued a centre for finishing cloths manufactured elsewhere. At the same time a modest increase may be noticed in the admissions of linen-weavers and tapiters.[58]

Swanson has argued that the tapiters worked primarily to satisfy domestic demand, whereas the woollen cloth ordinarily produced in York was directed at the export market.[59] This would again accord with the decline in the numbers of mercantile traders and especially drapers. The only trade that appears to have expanded significantly, spilling across Ouse Bridge into St Crux parish, was that of the fishmongers. This accords with franchise material and is despite evidence for a contraction of the Scarborough fishing industry.[60] The metal trades as a whole display a degree of stability despite some structural changes. Most significant is the expansion of the pewter industry focused on the parish of St Helen, Stonegate. This industry took advantage of York's effective monopoly over the regional supply of lead from Swaledale, Wharfedale, and Nidderdale, which was distributed through York via Boroughbridge.[61] The decline in admissions and absence of wills relating to pinners, nailers, lorimers, spurriers, cutlers, and, associated with the cloth industry, cardmakers for the period after 1445 is suggestive of decline, but may tend to exaggerate real trends. The manufacture of bows at York seems also to have contracted over the fifteenth century.[62]

[58] Ibid. 37, 39.

[59] Ibid. 44.

[60] P. Heath, 'North Sea Fishing in the Fifteenth Century: The Scarborough Fleet', *Northern History*, 3 (1968), 53–69. Some quantities of fish may have been brought into the city from Hull.

[61] A. Raistrick and B. Jennings, *A History of Lead Mining in the Pennines* (Newton Abbot, 1965), 25–8; Swanson, *Medieval Artisans*, 95.

[62] Some of these crafts were organized on a piece-rate basis and there would thus have been no necessity for all craft members to have been enfranchised: Swanson, *Medieval Artisans*, 72, 129.

GROWTH AND RECESSION IN LATE
MEDIEVAL YORK

Topographical evidence thus suggests certain patterns that broadly coincide with the franchise data. It is possible to describe two parallel trends. On the one hand, there were real changes in the patterns of demand and consumption. Thus changing fashions dictated that demand for furs would decline through the fifteenth century, but that the wares of the capper and the hatter would be increasingly in vogue. This is fully reflected in the changing levels of admissions of skinners and cappers respectively. The same must be true of the expanding market for pewter over pottery utensils, though some pewter was also exported.[63] The popularity of brick as an inexpensive, durable, and versatile building material explains the steady rise in the numbers of tilers enfranchised. On the other hand, changes in the structure of the regional economy and in overseas markets exerted perhaps still more profound influences on employment within the city.

Much of the available evidence relates to the city's cloth industry. This has been seen by Bartlett to have expanded through the fourteenth century and to have contracted subsequently.[64] His analysis of the expansion through the earlier fourteenth century depends upon a somewhat uncritical use of franchise data, a fragile source in respect of the numbers of weavers active within the city at any given date. Swanson argues that many weavers worked for others on piece-work contracts, and that weavers manufacturing for export, and not for sale within the domestic market, were not obliged to be citizens. Using the weavers' apprenticeship register that survives for the end of our period, she notes that 30 master weavers of 115 observed were not included in the freemen's register and that only 45 of 375 apprentices were subsequently recorded in the register.[65] Thomas Clynt, d. 1439,

---

[63] Swanson, *Medieval Artisans*, 163; J. Hatcher and T. C. Barker, *A History of British Pewter* (London, 1974), 40, 66, 70–2, 265.

[64] For a discussion of the industry in the 12th and 13th cents. see Heaton, *Yorkshire Woollen and Worsted Industries*; E. Carus-Wilson, 'The English Cloth Industry in the Late Twelfth and Early Thirteenth Centuries', *Economic History Review*, 14 (1944), 32–50; Miller, 'The Fortunes of the English Textile Industry during the Thirteenth Century', 64–82.

[65] Swanson, *Medieval Artisans*, 36; Swanson, 'Craftsmen and Industry', 38, 41.

described as a merchant, but clearly a textile entrepreneur, left money to all the weavers working for him in York and its suburbs in addition to the fullers similarly engaged in both York and Tadcaster 'and to each spinster of my wool'.[66] Since these workers were all presumably Clynt's employees engaged at piece-rates, it is unlikely that many would appear within the franchise register.

The growth of an export trade in English cloth is well documented, as is the involvement of York merchants trading through the port of Hull. What cannot be determined is how far York cloth was manufactured exclusively for export from the later fourteenth century. Hull customs accounts show an upward trend in cloth exports from the very eve of the Black Death, but it was not until the 1380s that the actual level of exports moved from a mean of under one thousand per annum to between three and four thousands.[67] It may be supposed that demand for cloth within the region itself may have increased as wages tended upwards in response to the shortage of labour. Certainly the most dramatic influx of new admissions of textiles craftsmen dates to the 1360s, i.e. two decades before the upswing in cloth exports. Although this high rate of admissions is in part a simple reflection of the extent of plague losses, the proportion of textiles admissions to all admissions was higher than in most subsequent periods. This is shown in Table 2.8. For want of more substantial evidence relating to regional cloth production and consumption, it is thus possible to suppose that cloth woven at York continued to have a domestic market through the fourteenth century despite the growing importance of overseas markets. Indeed, if it is the case that not all weavers producing for the export market would have been enfranchised, then a growth in the proportion of textiles admissions may more readily indicate an expansion of production for the domestic market than for overseas markets. It may consequently be unwise to describe the fortunes of the York cloth manufacture exclusively in terms of the overseas market.

The volume of cloth sent through Hull appears to have reached a peak at the end of the fourteenth century. Over the subsequent two and a half decades cloth exports were somewhat depressed due

---

[66] 'Et cuilibet Filatrici lane mee . . .': BIHR, Prob. Reg. 3, fo. 567ᵛ.
[67] Calculated from E. Carus-Wilson and O. Coleman, *England's Export Trade, 1275–1547* (Oxford, 1963).

TABLE 2.8. *York textiles admissions per decade, 1351–1521 (% of all admissions)*

Decade	Weavers	Dyers	All textiles	Total all admissions
1351–61	5.4	3.1	12.3	813
1361–71	6.6	2.6	14.5	1049
1371–81	6.4	2.8	15.6	823
1381–91	4.4	2.7	12.7	931
1391–1401	5.4	2.8	12.6	1183
1401–11	4.3	1.8	8.5	785
1411–21	3.7	2.2	9.7	1185
1421–31	3.1	2.1	10.2	1037
1431–41	4.2	1.6	10.2	856
1441–51	5.3	2.7	13.0	962
1451–61	5.4	2.7	14.7	639
1461–71	4.2	2.0	11.9	738
1471–81	2.9	3.4	11.3	806
1481–91	2.2	1.6	8.5	675
1491–1501	3.6	2.4	12.4	580
1501–11	1.7	1.5	7.4	542
1511–21	1.7	1.1	10.0	531

Source: Bartlett, 'Expansion and Decline of York', table 1, p. 22.

to a disruption of the Hanseatic trade, but revived over the period *c.*1425–49, despite an attempted Hanseatic trade embargo between 1434 and 1437. The capture of the Hanseatic Bay fleet in May 1449, however, heralded a sustained downturn in cloth exports out of Hull. This was only briefly reversed in the period *c.*1475–85 and again at the end of the century.[68] With the contraction of North European trade, York also lost its geographic advantage. The focus of trade on France and Iberia favoured London and the ports of Bristol and Exeter, and drew from the textiles regions of East Anglia and the West Country respectively.[69] This chronology does appear to coincide with the evidence for recession within the textiles trades and subsequently in those trades that depended for

[68] M. M. Postan, *Essays on Medieval Trade and Finance* (Cambridge, 1973), 252–79.

[69] Darby (ed.), *A New Historical Geography of England*, 222–6, 238, 240–1, 245–7; Carus-Wilson, *The Expansion of Exeter*.

custom on textile manufacture. Although the fifty-year averages employed earlier are insufficiently sensitive to these trends, the proportions of admissions of textile workers fell during the earlier decades of the fifteenth century, but revived only to fall more sharply from *c.*1460. This pattern is more marked if only admissions of weavers are considered.[70] The surviving weavers' apprenticeship books further suggest that by the later fifteenth century the number of apprentices employed by each master was falling.[71]

This observed correlation between the level of admissions and the volume of exports may suggest that the domestic cloth market was of only secondary significance by the fifteenth century, but the growth of other regional centres, apparent as early as 1379 from the West Riding poll tax returns for such centres as Wakefield, Rotherham, Ripon, and Pontefract, and later in 1399 from an inquisition into breaches of the York Weavers' charter, ensured that York's share of this market, though it may not have declined significantly, was unable to increase to compensate for waning overseas markets. By the later fifteenth century Halifax, Leeds, and Bradford had established themselves alongside Wakefield as the focus of the West Riding manufacture.[72] At the same time York cloth may even have begun to lose ground within the city's own markets, either because city-produced cloth was unable to compete in terms of price or because of changes in fashion. West Riding and Kendal cloth was marketed within York and features prominently in the stock of John Carter, a city tailor who died in 1485.[73] In the 1490s five Kendal men were admitted to the city's franchise as mercantile traders.[74] It thus appears that York lost its pre-eminent position as a centre of both production and distribution at some point in the mid- to later fifteenth century. Equally significantly, Bartlett, Swanson, and Kermode all argue that West

[70] See Table 2.8.

[71] Swanson, *Medieval Artisans*, 36.

[72] Table 2.2 above; *Calendar of Miscellaneous Inquisitions*, vi (London, 1963), no. 212, pp. 242–9; Bartlett, 'Expansion and Decline', 29; Heaton, *Yorkshire Woollen and Worsted Industries*, 44; Swanson, *Medieval Artisans*, 142–4; J. I. Kermode, 'Merchants, Overseas Trade, and Urban Decline: York, Beverley, and Hull, *c.*1380–1500', *Northern History*, 23 (1987), 59.

[73] YML, L 1/17; Swanson, *Medieval Artisans*, 144; Bartlett, 'Expansion and Decline', 29; D. M. Palliser, 'A Crisis in English Towns? The Case of York, 1460–1640', *Northern History*, 14 (1978), 117.

[74] D. M. Palliser, 'A Regional Capital as Magnet: Immigrants to York, 1477–1566', *Yorkshire Archaeological Journal*, 57 (1985), 112.

Riding clothiers were by this period beginning to bypass York merchants and trade directly with London merchants.[75]

It has traditionally been argued that the 'urban' woollen industry at York lost ground to cheaper, 'rural' competition as a consequence of over-regulation through civic and gild control, and over-taxation.[76] It may be more true to suggest that York's regional economic function was eroded during the later fifteenth century by the development of an alternative and increasingly self-sufficient industrial and commercial base in the West Riding. There are several measures of urban vitality within the Riding. A number of small urban communities can be seen to have been flourishing as early as 1379 from the poll tax evidence. Wakefield appears to have supported a Corpus Christi Play from perhaps the middle of the fifteenth century. Parish churches were rebuilt on a grand scale through the century at Wakefield, Rotherham, Halifax, Sheffield, Doncaster, and Bradford.[77] The boroughs of Doncaster and Pontefract even achieved corporate status in 1467 and 1484 respectively.[78] An analysis of the place of origin of immigrants to York admitted to the franchise between 1535 and 1565 reveals significantly few migrants from these textile and metal districts of the West Riding.[79] This is late evidence, but it suggests that skilled labour was not being lost from that region to York as was true of the less economically developed regions north-west of York.[80] It may be, therefore, that York was not just losing its market for cloth, but for a whole range of manufactured goods within the West Riding and elsewhere. West Riding towns were coming of age as centres of manufacture and distribution. The household accounts of the north Derbyshire Eyre family for the 1470s, for example, show that they were able to make most of their purchases in Sheffield.[81]

[75] Bartlett, 'Expansion and Decline', 30; Swanson, *Medieval Artisans*, 144–5, 147; Kermode, 'Merchants, Overseas Trade, and Urban Decline', 59–70.

[76] e.g. Heaton, *Yorkshire Woollen and Worsted Industries*, 44.

[77] A. C. Cawley (ed.), *The Wakefield Pageants in the Townley Cycle* (Manchester, 1958), pp. xiv–xvii; N. Pevsner, *The Buildings of England: Yorkshire, The West Riding* (Harmondsworth, 1967), 31, 122, 181, 229–30, 418–20, 450, 527–9.

[78] M. Beresford and H. P. R. Finberg, *English Medieval Boroughs: A Handlist* (Newton Abbot, 1973), 190–1.

[79] Palliser, 'A Regional Capital as Magnet', 116.

[80] Ibid. 114–17.

[81] C. Dyer, 'The Consumer and the Market in the Later Middle Ages', *Economic History Review*, 2nd ser. 42 (1989), 316.

The case that York was undergoing real economic recession by the later fifteenth century, and that this recession was first felt within the textiles sector does thus appear to have real foundation. But this observation requires some qualification. It would be wrong to argue for a serious recession outside the cloth-manufacturing crafts before the middle of the century, though some recession was probably experienced within these crafts during the earlier decades of that century. Though recession became widespread, there were still some trades, and particularly service trades, that continued to prosper into the early Tudor period. This era of recession followed, moreover, a period of sustained economic growth which encompassed nearly every sector of the urban economy. It must be doubted that these trends can readily be matched against movements in the total population of the city, as both Bartlett and Palliser have elsewhere argued, since this last can only be calculated with any degree of certainty for 1377.[82] There are, however, some clues.

For the period before the Black Death, McClure has argued that the majority of migrants to the city (51 per cent in the period 1312–27) came from within a twenty-mile radius. By 1360–5 migrants were drawn from rather greater distances; as many came from distances between twenty and forty miles as from one to twenty miles.[83] Certainly demographic recovery after 1349 through migration from the countryside must have been both real and substantial to have achieved a total population in the order of 12000–13000 by 1377 despite continued epidemics.[84] This is indicative of a high degree of economic vitality to attract migrants from York's rural hinterland, but it would be foolhardy to project a real population increase over the pre-plague level in the absence of any reliable pre-plague statistics. The demographic trend after 1377 is still more uncertain; the pattern of epidemic mortality is relatively easy to map (and mortality in 1429 and 1438 seems to have been especially severe), but the level of migration cannot be

---

[82] Bartlett, 'Expansion and Decline'; Palliser, 'A Crisis in English Towns?', 113.

[83] P. McClure, 'Patterns of Migration in the Late Middle Ages: The Evidence of English Place-Name Surnames', *Economic History Review*, 2nd ser. 32 (1979), 177, 180.

[84] York's poll tax population in 1377 was 7248. Using a multiplier of 1.65, i.e. making only modest allowance for evasion or exemption, this would suggest a population of 12000.

assessed with any confidence.[85] Rees Jones has argued that a decline in rent income through the fifteenth century, faster in York than at Oxford or Winchester, may be explained in part by falling demand due to falling numbers. She has also suggested some correlation between years of epidemic and a sharp downturn in rent incomes.[86] This last may suggest that by the fifteenth century demographic attrition due to the ravages of pestilence was not made good through immigration from the countryside. Gild ordinances of the later fifteenth century, moreover, suggest a growing unwillingness on the part of the economic community to absorb unskilled migrant labour, and Rees Jones has shown that it was poorer properties that were least likely to find tenants.[87] By the early sixteenth century civic authorities were concerned with the problem of vagrancy.[88] To argue that by the earlier sixteenth century the city's population had fallen to only some 8000, however, rests on too slender statistical evidence and an over-simplistic correlation of demographic with economic trends.[89]

URBAN ECONOMIC FORTUNES:
THE NATIONAL CONTEXT

Similar problems of sources and methodology characterize many individual studies of medieval urban economies. To assess the typicality of the York experience is thus a hazardous exercise. The majority of larger urban communities studied have been ports by reason of the accessibility of enrolled customs accounts as a barometer of trade. But the level of overseas trade may not be a good measure of the economic vitality of the port community itself. For Southampton it is possible to describe with some confidence the regional and overland trade associated with the port, but this evidence does not demonstrate that Southampton greatly benefited from the volume of trade passing through at

[85] Goldberg, 'Mortality and Economic Change'.
[86] Rees Jones, 'Property, Tenure and Rents', 253–7.
[87] Ibid. 260–2.
[88] Cullum, 'Hospitals and Charitable Provision'.
[89] A. G. Dickens, 'Tudor York', in P. M. Tillot, (ed.), *VCH, City of York* (Oxford, 1961), 121–2; Bartlett, 'Expansion and Decline', 33; W. G. Hoskins, 'English Provincial Towns in the Early Sixteenth Century', *Transactions of the Royal Historical Society*, 5th ser. 6 (1956), 5.

least during the course of the fifteenth century.[90] Too little has been written on the economies of such inland towns as Nottingham, Leicester, or even Coventry before 1500 for a more balanced national overview to be realized. Regional patterns, furthermore, must have been influenced by the apparently increasing economic importance of the capital. Certainly London merchants are found operating in a variety of regional markets, as at Southampton or, by the later fifteenth century, in the West Riding, at the expense of local traders.

Despite the uncertainty of the economic evidence, certain observations are still possible. A number of east coast ports appear to have lost ground over the fifteenth century. Economic recession at York after *c.*1460 was directly matched at Hull, which greatly depended upon York trade.[91] Great Yarmouth appears to have suffered even earlier with the decline of its herring fair. Boston, Lynn, and Yarmouth all were affected by the decline in raw wool exports.[92] The towns to the north of York, Newcastle, Durham, and Carlisle, are, however, too sparsely documented to justify like economic analysis, but both Newcastle and Durham are known to have experienced declining rentals by the fifteenth century.[93] The port of Chester may have experienced economic recession by the later fifteenth century following a decline in the port's wine trade from the middle of the century and the Irish trade from the 1460s.[94] There is thus some evidence here that a number of communities reliant on overseas trade and located broadly within the northern and eastern halves of the country were experiencing an economic downturn by about the second half of the fifteenth century. This regional picture must be

[90] O. Coleman, 'Trade and Prosperity in the Fifteenth Century: Some Aspects of the Trade of Southampton', *Economic History Review*, 2nd ser. 16 (1963), 9–22.

[91] Kermode, 'Merchants, Overseas Trade, and Urban Decline'.

[92] A. Saul, 'English Towns in the Late Middle Ages: The Case of Great Yarmouth', *Journal of Medieval History*, 8 (1982), 75–88; Carus-Wilson and Coleman, *England's Export Trade*; E. M. Carus-Wilson, 'The Medieval Trade of the Ports of the Wash', *Medieval Archaeology*, 6–7 (1962–3), 182–201.

[93] R. B. Dobson, 'Cathedral Chapters and Cathedral Cities: York, Durham, and Carlisle in the Fifteenth Century', *Northern History*, 19 (1983), 15–44; A. F. Butcher, 'Rent, Population and Economic Change in Late-Medieval Newcastle', *Northern History*, 14 (1978), 67–77; Rees Jones, 'Property, Tenure and Rents', 257.

[94] K. P. Wilson, 'The Port of Chester in the Fifteenth Century', *Transactions of the Historical Society of Lancashire and Cheshire*, 117 (1965), 1–15.

qualified by the divergent pattern of growth suggested for the nascent textile and manufacturing towns of the West Riding, although it would be difficult to demonstrate that this growth was actually sustained over the entire period in all cases.

For the South-West a differing pattern emerges. Carus-Wilson has described the 'expansion' of Exeter in the period *c.*1480–1510 through the export of cloth manufactured in the city's Devonshire hinterland to markets in France, Spain, and Portugal. Local clothing towns, such as Cullompton, Tiverton, and Taunton, display considerable vitality at this same period.[95] In neighbouring Cornwall the fashion for pewter stimulated demand for tin.[96] Bristol may also have experienced a degree of prosperity in the last decades of the fifteenth century, and here again new markets in Spain and Portugal provided a stimulus. Too little is known, however, of that city's own manufacture or of the local cloth industry to be sure that the trend in overseas trade was reflected at all levels of the urban economy.[97] Cloth manufacture within the Cotswolds hinterland, as at Stroudwater and Castle Combe, is known to have prospered through the fifteenth century, and the expansion of trade at Wells has already been commented upon.[98] The worsteds manufacture in and around Norwich may also have grown by the end of our period.[99] Similar expansion in cloth manufacture may be associated with a region of north Essex and southern Suffolk, though Britnell would argue that the rapid growth of Colchester in the period after the Black Death was not sustained throughout the fifteenth century.[100]

On balance, therefore, it would appear that the sort of economic downturn experienced in the northern and eastern regions during the second half of the fifteenth century, and especially in those communities most involved in overseas trade, was not necessarily characteristic of southern and western England. This cautious observation is justified by a concern that too little attention has

---

[95] Carus-Wilson, *The Expansion of Exeter*, 17–20.

[96] Tin production nevertheless declined during the later 15th cent.: J. Hatcher, *English Tin Production and Trade before 1500* (Oxford, 1973).

[97] J. W. Sherborne, *The Port of Bristol in the Middle Ages* (Historical Association, Bristol Branch, Pamphlet, 43; 1965).

[98] Darby (ed.), *A New Historical Geography*, 222–6.

[99] I am most grateful to Andrew King for this personal communication based on his study of the financial administration of the late medieval city.

[100] Britnell, *Growth and Decline in Colchester*.

been paid to internal trade, manufacture for the domestic market, and the economic fortunes of inland towns. In the absence of a greater range of detailed studies of individual towns it becomes difficult to assess the typicality of York's experience. A number of towns associated with the textiles regions of the South-West and the South-East may have been spared the sort of difficulties encountered in York during the later decades of the fifteenth century. On the other hand, relatively few towns (Colchester may have been one) can have enjoyed such swift recovery and real growth in the decades following the Black Death. The need for more case studies employing the widest possible range of evidence can only be restated, together with the fear that the sometimes rather sterile debate over the fortunes of towns during the late Middle Ages has focused too much attention on extreme cases at selected moments in time.

3

Women and Work

Women workers are not inconspicuous in the records of medieval
town and countryside, yet, with the notable exception of the work
of such writers as Annie Abram and Eileen Power, it is only
relatively recently that they have been the focus of much attention.[1] On one level this is a reflection of the circumscribed role of
women in industrial society, a role challenged first by their
experience within the Great War and latterly by the growth of the
Women's Movement.[2] On another level it follows from an increasing awareness of and readiness to exploit sources previously
ignored by the political historian or relegated to the antiquarian
or genealogist. This last is especially true of wills, poll taxes, and
registers of persons admitted to the franchise. Though the contents
of the present chapter cannot claim to be entirely new, they are
designed to broaden the debate and stimulate further research.
The concern here has not been merely to catalogue the range of
trades and occupations in which women were at some time
engaged, for this alone only obscures a more subtle economic
structure. Rather it is additionally to locate women's work within
the context of both the familial economy and the wider urban and
rural economies. It has also been to consider how far women's
role was circumscribed by lack of access to wealth and training,
by marital status, by the particular needs of the local economy,
and by household and family responsibilities. Underlying this
concern is the question that first prompted this study, namely how
far were women able to support themselves, and how did this
change in response to secular movements in the economy.

[1] Abram, 'Women Traders'; Power, *Medieval Women*. Mary Dormer Harris
clearly shared these interests as is apparent from the introduction to her edition of
The Coventry Leet Book.

[2] Abram's study of women in the economy of medieval London was published
in 1916. It should be noted that women are still in a minority among English
academic historians and that many English medievalists do not see the study of
women as more than a peripheral concern; most recent work on medieval women
has been achieved by American women academics.

The specific literature on women in medieval English town society is as yet slender and limited in scope. Hutton's work on fourteenth-century Shrewsbury, though of interest, is hampered by insufficient source material.[3] Lacey stresses the legal restrictions placed upon London women, but her review of women's work tends towards the anecdotal and seems to obscure underlying secular trends. Her conclusion that women, despite these legal restraints, played a relatively full role in the economic life of medieval London, an observation first suggested by Abram, is nevertheless of real value.[4] The picture that emerges from Hilton's studies of small town society in the West Midlands is similarly inconclusive, though Hilton does draw attention to the role of the female huckster as an intermediary between the market-place and the small consumer. Hilton also suggests a relationship between the urban female trader, typified by the huckster, and an allegedly high level of female migration into towns like Halesowen in the pre-plague years.[5]

A much more substantial survey is that achieved for Exeter in the later years of the fourteenth century by Kowalesk: from a detailed analysis of a very full series of borough court rolls.[6] Kowaleski tends to draw a rather negative view of female economic activity, treating service as a low-status occupation and noting a surprisingly high proportion of prostitutes among her population of economically active women. A discussion of the possible bias of the source material would here be useful since certain types of activity, namely brewing, forestalling, regrating, and even prostitution, would be more likely to feature in a legal record than other pursuits less strictly regulated by the civic authorities. In that sense the court roll does not constitute a reliable source for evaluating the structure of female economic activity. Kowaleski's detailed analysis of debt litigation is, however, exemplary, and shows the regularity with which women appeared in the courts as petty debtors. This Kowaleski relates to

---

[3] D. Hutton, 'Women in Fourteenth Century Shrewsbury', in L. Charles and L. Duffin (eds.), *Women and Work in Pre-Industrial England* (London, 1985), 83–99.

[4] Lacey, 'Women and Work in Fourteenth and Fifteenth Century London', 24–82; Abram, 'Women Traders'.

[5] Hilton, 'Lords, Burgesses and Hucksters', 10; Goldberg, 'The Public and the Private'; Ch. 6 below.

[6] Kowaleski, 'Women's Work in a Market Town'.

women's lack of access to capital, a major additional limiting
factor in a job market already circumscribed by legal restrictions.
It may, however, only reflect economic conditions for women on
the eve of, rather than during, a period of expanding opportunities. How different a picture might have emerged if Kowaleski had
extended her study into the fifteenth century is an open question.[7]

Contributions to the study of women in English rural society
are only marginally more numerous. Hilton has a valuable chapter
on the subject, based on a variety of sources, in the published
edition of his Ford lectures. Penn has explored women's work
from the perspective of prosecutions under the Statute of Labourers, an important study derived from a still neglected source.
Hanawalt has pioneered the use of coroners' rolls as a source and
has some material relating specifically to women.[8] Her evidence is
not without interest, but, as observed before, it can only throw
light on occupational activity where this activity resulted in
accidental death. This may tend to exaggerate gender differences
in work patterns since two apparently hazardous occupations,
namely carting and drawing water, male and female activities
respectively, account for a significant proportion of all work-
related accidents. It follows that Hanawalt's assertion that women
were more likely to work in and around the home, whilst men
worked in the fields, may disguise a more complex division of
labour. Certainly it is not possible to agree that the source is
relatively free from bias simply because people appear 'on an
involuntary basis'.[9] The most important survey to date is, however, Bennett's detailed study of the manor of Brigstock prior to
the Black Death.[10] Her survey is based on the comparatively full
series of court rolls surviving for this ancient demesne manor. The
restricted focus of this study reflects the limitations of the source
material. The court was primarily a forum for those who owed it

---

[7] For a discussion of some writings on women in later medieval continental
towns see Ch. 1 above.

[8] Hilton, 'Women in the Village'; Penn, 'Female Wage-Earners'; B. A.
Hanawalt, *The Ties that Bound: Peasant Families in Medieval England* (New York,
1986). See Ch. 1 above for a fuller discussion of these and other related studies.

[9] B. A. Hanawalt, 'Seeking the Flesh and Blood of Manorial Families', *Journal
of Medieval History*, 14 (1988), 35; Goldberg, 'The Public and the Private'.

[10] Bennett, *Women in the Medieval English Countryside*.

suit by reason of holding tenements of the lord. Adult males are thus disproportionately well represented; women, children, servants, and the landless disproportionately poorly represented. Only certain activities, particularly those that contravened customary law, fell within the jurisdiction of the court. The record of the court then is in no sense a mirror of society, although it is perhaps tempting to confuse its distorted image for some wider reality.

The court rolls thus paint a rather negative picture of women, presented, for example, for illegal gleaning, theft of food, or 'unjustly' raising the hue and cry. They show women as victims of male violence and suggests their 'disadvantaged position before the court'. What Bennett fails sufficiently to illuminate is how this pattern relates to the world outside the court. Similarly, she is concerned to argue that women were subject to patriarchal subordination and that this subordination was rooted in the structure of the household and family. This may or may not be true, but it is in part an illusion created by the conventions of the court record. Because the status of the married woman in law differed from that of her unmarried sister, the court invariably recorded the marital status of those women that were from time to time the subject of its deliberations. Court rolls alone appear an insufficient record. Only by drawing upon other sources can a more lively and representative overview be hoped for. This is true not least of female economic activity. Female brewers, bakers, and petty retailers may often be found in manor court rolls since their activities were liable to bring them into conflict with statute and customary law, but many other employments will pass unnoticed.

The present chapter is concerned to explore the full range of female economic activity over a comparatively long period of time. This dynamic analysis is designed to throw light not just on the range of employment women had access to, but on how and why this changed within the period studied. A number of sources are available for the study of female participation in economic life, but each presents its own difficulties. Few allow any form of quantitative analysis. It is only sometimes possible to identify the marital status of individual women, especially before the later fifteenth century. Few women can be traced between different types of source, which in any case tend to be class-specific. It is thus virtually impossible to reconstruct the working career of any individual over time. The following analysis can consequently be only prosopographical and essentially impressionistic in approach. It will focus on York and its rural hinterland, notably the West Riding and Howdenshire, for which substantial poll tax evidence survives. By devoting so much attention to York it is possible to combine material from a range of sources and so avoid some of the dangers inherent in a single-source study. It is particularly unfortunate that the records of the city courts are almost entirely lost for the period, and thus it is not possible to attempt the sort of study made by Kowaleski using Exeter court rolls. The records of the ecclesiastical courts at York do nevertheless provide a rare and valuable insight into economic activity in the form of personal testimony. The very range of complementary material allows, moreover, for much fuller use of individual sources than might otherwise be possible. One of the more important of these is the poll tax.

WOMEN'S WORK IN URBAN SOCIETY: THE POLL TAX EVIDENCE

There is much documentary evidence for women traders in towns from at least the thirteenth century. Market women are recorded in number in the assessment rolls of the borough of Wallingford from 1227.[11] Women are similarly listed for market-trading offences in the Norwich leet rolls dating from 1288–9.[12] In York female victuallers are found in breach of the civic ordinances of 1301 in some number, especially as regraters, otherwise hucksters, and brewers.[13] Any substantial discussion of the economic role of urban women in the pre-plague era is, however, necessarily beyond the scope of the present work. Evidence does exist for a fuller study, but an impressionistic overview of scattered sources suggests that it was not until the economic expansion of the later fourteenth century that women moved beyond the most traditional female tasks, such as spinning and laundering, and outside the

---

[11] *Royal Commission on Historical Manuscripts, Sixth Report* (London, 1877), 577–9.

[12] NRO, NCR Case 5, shelf b.

[13] Prestwich (ed.), *York Civic Ordinances, 1301*.

market-place.[14] It may thus be useful to commence this present analysis with a review of the poll tax evidence of 1379–81. Despite the uncertain quality of the data, the later poll taxes do at least allow some insight into the relative contribution of women on a trade by trade basis through the full range of urban economic activity. Poll tax data also allow for comparison between communities and enable the case of York to be placed in a wider national perspective.[15] The sexual composition of households by occupation is shown in Table 3.1.

With the exception of the unusually detailed return for Howden in 1379, occupational data from urban poll tax sources are usually limited to household heads. An analysis of service sex ratios derived from the same material does, however, demonstrate occupational-specific patterns that lend support to the view that the economic activities of the servant group were determined by the occupation of the head of household.[16] There is some evidence to validate this supposition for other members of the household besides servants, notably resident daughters, but in many instances the only other household members are spouses.[17] The most direct indicator of female labour outside service thus lies in the record of occupations of female heads of household. It is unfortunate that one of the defects of the later returns is that this group is inadequately enumerated. This is especially true of the York returns for 1381. Here fifty-three female heads of household are noted merely as labourers, and it is evident from a comparison of poll tax material for 1377 and 1381 (for the parishes of St Sampson and St Martin, Coney Street) that these later returns often exclude female householders described in the first survey.[18] There appears here also a slight bias against textile-workers, but in favour of leather traders between the two assessments and this may follow from the non-inclusion of some female workers. Elsewhere the surviving returns are often more satisfactory and this is reflected in the greater compatibility of numbers of recorded tax-payers between the 1377 totals and those for 1381. Whereas only some 55.4 per cent of the 1377 total tax population is recorded in 1381 for York, 85.1 per cent of the equivalent

---

[14] Cf. Goldberg, 'The Public and the Private'.
[15] See Ch. 2 above.　　　　[16] See Table 4.5 below.
[17] See Table 3.4.　　　　[18] See Appendix II.

TABLE 3.1. *Sexual composition of households by occupation from poll tax sources for 1379 and 1381*

	Total households	Female-headed	Proportion households with servants	Total population	Proportion in service	Total sex ratio
1379						
CANTERBURY (PRO, E 179/123/47)						
Butcher	12	1	91.7	50	54	104.2
Mercantile	12	—	50.0	31	22.6	63.2
Carpenter	9	—	44.4	22	27.3	144.4
DONCASTER						
Tanner	7	2	28.6	17	29.4	88.9
Leather	18	2	33.3	45	24.4	95.7
Fuller	7	4	—	10	—	42.9
HOWDEN						
Butcher	9	—	66.7	26	34.6	136.4
LYNN						
Baker	5	—	40.0	14	42.5	250.0
Brewer	5	1	50.0	20	45	58.3
Hostiller	5	1	60.0	13	30.8	44.4
Victuals	23	2	43.5	62	35.5	87.9
Cordwainer	7	—	14.3	17	17.6	112.5
Tanner	6	—	66.7	21	42.9	125
Leather	18	—	44.4	56	35.7	122.7
Chaloner	3	—	66.7	13	61.5	160.0
Spinster	10	10	—	10	—	0
Weaver	10	—	10.0	23	13.0	130
Textiles	38	11	15.8	77	20.7	97.4
Tailor	18	—	—	34	—	106.3
Clothing	24	2	4.2	53	17.0	100.0
Mercantile	21	1	90.5	99	60.6	81.6
Smith	5	—	40.0	14	28.6	180.0
Metal	19	2	26.3	43	20.9	126.3
Building	7	—	28.6	18	22.2	80.0
Wood	7	1	—	13	—	85.7
Transport	26	—	11.5	54	7.4	92.9
PONTEFRACT						
Butcher	8	—	62.5	31	45.2	106.7
Ostler	12	1	66.7	40	42.5	100.0
Spicer	5	—	40.0	15	33.3	66.7

TABLE 3.1. (*Continued*)

	Total households	Female-headed	Proportion households with servants	Total population	Proportion in service	Total sex ratio
Victuals	40	1	42.5	118	33.1	100.0
Saddler	5	—	60.0	13	30.8	160.0
Skinner	4	—	50.0	11	36.4	83.3
Souter	10	—	20.0	24	12.5	84.6
Tanner	7	1	42.6	19	21.1	111.1
Leather	26	1	38.5	67	22.4	103.0
Dyer	5	—	40.0	17	41.2	88.9
Weaver	16	4	25	34	14.7	78.9
Textiles	30	4	20.0	67	17.9	91.4
Tailor	18	2	38.9	45	24.4	104.6
Clothing	24	5	33.3	54	22.2	92.9
Draper	5	—	40.0	20	50.0	122.2
Merchant	4	—	75	24	54.2	100.0
Mercantile	12	—	50.0	52	46.2	100.0
Smith	14	1	42.9	33	21.3	135.7
Metal	22	1	31.8	51	15.7	142.9
RIPON						
Brewer	4	1	75	11	36.4	37.5
Cordwainer	12	—	25	26	15.4	116.7
Dyer	4	2	50.0	8	25	60.0
Weaver	12	3	16.7	20	10.0	122.2
Textiles	21	8	19.0	34	11.8	88.9
Mercantile	9	1	66.7	29	48.3	107.1
ROTHERHAM						
Baker	8	1	37.5	20	25	100.0
Victuals	19	3	42.1	42	23.8	90.9
Textiles	15	1	26.7	39	12.8	85.7
SHEFFIELD						
Smith	13	2	7.7	26	3.8	116.7
TICKHILL						
Tanner	6	1	66.7	16	31.3	128.6
Weaver	6	4	16.7	9	11.1	28.6
WAKEFIELD						
Fuller	7	1	42.9	17	23.5	112.5
Weaver	7	2	28.6	16	25	166.7

TABLE 3.1.   (*Continued*)

	Total households	Female-headed	Proportion households with servants	Total population	Proportion in service	Total sex ratio
1381						
LICHFIELD						
Baker	5	—	80.0	16	37.5	128.6
OXFORD						
Baker	28	—	42.6	76	30.3	137.5
Brewer	28	5	50.0	96	43.8	113.3
Butcher	18	1	66.7	56	37.5	154.6
Cook	17	—	23.5	38	18.4	111.1
Fisher	10	1	50.0	25	20.0	127.3
Fishmonger	8	—	87.5	28	42.9	86.7
Hostiller	12	—	45.5	30	26.7	70.0
Miller	8	—	37.5	19	15.8	72.7
Spicer	6	—	66.7	32	62.5	146.2
Victuals	145	14	46.9	418	34.5	111.1
Corvisor	41	—	29.3	94	20.2	141.0
Saddler	8	1	37.5	21	33.3	162.5
Skinner	23	—	30.4	54	16.7	134.8
Tawer	17	—	17.6	44	22.7	158.8
Leather	94	1	27.7	225	24.4	144.6
Dyer	6	—	66.7	16	37.5	166.7
Fuller	14	—	28.6	34	20.6	142.9
Sherman	5	—	40.0	11	18.2	175
Spinster	39	39	12.8	46	8.7	0
Weaver	34	—	32.4	91	33.0	193.6
Textiles	102	41	26.5	205	24.4	93.4
Tailor	50	1	44	142	35.9	144.8
Clothing	74	13	33.8	183	30.6	117.9
Draper	8	—	75	34	52.9	100.0
Mercantile	17	—	58.8	74	56.8	146.7
Goldsmith	5	—	80.0	16	37.5	128.6
Ironmonger	6	1	50.0	17	43.8	100.0
Smith	6	1	66.7	17	29.4	188.3
Metal	36	2	47.2	95	28.4	137.5
Labourer	19	1	15.8	36	16.7	125
Mason	9	—	22.2	18	27.8	125
Slater	12	—	41.7	29	17.2	123.1
Building	52	1	21.2	107	18.7	132.6

TABLE 3.1. (*Continued*)

	Total households	Female-headed	Proportion households with servants	Total population	Proportion in service	Total sex ratio
Carpenter	17	—	11.8	33	6.1	106.3
Wood	26	—	15.4	49	8.2	113.0
Transport	20	—	10.0	42	4.8	100.0
Armaments	11	1	27.3	24	16.7	140.0
Chandler	11	1	22.6	31	38.7	93.8
SHREWSBURY						
Skinner	2	—	100.0	11	63.6	37.5
Tailor	10	1	20.0	24	20.6	84.6
SOUTHWARK						
Baker	5	1	60.0	13	30.8	160.0
Brewer	24	3	24.6	57	24.6	103.6
Butcher	4	—	50.0	15	46.7	87.5
Huckster	24	20	8.3	29	6.9	20.8
Ostler	22	2	54.5	67	38.8	103.0
Victuals	105	32	32.4	236	26.7	85.8
Corvisor	34	1	14.7	70	14.3	125.8
Saddler	8	1	50.0	18	27.8	125
Skinner	14	3	—	23	—	91.7
Leather	59	5	15.3	117	12.8	116.7
Spinster	26	26	—	26	—	0
Textiles	41	30	9.8	51	9.8	37.8
Tailor	45	4	3.8	78	5.1	136.4
Clothing	72	18	4.2	114	3.5	103.6
Metal	25	2	24	50	20.0	177.8
Carpenter	17	1	11.8	40	12.5	110.5
Wood	23	1	13.0	54	11.1	107.7
Boatman	17	—	17.6	35	11.4	150.0
Transport	32	—	15.6	67	11.9	131.0
Stewmonger	4	—	100.0	23	65.2	91.7
WORCESTER						
Butcher	4	—	75	17	52.6	112.5
Tanner	7	—	42.9	19	21.1	111.1
Dyer	3	—	66.7	12	50.0	200.0
Fuller	3	—	66.7	13	46.2	116.7
Tailor	6	—	33.3	15	20.0	114.3

Women and Work

TABLE 3.1. (*Continued*)

	Total households	Female-headed	Proportion households with servants	Total population	Proportion in service	Total sex ratio
YORK						
Baker	31	1	29.0	76	19.7	94.9
Brewer	7	3	42.9	17	29.4	30.8
Butcher	29	—	48.3	80	30.0	128.6
Fisher	24	—	4.2	45	2.2	110.0
Hostiller	20	—	45	51	25.5	82.1
Spicer	12	—	58.3	34	32.4	88.9
Victuals	145	4	32.4	350	21.1	96.0
Cordwainer	46	—	10.9	94	6.4	95.8
Saddler	23	—	39.1	54	20.4	157.1
Skinner	21	—	4.8	38	2.6	137.5
Tanner	44	—	29.5	106	19.8	112
Leather	151	—	19.9	328	12.5	114.4
Dyer	18	—	50.0	50	36.0	117.4
Weaver	72	2	2.8	134	3.0	121.7
Textiles	127	5	17.3	254	9.4	130.0
Tailor	73	—	8.2	138	5.1	128.3
Clothing	97	4	9.3	186	5.9	117.6
Chapman	22	—	27.3	47	17.0	88.0
Draper	31	1	54.8	88	36.4	72.5
Mercer	39	—	64.1	122	42.6	106.8
Merchant	21	—	76.2	84	51.2	100.0
Mercantile	113	1	56.6	341	39.6	95.0
Goldsmith	13	—	15.4	27	7.4	107.7
Girdler	18	—	33.3	37	16.2	184.6
Lorimer	13	—	46.2	30	20.0	150.0
Marshal	17	2	35.3	40	22.5	122.2
Pinner	14	1	—	25	—	108.3
Metal	139	3	19.4	287	12.2	133.3
Building	44	—	6.8	80	5	135.3
Wright	37	—	13.5	73	8.2	118.2
Wood	65	—	13.8	126	9.5	127.3
Transport	32	1	3.1	56	1.8	115.4
Armaments	22	2	18.2	45	13.3	104.5
Chandler	5	1	20.0	9	11.1	125

Sources: As Table II.1 below.

population is so recorded for Oxford over the same period. (Persons aged between 14 and 15 years are excluded at the later date.) 83.7 per cent of the 1377 Pontefract tax population is likewise found in 1379, despite the non-inclusion here of 14–16-year-olds.[19] The Oxford and Southwark assessments for 1381 are especially valuable and full sources and provide a unique view of the occupational structure of independent female workers at this date. An occupational analysis of female householders derived from these returns is given in Table 3.2.

It is immediately apparent that where independent women traders are most satisfactorily recorded, as at Southwark, the majority are accounted for by but a few specific occupations. Hucksters and spinsters alone comprise some 46.5 per cent of female householders with designated occupations there, and shepsters and laundresses a further 16.2 per cent. These same trades represent some 69.6 per cent of the corresponding Oxford population, despite the less satisfactory nature of the returns here. Elsewhere the surviving returns can only indicate the range, but not the actual structure of trades open to single women.[20] Indeed the record seems actually biased against these particular occupations and this must surely reflect the low status and poverty of women so employed. Accordingly, they are not included within the tax. Beside these four occupations a number of other tradeswomen are regularly observed, though not in any great number. More frequent among these are the brewer, tapster, and ostler or hostiller, the weaver, kempster and fuller, the tailoress and the capper, the smith and the marshal, the skinner and the chandler.

Analysed by occupational category, the greater number are discovered within the textile, victualling, and clothing categories (nearly 81 per cent in Southwark and over 86 per cent in Oxford), as is shown in Table 3.3. The equivalent proportion for the rural West Riding in 1379 is somewhat smaller at just over 60 per cent. The absence of women trading independently within the mercan-

---

[19] Calculated from J. C. Russell, *British Medieval Population* (Albuquerque, N.Mex., 1948), 141–3.

[20] It is characteristic of the 1379 returns less regularly to designate occupations than is generally true of the 1381 assessments, because in 1379 occupation was only specifically stated in the case of individuals assessed at the higher artisan rate.

TABLE 3.2.   *Occupational analysis of urban female householders from poll tax sources for 1379 and 1381*

1381	1379				1379 and 1381
York	Oxford	Southwark	Lynn	Pontefract	Other
brewer×3 baker	brewer×5 huckster×3 tapster×3 butcher fisher ale-bearer	huckster×20 brewer×3 cook×2 ostler×2 baker tapster fruiterer garlicmonger fishbearer	brewer hostiller	ostler	brewer: Shrewsbury×3; Howden×9; Ripon baker Doncaster; Rotherham butcher: Canterbury miller: Ripon waferer: Rotherham malt-maker: Rotherham ostler: Tickhill
	saddler	skinner×3 saddler cordwainer		tanner	tanner: Doncaster×2; Tickhill skinner: Rotherham
kempster×3 weaver×2	spinster×39 kempster×2	spinster×20 kempster fuller dyer	spinster×10 kempster	weaver×4	weaver: Tickhill×4; Ripon×3; Wakefield×2; Doncaster; Rotherham

						Other places
sempster×2 purser wimplester	shepster×9 sempster×3 tailor	shepster×10 tailor×4 capper×3 pointer	threadwife	sempster×2 tailor×2 purser	sempster capper	fuller: Doncaster×4; Sheffield; Wakefield spinster: Canterbury×8 kempster: Ripon×3 dyer: Ripon×2 sempster: Ripon×2; Howden; Doncaster tailors: Howden×2; Shrewsbury shepster: Canterbury×2 wimplester: Howden
draper				merchant		chapman: Ripon; Doncaster
marshal×2 nailer	smith ironmonger	girdler×2		goldsmith needler	smith	smith: Sheffield×2; Tickhill marshal: Sheffield; Rotherham goldsmith: Tickhill furbour: Ripon

TABLE 3.2. (*Continued*)

| 1381 | | 1379 | | 1379 and 1381 |
York	Oxford	Southwark	Lynn	Pontefract	Other
	labourer				thatcher: Wakefield
		carpenter	wright		cooper: Doncaster
					ark-maker: Rotherham
					porter: Tickhill
porter					
fletcher×2	stringer				chandler: Howden; Rotherham
chandler	chandler				
mattress-maker	laundress×4	laundress×6	laundress	parchmener	net-maker: Rotherham
	net-maker	barber	barber		
		upholder × 3	horner		
		gardener			
		midwife			
		featherman			

Source: As Table II.1 below.

TABLE 3.3. *Proportions of female householders engaged in various occupational categories from poll tax sources (%)*

Occupational category	Southwark (N = 99)		Oxford (N = 79)		Other urban* (N = 137)		West Riding** (N = 320)	
Victualling	32.3	⎫	17.7	⎫	19.7	⎫	19.1	⎫
Textiles	30.3	⎬ 80.8	51.9	⎬ 86.1	36.5	⎬ 71.5	31.3	⎬ 60.3
Clothing	18.2	⎭	16.5	⎭	15.3	⎭	10	⎭
Leather	5.1		1.3		3.6		4.4	
Mercantile	—		—		2.9		4.7	
Metal	2.0		2.5		9.5		10.9	
Building	—		1.3		0.7		2.5	
Wood	1.0		—		2.2		5	
Transport	—		—		1.5		2.5	
Armaments	—		1.3		1.5		0.9	
Chandlers	1.0		1.3		2.2		—	
Others	11.1		6.3		4.4		8.8	

* As noted in Table 3.2 above. Includes York, Lynn, Pontefract, Howden, Ripon, Doncaster, Sheffield, Rotherham, Tickhill, Wakefield, Canterbury, and Shrewsbury.
** Rural communities only.
Sources: As Table II.1 below.

tile sector is especially striking and cannot be explained purely in terms of the overall occupational structure of Oxford and Southwark since there is elsewhere little evidence of independent female participation in this sector. It may well be that single women were rather more active in the processes of weaving and finishing cloth, in addition to the primary processes, within the textiles category than at first appears. The Southwark returns demonstrate that there was no weaving industry established there and neither the Lynn nor the Oxford assessments provide evidence for any substantial female involvement in those towns. The York poll tax, and likewise those for Pontefract and a number of other West Riding towns noted for their rapidly expanding textile industries, include, however, a number of single female weavers and fullers, though not to the degree found in the pastoral villages of Yorkshire. There is indeed some evidence here for a distinct regional pattern with a much more feminized textiles industry in Yorkshire and the North than found elsewhere.[21] It may also be noticed that single women are found in the metal trades in all the more substantial returns.

The occupational structure just described tends to demonstrate some significant differences from that observed for female servants.[22] Textiles and clothing account for only some 6–20 per cent of female servants, but some 48–68 per cent of independent women workers. Conversely, the mercantile sector contains hardly any single female traders, but in many towns employed a significant proportion of female servants.[23] Perhaps the more significant observation is the apparent inverse correlation between independent female economic activity and the availability of servant labour generally and male servants in particular. Only some 7–27 per cent of male servants were employed in textile- or clothing-related households, whereas these sectors regularly comprise some 20–5 per cent of the total labour force as calculated from poll tax sources.[24] Similarly, it is found that the proportion of male servants engaged in mercantile households invariably exceeds, often considerably, the total proportion of the labour force so employed. It thus follows that single female traders are most frequently encountered occupying niches created by the shortage of trained, i.e. former servant, male labour. This is even true within the victualling trades, although in broad terms the proportion of male servants here adequately matched the equivalent proportion of the overall labour force. Within those trades that were most frequently practised independently by women, notably those of the huckster, the brewer, and the hostiller or ostler, male servants are relatively scarce. This observation may perhaps be extended to cover even more marginal cases. The presence of craftswomen in the metal trades at Sheffield can be observed alongside an apparent shortage of male servants. The 1379 Sheffield returns, however, record very few servants, though an unusual proportion of households contain adult children. In Ripon, likewise, the textiles industry is characterized by the number of independent craftswomen and the relative absence of

---

[21] The Carlisle returns of 1377 include, among others, a female weaver and a female dyer.
[22] See Table 4.6 below.
[23] These figures refer only to servants in economically active households.
[24] All figures refer to Lynn, York, Pontefract, Oxford, and Southwark.

male servants. At Tickhill weaving appears almost completely feminized, but this may only reflect a more rural pattern, where women turned to weaving as a by-employment, as the Howden-shire (1379) returns demonstrate.

A number of points follow which will be more fully discussed in the concluding chapter. Women are only infrequently found independently engaged in trades regularly employing servants, i.e. the more prosperous trades requiring some degree of capital investment. This last is especially true of the major mercantile and leather trades. Only with equal infrequency, therefore, can women have set themselves up in trades for which they had received formal training within service, although many performed traditional 'feminine' tasks, such as needlework and washing, for which they may have experienced informal training from an early age. It follows also that women must have been prepared to redirect work skills learned during service later in their careers in a way that cannot have been generally true of their male counter-parts. Herein lies a particular point of gender-difference in terms of work identity. Whereas a man might follow the same trade all his active life, a woman might have to change hers on leaving service, on marriage, and even after marriage.

This last poses the question of the actual marital status of these 'independent' women traders here discussed. They may either have been single, i.e. unmarried, or widowed. Some of the returns do, however, distinguish widows, though as a group they are perhaps particularly vulnerable to exclusion from these later assessments. The 1379 returns for Sheffield distinguish 31 widows, some 11.1 per cent of all householders. This compares with a mean of 12.9 per cent derived from 70 early modern parish listings.[25] The equivalent proportions for York and Lynn are only 6.7 and 5.9 per cent respectively (based on a total of 105 widows listed for York in 1381 and 29 from the fragmentary Lynn returns in 1379). A mere dozen widows are recorded for Lichfield, although here is found a group of female 'cottars' of equivalent size. That this last comprised single women cannot be demon-strated, but it is significant that four of these cottars, together with one widow, are included only within the additional Lichfield

[25] P. Laslett, 'Size and Structure of the Household in England Over Three Centuries', *Population Studies*, 23 (1969), table 9, p. 216.

return.[26] This is again indicative of the tendency of the later poll taxes regularly to underenumerate women.

It is equally significant that neither of the two returns that most completely distinguish independent female traders (Oxford and Southwark) specifies widows. One Sheffield widow is uniquely described also by trade: Magot' Barkar *vidua*, walker. It is probable that her occupation is so recorded only because she might otherwise be thought a barker, or tanner, as her surname suggests. It must follow that at Oxford and Southwark widows are included within the population of tradeswomen, but not so designated. The assessments are thus divided between those that distinguish women by marital status and those that distinguish women by occupation. It follows that in those returns where widows are listed in some number it cannot be concluded that these women were not themselves economically active. Much the same must be true of those returns that simply fail to identify female householders, at least in any numbers, as is true of Pontefract or Doncaster in 1379. The poll tax returns of 1379 and 1381 may, in conclusion, appear slightly disappointing sources for female economic activity, but they are certainly not evidence for inactivity.

It is not possible to derive any information regarding the economic role of married women from poll tax sources. Save for a small number of Howden wives distinguished independently from their husbands as brewster (*braciatrix*), the returns list married females alongside their spouses without comment.[27] Arguing from silence, this may suggest that women did not usually engage in major craft activity independently of their husbands, and that they invariably assisted their husbands apart from their domestic duties. This can only be tested from alternative sources. It is, however, possible to consider the case of the small numbers of daughters listed in the returns. The regularity with which adult children are enumerated can again be doubted, although the level of recording seems surprisingly uniform. It must remain a possibility that some young women are designated servant rather than

---

[26] PRO, E 179/177/22.

[27] The same is true of the rural Howdenshire returns for 1379 and some of the West Riding returns in the same year. The return for Asmunderby with Bondgate in Claro Wapentake, for example, includes a female mason and a female smith who were married to a shoemaker and a tanner respectively.

daughter within the parental home, but the poll taxes do show that most adolescents left home either as servants or otherwise. It thus appears significant that this group of resident daughters when analysed by occupation demonstrates a regular pattern. This is shown in Table 3.4.

The majority are found within the victualling, textiles, and, notably, leather categories. Their involvement in the first two categories, as assistants to brewers, bakers, weavers, fullers, and dyers, is in line with expectation. These are all trades in which females otherwise participated either as servants or as independent producers. Female assistants are likewise found regularly in wood-working occupations. Neither the tailor nor the cordwainer, both low-status craftsmen, seems to have engaged servants in any number and it seems likely that they sometimes turned to their daughters instead. Their skill as needlewomen, sewing the separate pieces of the leather to form the shoe, may have been retained preferentially within the family as a less costly option than the engagement of a servant.[28] The instances of daughters employed by tanners are more surprising, though female servants are certainly found within this trade and several independent female tanners have already been noticed. Finally, it must be observed that a number of daughters are also found associated with widows' households. This again may reflect the relative poverty of such households, where the daughter fulfilled a domestic function in preference to a female servant, likewise regularly found in such households. As earlier argued, however, at least some of these households headed by widows would have engaged in economic activity.

Poll tax sources do suggest a rather wider range of female economic activity by 1379–81 than appears, on more slender evidence, to have been true of the pre-plague era. The numbers of independent women engaged in textile, metal, and even leather trades cannot go unnoticed. Equally it must be acknowledged that the poll taxes hardly suggest an equal role for working women. They were most frequently found in low-status, traditionally 'feminine' forms of employment which enjoyed little formal

[28] F. Grew and M. de Neergaard, *Shoes and Pattens* (Medieval Finds From Excavations in London, 2; London, 1988), 48–9; Swanson, *Medieval Artisans*, 56.

TABLE 3.4. *Occupational analysis of resident daughters from poll tax sources by household*

	Victuals	Leather	Textiles	Clothing	Wood	Other
1377						
Carlisle						goldsmith
1379						
Bradfield		cordwainer		tailor		mason merchant smith
Canterbury		currier				
Doncaster					slay-maker	porter labourer†×2 smith
Howden	hostiller brewer			tailor		merchant
Pontefract	miller	tanner cordwainer skinner	weaver×2	tailor		
Ripon	spicer baker	cordwainer tanner×2	dyer		carter	
Rotherham			walker×2 dyer			plumber
Sheffield	baker			tailor		
1381						
Oxford	brewer×2 cook	saddler skinner	spinster×2	tailor		laundress
Southwark		cordwainer skinner		tailor	cooper sawyer carpenter	barber

Worcester	baker×2	tanner*	fuller	labourer†
York	fishmonger	tanner	weaver	
		cordwainer	chaloner	

† Female-headed households.
* Sister of household head.
Source: As Table II.1 below

training. Within the mercantile sector they were hardly found at all. The assessors, moreover, seem often to have thought the marital status of a female taxpayer more significant than her occupational status. The picture is thus distorted inasmuch as the returns provide evidence not of all women's economic activity, but only that of a selected few, notably single women. Outside of service, the majority of adult women were married. The potentially considerable productive contribution of women within marriage, however, fell outside the scope of the subsidy. If the returns were used to study the economic role only of single males, then a similarly much more limited view of male activity within the urban economy would emerge. It is here appropriate to consider the full range of trades known to have been practised by women within the period as reflected in a variety of sources. This analysis will again use the broad occupational categories previously adopted by way of a framework.

THE OCCUPATIONS OF TOWNSWOMEN
c.1300–1520

Victualling

It was in the victualling trades that women were most conspicuous within the medieval urban environment. This was not merely a product of the economic expansion of the later fourteenth century. The retail of ale, bread, fish, poultry, and dairy goods appear to be areas especially dominated by women and they attracted rural vendors in addition to resident townswomen into the market place. Indeed the Nottingham poultry market was anciently known as the Womanmarket.[29] Fifteen of the twenty poulterers listed in the Wallingford assessment roll for 1290–1 were female.[30] The earliest surviving Norwich leet rolls and the record of fines for breach of the York civic ordinances of 1301 also illustrate the extent to which women were involved in the marketing of a variety of foodstuffs.[31] Alewives

---

[29] Stevenson (ed.), *Records of the Borough of Nottingham*, ii. 149.
[30] *Royal Commission on Historical Manuscripts, Sixth Report*, 579.
[31] NRO, NCR Case 5, shelf b; Prestwich (ed.), *York Civic Ordinances, 1301*, 22–8.

and women bakers are noted in the records of the fair of St Ives of the late thirteenth century, and likewise in considerable number in the records of the University of Oxford through the first half of the fourteenth century.[32] It is from such a range of independent sources that a more detailed analysis must be attempted, but it is a product of this diversity that it is hardly possible to detect any real secular or regional patterns. This last may be achieved through a comparative analysis of court roll data, as those for Nottingham, Exeter, and Colchester or some smaller boroughs, over a long time period, in itself a massive exercise.[33] The material considered here does, however, allow some form of trade-specific analysis which seems to enjoy a wider significance.

There is much evidence that women monopolized the trade in poultry and dairy products. The poulterers of Wallingford have already been noted. Using later fourteenth-century market fine evidence, Kowaleski has remarked upon the numbers of women dealing in poultry or eggs, butter, and cheese at Exeter.[34] In 1395 a Nottingham jury described the *auxiatrices* or women poulterers of the town as selling butter, cheeses, salt, garlic, flour, and even tallow candles.[35] At Lynn the 'mylk wymen' are the subject of an ordinance directing them to sell only fresh, unadulterated milk, cream, and butter, and all those fined for regrating cheese listed in the earlier Norwich leet rolls are females.[36] Women are likewise presented as regraters of chickens, capons, eggs, as well as fish at Queenshythe in 1422.[37] It is thus somewhat surprising that the poulterers cited in the Norwich leet rolls are exclusively male and that there are equally no independent female poulterers observed from poll tax sources.[38] This last would appear less remarkable if it could

---

[32] E. Wedermeyer, 'Social Groupings at the Fair of St Ives (1275–1302)', *Medieval Studies*, 32 (1970), appendix, table 6, pp. 56–8; Salter (ed.), *Medieval Archives of the University of Oxford*, 143–265.

[33] Although differing record conventions within and between sources could make comparative analysis difficult.

[34] Kowaleski, 'Women's Work in a Market Town', 5.

[35] Stevenson (ed.), *Records of the Borough of Nottingham*, i. 270.

[36] Owen, *The Making of King's Lynn*, 422; NRO, NCR Case 5, shelf b, 6–8, 19.

[37] Thomas (ed.), *Calendar of Plea and Memoranda Rolls, 1413–37*, 138.

[38] NRO, NCR Case 5, shelf b, 8, 19.

be shown that most women poulterers were married since their husbands' names may appear only because responsible for their wives' debts, but in practice it is seldom possible to determine the marital status of women traders in any number from nominative sources before the later fifteenth century.

It is no easier to determine whether these female traders were normally resident within the town or were countrywomen bringing produce to market. One Elena Scott, 'huswyff' of Bradmore, was presented by jurors of the neighbouring town of Nottingham in 1482 for regrating eggs, butter, and cheese in the market there. Many of the women that appear in the records, however, do so as forestallers of the market, i.e. persons going out to buy goods from country producers before they reach the market in order to resell them at a profit, and are therefore presumably residents.[39] The terms 'forestall' and 'regrate' in fact tend to be used rather indiscriminately. The London women presented in 1422 were said to have bought directly from the boats bringing produce into the city by meeting them early in the morning or in the evening, and one Agnes Drew, poulterer, was committed to Newgate for buying up poultry in Leadenhall market before prime.[40] A similar indictment was made at Nottingham in 1395 of a group of seven women, four of whom are described as wives, and two men. Significantly one of these forestallers of poultry was named Anna Hukkester.[41] Of the handful of women so fined in the later leet rolls of Norwich, dated 1374–5 and 1390–1, all were married. One Peter Brasiere is stated to have forestalled poultry, doves, meat, and fish through his wife and servants, but it is his name that is recorded.[42]

The evidence just presented suggests a more complex pattern than at first appears. Though the larger towns were undoubtedly dependent on the surrounding countryside for the supply of foodstuffs, and though the trade in poultry and dairy products must, in the market place at least, have been invariably conducted by women, just as the rearing of poultry and the

---

[39] Stevenson (ed.), *Records of the Borough of Nottingham*, ii. 324.

[40] Thomas (ed.), *Calendar of Plea and Memoranda Rolls, 1364–81*, 21; *1413–37*, 138.

[41] Stevenson (ed.), *Records of the Borough of Nottingham*, i. 276.

[42] NRO, NCR Case 5, shelf b, 17, 18.

running of the dairy were traditionally female concerns, it is not these market-day visitors that feature in the records.[43] It is another class of trader that is observed, one that appears to be resident and, so far as the sources allow, is frequently married. These women bought up quantities of such goods to resell at a higher price, as the wife of Henry Lane who bought poultry in the market on Saturday in order to resell it on the Sunday.[44] They were thus but one element of a more general category of female trader, namely the regrator or huckster.[45] It should be noted that the regular poulterer, trading from his shop rather than in the market place, appears from poll tax and franchise sources to be exclusively male. They are not, however, observed in any quantity and it is likely that much of the demand was filled by the market trader and her shadowy counterpart, the regrater of poultry.

The fish trade is another area in which women were regularly found, both as legitimate traders or as forestallers. A group of eight women and one man were presented by a Nottingham jury in 1396 for forestalling herring above the authorized price, and there are numerous references to women trading in herring and other fish in the early court rolls of Colchester. In 1311 a group of fishwives bought fish in Hythe to resell at a higher price in Colchester, but the fish were found to be rotten when offered for sale.[46] In 1350 the wife of a Norwich fishmonger was herself presented for forestalling fish at Surlingham on the Yare outside the city.[47] A York woman was fined for a trading offence in respect of some red herring in 1486–7, and the involvement of women in the preparation and merchandising of fish is implicit in an entry in the leet book for Coventry in

---

[43] There is some early 16th-cent. evidence from Norwich for countrywomen selling butter in the market there: NRO, NCR Case 16, shelf a, 2, mayor's court book, 1510–32, 110, 192, 324. For women manufacturing butter and cheese see Shahar, *The Fourth Estate*, 241.

[44] NRO, NCR Case 5, shelf b, 18.

[45] To regrate was to sell goods in small, invariably non-standard quantities, often at a higher price than the same goods when sold in more standard quantities within the regular market.

[46] Stevenson (ed.), *Records of the Borough of Nottingham,* i. 322; W. G. Benham (ed.), *Court Rolls of the Borough of Colchester,* i. *(1310–1352),* trans. I. H. Jeayes (Colchester, 1921), 7, 19, 29; Britnell, *Growth and Decline in Colchester,* 37.

[47] NRO, NCR Case 8, shelf a, 8.

1512.[48] The leet records for Norwich may serve to place this involvement in perspective in a manner not possible from purely anecdotal evidence. Only about 5 per cent of some hundred persons fined in the earlier rolls for forestalling fish were female, though it is very possible that the wives of some of the men fined were themselves active.[49] Britnell, working from borough court evidence, argues that in Colchester, where fish was a major commodity, the majority of forestallers were women, 'the wives of stall holders, who hung around the lane ends in the hope of earning a quick penny'.[50]

A rather fuller analysis of female stallholders in Norwich fish market is possible for the period from the late fourteenth century, when the stalls were bought up by the council, until the early sixteenth century.[51] Here the proportion of stalls leased by women varied between 10 and 35 per cent of all stalls. Often a female stallholder can be identified as the widow of the previous lessee, an observation that differs markedly from that observed for the butchers' stalls in the same market, and suggests that the wife too enjoyed a full role in the merchandising of fish. Indeed, where a man rented more than one stall, his wife might manage one of the additional stalls independently. In London Margaret Salisbury, the widow of a fishmonger, was said in 1440 to have long traded as *femme sole*.[52] When the keeper of the assay of oysters farmed his office to women in Queenshythe, however, the authorities held it contrary to the 'worship' of the City of London 'that women should have such things in governance'.[53]

The evidence for women acting as butchers is very slender. As noted, hardly any of the butchers' stalls in Norwich market ever fell into female hands, though Alice, the widow of Thomas Cole, may be briefly observed trading from his old stall immediately after his death.[54] A Nottingham woman,

[48] Dobson (ed.), *York Chamberlains' Account Rolls,* 177; Harris (ed.), *Coventry Leet Book*, 635. For equivalent German evidence see Wiesner, *Working Women in Renaissance Germany*, 119.

[49] NRO, NCR Case 5, shelf b, 3, 7, 8.

[50] Britnell, *Growth and Decline in Colchester*, 40.

[51] NRO, NCR Case 18, shelf a.

[52] Jones (ed.), *Calendar of Plea and Memoranda Rolls, 1437–57*, 35–6.

[53] Thomas (ed.), *Calendar of Plea and Memoranda Rolls, 1413–37*, 139.

[54] NRO, NCR Case 18, shelf a, fo. 81.

Elizabeth Stafford, described as a 'housewife', was presented in
1496 for selling bad meat, but it is unlikely that she was a
butcher as such.[55] Wives may, however, have assisted their
husbands to prepare the meat after slaughter, and at Norwich
several butchers' wives are noted selling puddingstock in the
market there.[56] The manufacture and sale of black puddings
appears to have been 'women's work' and whereas the wives of
butchers had ready access to the raw materials, it is possible to
find examples of women purchasing animal intestines for this
purpose. Thus the Selby Abbey kitchener's account for 1416–17
records the sum of £1. 12s. 11d. paid by one Agnes Bernard
for animal intestines at the rate of 5d. per beast. The same
Agnes was elsewhere employed by the Abbey as a 'preparer of
offals'.[57] Wiesner has observed a similar pattern in early
modern German towns, where it was women that made saus-
ages and cleaned and sold offal and tripe.[58]

Women are observed as bakers and, more frequently, as
vendors of bread, the latter group again overlapping with that
more general class of petty trader, the huckster. Baking was
perhaps a traditional female domestic activity, the uncooked
bread being brought to a communal oven. In the more com-
mercialized context of the medieval town, however, professional bakers are found in number and these tend to be male.
Only seventeen of the sixty bakers observed trading at the St
Ive's fair in the period 1275–1302 were female, and only one
single female trader together with two married women, listed
alongside their husbands, are recorded within a group of thirty
bakers in Oxford in 1329 resisting the payment of a weekly
penny rent.[59] One Alice Baxter had a brass pot seized in lieu
of a similar payment at Nottingham in 1378.[60] Katherine Patan,
fined for a trading offence in respect of horse-bread in 1486–7,

---

[55] Stevenson (ed.), *Records of the Borough of Nottingham*, iii. 46–8.
[56] NRO, NCR Case 18, shelf a, fos. 53ᵛ ff.
[57] J. H. Tillotson (ed.), *Monastery and Society in the Late Middle Ages: Selected Account Rolls from Selby Abbey, Yorkshire, 1398–1537* (Woodbridge, 1988), 124–5. She also purchased wool from Selby Abbey.
[58] Wiesner, *Working Women in Renaissance Germany*, 114–115.
[59] Wedemeyer, 'Social Groupings', 56–8; Salter (ed.), *Munimenta Civitatis Oxonie*, 75–8.
[60] Stevenson (ed.), *Records of the Borough of Nottingham*, i. 196.

had the previous year been in service with a York capper.[61] Some of these bakeresses may have exploited a domestic skill to generate an income, perhaps to supplement a husband's earnings or as a means of livelihood as a widow. The wife or widow of one Thomas Milner, saddler, was fined in York for underweight bread and another woman similarly fined may have been the widow of a shearman. The record uses the term wife (*uxor*), but this usage is ambiguous and certainly sometimes refers to widows. It is unclear whether these women were marketing their own bread or were merely bread-sellers.[62]

If the bakeress was uncommon, the female bread-seller is widely and regularly discovered. In York Agnes, widow of John Alan, is recorded paying stallage to trade in this capacity between 1462–3 and 1475–6. She may perhaps be identified with the Agnes Aleyn who was admitted to the franchise in 1478–9 as a stringer.[63] Yet the ordinances of the bakers for the same city in the late fourteenth century had attempted to proscribe the 'huksters of brede' since they were perceived to be a threat to trading standards. Clearly this policy had little effect. By 1479 they limited themselves to preventing the hucksters trading in bread manufactured by country bakers, a more immediate threat to the urban industry.[64] At Leicester the civic authorities likewise attempted to regulate the bread-sellers (*regratrices*) in 1357 by restricting them to their shops (*fenestris suis*) and to the sale of bread as an individual item.[65] In Coventry in 1431 a civic ordinance ruled that the bakers were not to sell to hucksters.[66] It must be doubted how far such provisions were effective inasmuch as the female bread-seller filled a necessary role in distributing a staple commodity throughout the urban community to even the most humble consumer. In some instances the vendor might be the wife of the baker. There is some evidence for this from an analysis of names of persons fined for selling underweight bread in Oxford early in the four-

[61] Dobson (ed.), *York Chamberlains' Account Rolls*, 179; BIHR, Prob. Reg. 5, fo. 275ᵛ.

[62] Dobson (ed.), *York Chamberlains' Account Rolls*, 177, 197.

[63] Ibid. 105, 122, 147; Collins (ed.), *Register of the Freemen of the City of York*, i. 200.

[64] Sellers (ed.), *York Memorandum Book*, i. 167–71.

[65] Bateson (ed.), *Records of the Borough of Leicester*, ii. 107.

[66] Harris (ed.), *Coventry Leet Book*, 139.

teenth century. A York woman similarly fined in 1454–5 may have been the widow of a baker continuing the business in her own right, and the wife of a York baker, John Haddon, was fined in 1451–2 for selling underweight horse-bread.[67]

The involvement of women in the production of another staple, ale, was also traditional, but probably rather more extensive even in an urban context than has been seen to be true of bread. In the absence of a pure water supply, ale was drunk in quantity. It may additionally have possessed some real nutrient value. In rural society local demand was probably satisfied by the periodic brewings of village women.[68] Poll tax evidence does, however, record a number of urban women, whose livelihood was apparently dependent upon brewing, alongside male brewers, who are nevertheless in an apparent majority. At Howden, perhaps the most rural and least industrialized of the 'urban' sample, the rural feminized pattern prevails. But the more detailed returns here also describe a number of married women occupied as brewsters independently of their husbands. In several instances these women are married to men who are themselves concerned in the victualling trades, namely two butchers, a fishmonger, and a spicer or grocer.[69] It is striking that in every household in which the wife was active as a brewster there is recorded a female servant (with the exception of two of the eleven households in this category for which no servant is recorded). The Howdenshire returns provide some insight into the true level of female participation in the brewing trade which is not otherwise apparent from poll tax or even more general sources.

The Norwich leet rolls contain extensive lists of persons in breach of the assize of ale. Here as elsewhere, fines were so regularly imposed as to form a levy on trade rather than a serious attempt to enforce trading standards.[70] The numbers of

---

[67] Salter (ed.), *Medieval Archives of the University of Oxford*, 1–181; Dobson (ed.), *York Chamberlains' Account Rolls*, 86; YCA, CC 1A, fo. 108ᵛ; BIHR, Prob. Reg. 2, fo. 250ᵛ.

[68] For a fuller discussion of brewing in the countryside see below.

[69] Two others are married to a draper and a cordwainer respectively. In five further instances the husband's trade is unknown: 'Assessment Roll of the Poll-Tax for Howdenshire'.

[70] Cf. The Old Usages of Winchester: Smith (ed.), *English Gilds*, 355. The same was true of Colchester: Britnell, *Growth and Decline in Colchester*, 90.

women among those so fined identified not as wife to another,
but by their personal name are but few. Some of these can be
identified as widows. Of the 500 persons listed in the earliest
roll, dated 1288–9, only 44 (8.8 per cent) are single women,
eight of whom are designated widows.[71] Whereas the earliest
surviving rolls record mostly married couples or alternatively
wives, identified only by reference to their husbands' names,
the later returns, including those that survive for the late fourteenth century, list mostly male names without reference to
possible spouses; only 18 females as against 221 males are listed
in the most recent surviving leet roll dated 1390–1.[72] If married
couples listed in 1288–9 are counted as one rather than two
persons, then this represents a real decline in numbers over the
century and a more marked apparent decline in the proportion
of independent females.[73] It would thus appear that the later
record is limited to the individual actually responsible for payment of the fine, but not necessarily to the individual, invariably female, whose activities incurred the fine.

The same is certainly true of the extensive register of brewing fines contained within the two surviving York chamberlains'
books of account dating to the period 1446–54.[74] The majority
of the women here described as wives (*uxor*) can be demonstrated from testamentary sources to be in fact widowed. The
other independent women listed may be either widows or
unmarried daughters. Thus the 'Ottryngton wyff', otherwise the
wife of Robert Ottrington, observed paying brewing fines
throughout the record period can be identified from Robert's
will dated 1443 as his widow.[75] Margaret Colton is found paying
brewing fines for two years following her enfranchisement as a
brewster in 1448–9. She had earlier been employed in service
and may thus have been unmarried during her two-year brewing career, but is lost from the record on marriage.[76] It may
also be that the extensive list of London brewers *c.*1420, which

---

[71] NRO, NCR Case 5, shelf b, 3.

[72] NRO, NCR Case 5, shelf b, 18.

[73] 7.5 as against 15.7%.

[74] YCA, CC 1, 1A.

[75] YCA, CC 1, pp. 18, 58, 96; CC 1A, fos. 39, 42^v, 46; BIHR, Prob. Reg. 2,
fo. 51^v.

[76] Collins (ed.), *Register of the Freemen of the City of York*, i. 169; YCA, CC 1,
p. 140; CC 1A, fo. 35^v; BIHR, Prob. Reg. 2, fo. 23.

distinguishes four widows, includes married women under their husbands' names.[77] Kowaleski argues that this was true of Exeter records in the late fourteenth century.[78] It is explicit in Britnell's analysis of the brewing trade at Colchester that most ale there was brewed by women, including the wives of leading burgesses.[79] It is noteworthy that the York record is entitled 'finibus et amerciamentis brasiatricum', i.e. of the brewsters.

Financial records are not the only source suggestive of a high level of female involvement in ale-brewing. Bequests of brewing equipment are very commonly observed in wills, especially those made by females. One Emma de Stonegate allowed her servant Agnes the use of her house and brewhouse for a year following her death and bequeathed her malt on condition that the ale made from it be sold and the profit returned to the executors. Agnes was also to provide a quantity of best ale for the poor.[80] A merchant of York, Alan de Hamerton, d. 1406, forgave Beatrix Sleford of Hull a debt of 50*s.* she owed him for the purchase of brewing vessels.[81] It is evidence of this kind that points to brewing as the occupation of the wives and widows not of the poorer, but, as has already been observed for Colchester, of the more substantial artisans and traders. The example of Margery Kempe, the early fifteenth-century bourgeoise and visionary, is well known, but still illustrative. She claims to have turned to brewing 'for pure covetyse and for to maynten hir pride', that is to outshine her neighbours in dress. This remark is to be treated with caution, but it may indicate that Margery had control over her profits. She also maintained servants to assist her in her trade.[82] The York widow Agnes Grantham, who supplied among others the household of the master of St Leonard's hospital, may have depended upon her trade for a livelihood, but she also appears to have been a person of some means and maintained a household of several servants in addition to her son Thomas.[83]

A number of the brewsters identified in the York chamber-

---

[77] Sharpe (ed.), *Calendar of Letter-Books: 'I'*, 233–5.
[78] Kowaleski, 'Women's Work in a Market Town', 151. See also Hilton, 'Small Town Society', 60 and n. 13.
[79] Britnell, *Growth and Decline in Colchester*, 89–90.
[80] YML, D/C Reg. 1, fo. 52.   [81] BIHR, Prob. Reg. 3, fo. 244.
[82] Meech and Allen (ed.), *The Book of Margery Kempe*, 9–10.
[83] BIHR, CP. F. 36 (1410).

lains' books of account were the widows of freemen. Several women were themselves admitted as brewsters to the city's franchise in the period before 1500, one of whom, Juliana de Bramwyth 'de Doncastre' is recorded as household head, despite being married, in the 1377 poll tax.[84] Another substantial widow engaged in brewing was Katherine Lakensnyder. She maintained a large household of servants including, like Agnes Grantham, a tapster or taverner and was also a contemporary of Juliana de Doncastre, in whose parish of St Martin, Coney Street, she lived. She may perhaps further be identified with Katerina de Barneby listed in the 1377 poll tax. She was certainly active between 1381 and her death in 1394.[85] The evidence for female involvement in the brewing industry in towns is thus considerable, but it is probable that the professional male brewer took an increasingly large share of the trade from the later fourteenth century. This is reflected in the declining numbers of women observed paying brewing fines (assuming married women are represented by their husbands). Conversely, the number of male brewers admitted to the franchise of York increased in the fifteenth century. It may be that the use of hops by the same period favoured the larger, invariably male, professional brewer of beer over the part-time female brewster of ale given the longer product life of the former. This has been documented by Britnell in the case of Colchester. Many of the beer brewers found there from about the middle of the fifteenth century were immigrants from the Low Countries or Germany and it may be that initially they catered for Dutch and German mariners using the port.[86] The same may have been true at Hull, where some beer was imported from the Low Countries from the later fourteenth century. In 1428 one William Beerbrewer was allowed to settle and trade there, and other Dutch and German brewers of beer are recorded there and at Scarborough in subsequent years.[87]

[84] Collins (ed.), *Register of the Freemen of the City of York*, i. 75; Leggett (ed.), 'The 1377 Poll Tax Returns for the City of York', 137. The York 1381 returns are defective at this point.

[85] Lakensnyder is a contemporary Flemish term for a trader in cloth. Collins (ed.), *Register of the Freemen of the City of York*, i. 44; Leggett (ed.), 'The 1377 Poll Tax Returns for the City of York', 136; Bartlett (ed.), *Lay Poll Tax Returns for the City of York*, 41; BIHR, Prob. Reg. 1, fo. 72.

[86] Britnell, *Growth and Decline in Colchester*, 196–7.

[87] Allison (ed.), *VCH, York, East Riding*, i. 52.

The tapster, taverner, tippler, or huckster of ale was as a class much more exclusively female and extended much lower down the social scale. Certainly some brewers, as just observed, sold ale by the measure, even employing servants for this purpose, but many retailers may have depended upon others for the supply of the ale they sold. The evidence here is ambiguous. Brewers were fined under the Assize of Ale indiscriminately, as at Norwich, but the register of fines at Oxford during the first half of the fourteenth century does regularly distinguish the actual brewer (*braciator*) from the retailer (*regrator*).[88] The proportion of retailers is consistently larger than that of brewers and this proportion is observed to rise immediately following the Black Death. The proportion of all individuals fined described as 'regrator' in the period 1311–45 is 54.3 per cent. In the period 1350–1 it had risen to 68.4 per cent, although the total numbers fined falls markedly from a mean of 241 to 115.5. A number of those named in the York chamberlains' accounts are similarly designated 'tipler'. Tipplers, tapsters, and victuallers are also noted among the trades of women *intrantes* at Canterbury and women were likewise licensed to trade in Nottingham. No less than four of the eleven women licensed there in 1478–9 are designated 'tippler', one of whom, Alice Chadwyk, is first noticed so engaged in 1459–60.[89] Such women regularly ran taverns, in effect the front room of their house or shop, where ale was sold by the cup. These taverns were evidently distinguished by a sign. Two London taverners prosecuted in 1355 for selling ale contrary to the ordinance were appropriately known as Margery atte Cocke and Alice atte Harpe. A third was known as Englesia la Huxtere.[90] Of 26 persons presented by a Queenshythe jury for selling ale in their houses by hanaps or mugs in 1422, 21 were female, 14 of whom were married.[91] Six of the seven hostillers paying maltot at New Romney in 1384–5 were female.[92]

[88] Salter (ed.), *Medieval Archives of the University of Oxford*, 184–265.
[89] Cowper (ed.), *Intrantes*; Stevenson (ed.), *Records of the Borough of Nottingham*.
[90] Thomas (ed.), *Calendar of Plea and Memoranda Rolls, 1323–64*, 254–5.
[91] Thomas (ed.), *Calendar of Plea and Memoranda Rolls, 1413–37*, 140.
[92] *Royal Commission on Historical Manuscripts, Fifth Report* (London, 1876), 533.

The regulation of these 'alewives' and alehouses they kept was a matter of continual concern to the civic authorities. On the one hand, the retail of ale in this way was seen as a threat to the policy of price control, itself an aspect of wage regulation. Following from this was an insistence that standard measures only be used. Thus in Norwich one Margaret de Brundale, whose name does not appear within the list of brewers paying fines, was indicted for selling ale using an unauthorized earthen vessel, and in Leicester the tipplers were instructed in 1499 only to use authorized wooden pots and again in 1501 to bring these pots to be sealed.[93] Women were likewise presented in Lynn in the late fourteenth century for selling ale in unsealed vessels.[94] A London ordinance of 1411 demanded that all who sold ale out of their own homes should 'provide themselves with pewter pots . . . . sealed with the seal of the Chamber'.[95] Of at least equal weight, however, was the threat posed by taverns to order and good government. Repeatedly the civic authorities ordered that alehouses should close at nine at night, as at Beverley in 1405 or at Lynn in an instruction to 'alle camerers tapsterys gannokers and sellers of ale'. The Lynn order distinguishes the 'braciatrix' from the 'venditrix dicta tipeler'.[96] The concern is made explicit in the indictment of Letice Dodsworth and Elizabeth Fox 'on account of their evil conversation and their unlawful keeping of a tavern after nine o'clock at night' contrary to the Nottingham ordinance of 1463.[97] Often the tavern was associated with prostitution and crime. By 1492 the Coventry authorities were sufficiently disturbed as to direct that, 'no person from this Cite ffrohensfurthe kepe, hold, resceyve nor favour eny Tapster, or Woman of evell name, fame or condition to whom eny resorte is of synfull disposicion, hauntyng the synne of lechery . . .'. In the margin of this entry is written 'For Tapsters & harlattes'.[98] By the mid-sixteenth century in the depths of depres-

---

[93] NRO, NCR Case 5, shelf b, 7; Bateson (ed.), *Records of the Borough of Leicester*, ii. 358, 362.

[94] Owen (ed.), *The Making of King's Lynn*, 421.

[95] Sharpe (ed.), *Calendar of Letter-Books: 'I'*, 97.

[96] Leach (ed.), *Beverley Town Documents*, 15; Owen (ed.), *The Making of King's Lynn,* 422.

[97] 'Occasione malae conversationis et inhonestae gubernationis et custodiendae tabernam per horam novenam noctanter': Stevenson (ed.), *Records of the Borough of Nottingham*, ii. 277, 425.

[98] Harris (ed.), *Coventry Leet Book*, 544.

sion, the city authorities saw in the numbers of brewers and tipplers able to make a living out of excessive charges the cause of the decline of more substantial industries 'Wherby almyghtie God is highlie displeased, the comen-Welthe of this Citie greatlie decayed, and vice, Idlenes, & other innumerable myscheves norisshed and encreased . . .'.[99]

Throughout the victualling trades just described, and even beyond, the name of the huckster has frequently been observed. The term, though invariably applied to female traders, referred generally to any retailer and overlaps in usage with the upholder and the chapman. Women hucksters or regrators are found most frequently in those areas of the retail trade which were most feminized, hence their particular association with the victualling sector. Such traders often engaged in a range of related activities. Thus a group of London women presented in 1422 as regrators of fish, eggs, chickens, and capons were also indicted for forestalling butter and cheese. Similarly, the women poulterers of Nottingham were said in 1395 to sell additionally garlic, flour, salt, butter, cheese, and tallow candles, all at excessive prices.[100] One Katherine Hukster sold candles to the city authorities in Norwich, whereas the hucksters of Winchester were presented in 1372 for selling charcoal, *bikermans*, cheese, eggs, and corn at 'excessive' prices.[101] In Leicester the authorities attempted to legislate in 1357 against regrators of bread who regularly sold in addition butter, cheese, and eggs.[102] Women also sold fruit and vegetables. Selby Abbey, for example, purchased leeks and cabbages from one Alice Spaldyng in 1416–17.[103]

The huckster emerges as a general petty retailer whose customers were too poor to buy in bulk in the regular market. She was able to supply a range of necessities in however small a quantity was required and could operate outside the market place near to her customers. But her activities were frequently in

[99] Ibid. 771; cf. also 786, 801.
[100] Thomas (ed.), *Calendar of Plea and Memoranda Rolls, 1413–37*, 138; Stevenson (ed.), *Records of the Borough of Nottingham*, i. 270.
[101] NRO, NCR Case 18, shelf a, fo. 153; D. Keene, *Survey of Medieval Winchester* (2 vols.; Winchester Studies, 2; Oxford, 1985), i. 390.
[102] Bateson (ed.), *Records of the Borough of Leicester*, ii. 107.
[103] Tillotson (ed.), *Monastery and Society*, 126; Wiesner, *Working Women in Renaissance Germany*, 120. There were female fruit-sellers on Ouse Bridge in York: Sellers (ed.), *York Memorandum Book*, i. 198.

contravention of civic trade regulations designed to hold down prices and localize marketing so as to facilitate the enforcement of trading standards. Female hucksters are found purchasing licences to trade, as at York or Canterbury, but most often they appear in court records. There is, however, little to suggest that regulation was ever very effective and the mere fact that women were admitted as hucksters to the franchise in York hardly supports Hilton's thesis of an anti-huckster ethos characteristic of larger towns.[104] Langland's much cited Rose the Regrator is not an archetype but rather a dramatic synthesis. Hilton may, however, be correct to associate the huckster with the small town more than the city. Whereas in the larger community trade specialization was the norm, in small town society, with its more immediate linkage to a rural hinterland, there may have been a fuller scope for the female general trader in foodstuffs.

Textiles

There exists much qualitative evidence for the involvement of women in all stages of the textiles industry, but especially within the primary, but essential, processes of spinning and carding wool. Large numbers of such workers were required to support the output of a single loom and there were probably few women who did not supplement the familial income in this way, however otherwise generally employed. Cause paper evidence, which allows a rare insight into such everyday activities, provides two particular examples. Katherine, wife to James Sadler, primarily assisted her husband in his work, but she also worked at 'kempstercraft' or wool-carding. Marion de Walde, married to a York potter, is observed working a spinning-wheel, to which she hurriedly returned so as to avoid detection by her husband, whom she suspected of being unfaithful.[105] Many women, unmarried and widowed alike, must have been solely dependent on these crafts for their livelihood. It is evident from the wills of several York entrepreneurs that individuals often employed spinsters in number. Thus the draper William Shipley, d. 1435, bequeathed 6*d.* 'cuilibet pauperi mulieri que michi operari et filare consuevit'

---

[104] Hilton, 'Lords, Burgesses and Hucksters', 7–8.
[105] BIHR, CP. E. 159 (1393); CP. E. 111 (1372).

and the dyer William Crosseby similarly remembered the 'poor women' who worked as spinsters and carders for him, directing that twenty shillings be divided between them.[106] The wills of Thomas Clynt, d. 1439, and Alice Chellow, a merchant's widow, d. 1466, may also be noted for similar bequests to spinsters of 4*d.* each.[107]

The modest nature of such bequests and the repetition of the epithet 'poor' tells its own story. Other sources tend to confirm the view that poverty and exploitation was often the lot of the humble spinster. Employers often cheated spinsters, who worked on a piece-rate basis, by substituting false weights when measuring wool for spinning. Langland's Rose the Regrator is thus guilty. The repeated injunctions found in the leet book of Coventry that standard weights only be used confirm that the practice was not confined to fiction.[108] The requirement to adopt standard 2½ lb. wool weights is likewise found among the 1467 ordinances of Worcester, and here also is an injunction that spinsters' wages be paid only in cash and not in kind.[109] The poverty of spinsters is further reflected among deponents in York causes. One Pontefract girl, Isabella Foxhole, noted in a cause dated 1418, was said to make a meagre living by carding and spinning wool. She was the daughter of a villein and had previously been in service to one John Carrow of Pontefract who was married to her aunt. Her status again made her vulnerable to allegations of immorality, and it was alleged that her motives for trying to enforce a contract of marriage against a Pontefract man she had known and slept with as a servant were purely financial. The court, however, ruled in her favour.[110] Alice de Bridelyngton of Beverley, a deponent in a matrimonial cause of 1367, was described as 'non coniugata operatrix lane anglice spynner'. She lived with another spinster, who had allegedly left her husband, and was herself accused of prostitution.[111] The exigencies of their regular employment may indeed have forced some spinsters to resort to theft and prostitu-

---

[106] Crosseby's will is dated 1466: BIHR, Prob. Reg. 3, fo. 437; 4, fo. 70.
[107] BIHR, Prob. Reg. 3, fo. 567ᵛ; 4, fo. 72.
[108] W. W. Skeat (ed.), *The Vision of William Concerning Piers the Plowman* (EETS 38; 1869), B-Text, passus v, 11. 216–17; Harris (ed.), *Coventry Leet Book*, 243–5, 271, 640, 658, 707, 777.
[109] Smith (ed.), *English Gilds*, no. 17, 383; Swanson, *Medieval Artisans*, 31.
[110] BIHR, CP. F. 81 (1418).
[111] BIHR, CP. E. 102.

tion. Numbers of spinsters, not all of whom were unmarried, are
listed as prisoners in the early sixteenth-century records of the
Quarter Sessions at Norwich and spinsters at Nottingham were
presented for receiving goods and petty theft.[112] The poverty of
the spinster outlasted the medieval era. It was argued in York in
1561 that the city's textile industry was in decline because the
carders and spinsters could no longer afford to live there.[113]

With the possible exception of the wheel, for which the distaff
remained the regular alternative, the craft of the spinster and the
kempster demanded little capital investment. This was not true of
the webster, but nevertheless women are found working as
weavers.[114] There is ample gild evidence to show that wives and
daughters of weavers helped operate the loom and it is likely that
many of the women weavers working independently were in fact
widows of weavers. The York tapiters' ordinances provide for
wives to work and it is implicit in the Coventry weavers' ordinances of 1453 that wives and daughters had regularly assisted
husbands prior to that time.[115] John Walton and John Nonhouse,
weavers of York, both left looms to their widows, and Henry
Browne and John Kendale made similar provision for their
apprentices to continue to serve their mistresses.[116] Isabella, the
widow of John Nonhouse was actually admitted to the city's
franchise as a weaver following her husband's death.[117] A woman
was licensed to trade as a weaver in Nottingham in 1478–9 and
likewise at Canterbury 1415–16.[118] The high rate of participation
of females in the industry in parts of Yorkshire in the later
fourteenth century suggested from poll tax sources is confirmed
elsewhere. The York weavers' ordinances of 1400 permitted
women to work in the trade provided they could demonstrate

[112] NRO, NCR Case 20, shelf a; Stevenson (ed.), *Records of the Borough of Nottingham*, iii. 48, 353.

[113] Palliser, 'A Crisis in English Towns?', 116.

[114] There is a good 14th-cent. line drawing of a woman working a loom in British Library, Egerton MS 1894, fo. 2ᵛ.

[115] Sellers (ed.), *York Memorandum Book*, ii. 190; Phythian-Adams, *Desolation of a City*, 87–8.

[116] BIHR, Prob. Reg. 2, fos. 188, 312; 3, fo. 596; 5, fo. 424.

[117] Collins (ed.), *Register of the Freemen of the City of York*, i. 158; Swanson, *Medieval Artisans*, 35.

[118] Cowper (ed.), *Intrantes*; Stevenson (ed.), *Records of the Borough of Nottingham*.

their skill.[119] The report of an inquisition dated 1399 into the
infringement of the York weavers' charter of Henry II lists some
fifteen female weavers, six of whom, as against only three male,
were associated with Wakefield and a further seven with the
neighbouring villages of Sharlston, Crofton, Altofts, and
Thornhill.[120]

It is not possible to identify the marital status of these weavers,
although several may have been unmarried. One Joan Bager of
Wakefield had regularly produced four cloths between November
and February, a slack agricultural period, for the previous twenty
years. There is evidence that some workers were provided with
looms by other weavers for whom they worked. This practice was
forbidden in the restrictive worsted weavers' ordinances of Norwich of 1511, but at Nottingham the loom of one Alice, wife to
John Baxter, is recorded among the goods of the weaver Henry
de Sutton, and in 1410 a Margaret Webster was found to be
unjustly detaining weaving equipment belonging to one Thomas
de Gedyngton.[121] A York weaver, Thomas del Syke, left 20*d*. to
Christina and Beatrix living in the neighbouring village of Hun-
tington who served him in his craft. It must be admitted, however,
that these workers are as likely spinsters as weavers.[122]

Qualitative evidence for the participation of women in other
sectors of the textiles trade is but slight, but not of itself inconsistent with the pattern suggested from poll tax sources. A woman
was licensed to trade as a dyer in Canterbury in 1427–8, and two
female dyers have already been noted from the Ripon poll tax
returns of 1379.[123] The York dyers' ordinances of 1472 refer to
female workers and the (?)late fourteenth-century ordinances of
the same craft gild were attested by two women masters, one of
whom was a widow. The marital status of the other is not clear,
but she may have been a relation of another master.[124] These
latter ordinances were, however, actually restrictive in as much as
widows were only allowed to trade for a year after their husband's

---

[119] Sellers (ed.), *York Memorandum Book*, i. 243.
[120] *Calendar of Miscellaneous Inquisitions*, vi, no. 212, pp. 242–9.
[121] Hudson and Tingey (eds.), *Records of the City of Norwich*, ii. 377; Stevenson
(ed.), *Records of the Borough of Nottingham*, ii. 22, 68–70.
[122] BIHR, Prob. Reg. 3, fo. 49ᵛ.
[123] Cowper (ed.), *Intrantes*; Table 3.2 above.
[124] Sellers (ed.), *York Memorandum Book*, i. 112; ii. 212.

death, unless their servant was admitted to the franchise.[125] A widow was licensed to trade as a fuller in Canterbury between 1426 and 1428 and a York fuller, Thomas Wod, left his widow Margaret his fulling mill at his death in 1484.[126] John Harpham of York bequeathed his tools, workshop, and tenters jointly to his wife and his blood relative Thomas.[127] Again, from probate sources it is possible to conclude that Alice Byngley had pursued her late husband's craft of shearman until her death in 1464, for she bequeathed the tools of her trade to her male servant. Alice's husband had died some years before.[128] Such evidence adds little to what might be gleaned from the poll tax returns, but it seems probable that had single women, other than widows, engaged independently in these trades more often, then this would be reflected in the sources.

Clothing

The evidence for female involvement in the clothing trades is a little more substantial. The seamstress or 'sempster', as she regularly appears in the records, is apparently ubiquitous and may regularly be identified with single, unmarried females. One such woman, Marjory Wadyngton of York, was involved in matrimonial litigation for the hand of Robert Tavarner.[129] Of the handful of York female testators dying unmarried, three described their trade as sempster, namely Margaret de Knaresburgh, d. 1398, Margaret Crosseby, d. 1432, and Margaret Firbanke, d. 1438.[130] A number of the women admitted to the city's franchise, including several admitted by right of patrimony, were described as sempsters. The majority of such women must, however, have remained obscure.[131] Much the same must be true of the shepster or dressmaker, so far as her trade can be distinguished from that of the sempster or even the tailoress observed in certain poll tax returns. A Canterbury woman, Agnes Rogger, was, for example,

[125] Sellers (ed.), *York Memorandum Book*, i. 114.
[126] Cowper (ed.), *Intrantes*; BIHR, Prob. Reg. 5, fo. 235ᵛ.
[127] BIHR, Prob. Reg. 3, fo. 94.
[128] BIHR, Prob. Reg. 2, fo. 331ᵛ; 3, fo. 291.
[129] BIHR, CP. F. 103, 108 (1433).
[130] BIHR, Prob. Reg. 2, fo. 603; 3, fos. 14, 527ᵛ.
[131] Collins (ed.), *Register of the Freemen of the City of York,* i; Swanson, *Medieval Artisans*, 46.

licensed to trade between 1418 and 1421 as variously *sartrix* and shepster.[132] Like the spinsters, relative poverty must have been the common lot of these workers who were regularly employed on a piece-work basis. Kowaleski cites the example of Joan Shippestere, who was frequently fined over ten years in Exeter for cutting and marketing cloth outside the franchise. She was also the subject of theft charges by two of her employers.[133] There is little reason to doubt the typicality of this case, although the lack of equivalent court data for York is to be regretted.

A small proportion of women engaged in fine needlework are identified as embroiderers. Alice Legh, a York widow, was owed the not inconsiderable sum of 26*s.* 8*d.* by her employer Robert Loksmith, vestment-maker for 'fyne hemynge of broderye' at his death.[134] Even York, however, regional capital and ecclesiastical centre though it was, does not appear to have supported many such workers of either sex, and relatively few embroiderers or vestment-makers are recorded as admitted to the franchise.[135] London alone appears to have acted as a centre attracting female apprentices from all parts of the country.[136] There is good evidence here that women worked alongside men to produce the so-called *Opus Anglicanum* for royal, noble, and ecclesiastical patrons, and also for the export market.[137] London also monopolized the equally specialized, but entirely feminised trade of the silkworker, but a silkwoman is found amongst the enfranchised at York.[138] Another such worker at York is known from her will, namely Agnes Setter, who died unmarried in 1435.[139] It may be that these women were former London apprentices. Their relative prosperity is implicit in the sources in which they are discovered.[140]

---

[132] Cowper (ed.), *Intrantes.*

[133] Kowaleski, 'Women's Work in a Market Town', 153.

[134] Swanson, *Medieval Artisans,* 52.

[135] Miller, 'Medieval York', 114. A Ripon woman, Elena Fulford, apparently supported herself by embroidery as is apparent from her will: BIHR, Prob. Reg. 2, fo. 278.

[136] Thomas (ed.), *Calendar of Plea and Memoranda Rolls, 1381–1412,* 240; *1413–47,* 42, 146–7, 176.

[137] R. Parker, *The Subversive Stitch: Embroidery and the Making of the Feminine* (London, 1984), 40–59.

[138] Elena Arnald was admitted in 1436: Collins (ed.), *Register of the Freemen of the City of York,* i. 150; Dale, 'The London Silkwomen of the Fifteenth Century', 324–35.

[139] YML, D/C Reg. 1, fo. 241.

[140] One exception is Katherine Burton, silkwoman, presented for fornication in

One further area of the clothing trade for which there is much evidence for female involvement is cap manufacture. The ordinances of the Oxford gild of cappers, dated 1499, provide for the employment of female cap-knitters, and equivalent ordinances of 1496 at Coventry entitled members to teach their wives, although no females are included in the list of masters there.[141] Further Coventry ordinances of 1520 refer to the employment of spinsters and knitters of caps, but it is evident from the context that these are exclusively female; a new worker is to prove 'that she have well & Trewly usid herself or noo in good work and puttyng in her stuf . . .'.[142] Women cappers are also observed purchasing licences to trade in Nottingham late in the fifteenth century and Canterbury in the early sixteenth century.[143] At York several women were admitted to the franchise as cappers, and the ordinances of the cap-makers there, dated before 1439, refer specifically to female as well as male members.[144] The expansion of cap manufacture in response to changing fashions from the later fifteenth century would thus appear to have led to an appreciable level of female employment. Of other related crafts evidence is only slight, though it may be noticed that one Agnes Kepewyk is listed among the master glovers of York attesting to gild ordinances late in the fourteenth century.[145] For a fuller range of craft activity, poll tax sources again prove the more satisfactory.

Mercantile Trades

The association of women with textiles extends beyond their manufacture and working to their merchandising. It is not difficult to find examples of wealthy merchants' widows trading in their

---

1430. It is possible she is the same Katherine Burton, alias London, noted living in Bootham in 1432 and then aged 30 or more. This identification would suggest that Katherine was supporting herself through trade and her alias may even imply that she had learned her craft in the capital: BIHR, D/C AB. 1, fo. 82; CP. F. 104.

[141] Salter (ed.), *Munimenta Civitatis Oxonie*, 235; Harris (ed.), *Coventry Leet Book*, 573–4; Swanson, *Medieval Artisans*, 51.

[142] Harris (ed.), *Coventry Leet Book*, 672–3.

[143] Stevenson (ed.), *Records of the Borough of Nottingham*; Cowper, *Intrantes*.

[144] e.g. Collins (ed.), *Register of the Freemen of the City of York*, i. 187–8 (Agnes Croft and Alice Gaynford); Sellers (ed.), *York Memorandum Book*, i. 77–8.

[145] Ibid. i. 50, 82.

own right and the somewhat exceptional cases of Margery Russell of Coventry and Rose Burford of London are already well known.[146] Nichola de Irby, a York merchant's widow, left a ship, the *Anneys de Yhork*, by her will made in 1395, and another such widow, Alice Upstal, bequeathed pack saddles to her one male servant. She further bequeathed 6s. 8d. to be divided 'inter mulieres que fuerint operarie mee'.[147] Kowaleski is able to cite a number of further examples of such widows drawn from the port towns of Bristol, Exeter, and Dartmouth, but concludes that they 'were both few in number and compared to men enjoyed a much less active mercantile career'.[148] The career of Marion Kent of York may be illustrative. She was widowed in 1468 whilst her children were still minors and actively continued her late husband's business, supplying *inter alia* wood to the Corpus Christi Gild and iron to the Minster. She appears, however, to have been most active only in the decade following her husband's death. It was during this time (1474–5) that she is recorded as serving on the council of the York mercers' gild. There is little evidence that she remained active once her children achieved adulthood and up to her own death in 1500.[149]

If such general merchants were rare, though comparatively well documented, aulnage accounts do suggest that women were frequently concerned in the marketing of cloth, albeit in small quantities. Some 113 women are accounted for in the aulnage rolls for York in 1394–5 as against 341 men.[150] Only one of these women, Joan de Calthorn, is known to have been of the franchise, but she was not in fact admitted as an 'uphalder' until 1414.[151] Most women are observed merely once during the course of the year and must consequently have depended upon other means of livelihood. Several women, however, appear more regularly, as

---

[146] Power, *Medieval Women*, 56–7.

[147] BIHR, Prob. Reg. 1, fo. 89; 2, fo. 640.

[148] M. Kowaleski, 'Women and Work in Medieval English Seaports', typescript paper (Berkshire Conference on Women's History, Smith College, 1984).

[149] BIHR, Prob. Reg. 3, fo. 320; 4, fos. 34ᵛ, 53ᵛ; Swanson, 'Craftsmen and Industry', 367; Swanson, *Building Craftsmen*, 29; Sellers (ed.), *The York Mercers*, 64, 67.

[150] Lister (ed.), *Early Yorkshire Woollen Trade*, 48–94. These figures differ from those cited by Swanson, perhaps because I have counted names rather than entries. Swanson's analysis further suggests that those paying aulnage are producers and not, as here suggested, merely traders: Swanson, *Medieval Artisans*, 35.

[151] Collins (ed.), *Register of the Freemen of the City of York*, i. 120.

TABLE 3.5.   *York aulnage accounts, 1394–1395: Proportional*
frequency of appearances by sex

Appearances	1	2–3	4–6	7+	
% male traders	68.3	20.2	7.6	3.8	N = 341
% female traders	74.3	17.7	8.0	—	N = 113

Source: Lister (ed.), *Early Yorkshire Woollen Trade*, 48–94.

for example Joan de Burton and Agnes Wellom, and in general
there is little difference in the frequency traders of either sex
appear within the rolls, as Table 3.5 shows. The proportion of
female traders thus observed is comparatively high, being almost
one quarter (24.9 per cent) of the total. This contrasts markedly
with an equivalent proportion of only 6.9 per cent (11 of 159
traders) listed in the aulnage account for the same year at
Winchester.[152] This may be further evidence of a regional pattern
in female economic activity at this date. Significantly a few of the
female traders at York are given the trade surname of 'huckster'
and it is elsewhere evident that the term huckster might indicate a
petty cloth trader. Thus Matilda de Alnewyk noted in her will a
coverlet purchased from one Magota le Hukkester.[153] Franchise
evidence suggests that the terms 'clathseller', 'uphalder', and
'chapwoman', as also 'huckster', were used indiscriminately and
women under these categories are relatively well represented
among the population of York freemen.[154] Most of this enfranchised élite appear to have been single at entry. Agnes Kilburn,
'puella', left several ells of linen cloth in her will dated 1477 and
these may represent her stock in trade.[155]

Aulnage evidence indicates a few other women cloth traders
working in other Yorkshire cloth towns, notably Pontefract, but
outstanding is the Wakefield widow Emma Erle, who accounted
for some 48 cloths in 1395–6.[156] She can be identified as a widow

---

[152] Keene, *Survey of Medieval Winchester*, i. 389.
[153] YML, D/C Reg. 1, fo. 62ᵛ.
[154] e.g. Collins (ed.), *Register of the Freemen of the City of York,* i. 73–4, 120,
127, 131–2, 135 (Midellton, Hopirton, Aldefeld, Calthorn, Lastyngham, Claxton,
Passelewe, Hill, Clark, and Duffeld).
[155] BIHR, Prob. Reg. 5, fo. 18.
[156] Lister (ed.), *Early Yorkshire Woollen Trade*, 40, 90–5.

from a matrimonial cause of 1381 which refers to a child born of her.[157] A York cause of 1503 concerns a widow, Elizabeth Foster, trading in cloth.[158] For later fourteenth-century Exeter Kowaleski is able to identify three female cloth sellers, all the widows of cloth merchants.[159] Isabella, wife to John Yerdele, is noted manufacturing and trading in cloth as *femme sole* in London in 1374.[160] Female mercers are found among a group of London debtors in 1367, and the authorities in Coventry made some provision for the petty female cloth trader there.[161] Whereas cloth traders were normally restricted to the drapery on Fridays, 'a woman that bereth a dossen in her armes' was exempt. It is of interest to note that female cloth traders have also been recorded in the towns of later medieval Denmark.[162] One early sixteenth-century merchant of Malmö, Ditlev Enbeck, retailed through some thirty-three female mercers, as against only six male, in his employ. Seventeen of these can be identified as the wives or widows of artisans not connected with the trade. Much the same structure of marketing may well have operated in English towns.

Metal, Leather, and Miscellaneous Service Trades

For most other manufacturing and service professions qualitative evidence relating to the role of women is invariably slight and much reliance has necessarily been placed here on probate sources. In the metal crafts women appear moderately active. The surviving late fifteenth-century accounts of the London black-smiths' company include quarterage payments of female craft members, and the ordinances of the York ironmongers of 1490 applied equally to male and female members.[163] In 1429 a London apprentice sued his former mistress Beatrix Goscelyn, the widow of an ironmonger, 'who by the law and custom of the city and will

[157] BIHR, CP. E. 124.

[158] BIHR, CP. G. 8.

[159] Kowaleski, 'Women's Work in a Market Town', 152.

[160] Thomas (ed.), *Calendar of Plea and Memoranda Rolls, 1381–1412*, 19–20.

[161] Ibid. 75; Harris (ed.), *Coventry Leet Book*, 100.

[162] G. Jacobsen, 'Women's Work and Women's Role: Ideology and Reality in Danish Urban Society, 1300–1550', *Scandinavian Economic History Review*, 31 (1983), 6–9.

[163] A. Adams, *The History of the Worshipful Company of Blacksmiths* (London, 1951), 22, 25; Sellers (ed.), *York Memorandum Book*, i. 201, 203.

of the deceased ought to have kept up his household and instructed his apprentices', but had instead sold the business and dismissed the apprentice.[164] It is evident that female servants were sometimes trained in the craft, that wives assisted their husbands, and that widows sometimes continued to run businesses after their husbands' demise. In the earlier fourteenth century, for example, William le Ferour left his servant Alice all the tools of his trade.[165] The ordinances of the York founders, dated 1390, record that members were allowed to instruct their wives and it is significant that one master was allowed a second apprentice because he had no wife to assist him ('. . . sauve que le dit Gyles [de Bonoyne] puisse avoir deux apprenticz ensemble a cause qil nad nulle femme').[166] A York dyer, James Robynson, purchased a licence in 1501 that he and his wife might trade as ironmongers, and Palliser cites the example of a mayor's widow so trading in 1487 and eligible for gild office.[167] Will evidence also shows that Margaret Soureby continued her late husband's craft as a founder for she bequeathed the tools in her shop to her servant, Thomas de Burton.[168] Similarly, Hugh Leyfeld, smith, left his anvils to his widow Alice at his death in 1485.[169]

Women are also found in the small metal trades and this accords with the poll tax evidence. Adam Hecche, a York armourer, who died in 1404, left his tools for 'maylework' to his daughter Agnes, whereas his son received his tools for 'fourbourcraft'.[170] Two York goldsmiths provided for their apprentices to serve their widows, namely John de Parys, d. 1393, and John Luneburgh, d. 1458.[171] In Canterbury a Marion Goldsmyth was licensed to trade in the years 1427 to 1431: it is clear from the context that her trade coincided with her surname.[172] Medieval folklore had it that it was a female blacksmith that fashioned the nails for Christ's crucifix-

---

[164] Thomas (ed.), *Calendar of Plea and Memoranda Rolls, 1413–37*, 230–1.
[165] YML, D/C Reg. 1, fo. 3.
[166] Sellers (ed.), *York Memorandum Book*, i. 106; Swanson, *Medieval Artisans*, 74.
[167] YCA, C 5: 1; D. M. Palliser, *Tudor York* (Oxford, 1979), 150.
[168] YML, D/C Reg. 1, fo. 175ᵛ; Swanson, *Medieval Artisans*, 74.
[169] YML, D/C Reg. 1, fo. 360ᵛ.
[170] BIHR, Prob. Reg. 3, fo. 102; Swanson, *Medieval Artisans*, 71.
[171] YML, D/C Reg. 1, fo. 106; BIHR, Prob. Reg. 2, fo. 388ᵛ.
[172] Cowper (ed.), *Intrantes*.

ion.[173] Several female pin manufacturers are also observed from wills. It is probable that Elena Couper, a pinner's widow, had continued to follow her husband's trade for she employed the unusual number of five female servants at her death.[174] Marjory Kyrkeby, formerly servant to Thomas Bracebrigg, a York merchant, was working as a pinner by the time Thomas made his will in 1436.[175] Pin manufacture in fact became largely feminised over a wide area. Pin and needle manufacture were regarded as 'women's work' in early modern German towns, and in sixteenth-century Lyons it remained the one area of the metal trades open to women. By the early modern era it had become a sweated industry.[176]

The slight evidence relating to women in the leather trades perhaps reflects the relative paucity of women engaging independently in this area. The York curriers' ordinances of 1423–4 forbade the employment of any women assistants other than the wives of the masters, but it is not clear how far this rule represented a restrictive modification of earlier practice or merely a definition of established custom.[177] Certainly documentary evidence suggests that it was not unusual for the wives or widows of artisans in leather to assist in or take over the running of the business. Kowaleski, for example, has found a number of women working in the leather trades of late fourteenth-century Exeter, some of whom were married to husbands employed in the same craft.[178] It is known from a cause of 1393 that Juliana, wife of Roger del Grene, besides work as a kempster, 'she practises the craft of saddler with her husband'.[179] This last observation is particularly valuable because such direct evidence is so very rare. Margaret Burton, who can be identified as the widow of the York tanner John Burton who died in 1479, must have continued his business for she was fined one mark in 1486 for a trading offence

---

[173] M. D. Anderson, *Drama and Imagery in English Medieval Churches* (Cambridge, 1963), 106.

[174] BIHR, Prob. Reg. 4, fo. 135ᵛ.

[175] BIHR, Prob. Reg. 3, fo. 487ᵛ.

[176] Davis, 'Women in the Crafts', 62; Wiesner, *Working Women in Renaissance Germany*, 169; Clark, *Working Life of Women*, 193.

[177] Sellers (ed.), *York Memorandum Book*, ii. 169.

[178] What these trades are is not specified: Kowaleski, 'Women's Work in a Market Town', 152.

[179] 'Utitur artificio selarii cum marito suo': BIHR, CP. E. 159.

as a tanner.[180] Emmota Pannall, a saddler's widow, likewise continued to trade and bequeathed the tools in her workshop to her servant Richard Thorp.[181] Alice Hairester, a barker (i.e. tanner) noticed paying stallage at York in 1448–9 may likewise have been widowed.[182]

There is little evidence for female shoemakers, though Langland does include a 'souteress' amongst the patrons of the tavern visited by Gluttony.[183] Female skinners are apparently equally uncommon, but Veale, in her study of the fur trade, has identified a few widows trading and, more rarely, women acting as *femme sole*.[184] In Norwich women appear responsible for lining the mayor's hat with beaver fur. Thus Juliana Bury is employed in 1419–20 and Margery Craston in 1431–2. The same Juliana Bury displays a versatility that was characteristic of female traders, however, for she also engaged to supply the city with wooden boards in 1418–19.[185]

The Norwich source just cited provides further examples of women apparently trading in imported timber, but otherwise references to women labouring in either the woodworking or the building trades are rare. Davis has drawn attention to the role played by women as semi-skilled labour in all forms of building and construction work in Lyons in the sixteenth century, but it is unclear how far this might have been true of England at a slightly earlier date.[186] Poll tax evidence discussed earlier does, however, point to the frequency with which masons, tilers, and wrights employed female assistants. The widow of a York tile (i.e. brick) manufacturer, Isabella de Copgrave, d. 1400, evidently continued her late husband's business for she still possessed his tilehouses in Fishergate at her death, and in Beverley an Agnes Tiler was paid for a thousand tiles purchased during the construction of the North Bar in 1409–10.[187] The wife of one John Grew supplied

[180] Dobson (ed.), *York Chamberlains' Account Rolls*, 178; BIHR, Prob. Reg. 5, fos. 149, 331ᵛ.
[181] BIHR, Prob. Reg. 2, fo. 363ᵛ.
[182] YCA, CC 1, 108.
[183] Skeat (ed.), *Piers the Plowman*, B-Text, passus v, l. 315.
[184] E. M. Veale, *The English Fur Trade in the Later Middle Ages* (Oxford, 1966), 100.
[185] NRO, NCR Case 18, shelf a, fos. 124, 127ᵛ, 128, 182ᵛ.
[186] Davis, 'Women in the Crafts', 59.
[187] BIHR, Prob. Reg. 3, fo. 40ᵛ; A. F. Leach, 'The Building of Beverley Bar', *Transactions of the East Riding Antiquarian Soc.* 4 (1896), 31.

Selby Abbey with plaster in 1434–5.[188] Alice Alban continued her husband's trade as a painter for she bequeathed a stone for mixing colours to each of her two male servants in 1361.[189] Similar probate evidence indicates that the widow of a carpenter, a cooper, and a pattener had the opportunity to continue trading as provision was made for apprentices to remain in service with their mistresses.[190] Women appear regularly to have assisted thatchers by 'drawing' or preparing the straw or reeds to be used and by carrying thatch. It may be supposed that male thatchers were sometimes assisted by their wives. This is implicit from the deposition in a matrimonial cause dated 1356 of one Margaret, whose husband William Theker was then employed thatching houses at Acaster Selby.[191] A woman was paid 6*d.* for drawing 34 thraves of reed at Selby in 1416–17, whereas the thatcher himself was paid 2*s.* 1*d.* and his servant 1*s.* 10*d.* for their five days' thatching. In the same year women were employed to carry thatch from the water-mills at Selby to a house that was being thatched.[192] Women are more rarely found as assistants to tilers as at Oxford in 1372 or Cuxham in 1315 or 1358.[193] At Selby in 1446–7 a woman was paid 2*d.* for carrying 1500 roofing tiles from the boat to a cart.[194]

Some further examples of female artisans may briefly be noted. The York stringers' ordinances of 1420 refer equally to male and female craft members and provide, somewhat exceptionally, for a four-year apprenticeship.[195] A Canterbury woman was licensed to trade as a fletcher in 1443–4, and a York bowyer provided that his apprentice remain in service with his widow. The Canterbury woman is described as 'uxor' and, from the context, may perhaps be identified as a widow.[196] Isabella de Morland appears as one of

[188] Tillotson (ed.), *Monastery and Society*, 247. John Grew was keeper of the ferry in 1441–2.
[189] YML, D/C Reg. 1, fo. 36; Swanson, *Medieval Artisans*, 80.
[190] YML, D/C Reg. 1, fo. 145 (Awstyn, d. 1408); BIHR, Prob. Reg. 4, fo. 161ᵛ (Ball, d. 1471); 2, fo. 504 (Tunstall, d. 1427).
[191] BIHR, CP. E. 70.
[192] Tillotson (ed.), *Monastery and Society*, 97, 106–7, 173–5.
[193] J. E. T. Rogers, *A History of Agriculture and Prices in England* (8 vols.; Oxford, 1866–1902), ii. 292, 315, 319.
[194] Tillotson (ed.), *Monastery and Society*, 227.
[195] Sellers (ed.), *York Memorandum Book*, ii. 122–3; Swanson, *Medieval Artisans*, 103.
[196] Cowper (ed.), *Intrantes*; BIHR, Prob. Reg. 3, fo. 539 (Gilliot, d. 1438).

only four master parchment-makers (parchmeners) agreeing to craft ordinances at York late in the fourteenth century.[197] A female bookbinder appears in a London record of 1311–12 and an Agnes Bookbynder was fined at Norwich for trading outside the franchise in 1374–5.[198] A tailor of York was fined in 1454–5 because his wife and servants worked as card-makers.[199] A York horner's widow continued to trade at the end of the fifteenth century and left her tools to her male servant in her will.[200] A water-leader similarly provided for his servant to continue to work for his widow for a year after his death.[201] There is evidence that women were regularly employed as wool-packers. An early fourteenth-century Leicester source refers to sworn women wool-packers and Southampton regulations of 1503 suggest that women wool-packers and porters there were allowed some form of gild organization.[202] Certainly there was nothing unusual about employing women to carry heavy loads. Manuscript sources show that it was frequently women that carried the bulging sacks of grain to the mill. Women were employed carrying turves, used as fuel, at Selby. A team of eighteen women were engaged for a full day in 1401–2 to unload a ship carrying turves. Each was paid 3*d.* plus food to a similar value, including a pennyworth of ale.[203]

Two further non-service trades are rather better documented. The second-hand clothes dealer or upholder must have been a common figure in medieval town life. In a society where even the wealthy bequeathed their clothes by will item by item, she must have played a crucial role in satisfying the needs of poorer members of the urban community. The term 'upholder' unfortunately appears to embrace a variety of petty traders, particularly traders in cloth, and it is not possible to identify individuals precisely. Upholders are, however, widely found; a Nottingham widow, Margery Wood, was licensed in the trade in 1467–8 and

---

[197] Sellers (ed.), *York Memorandum Book*, i. 82.
[198] Sharpe (ed.), *Calendar of Letter-Books: 'D'*, 278; NRO, NCR, Case 5, shelf b, 17.
[199] Dobson (ed.), *York Chamberlains' Account Rolls*, 86; Swanson, *Medieval Artisans*, 72.
[200] YML, D/C Reg. 2, fo. 1 (Brown).
[201] BIHR, Prob. Reg. 2, fo. 103ᵛ (Mountane, d. 1445).
[202] Bateson (ed.), *Records of the Borough of Leicester*, ii. 18–23; Power, *Medieval Women*, 61.
[203] Tillotson (ed.), *Monastery and Society*, 201, 138 (stacking turves).

again in 1478–9, and some dozen women, several of whom were probably widows, were similarly licensed in Canterbury during the course of the fifteenth century.[204] On a wider perspective Wiesner has found that in sixteenth-century Nuremberg a group of women, known as *Keuflinnen*, enjoyed an effective monopoly in the marketing of second-hand clothing and other goods.[205] More evidence yet survives concerning the feminised craft of the tallow chandler. The York ordinances of the sauce-makers, dated 1417, show that butchers' wives were regular manufacturers of Paris or tallow candles. The craft was concerned, however, that the wives of skinners and other artisans operating outside the Shambles 'in magna multitudine' were also converting the tallow available to them to manufacture candles, but were refusing to contribute to the saucers' pageant according to custom.[206] In Coventry in 1494 it was similarly directed that wives manufacturing and selling candles should be contributory to the smiths' pageant.[207]

Examples of women chandlers are common in medieval urban records. Women are observed indicted for trading offences relating to the manufacture and sale of candles in London in the earlier fifteenth century, and similarly in Exeter and Norwich. The Norwich leet roll evidence is ambiguous as it is likely that only single female traders are named in person, married women being represented by their husbands' names. The record thus understates the true level of female activity.[208] In Nottingham women traders were presented for selling candles without cotton wicks, and in 1299–1300 the chandlers of Mancroft in Norwich were presented for forming a price-fixing cartel.[209] From York there exists also some evidence that women worked as wax-chandlers, especially within the Croxton family. Agnes Croxton, dying single in 1418, is described in her will as a chandler and Edonea Croxton apparently pursued her late husband's trade for she left a wax-

---

[204] Stevenson (ed.), *Records of the Borough of Nottingham*; Cowper (ed.), *Intrantes*.

[205] Wiesner, *Working Women in Renaissance Germany*, 134–40.

[206] Sellers (ed.), *York Memorandum Book*, i. 155–6.

[207] Harris (ed.), *Coventry Leet Book*, 555.

[208] Sharpe (ed.), *Calendar of Letter-Books: 'F'*, 278; NRO, NCR, Case 5, shelf b, 8, 19.

[209] Stevenson (ed.), *Records of the Borough of Nottingham*, i. 270, 314; NRO, NCR, Case 5, shelf b, 8.

board and moulds to her male servant at her death in 1486.[210]
Margaret Bettes may similarly be shown to have traded as a widow
until her death in 1507.[211] The trading activities of another York
chandler, Margaret Harman, who can be identified as the wife of
a weaver, appear to have been fairly substantial; she is observed
in a cause dated 1430, but relating to events two years before, to
have purchased candlewick to the value of 23s. 10d., a sufficiently
large quantity as to require assistance to carry the purchase
home.[212] Margaret Harman's status as a wax- or tallow-chandler is
uncertain, but on balance the wax-chandler's craft does not appear
to have been significantly feminised and this must reflect the very
much greater capital cost of the raw material. A Maud 'la
Wexmangere' is, however, to be observed at the borough of
Wallingford in 1230.[213]

Women are prominent within a number of service trades and
are regularly found in the records. This is especially true of women
employed as nurses engaged privately to care for the sick,
although women were also employed in hospitals. Payments and
bequests to sick nurses are commonly found in wills. Thus Joan
Bedale left 12d. to 'mulieri custodienti me in infirmitate mea' at
her death in 1438.[214] In London a skinner, Robert de Eye,
recovered 26s. 8d. and a bed earned by his wife over a four-year
period nursing one William de Longford.[215] Similar litigation to
recover a debt owed to a woman caring for a sick girl whilst she
was single is found in an early sixteenth-century Nottingham
record.[216] In York one Margaret Esyngwald deposed in a cause
dated 1393 that she had care of a married woman during an illness
and it is implicit in her testimony that she lived with the family for
that time.[217] The great hospital of St Leonard's at York appears
to have employed lay female staff in addition to the regular sisters.
Some five, including the cook's wife, were working there in 1295
besides other female domestic staff, and female workers associ-

---

[210] YML, D/C Reg. 1, fos. 184ᵛ, 366ᵛ; Swanson, *Medieval Artisans*, 100.

[211] J. Raine (ed.), *Testamenta Eboracensia*, iv–v (Surtees Soc. 53 and 79;
1869–84), iv, no. 151, pp. 261–2.

[212] BIHR, CP. F. 174; Prob. Reg. 2, fo. 539ᵛ.

[213] *Royal Commission on Historical Manuscripts, Sixth Report*, 577.

[214] BIHR, Prob. Reg. 3, fo. 556A.

[215] Thomas (ed.), *Calendar of Plea and Memoranda Rolls, 1364–81*, 25.

[216] Stevenson (ed.), *Records of the Borough of Nottingham*, iii. 112–14.

[217] BIHR, CP. E. 159.

ated with St John's hospital in Oxford are observed in 1391.[218] Well-to-do families may sometimes have employed wet-nurses and child-minders. Elizabeth, the wife of Thomas de Swanland, a Beverley draper, for example, remembered her former nurse Alice in her will dated 1404. St Leonard's employed a sister to care for orphaned children in the appropriately named 'barn-house'.[219]

Three further service trades, those of the barber, the miller, and the laundress, may also be considered from urban sources. The latter trade was, unsurprisingly, totally feminised. Town authorities seem to have been concerned that water supplies were being polluted by washerwomen; at Leicester in 1467 women were forbidden to wash clothes at the common wells, and in Coventry a year later women were similarly restricted from using the city conduits.[220] St Leonard's hospital in York employed its own laundress, and a 'lavendar' was licensed to trade in Canterbury in 1415–16.[221] Early churchwardens' accounts regularly include payments to women for washing vestments, though these women may sometimes be identified as the wives of the churchwardens.[222] A woman employed washing vestments at Selby Abbey in 1446–7 was the wife of the embroiderer called in to repair the same vestments.[223] Numbers of women were presented in the consistory court of Durham for washing clothes on feast-days, though it is not certain that these were laundresses.[224]

The importance of hand-mills worked by women is suggested by the conflict concerning their use between the townsfolk and the abbey at St Albans in the fourteenth century. In the mid-fifteenth century a Wakefield woman, Alice Barlawe, bequeathed a set of millstones ('j *par molar*'). It may be remembered that some years

---

[218] LJRO, QQ 2; Salter (ed.), *Medieval Archives of the University of Oxford*, 26.

[219] BIHR, Prob. Reg. 3, fo. 105ᵛ; LJRO, QQ 2.

[220] Bateson (ed.), *Records of the Borough of Leicester*, ii. 291; Harris (ed.), *Coventry Leet Book*, 338.

[221] LJRO, QQ 2, 10; Cowper (ed.), *Intrantes*.

[222] e.g. St Dunstan's, Canterbury: J. M. Cowper (ed.), *Accounts of the Church-wardens of St Dunstan's, Canterbury, 1484–1580* (London, 1885), 12. I am grateful to Mrs Julia Carnwath for the information that the wives of churchwardens were often responsible for cleaning vestments.

[223] Tillotson (ed.), *Monastery and Society*, 222–3.

[224] J. Raine, *Depositions and other Ecclesiastical Proceedings from the Courts of Durham* (Surtees Soc. 21; 1845), 30, 33.

before Margery Kempe, then married to a Lynn merchant, had herself briefly supervised a horse-mill worked by a male servant with two horses.[225] Horse mills are by no means uncommon within urban records, but it is unclear whether the example of Margery Kempe is representative. That it may be so is suggested by the wills of two York widows dating to the early years of the sixteenth century. Jane Bukkill left her horse-mill and horse to one Adam Silbarnt and, similarly, Isabel Roger bequeathed two horses belonging to a mill to Christopher Richerdson.[226] That Jane and Isabel failed to bequeath these through the female line suggests, however, that women enjoyed no monopoly over this form of milling.

The barbers' craft ordinances at Oxford and at York both provide for employment of women.[227] Women are noticed purchasing licences to trade as barbers in Nottingham in 1478–9, Canterbury during the earlier part of the fifteenth century, and York in 1454–5.[228] Those licensed at Canterbury appear to have been married or, more especially, widowed. From a cause dated 1439 it is apparent that one Agnes Barebour traded and employed servants in the craft in York whilst still single, and she also was active as a brewer.[229] One further service trade regularly observed in female hands is that of the boatman or ferryman. Margaret Calf of Norwich was, for example, paid by the city for making four journeys in her boat in 1387–8, and Agnes de Kendale in 1343–4 and Alice de Wetherall in the 1370s are found employed as ferrywomen for St Leonard's hospital in York.[230] Ferrywomen are by no means restricted to the English later Middle Ages. They are, for example, also documented in medieval Denmark, early modern German towns, and Lyons at the same period. Perhaps this trade should be looked upon as a by-employment and that

---

[225] R. Faith, 'The "Great Rumour" of 1377 and Peasant Ideology', in R. H. Hilton and T. H. Aston (eds.), *The English Rising of 1381* (Cambridge, 1984), 68; BIHR, Prob. Reg. 2, fo. 239; Meech and Allen (eds.), *The Book of Margery Kempe*, 11.

[226] BIHR, Prob. Reg. 8, fo. 70; 9, fo. 75ᵛ.

[227] Salter (ed.), *Munimenta Civitatis Oxonie*, 110; Sellers (ed.), *York Memorandum Book*, i. 209–10.

[228] Stevenson (ed.), *Records of the Borough of Nottingham*; Cowper (ed.), *Intrantes*; Dobson (ed.), *York Chamberlains' Account Rolls*, 87.

[229] BIHR, CP. F. 182; YCA, CC 1, pp. 17, 59, 120, 139; CC 1A, fos. 22ᵛ, 35ᵛ, 39, 42ᵛ, 46ᵛ.

[230] NRO, NCR, Case 18, shelf a, fo. 14; YML, M2/6e, fos. 6, 23, 39ᵛ, 62ᵛ.

women so employed would engage in other activities when their services were not required, although Wiesner notes of German towns that ferrywomen there were often older females or widows.[231]

WOMEN'S WORK IN THE COUNTRYSIDE

The economic role of women in the English medieval countryside has not commanded much attention, but interest has grown somewhat of late years. Manor court rolls highlight women's role as brewers and bakers since these activities were regulated by the Assizes of Ale and of Bread.[232] The activities of women as paid agricultural labour are also to be glimpsed from manorial account rolls, and perhaps more substantially from records of prosecutions under the Statute of Labourers.[233] This present review draws upon two hitherto under-utilized sources to gain a still broader impression of the range and types of employment women engaged in and how these may have varied from one agricultural region to another. The principal source explored here are the returns of the 1379 poll tax for the entire West Riding and for Howdenshire in the East Riding. This tax was levied on adult lay persons and includes substantial occupational data for males and females alike. Some additional information may be gleaned from the depositions recorded within the York cause papers, but these are a generally less satisfactory source for the identification of the kinds of work rural women were engaged in. A cause from 1361, for example, describes how Elena Wright served her 'husband' by winnowing and selling grain and, enigmatically, 'in other tasks which pertain to a materfamilias'.[234] A mid-fifteenth-century cause refers only to Alice Vasour as working in the fields, whereas at an earlier date Alice Reding is described simply as 'mulier bone industrie'.[235]

The West Riding poll tax returns for 1379, long ago published by the Yorkshire Archaeological Society, vary in quality between

---

[231] Jacobsen, 'Women's Work and Women's Role', 19; Davis, 'Women in the Crafts', 62; Wiesner, *Working Women in Renaissance Germany*, 127.

[232] Cf. Bennett, *Women in the Medieval English Countryside*.

[233] Cf. Hilton, 'Women in the Village'; Penn, 'Female Wage-Earners'.

[234] BIHR, CP. E. 84.

[235] Alice may have woven cloth: BIHR, CP. F. 191; E. 92.

the twelve constituent wapentakes, although none is as detailed as the equivalent Howdenshire returns.[236] The second poll tax was levied in theory on all lay persons over the age of 16. Married couples were assessed together and a differential assessment with a minimum rate of 4*d*. was employed. Artisans and other more substantial persons, including franklins and farmers of manors, were taxed at 6*d*., 1*s*., or more.[237] Within these Yorkshire returns such higher-rate taxpayers are invariably described by occupation, although there may be numbers of craftworkers not deemed to be of sufficient substance to be taxed as artisans. It may be that there is some justification in the case of craftswomen for using occupational by-names as evidence for occupations in such cases since surnames still appear unstable at this date within this region. Millers, for example, are very rarely designated, though the surname 'Milner' is often encountered. In the Ainsty a few individuals so named are assessed at sixpence, indicative that these were indeed millers and that the assessors here chose to class them as artisans. For the purposes of this present analysis single women having an occupational by-name will be presumed to be of that calling unless there is evidence that this is a family name possessed by other members of a particular community. This method will inevitably introduce a margin of error, but it may be noted that the pattern of occupations so derived is remarkably consistent and corresponds well with the evidence for female craft work derived from occupational designations of higher-rate female taxpayers only. Some occupational by-names are, moreover, specifically feminine, as, for example, semester, sewester, laundere, norys or *nutrix*, all professions unlikely to merit taxation at the higher rate.[238]

Other than for Howdenshire the returns rarely note the occupation of a married woman where this differs from or is in addition

---

[236] 'Rolls of the Collectors in the West Riding'; 'Assessment Roll of the Poll-Tax for Howdenshire'. All further material in this section is derived from these unless otherwise indicated. The West Riding returns were first used as a source for women's work by Power in her *Medieval Women*, 65.

[237] *Rotuli Parliamentorum*, iii. 57–8.

[238] These surnames are unlikely to be inherited and may reasonably be regarded as accurate designations in most instances. To apply a similar methodology to rural males possessing occupational surnames would, however, be unwise since it would be much more difficult to distinguish between inherited surnames and occupation-specific surnames.

to that of the husband. For Claro Wapentake, however, the husband's occupation is stated after his own name and not that of the couple as is more usual elsewhere. Where the occupation is stated after the wife's name, therefore, this may be assumed to refer specifically to the wife. In nearly all these cases the wife is stated to be a 'brewster'. Joan, the wife of William Palfrayman of Kirk Deighton, however, is assessed as a weaver (*textrix*) separately from her husband. Dependants, i.e. children, servants, and other relatives, are often recorded immediately following the head of household, but for the wapentakes of Barkston Ash, Morley, Skyrack, Staincliffe, and Ewecross single persons are regularly listed together at the end of the return for each community without any indication of the household unit to which they might belong. This is also true of the returns for individual communities within the other wapentakes, but sometimes details of household affiliation are provided and household units can thus be reconstructed. For the wapentakes of Strafforth, Tickhill, Staincross, Osgodcross, Agbrigg, and Claro, a variety of measures relating to household and occupational structure may thus be derived. It is further possible to compare measures derived from specifically rural communities primarily engaged in agriculture against those derived from more urban, craft-based communities. Occupational patterns as observed between the rural West Riding and other urban communities are broadly similar, but female metal traders, notably smiths and marshals, are proportionately more numerous and clothing traders less so.[239] These patterns may suggest structural differences between town and country. Whereas rural households may have relied less on the market, and thus on tailors and sempsters, for their ordinary clothing requirements, than may have been true of townsfolk, the need for non-specialist smiths was universal in rural society. Conversely, greater craft specialization in urban communities may have militated against the independent female trader.

Pastoral agriculture, that typified Howdenshire and much of the West Riding, tended to be less seasonalized and to draw upon female labour for various specific occupations, notably washing and shearing sheep, milking both cows and sheep, and the manufacture of butter and cheese. The wages of women for

---

[239] See Table 3.3 above.

washing and shearing sheep are, for example, noted in the kitchener's accounts for Selby Abbey.[240] Evidence from the York cause papers likewise demonstrates that women engaged in a variety of other part-time activities associated with sheep farming and the production of woollen cloth, such as spinning and carding wool, and weaving. The majority of more specific tasks performed by women as noted from rural cause papers were also agricultural in nature; women are observed weeding crops, reaping, winnowing, milking cows, and even purchasing sheep. The fifteenth-century 'Ballad of a Tyrannical Husband' describes a wife that milks the cows, makes butter and cheese, feeds the chickens and ducks, pastures the geese, brews and bakes, swingles flax, cards wool, spins, and weaves cloth in addition to caring for her husband and children. 'The goodwyf', the poet explains, 'hade meche to doo, and servant had se none.'[241] In a sense these are the invariably unremarked 'tasks which pertain to a materfamilias', the 'mulier bone industrie'.[242] They are only substantially documented where women engaged in them for wage or profit. Thus manorial account rolls demonstrate the range of tasks in which women might be employed, but fail to indicate more generally the gender-specific structure of the labour force. Evidence of indictments under the Statute of Labourers, as Penn observes, may be a more satisfactory source.[243] This last is, however, limited to persons actually presented. These may not be entirely representative of the labouring population as a whole. The poll taxes constitute an alternative and potentially less problematic source. Even in this respect the West Riding poll tax is, however, a slightly disappointing source: such low-status occupations as spinster, shepster, huckster, and lavender or laundress, so well represented in the 1381 returns for Oxford and Southwark, are rarely recorded. It is still less satisfactory a source for those women whose livelihood was exclusively on the land.

The poll tax rarely distinguishes widows from other single

---

[240] Tillotson (ed.), *Monastery and Society*, 167.

[241] 'Ballad of a Tyrannical Husband', in T. Wright and J. O. Halliwell (eds.), *Reliquae Antiquae* (2 vols.; London, 1843), ii. 196–9. For evidence of women employed in weeding crops see D. Postles, 'Cleaning the Medieval Arable', *Agricultural History Review*, 37 (1989), 134.

[242] BIHR, CP. E. 84; E. 92.

[243] Penn, 'Female Wage-Earners', 2–3.

women, though it may reasonably be assumed that all those female-headed households containing children and most such households containing servants represent widows. In Rutland female-headed households were as likely to contain male dependants as female, but in the West Riding male dependants are comparatively uncommon. Thus in Rutland of 44 female-headed households, 17 contained male children as against 19 that contained female children, and 13 contained male servants as against 8 that contained female servants. In Strafforth Wapentake, out of 63 such households, only 14 contained sons as against 42 that contained daughters. Much the same pattern is found again for Tickhill and Staincross wapentakes. Taking the two together, female-headed households containing daughters appear to be twice as common as those containing sons. Households containing servants are more rare, but again the balance is tilted in favour of females. It may thus be that for widows holding dower land, male labour was at a premium in arable Rutland, but that in a pastoral economy female labour was actually preferred. This accords with the range of work already outlined as available to women within a pastoral economy. Women with little or no land might work as labourers. In this respect also women may have found more opportunity within a pastoral economy caring for livestock and dairy herds than within an arable, though it is difficult to assess the significance of such by-names as 'cowhird' and 'calfhird' as borne by women at Kirk Deighton near Wetherby and Rufforth near York. It thus appears that opportunities for single women to support themselves were actually wider within a pastoral than an arable economy.[244]

One of the most common by-employments for women was brewing. The prominence of rural women, especially married women, as brewsters is readily attested from manor court rolls. Women were regularly presented for breach of the Assize of Ale, though it is apparent that some court rolls record women with far greater regularity than others. Bennett has argued that these patterns reflect real differences in the degree to which women participated in the rural brewing trade according to the prevailing agrarian economy. In the open-field arable economy of Houghton-cum-Wyton, Huntingdonshire, and more especially in the forest

---

[244] See Ch. 6 below.

economy of Brigstock, Northamptonshire, women dominated the brewing trade as males were fully occupied by other activities. In the less labour-intensive pastoral economy of Iver, Buckinghamshire, however, most brewing was apparently done by men.[245] This view may be questioned on two grounds. As has been shown before, the court was concerned to extract fines and thus might record the names not of those married women who brewed, but of their husbands who were in law responsible for their wives' debts. The gender-specific pattern of the names listed may thus reflect local practices of record-keeping. The only females listed at Iver may, therefore, be exclusively widows or single women. Graham suggests another possibility, namely that the court may have recorded the names of those who actually paid the fine. Where a woman engaged in brewing was married to a manorial tenant who would thus ordinarily be present at the court, then the husband would pay the fine. In the case of poorer peasants not owing suit of court, the wife would often be asked to pay the fine.[246] This accords with Bennett's own observation that poorer women were better represented in the manorial court than their more substantial sisters. Poll tax evidence is free from these sorts of difficulty, and the 1379 returns for Howdenshire, a pastoral region, demonstrate that the trade there was almost exclusively in the hands of women.

The rural West Riding and Howdenshire poll tax returns tend to support the observation that brewing was primarily, but not exclusively, the responsibility of the married woman. The West Riding returns list some thirty-one brewsters, and the Howdenshire returns, which record the occupations of married women with much greater consistency, a further forty-four. Since the poll tax material generally fails to record the occupations of wives, and brewing was in any case only an occasional employment, these figures must be regarded as seriously deficient. Only for the wapentakes of Claro and the Ainsty do the West Riding returns list brewsters in any numbers, though these same returns also apparently include a number of male brewers. It may merely be that the assessors for these two wapentakes chose to regard

---

[245] Bennett, *Women in the Medieval English Countryside*, 125–6.
[246] H. Graham, '"A Woman's Work . . .": Labour and Gender in the Medieval Countryside', in P. J. P. Goldberg (ed.), *Woman is a Worth Wight: Women in English Society c.1200–1500* (Stroud, 1992), 126–48.

brewing as an activity that merited a higher level of taxation, but the proximity of these wapentakes to York, the only substantial city within the wider region, may be significant. The presence of some male brewers suggests that the industry here was on a large scale and it seems probable that some ale was sent to York, where there was demand not just from a resident population, but from numerous visitors to the markets and shops or on various kinds of business. The majority of brewsters appear, nevertheless, to have been married women, though some were clearly widows. This is apparent from the small number of brewsters assisted by their daughters, as for example Margaret Broune of Wetherby, and is explicitly stated in a few instances within the Howdenshire returns, for example Isabella Wryght, brewster of South Duffield.

It is unlikely that many unmarried women are represented as independent brewsters as brewing required a degree of capital investment rarely open to the young and single, but an interesting partnership between Agnes Milner, webster, and her daughter Agnes, a brewster, is recorded at Barmby on the Marsh in Howdenshire. A number of married brewsters are associated with households containing dependants including servants, though only occasionally is the husband also associated with a trade. This observation would tend to confirm McIntosh's findings from the court rolls of the manor of Havering for the period 1380–1460 that the majority of brewsters were married to agriculturalists, and to 'men of middling economic level'.[247] A small number of women are also found as hostillers, but these were probably mostly widows.

It is difficult to assess how the level of female participation in the brewing business may have changed over time. Urban sources suggest that the introduction of beer brewed with hops may have resulted in a growth in male interest in the trade, but most brewing in the countryside probably remained small-scale and occasional. There is thus little reason to believe that the brewing of ale by women should have declined before the early modern era. Bennett, drawing on pre-plague evidence, has, however, suggested the interesting thesis that women's participation in the economy as reflected in baking and brewing expanded in the face of recession. Thus she suggests that an increasing proportion of

[247] McIntosh, *Autonomy and Community*, 173–4.

female brewsters to male brewers recorded at Houghton-cum-Wyton and at Iver during the decades culminating in the Agrarian Crisis and again on the eve of the Black Death is indicative of a real trend consequent upon a concentration of male activity in more profitable areas.[248]

Uncertainties of record-keeping, as outlined above, render these findings doubtful. It may simply be that more widows are recorded as the period may have been marked by high mortality and consequently numbers of broken marriages, but also the numbers of women remaining single following the death of a husband itself may have increased. Graham's suggestion that it is persons paying the fines who are recorded would also explain a growing proportion of females recorded since Bennett herself notes that women were more active in the land market and also more likely to be presented for criminal activity in times of hardship. It follows that a higher proportion of women would have been present at the regular sessions of the manor court and thus in a position to pay brewing and other fines in person. The statistical basis upon which Bennett's thesis rests is, moreover, very selective and does not accord with Graham's findings for the Staffordshire manor of Alrewas. Clearly this is a subject that needs to be explored at greater length than is possible here.

Poorer women, including the young and unmarried, may often have relied on the spinning and carding of wool to earn or supplement a meagre living, whilst others traded as seamstresses. William Langland, for example, movingly describes the plight of poor spinsters and carders of wool.[249] In the 'Second Shepherd's pageant' of the Wakefield Corpus Christi cycle, Gyll, Mak the sheepstealer's wife, continues to spin after darkness falls and refuses to be interrupted, such is the need to augment their slender income:

> I am sett for to spyn; I hope not I myght
> Ryse a penny to wyn, I shrew them on hight![250]

These occupations were not generally regarded by the poll tax assessors as of sufficient substance to merit artisan status. The

[248] Bennett, *Women in the Medieval English Countryside*, 126.
[249] Skeat (ed.), *Piers the Plowman*, C-Text, passus x, ll. 71 ff.
[250] 'The Second Shepherd's Pageant', in Cawley (ed.), *The Wakefield Pageants*, ll. 298–9.

Howdenshire returns do include two kempsters, though only one is assessed at the sixpenny rate, whereas at Cliffe one Margaret Semester is assessed as an artisan and at Lindeley in Claro Wapentake, Matilda Schawe is supported by her daughter Margaret, 'semster'. Altogether the West Riding returns allow twenty-one seamstresses or sempsters to be identified, almost exclusively from surname evidence. Kempsters and spinsters are even more poorly represented since these employments were too universal to constitute useful by-names. How many spinsters worked with the more productive wheel rather than the traditional, though highly versatile distaff is uncertain. An Isabella Whelespynner is found at Bishopthorpe, just south of York, and this by-name might suggest that the wheel was still uncommon in 1379. By the fifteenth century spinning-wheels are not infrequently noted within wills and they may have become increasingly common, but perhaps more especially in towns.[251] Swanson suggests that women often rented rather than owned their own wheels.[252] This would have served to reduce any advantage in terms of earning-power of the wheel over the much cheaper distaff. It is further possible that any increase in productivity consequent upon technological advance would only have served to depress the wages paid to spinsters. A number of spinsters from within the county are known to have been presented between 1360 and 1364 for receiving 'excessive' wages. Two, Matillis Swan and Alice de Skyren (Skerne, near Driffield), were also presented under the same statute as weavers, and Margaret Pocher was similarly presented as 'filatrix et messor'.[253] The strong bargaining position of wage labour at the time of the second plague is, however, unlikely to have continued through the fifteenth century, and it may be remembered that by the mid-sixteenth century West Riding cloth was said to be more competitive than that of York because spinsters and carders could not afford the high cost of living in the city.[254]

The regional economy depended on large numbers of carders and spinners of wool to support the manufacture of woollen cloth.

---

[251] e.g. YML, M2/6e, fo. 36 (Margaret Usburn, York); BIHR, Prob. Reg. 2, fo. 140 (William Lydeyate, York); 5, fo. 40 (Agness Ragett, Coxwold).

[252] Swanson, *Medieval Artisans*, 31; Britnell, *Growth and Decline in Colchester*, 102.

[253] Putnam (ed.), *Yorkshire Sessions of the Peace*, 58, 69, 71.

[254] Heaton, *The Yorkshire Woollen and Worsted Industries*, 55.

The craft of the weaver is much better represented within the surviving returns as its status as an artisan craft is unambiguous. 199 weavers, both male and female, may be identified from designations alone for the rural parts of the Riding. In general, female websters are found most in those parts of the Riding where male weavers are also most common. Altogether some seventy-seven websters can be identified from designations and by-names, the greatest concentration being in Claro Wapentake north-west of York. In rural Howdenshire at the same date twenty-four female websters are recorded, six in the village of Barmby on the Marsh alone. A number of these women are associated with adult children and this pattern would again indicate that many websters were widows. Margaret de Skyres of Hoyland (Tickhill Wapentake) even retained two sons and two daughters in her household. Sometimes, however, it is the daughter that is described as 'webster' or 'textrix' as in the case of Isabella, the daughter of Elena Wall of Hunsingore, or Isolda, the daughter of Richard Broune and his wife of Burton Leonard. A number of others maintained servants. The household of Elizabeth de Snayth, webster, assessed at 11s., contained her daughter, another female relative, and a male servant. Much more rarely married women are distinguished, as for example the wife of John del Croft of Wetherby, 'textrix'. Given the failure of the poll tax consistently to record the occupations of married women, it seems probable that a number of other married women may have worked as weavers without being so described.

A further nineteen websters may be found in such urban communities as Pontefract, Ripon, and Tickhill, and only two in the surviving York returns for 1381. This pattern might suggest that the female webster was more commonly located in the country than the town. This may be related to the rural economy of the West Riding and Howdenshire. The evidence of an inquisition into breaches of the York weavers' charter of Henry II dated 1399 suggests that much rural cloth weaving was seasonal, most cloths being produced in winter or in April and May.[255] These represent slack seasons within an essentially pastoral economy and it may be concluded that much weaving constituted a by-employment within an agricultural community rather than a full-

---

[255] *Calendar of Miscellaneous Inquisitions*, vi, no. 212, pp. 242–9.

time means of support. The same may also be true of such small
'urban' communities as Wakefield and Tickhill. The inquisition
data are generally biased towards recording only male weavers. It
may be that female websters were often overlooked in this source
because of the occasional nature of their work and their subordin-
ate position within the familial economy. The data do, however,
suggest a rather higher concentration of female websters in and
around Wakefield than the poll tax would allow. The poll tax
returns may likewise not record websters consistently, but the
evidence would equally support a real growth in the industry over
the two decades following the poll tax. This would be consistent
with the evidence for the continued growth of the textile districts
of the West Riding over the course of the fifteenth century, but it
is more difficult to assess the implications of this for female
employment since the industry may also have become more
urbanized.[256] In pastoral Herefordshire a similar pattern of high
female involvement in the weaving industry has been suggested by
Penn from the assize roll of 1355–6, and numbers of female
weavers are likewise to be found in Somerset in 1358.[257]

Female hucksters and chapmen can be identified from a variety
of sources as general traders and may be associated with a number
of communities noted within the 1379 poll tax returns for the West
Riding. From these it is possible to distinguish ten female chapmen, three merchants, and a pedlar. Half the female chapmen are
located in Strafforth Wapentake in the south-east of the Riding
and it is probable that this reflects the greater willingness of the
collectors there to assess such women at the artisan rate of 6*d*.
The actual number of female general traders throughout the
Riding is therefore likely to have been much higher. Most of the
women recorded were probably widowed, as for example Alice
Broune of Wath, who was assessed alongside her daughter.

Turning to other craft activities represented in the 1379 poll tax,
women are frequently noticed trading as smiths and marshals.
Some twenty-seven are noticed from the rural West Riding and a
further nine in the towns of the region. Often they can only be
identified from by-names, but they are specifically designated as
artisans paying the tax at a higher rate with sufficient regularity as

[256] Lister (ed.), *Early Yorkshire Woollen Trade*, 48–94.
[257] Penn, 'Female Wage-Earners', 5–6.

to allow some confidence in this method. A few smiths are known to be widows since they were assisted by their children, as for example Alice Wod, smith, who had both a son and a daughter over the age of 16 living with her at Hiendley in Staincross Wapentake. The marital status of other independent female smiths and marshals is less certain, especially in view of the numbers of daughters trained in smithcraft identified from the same returns, though in Claro Wapentake the wife of William Brame, tanner, is described as a smith, and the couple are assessed together at 1*s*. In this same village the wife of Nicholas Hamund, sutor, is specifically designated a mason, and elsewhere in Claro an Isabella Mason is assessed in association with her son and a female servant. The by-name 'wright' is similarly encountered in association with single women, but here there are no examples of such women being assessed at the higher rate. This is despite the evidence that wrights or carpenters frequently made use of the labour of their daughters. The evidence for female tanners is likewise inconclusive.

Three service occupations may also be noted, those of the miller, the laundress, and the nurse. Only three laundresses and a 'kerchieflavender' are noted from by-name evidence. This was an exclusively female occupation, though probably only part-time in most cases, and women were often presented for washing clothing on Church festivals.[258] The female miller, again noted from by-name evidence, is more commonly noticed and may represent an operative of a hand-mill or quern. Equally it could signify the owner of a horse-mill since the numbers of women who possessed querns was probably too large to usefully identify such women as 'miller'. The nurse is particularly well represented since in this instance there seems little reason to doubt by-name evidence. In total, fifteen nurses are listed within the West Riding returns. The rural aristocracy in particular appear to have demanded wet-nurses for their children as is suggested from a matrimonial cause of 1366.[259] When Elena, the wife of Gervase de Rouclif, gave birth to a son one Martinmas, Elena, subsequently the wife of Thomas Taliour of Skelton, was asked to act as wet-nurse; she had just left service having herself given birth the previous month.

[258] Raine (ed.), *Depositions and other Ecclesiastical Proceedings,* 30, 33.
[259] BIHR, CP. E. 89.

On this occasion Elena refused because she said she loved her baby and did not wish to prejudice its survival by suckling another. One and a half years later, however, she was still feeding her child when Elena de Rouclif gave birth to a daughter. This time Elena agreed to become her wet-nurse, and the same day she was born took the infant to be baptized two and a half miles away in the parish church of St Olave's in York. How Elena managed to support herself and her baby between these two dates is sadly unrecorded. The same source contains the deposition of one Cecily de Shupton, then of York, who was employed in the home of Elena de Rouclif for a month between her giving birth and being churched (to use nineteenth-century terminology), as a monthly nurse.

PROSTITUTION

There remains one other service occupation that demands fuller examination, not least because the subject has recently generated a body of literature that allows the English evidence, and in particular the evidence surviving from York, to be set within a wider European context. If the regional evidence relating to prostitution is typical, and the indications are that it is, then there is little to suggest that many English women turned to prostitution as a profession; some may have been forced into prostitution from time to time to supplement wages in times of hardship, that is casual prostitution, and this may have been particularly true, for example, of the early fourteenth and later fifteenth centuries. The attitude of English civic and ecclesiastical bodies to prostitution seems to have been ambivalent. In a few towns prostitutes and even brothels were regulated. There is evidence for the regulation of prostitutes at Southampton by the late fifteenth century, but it is most fully documented in the case of the municipal brothel at Sandwich, which itself only dates to 1475, and the stews of Southwark within the liberty of the bishop of Winchester.[260] One of the purposes of the Sandwich regulations and of the surviving

---

[260] Anderson (ed.), *The Assize of Bread Book*, 16, 31 ff.; J. B. Post, 'A Fifteenth-Century Customary of the Southwark Stews', *Journal of the Society of Archivists*, 5 (1977), 418–28; R. M. Karras, 'The Regulation of Brothels in Late Medieval England', *Signs*, 14 (1989), 411.

fifteenth-century customary for the Southwark stews was ostensibly to safeguard the interests of the prostitutes. Even these cases, exceptional by English standards, fall short of the level of control over prostitution apparently common in the towns of southern and eastern France, Spain, northern Italy, or even southern Germany, where civic brothels are the norm and prostitution a necessary social institution.[261]

Most English evidence suggests, however, a much more *laissez-faire* attitude on the part of both ecclesiastical and civic authorities. As Karras has argued, prostitutes were viewed as traders offering a commodity that was of service to a wider community. Like other trades, it was subject to regulation. Prostitutes were permitted wages for their work, but were not allowed to be selective of their clients. They were indeed to be 'common women'.[262] A number of towns attempted with varying degrees of enthusiasm and success to keep prostitution outside the walls and, by implication, beyond their area of jurisdiction. This was true, for example, of Coventry in 1445, and Leicester in 1467.[263] From 1394–5 in Hull an area of land by the Humber just outside the town walls and three arches of the walls themselves were leased by the borough to prostitutes at an annual rent of £3. 6s. 8d., an action that also implies a significant degree of group solidarity among the women concerned.[264] Such a policy made attempts to keep prostitutes outside the walled area of the town at least credible. In 1312–13 the bailiffs at Norwich were attacked when attempting to expel some prostitutes from the city. In Winchester, however, an earlier policy of expelling prostitutes was replaced in the fifteenth century by one of levying fines.[265] The civic authorities in Exeter appear likewise to have profited from regular fines imposed on prostitutes.[266] Karras has suggested that in many towns fines were imposed on brothel-keepers with such regularity that, like brewing fines, they constituted no more than a licence

[261] Karras, 'Regulation of Brothels', 399–401.

[262] Ibid. 425–6; J. W. Baldwin, *Masters, Princes and Merchants*, i (Princeton, NJ, 1970), 134.

[263] Karras, 'Regulation of Brothels', 407 n. 33.

[264] Allison (ed.), *VCH, York, East Riding*, i. 75; Karras, 'Regulation of Brothels', 405 n. 28.

[265] Hudson (ed.), *Leet Jurisdiction*, 58–9; Keene, *Survey of Medieval Winchester*, i. 390–1.

[266] Kowaleski, 'Women's Work in a Market Town', 154.

fee.[267] Ecclesiastical bodies gained both from their position as urban landlords and from their spiritual jurisdiction in matters of morality. Keene has observed that the major landlords of Winchester prostitutes were the abbot of Hyde and the wardens of the Trinity chapel and St John's hospital.[268] In York the Vicars Choral rented cheap tenements to known prostitutes whose clients were often themselves vicars choral. The consistory court there additionally employed professional prostitutes to act as jurors to investigate the virility of husbands in cases where annulment of marriage was sought on grounds of impotence.[269]

The prostitutes themselves are generally obscure. This obscurity is itself the corollary of their poverty, evident from their concentration in cheap cottage and tenemental properties often in marginal inner urban areas or alternatively in the suburbs.[270] In York large numbers of prostitutes, as has been observed, can be associated with a group of cottages owned by the Vicars Choral on the corner of Aldwark and St Andrewgate. Rents here were very small—only 4*s*. to 6*s*. per annum in the later fourteenth and fifteenth centuries.[271] They seem to have moved around frequently, rarely staying in one place more than a few years at a time. Thus one Matilda del Wodde was presented for fornication in St Andrewgate in 1423 and in suburban Bootham in 1424 and 1425 before moving out of the jurisdiction of the Dean and Chapter, if not the city.[272] Joan Cryspyn was similarly presented whilst resident in Goodramgate in 1440, Aldwark in 1442 and again in 1448, before finally settling in Swinegayle from 1452.[273] Few women, however, were presented as regularly as Joan Cryspyn and, even allowing for the relative ease with which York prostitutes at least might move from one jurisdiction to another, it is evident that many women turned to prostitution only occa-

---

[267] Karras, 'Regulation of Brothels', 407.

[268] Keene, *Survey of Medieval Winchester*, i. 390.

[269] For two such jurors, Joan Laurence and Isabella Eston, see BIHR, CP. F. 111; D/C AB. 1, fos. 83ᵛ, 85ᵛ (Laurence); CP. F. 43; YML, H2/1, fo. 6ᵛ (Eston). Cf. J. A. Brundage, 'The Problem of Impotence', in V. L. Bullough and J. A. Brundage, *Sexual Practices and the Medieval Church* (Buffalo, 1982), 140; id., *Law, Sex, and Christian Society in Medieval Europe* (Chicago, 1987), plate 14.

[270] As at Winchester: Keene, *Survey of Medieval Winchester*, i. 392.

[271] YML, VC 4/1/1–16; VC 6/2/1–78.

[272] BIHR, D/C AB. 1, fos. 64ᵛ, 67, 69ᵛ.

[273] BIHR, D/C AB. 1, fos. 97ᵛ, 98ᵛ, 102, 112, 116ᵛ, 122ᵛ, 130, 131ᵛ, 135ᵛ, 139, 139ᵛ.

sionally, when trade was slack and legitimate forms of employment scarce. This is demonstrated, as Keene found at Winchester, by the frequency with which women with by-names of spinner, shepster, and kempster are noticed.[274] In York the by-names of cook and sempster are especially common. A number of women there also bore the surname Scott and this may indicate that local prejudices effectively denied these northern migrants access to regular employment. That migrants generally were especially well represented among women involved in prostitution is suggested by both Keene and Kowaleski in their studies of Winchester and Exeter respectively.[275] Little is known of their earnings. Karras suggests that a penny was the normal rate, but cites an example of a London woman who was given 4*d*. by a priest client for one night and a farthing cake and farthing-worth of ale for a second.[276] A Lichfield woman, however, claimed in 1466 to have earned the princely sum of six royals by entertaining members of the household of the duke of Clarence.[277]

The clients of prostitutes were frequently, but by no means exclusively, religious.[278] Kowaleski, in her study of fourteenth-century Exeter, has been able to show that one professional prostitute, Emma Northercote, actually pursued her clients, who included priests, through the borough courts to recover debts owed for her services.[279] In York in 1424 Elizabeth Frowe was presented as a procuress for the Austin friars and Joan Scryvener as such for friars and priests generally.[280] Local clergy are likewise conspicuous among the clients of prostitutes in Lichfield in 1466.[281] In London in 1385, Elizabeth Moryng was presented for procuring women to serve a clientele of friars and chaplains and in 1500

[274] Keene, *Survey of Medieval Winchester*, i. 392.

[275] Ibid.; Kowaleski, 'Women's Work in a Market Town', 154. In Augsburg in the early 16th cent. this pattern was formalized by regulations preventing the civic brothel from employing local women: L. Roper, *The Holy Household: Women and Morals in Reformation Augsburg* (Oxford, 1989), 98–9.

[276] Karras, 'Regulation of Brothels', 418 n. 74.

[277] A. J. Kettle, 'City and Close: Lichfield in the Century before the Reformation', in C. M. Barron and C. Harper-Bill (eds.), *The Church in Pre-Reformation Society* (Woodbridge, 1986), 165–6.

[278] Cf. Keene, *Survey of Medieval Winchester*, i. 392; Kowaleski, 'Women's Work in a Market Town', 154; Karras, 'Regulation of Brothels', 425.

[279] Kowaleski, 'Women's Work in a Market Town', 154.

[280] BIHR, D/C AB. 1, fo. 67.

[281] Kettle, 'City and Close', 166–7.

William Bell, the warden of the Franciscans of Nottingham, was presented as a common pimp.[282] Married men and unmarried, including servants, are also found among the recorded clients of prostitutes, though servants seem comparatively uncommon. A few men, as for example Sampson Pere of Lichfield or John Sadeler of York, seem regularly to have fornicated with both casual and professional prostitutes, but perhaps with other women also.[283] The observed pattern thus differs from what might be expected from continental evidence, where the clients of prostitutes were chiefly young, unmarried males and prostitution was seen as a necessary evil designed to provide a sexual outlet for the young male without prejudice to the virtue of 'respectable' women.[284] This perhaps suggests something of the difference between English and, for example, Mediterranean social structure. In Mediterranean culture marriage for males was often very late, but their youthful brides were expected to be virgins.[285] In later medieval England, marriage may not have been so long delayed for males, but marriages were companionate, and virginity before marriage seems not to have been so highly valued.[286]

The evidence suggests that areas where prostitutes were concentrated were relatively well defined and well known, and this is reflected in the perdurance of certain locations as centres for prostitution. Thus many York streets associated with prostitution in the later Middle Ages retained their identity well into the nineteenth century.[287] Some streets most closely identified as the haunts of prostitutes often bear names equivalent to the 'Hot Streets' (*Carreria Calida*) of the Languedoc. Love Lane, Cock's Lane, and Grape Lane (from Grape- or Gropecunt Lane) are especially common. London's Cheapside had a Popkirtle Lane. The frequent location of these streets near major religious houses appears to add weight to the notion that in an English context the

---

[282] Sharpe (ed.), *Calendar of Letter-Books: 'H'*, 271; Stevenson (ed.), *Records of the Borough of Nottingham*, iii. 74.

[283] Kettle, 'City and Close', 165; BIHR, D/C AB. 1, fo. 145.

[284] J. Rossiaud, *Medieval Prostitution*, trans. L. G. Cochrane (Oxford, 1988), 38–44; Roper, *The Holy Household*, 100.

[285] Rossiaud, *Medieval Prostitution*, 15–18; Smith, 'The People of Tuscany'. The same was true of early modern Augsburg: Roper, *The Holy Household*, 135–8, 143–4.

[286] See Ch. 5 below.

[287] Cf. F. Finnegan, *Poverty and Prostitution* (Cambridge, 1979).

clergy were often the principal clients of prostitutes. York's Grape Lane was near the Minster, as were other streets there associated with prostitution. Whitby's Grape Lane was located on the east side of the River Esk near the abbey, rather than on the west or town side. In Westminster prostitutes were likewise concentrated near the abbey.[288] Within these areas it is possible to identify actual brothels, some of which were managed by women. Joan Plumer is thus observed operating in Goodramgate, York, early in the fifteenth century and Margaret Clay likewise during the 1450s.[289] Much soliciting seems, however, to have been done through procuresses. Agnes Hudson of Swinegayle was presented in 1447 for leading a woman to spend the night with one Thomas Peny in his house.[290] In London, where prostitution within the city was outlawed, one Margery and a Joan Wakelyn appear to have worked in partnership. On one specified occasion Margery procured Joan to go to a Lombard's house and Margery received 4*d.* of the 12*d.* Joan earned from this transaction.[291]

Professional pimps and procuresses may have been responsible for first involving girls, with or without their consent, in prostitution. There are several instances of York prostitutes procuring their own daughters, and in London in 1439 it was found that a girl, Elizabeth Lane, was procured against her will by Margaret Hathewyk acting for Lombard clients.[292] The histories of most prostitutes are, however, obscure. Joan Lawrence of York was said to be 36 when she acted as a juror in an impotence case. If she can be identified with the person indicted for fornication in Bishophill in 1412, she would then have been only 16. She was presented again for fornication between 1431 and 1432, at which time she was living in one of the Aldwark tenements of the Vicars Choral. When she left that property she moved from the Dean and Chapter's jurisdiction and is thus lost from record.[293] Isabella

---

[288] For Grapecunt Lane in York see BIHR, D/C AB. 1, fo. 241ᵛ. In early 16th-cent. Augsburg unregulated prostitutes lived near the cathedral: Roper, *The Holy Household*, 9.

[289] YML, M2/lf, fo. 49ᵛ; BIHR, D/C AB. 1, fos. 27, 44, 48ᵛ, 49 (Plumer); fos. 119ᵛ, 125ᵛ, 127ᵛ, 129, 132ᵛ (Clay).

[290] BIHR, D/C AB. 1, fo. 110ᵛ.

[291] Jones (ed.), *Calendar of Plea and Memoranda Rolls, 1437–57*, 13.

[292] Ibid.; Margaret Cadde was procured by her mother Joan in 1453: BIHR, D/C AB. 1, fo. 123ᵛ.

[293] YML, H2/1, fo. 4ᵛ; VC 6/2/51, 53.

Wakefeld is first noticed as an apprentice to Christine de Knarisburgh, sempster. In 1402 she unsuccessfully attempted to enforce
a contract of marriage in the Church court with one Thomas Fox,
with whom she had had sexual relations. From 1403 to 1432 she
was regularly presented as a prostitute, procuress, and brothel-
keeper. From at least 1409 she was living in St Andrewgate and
was several times a tenant of the Vicars Choral. In 1414 she was
described as living with a priest named Peter Bryde. Sometime
after 1432 she must either have left or, more probably, died, for
her name disappears from the Vicars Choral rentals and the
surviving capitular court book. She would then have been aged
about 50.[294]

By the later fifteenth century more women may have been
forced into prostitution as they were increasingly denied access to
other forms of employment in the wake of growing economic
recession. The York evidence may be compatible with a growth
both in prostitution and the areas where prostitutes were congregated.[295] Certainly it is possible to detect a note of increasing
alarm in the attitudes of civic authorities. The Nottingham ordinances of 1463 have been cited earlier, and numbers of people
were subsequently presented there for running brothels, receiving
servants with their masters' goods and allowing servants to play at
dice.[296] An ordinance proscribing brothels in Leicester was issued
in 1467.[297] The most far-reaching civic legislation was, however,
that attempted at Coventry in 1492. This included an ordinance
'that no senglewoman, beyng in good hele and myghty in body to
labour within the age of l yeres, take nor kepe frohensfurth housez
nor chambres to themself . . . but that they go to service til they
be married'.[298]

The success of such social engineering designed to eradicate
prostitution in a city experiencing severe economic dislocation
must be doubted, and this particular clause was modified only
three years later.[299] But the implication of this legislation, namely

---

[294] YML, H2/1, fos. 8, 8ᵛ; VC 6/2/44, 48, 51, 53; BIHR, CP. F. 22; D/C AB. 1,
fos. 27 ff.

[295] BIHR, D/C AB. 1. I hope to explore this hypothesis more fully elsewhere.

[296] Stevenson (ed.), *Records of the Borough of Nottingham*, ii. 324–6, 330,
346–8.

[297] Bateson (ed.), *Records of the Borough of Leicester*, ii. 291.

[298] Harris (ed.), *Coventry Leet Book*, 544.

[299] Ibid. 568.

that women were not presumed to have any independent livelihood, but were expected to accept instead the submergence of
their identity within the family either as servants or as wives,
cannot go unnoticed. To provide for the daughters of the poor
and dowryless that they might marry, and thus protect marriage
and the family from the pernicious influence of poverty became,
in York at least by the latter decades of the century, important
works of charity. Thus John Carre, a former mayor of York in a
will dated 1487 left 40*s*. to each of 'xv pore madyns well disposed
to mariage' and 'xxli. to pure women wedded kepyng housold
togeder where most nede is w'in the Fraunches of York'.[300]
Margaret Bramhowe likewise left her household utensils to be
divided amongst recently espoused couples in need ('inter vivos et
mulieres nuper disponsatos necessitatem habentes').[301] Joan
Chamberlayn of York, d. 1502, whose position as a wealthy
resident of one of York's poorest parishes may have made her
more acutely aware of the hardships faced by her poor neighbours,
left her house on Hungate to be sold to provide funds 'to the
exhibicion of pure chylder apte to lerne to scoles, pore maydens
well dysposyd to mariages, and to wayes or briges brokon
. . . amendynge and repariage'.[302] A similar pattern is apparent in Somerset. Sir Richard Newton, for example, left five marks
in 1448 for five poor maids to marry 'in recompense that y have
don in synnes of flesshe'.[303] In Bristol a number of merchants'
wills dating to before 1390 provide for the marriages of poor
maidens, but significantly this form of pious bequest, with one
exception dated 1436, is not repeated until after 1450.[304] This
observation suggests that there too young women of humble

---

[300] BIHR, Prob. Reg. 5, fo. 327^v. Similar provision was made by Sir John
Gilliot: Raine (ed.), *Testamenta Eboracensia*, v. 14.

[301] BIHR, Prob. Reg. 4, fo. 34^v. The will is dated 1471.

[302] BIHR, Prob. Reg. 6, fo. 34^v.

[303] Three Somerset wills registered in the Prerogative Court of Canterbury after
1400 make provision for poor maids' marriages. These are dated 1441, 1448, and
1458: F. W. Weaver (ed.), *Somerset Medieval Wills* (3 vols.; Somerset Record
Society, 16, 19, 21; 1901–5), i. 148, 182; ii. 352. It may be that the absence of such
wills at a later date is a reflection of the relative prosperity of the region in the late
15th cent., but it would be unwise to reach conclusions without examining wills
proved within the more local courts.

[304] T. P. Wadley, *Notes or Abstracts of Wills Contained in the Volume Entitled
the Great Orphan Book and Book of Wills* (Bristol and Gloucester Archaeological
Society, 1886), 6, 17, 20–1, 24, 27, 128, 133, 160, 180, 185, 192.

background were considered well able to support themselves by the earlier decades of the fifteenth-century, but that this perception was eroded during the second half of that same century. Some early fifteenth century London wills do continue to provide for poor maids, but it may be that circumstances in the capital were atypical.[305] In York, as elsewhere, charitable provision for the marriage of 'poor maidens' was to survive the Reformation and examples can even be found in the reign of Elizabeth.[306]

[305] F. J. Furnivall (ed.), *The Fifty Earliest English Wills* (EETS 78; 1882), 15, 23, 79.

[306] e.g. William Scarthe, Shipmaster of Hull, left 6*s.* 8*d.* for the marriage of four poor maids at his death in 1578: BIHR, Prob. Reg. 21: ii, fo. 437. I am most grateful to Prof. M. C. Cross for this reference.

4

Servants and Servanthood

Any relationship between master or mistress and employee might technically be seen as one of service. The employee was the master's servant. A variety of words were used to describe such individuals: namely in the case of females, *serviens*, *famula*, *ancilla*, *mainpast*, and even *apprenticia*. In practice the term was often used in a narrower and more specific sense, well known to scholars of the early modern and modern eras, to describe invariably young and unmarried individuals living under the same roof as their employer.[1] The evidence considered here points to servants being drawn from all social status groups to work for masters and mistresses who may have been former servants themselves. Many former servants married after leaving service, sometimes to other former servants and workmates, set up house, and employed servants themselves. It thus appears unhelpful to identify servants as a 'class'; rather they may more usefully be described in life-cycle terms. Certainly it is possible to identify some servants that were married or servants that did not live with their employer and share his or her table, but these are the exception.[2] This chapter is concerned with describing the great majority of servants in life-cycle terms. But as an element in the labour force servants had an economic function also. Changes in the economy are reflected in changes in the demand for, and conditions of service of, servants in both town, where servants appear to have been especially numerous, and country, where servants are less well documented and probably less numerous. These are the themes that will be considered here.

Some idea of the proportions of servants found within late

---

[1] Cf. A. Kussmaul, *Servants in Husbandry in Early Modern England* (Cambridge, 1981); McIntosh, 'Servants and the Household'; P. Laslett, 'Characteristics of the Western Family Considered over Time', in id., *Family Life and Illicit Love in Earlier Generations* (Cambridge, 1977), 12–49.

[2] A few married servants are, for example, listed in the 1379 poll tax returns for Howdenshire: 'Assessment Roll of the Poll-Tax for Howdenshire'.

medieval English communities may be derived from the first poll tax of 1377. These data are limited to the tax population, i.e. persons over 14 years, and the probability that servants, especially female servants, were most likely to evade the tax must be considered.[3] Entry into service may well have been as early as 12 years, moreover, yet in the absence of substantial knowledge of birth-rates and infant mortality it would be difficult to extend the poll tax evidence to attempt a measure of the proportion of servants within the entire population. The poll tax data suggest that between 20 and 30 per cent of the urban population were servants, but only 10 per cent of the population of Rutland villages, and little over 7 per cent of villages in the Coquetdale ward of Northumberland.[4] The relatively lower proportions observed for Colchester, Carlisle, and Rochester may be explained by the presence there of unusually high proportions of single persons, some of whom were probably in service but are not specifically designated. The high York figure is likely to be a little exaggerated due to the unrepresentative nature of the partial surviving returns.[5] Despite these qualifications, and even allowing for some doubts as to the quality of the Coquetdale material, it is clear that the proportions of servants associated with towns are all significantly higher than those suggested by the surviving rural nominative returns in 1377.

Servants are recorded by name, and so are identifiable by sex, for but a few of the 1377 urban returns.[6] The limited evidence does, however, indicate urban sex ratios in excess of, but not very much so, one hundred.[7] The high measures achieved for Colchester may again reflect the less satisfactory nature of the return here. These figures again differ significantly from those indicated by the Rutland returns. Here the mean service sex ratio was as high as 161.9, a degree of difference that cannot be explained simply in terms of evasion, even although, given the lower proportion of servants, evasion by female servants might disproportionately affect service sex ratios. The equivalent ratio for Coquetdale was even higher at 194.1, i.e. male servants outnum-

[3] Goldberg, 'Urban Identity and the Poll Taxes'; Ch. 2 above.
[4] See Table II.1 below.
[5] The poorer suburban parishes are largely missing. See below.
[6] Notably for Carlisle, Colchester, Hull, and two parishes in Oxford.
[7] See Table II.2 below.

bered females by nearly two to one. Strafforth Wapentake in the
West Riding, however, a predominantly pastoral region, enjoyed
a more balanced service sex ratio (SSR) of 104.8 according to the
1379 returns.[8] For Reims in 1422 the parishes of St Pierre and St
Hilaire demonstrate characteristically urban service ratios of 100
and 108.3 respectively.[9] It is unfortunate that Laslett's analysis of
62 parish listings drawn from the period 1574–1821 fails to
distinguish urban from rural communities and makes no allowance
for probable secular variation. His mean service sex ratio of 106.6
is probably thus of limited value, though rather higher ratios are
observed at Ealing in 1599 (SSR = 166) and Crosby Ravensworth
in 1787 (SSR = 150).[10] Using Marriage Duty Act data of c.1700,
Wall has described low sex ratios within three urban communities,
namely Southampton (SSR = 91.6), London (SSR = 84.8), and
Shrewsbury (SSR = 70.6), but a markedly higher service sex ratio
within the county of Kent as a whole (SSR = 226.5). In pastoral
Wiltshire, however, the composition of servant groups was more
balanced (SSR = 100).[11] The poll tax evidence may thus accord
with a wider historical pattern which saw service to be more
feminised in urban and pastoral communities than rural, arable
communities. It is evident, however, that the sexual composition
of servant groups varied over time as well as between communities. In this respect urban service sex ratios appear to have been
higher at the time of the first poll tax than was true of the last
years of the seventeenth century.

Poll tax data may similarly be used to calculate the distribution
of servants through households. Not all the returns are arranged
such that individual households can readily be identified and it is
not possible to allow for such households as contained only
servants under taxation age. It may be that the proportions
derived are thus understated, but this may be balanced by the

---

[8] The quality of the 1379 returns must, however, be regarded as inferior to the
surviving nominative listings for the first poll tax. Servants below the age of 16,
moreover, were not recoded in 1379.

[9] P. Desportes, 'La Population de Reims au XVᵉ siècle', *Moyen Âge*, 72 (1966),
491 n. 87.

[10] Laslett, 'Size and Structure of the Household', table 13, p. 219; id., 'Characteristics of the Western Family', table 1.6, pp. 32–3.

[11] R. Wall, 'Regional and Temporal Variations in English Household Structure
from 1650', in J. Hobcraft and P. Rees (eds.), *Regional Demographic Development*
(London, 1980), table 4.10, p. 107.

TABLE 4.1 *Proportions of servant-keeping households and servant groups from the 1377 poll tax returns*

	% of servant-keeping households	mean size servant groups
Coventry, Bailey Lane	83.6	2.8
Carlisle	23.9	1.5
Dartmouth	30.3	1.5
Hull	14.8	2.1
Northampton†	36.2	2.1
Oxford		
St Peter in the East	29.2	2.3
St Mary the Virgin	26.8	2.3
York†	38.4	2.1

† Incomplete return.

Source: As Table II.1 below.

possible failure to record some solitary households. The results achieved are shown in Table 4.1. The Carlisle proportion is probably underestimated, whereas the proportion for Bailey Lane, Coventry, is atypically high. In general, allowing for the exclusion of servants aged below 14 years, it would appear that some one-third of urban households contained servants, about twice the proportion suggested for rural Rutland. This compares with a calculated mean of 39.4 per cent in Coventry as a whole in 1523 and of 37.0 per cent for the mixed Norwich suburb of Trowse in 1512–13.[12] It stands comparison also with the Poorterie quarter of Ypres in 1506, where 30.5 per cent of households contained servants, but is rather less than the proportions found in 1422 for two wealthy Reims parishes of St Pierre and St Hilaire (49 and 46 per cent respectively).[13] Had data survived for the other eleven Reims parishes then a rather lower mean may perhaps have been found there also. Wall found that 26.2 per cent and 30.0 per cent of households at Southampton and Shrewsbury respectively in

[12] Phythian-Adams, *Desolation of a City*, 204; NRO, NCR Case 7, shelf i, subsidy roll 4 Hen. VIII. Cf. M. Mitterauer, 'Servants and Youth', *Continuity and Change*, 5 (1990), 18–20.

[13] Calculated from H. Pirenne, 'Les Dénombrements de la population d'Ypres au XVᵉ siècle', *Vierteljahrschrift für Social- und Wirtschaftsgeschichte*, 1 (1903), 13, 15, 19; Desportes, 'La Population de Reims', 489 n. 84.

*c.*1700 contained servants. A proportion of 58.0 per cent for a London sample is atypical, but may reflect the concentration of wealth within the capital. In Wiltshire at the same date, however, only some 14.0 per cent of households contained servants, a proportion strikingly similar to that found for Rutland over three hundred years before.[14]

These broad levels of uniformity in rural and, more especially, urban proportions of servant-keeping households are surprising since the underlying numbers of recorded servants within the populations vary considerably. The explanation must lie in the structure of the economic communities and the broad division of the society into those who employed labour and those who worked for others. Phythian-Adams has estimated that in early sixteenth-century Coventry, employers, whom he identifies as the civic élite, members of the two leading gilds, and small masters, constituted some 780 or some 40 per cent of the city's households. Journeymen, labourers, out-servants, and poor widows, on the other hand, made up the remaining 60 per cent of households.[15] The proportion of labour-employing households to all households thus coincides very closely with the equivalent proportion of urban households containing servants.

In York, where a relatively wide franchise operated, the labour-employing classes can be closely identified with the enfranchised. Many heads of households containing servants listed in the surviving 1377 returns are listed in the freemen's register or are the widows of freemen. Conversely, individuals described as labourer (*laborarius*) in the 1381 returns, and therefore designated employees rather than employers, cannot be associated with servants in the appropriate sections of the 1377 returns, even where these individuals are apparently identified with specific trades in the freemen's register.[16] It is probable, therefore, that if allowance is made for individuals excluded from the register, as for example those admitted by right of patrimony, then the majority of servant-keeping households could be identified with freemen or their

---

[14] Wall, 'Regional and Temporal Variations', table 4.10, p. 107.

[15] Phythian-Adams, *Desolation of a City*, table 9, p. 131.

[16] e.g. Thomas de Kirkham, walker or fuller of the parish of St Mary, Bishophill Senior, or Thomas Mareschall, weaver of St Helen's, Stonegate. These are both crafts regularly employed on a piece-rate basis by textile entrepreneurs: Swanson, *Medieval Artisans*, 129.

widows.[17] The right to keep servants was, however, restricted to the citizen class only in the instance of apprentices. Thus at Norwich, where a more restrictive franchise was maintained, fines were not infrequently levied on persons, including women, for maintaining apprentices although outside the franchise.[18] In general, Phythian-Adams' observation that servant-keeping was 'a palpable expression of a householder's status' appears to hold.[19]

This last is reflected in the concentration of households containing servants in the more commercial and industrial parts of towns. The very high proportion of such households observed for Bailey Lane, Coventry, in 1377 compares favourably with that found for the same ward in 1523 (67.9 per cent).[20] Bailey Lane was indeed the commercial centre of medieval Coventry for here were congregated the city's mercers together with other high-status craftsmen including goldsmiths.[21] Bailey Lane, together with the city's other wards, also demonstrates a rough correlation between the proportion of households with servants and the quality of housing stock. Using rental values as listed in 1522, Phythian-Adams has found that some half of houses assessed at 12*s.* or more per annum contained servants in 1523 and that such property was distributed less than equally through the city, and was especially concentrated in the wealthier wards.[22]

The concentration of servant-keeping households within those York parishes included in the surviving 1377 returns is given in Table 4.2. It is unfortunate that the fragmentary nature of the surviving returns only allows a rather small and possibly unrepresentative sample of households to be analysed for some parishes. There is, moreover, a clustering of parishes within the central area north-east of the Ouse, but only one south-western parish (St Mary, Bishophill Senior) and only one suburban district (Bootham). Nevertheless, the wealthy parishes of St Martin, Coney Street, and St Crux, conspicuous for its mercantile house-

[17] Cf. Bartlett, 'Expansion and Decline', 22 and n. 1; Dobson, 'Admissions to the Freedom'.
[18] NRO, NCR Case 5, shelf b, 17, 18.
[19] Phythian-Adams, *Desolation of a City*, 205.
[20] Ibid., table 17, p. 206. See also Ch. 7 below.
[21] Ibid. 160, 311–15.
[22] Ibid. 163–5, fig. 2, p. 164.

TABLE 4.2.   *Servant-keeping households and servant groups by parish*
from the York poll tax of 1377

Parish	Total households	% households containing servant	Mean size servant groups
St Martin, Coney Street	93	65.6	2.2
St Crux	120	48.3	2.1
St Mary, Bishophill Senior	45	40	1.7
St Helen, Stonegate	82	37.8	2.1
St Sampson	160	36.9	2.0
St Denys, Walmgate	52	34.6	2.5
St Saviour	88	34.1	2.2
All Saints, Pavement	18	33.3	2.3
Bootham	103	11.7	1.7

Note: The partial return for St Mary, Bishophill Senior, forms a separate membrane in the original returns and is not an extension of the return for the parish of St Denys as shown in Leggett's edition.

Sources: Leggett (ed.), '1377 Poll Tax Returns for the City of York'; PRO, E 179/217/13.

holds, are both characterized by high proportions of servants.[23] Conversely, the extra-mural suburb of Bootham demonstrates an exceptionally low proportion of households containing servants, lower even than that found for any of the wards of Coventry in 1523. In structural terms Bootham appears more rural than urban, and in historical terms the area was claimed as a franchise of St Mary's Abbey until 1354.[24] It seems likely that in this economically underdeveloped suburb journeyman and piece-work labour predominated, as is suggested by the concentration of *laborarii* listed in the 1381 returns.[25] Thus the broadly similar proportions of servant-keeping households that characterize larger towns as a whole disguise real variation between one area and another within individual towns.

---

[23] St Martin's was a comparatively industrialized parish with a high concentration of leather-workers, though a number of mercantile families are also listed in the poll tax.

[24] Miller, 'Medieval York', 68–9.

[25] Bartlett (ed.), *Lay Poll Tax Returns for the City of York*, 50–2. The metal trades are also well represented in these later returns.

THE STRUCTURE OF RURAL SERVICE:
THE WEST RIDING IN 1379

It remains to explore the structure of rural service in greater depth. In this respect the 1379 West Riding poll tax returns are an invaluable source.[26] They permit a detailed regional survey of the pattern of servant-keeping between town and country and between agricultural- and trade-related households. It has already been observed that towns tended to be characterized by a relatively low adult sex ratio, i.e. women outnumber men, and by a relatively high proportion of servants. Thus the poll tax sex ratios for Howden and Pontefract were 84.7 and 92.8. The proportions of servants to all taxpayers in Pontefract was 17.4 per cent. This contrasts with a sex ratio of 99.2 and a proportion of the population in service of only 4.5 per cent for Strafforth Wapentake (excluding Doncaster, Bradfield, Rotherham, and Ecclesfield). For rural Howdenshire, where the returns are rather more comprehensive, the total sex ratio was somewhat higher than for Howden itself at 94.4. The structure of urban craft- or trade-related households also demonstrates certain specific characteristics. A very high proportion of all servants can be associated with such households, but relatively few contain adolescent children, i.e. those over 16 years and thus of age to be taxed. The ratio of children to servants tends thus to be very low for many urban communities, 0.14 at Pontefract, 0.16 at Ripon, and 0.18 at Doncaster. This may be compared against equivalent ratios of 0.53 for Claro, 0.86 for Strafforth, and 1.40 for Tickhill Wapentake. The proportions of servants specifically associated with craft households tend to be rather smaller in rural communities, but these proportions are not insignificant considering the relatively small numbers of households known to be engaged in craft activity. On the basis of this analysis some larger communities that could be considered urban on the basis of size and occupational structure appear anomalous. Ecclesfield and Bradfield, for example, with tax populations of 313 and 398 respectively are

---

[26] All references in this section are to the 'Rolls of the Collectors in the West Riding' and 'Assessment Roll of the Poll-Tax for Howdenshire' unless otherwise stated.

thoroughly rural in structure despite possessing rather larger numbers of artisans than their neighbours. The same is also true of Sheffield with a tax population of 527, but relatively few servants and a high child to servant ratio (1.13).

The same pattern of analysis may be applied to specific occupations. The trades of tailor, souter or shoemaker, weaver, smith or marshal, and wright or carpenter have been considered here since they are well represented in both village and town. The rural sample is drawn from Strafforth, Tickhill, Staincross, Osgodcross, Aggbrigg, and Claro wapentakes, and the urban sample from Pontefract, Wakefield, Ripon, Doncaster, Tickhill, and Rotherham, towns with a combined tax population of 3275. Sex ratios associated with servants do not differ radically between town and country save in weavers' households. Here female servants are rather more common in rural districts (urban SSR = 400, rural SSR = 150) and this would accord with other evidence that weaving was more feminised outside the town.[27] Servant groups associated with wrights and carpenters tend to be comparatively feminised in both town and country (urban SSR = 75, rural SSR = 80). Conversely, servant groups associated with smiths and marshals tend to be male dominated (urban SSR = 260, rural SSR = 200). The striking difference between town and country is again seen in the high proportion of children retained in rural artisan households. Children are here clearly retained in preference to the employment of servants. Whereas the child to servant ratio in the group of towns ranges between 0.07 for wrights and carpenters, and 0.17 for weavers, for the rural sample the equivalent ratios range from 0.55 for souters to 1.72 for wrights and carpenters. The sex ratios associated with these children tend to be more balanced and thus show little correlation with service sex ratios. Within the households of smiths and marshals over the six wapentakes, for example, there are 23 daughters and 28 sons recorded as against 22 female servants to 44 male. In the cases of souters and weavers dependent female children actually outnumber male children, though sample sizes are comparatively small. Since the poll tax was levied only on persons aged 16 and over, there can be little doubt that such retained children and servants of either sex were economically active. At Howden retained

---

[27] See Ch. 3 above.

children are specifically, albeit confusingly, described as servants to indicate their economic status. This is sometimes made explicit within the tax records. Isolda, the daughter of Richard Broune and his wife, is described as 'textrix' and separately assessed at the higher rate. Likewise Emma, one of four recorded servants of John Dicas, a tanner of Fryston, is assessed as a webster also at the higher rate.

The West Riding poll tax evidence thus supports the notion that service as an institution was comparatively widespread, but that it was less comprehensively developed within rural areas than was true of the towns. In rural communities the retained labour of children represents a significant productive element within the household alongside or in place of servants. Young country-women, moreover, were at least as likely to be found living in their parental homes as dependent labour than as servants in the households of others, whereas young men were more likely to be found as servants. Service sex ratios associated with rural craft households tend, therefore, to be relatively high; male servants outnumbered female by three to two, as in Strafforth (craft SSR = 140.7) and Claro Wapentake (craft SSR = 150), although ratios for all servants are often lower. In the towns the equivalent ratios are rather lower, as at Pontefract (craft SSR = 117.9) or Ripon (craft SSR = 88.5).

These patterns are mirrored in the 1377 poll tax returns for the county of Rutland and for the Coquetdale Ward of Northumberland.[28] These earlier returns are assessed on a population aged 14 or more. Using by-name evidence alone to identify craft households, the frequency with which children are retained in such households is again apparent. Indeed for Rutland excluding Oakham (tenants of the king) the craft child to servant ratio is 1.44, but for the small town of Oakham itself it is only 0.11. The craft servant sex ratio in rural Rutland is especially high at 242.9, though the sex ratio for the entire tax population is lower at 161.9. Significantly the sex ratio of dependent children is much lower, i.e. more feminised, in craft households (sex ratio = 69.6) than in all households (sex ratio = 101.0). This would suggest that in rural Rutland crafts drew disproportionately upon male servants and female children. It is tempting to conclude that the retention of

---

[28] PRO, E 179/269/51; E 179/158/29.

female children between the ages of 14 and 16, an age group
excluded from the 1379 poll tax, was an especially common
phenomenon in craft households.

SERVANTHOOD: TERMS AND CONDITIONS

It is perhaps appropriate here to turn away from this broad
structural analysis so as to consider in more detail the actual
circumstances of service. The only substantive evidence for the
age at entry into service and customary length of service is that
contained in depositions. Servants indeed form a significant proportion of all deponents within the sample of York cause papers
explored here. This merely reflects the ubiquitous presence of
servants in households to overhear and witness the conversation
and activities of other household members. Over sixty servants or
former servants of both sexes can be identified out of a total of
1094 deponents. Of these twenty-four male and twenty-three
female servants can be known by age directly from the descriptive
data. A further sixteen male and thirteen female former servants,
whose ages are given, can be identified retrospectively from their
actual depositions; some were still in service when called as
witnesses. The ages so derived represent the ages either at which
the deponent testified or at the time of the events at issue in the
cause. It follows that while the range of ages at which service was
common is well represented, the customary age of entry or leaving
is less clear. The ages of female and male servants derived from
this deposition evidence are represented diagrammatically in
Table 4.3.

No servant significantly under the age of 12 was encountered
among the deposition population. One witness, Cecily, wife of
William Redeness, was aged 24 or more at her deposition and had
been in service when she was present at a marriage thirteen years
earlier. This would have made her at least 11 at the time, but
perhaps a year or so older.[29] Agnes de Polles is stated to have
entered service, probably for the first time, fourteen years earlier.
Since her age is given as 26, this would have made her 12 at the
time.[30] Another girl, aged 15 at her deposition, claimed to have

[29] BIHR, CP. F. 56 (1410).
[30] BIHR, CP. E. 89 (1366).

known a fellow servant for three years. As the acquaintanceship probably represents her length of service in the same household, she can be assumed to have entered service at 12.[31] Examples of girls in service in their teens are not uncommonly found, though most commonly in the later fourteenth century, and it may be tentatively concluded that the minimum and perhaps the most common age for commencing service was 12 years. This coincides with the canonical age of majority for girls and may have been regarded as the age at which girls ceased to be regarded as children dependent upon their mothers. The *Italian Relation* would suggest a still more precocious age of 7–9 years by *c.*1500, but this must be an untrustworthy source.[32] The narrative is designed to draw attention to cultural contrasts between north Italy and the author's perception of England, itself based almost exclusively on the well-to-do citizens of London. Thus the author exaggerates the youth of servants, and the supposed want of affection ('il poco amore delli Inglesi') of parents, when describing an institution that was largely alien to him.[33] Ironically, child-servants were to be found in a Mediterranean context. In both late medieval Florence and Barcelona girls as young as 8 were placed as servants for a period of years on the understanding that the employer would give the girl a dowry on her marriage sometime in her mid- to late teens.[34]

The age at which individuals normally left service in late medieval Yorkshire is less well documented than age at entry, but clearly it was much later than was true of many servants in Southern Europe. Nor was service so explicitly a means to marriage as a livelihood. A small number of males are observed

---

[31] BIHR, CP. E. 121 (1372).

[32] C. A. Sneyd (ed.), *A Relation . . . of the Island of England . . . About the Year 1500* (Camden Soc. 37; 1847), 24–5.

[33] Ibid. 24. Blanchard in a review of Smith, 'Hypothèses sur la nuptialité' suggests that age of service in England may have declined between the late 14th cent. and the time of the *Italian Relation*, but this is to ignore the inherent bias of this last: I. Blanchard, 'Reviews', *Economic History Review*, 2nd ser. 37 (1984), 118.

[34] C. Klapisch-Zuber, 'Female Celibacy and Service in Florence in the Fifteenth Century', in ead., *Women, Family, and Ritual in Renaissance Florence* (Chicago, 1985), 173–4; ead., 'Women Servants in Florence during the Fourteenth and Fifteenth Centuries', in Hanawalt (ed.), *Women and Work*, 68; T. M. Vinyoles, *Les Barcelonines a les darreries de l'edat mitjana* (Barcelona, 1976), 33–66. I am grateful to Mr P. Rycraft for making this last available to me.

TABLE 4.3. *Age distribution of female and male servants over time*

Period	Age observed
Female servants	
1301–49	12 ———————— 16
1350–99	12 ——————— 15
	12 15 16
	14+
	18 ———— 20 22 24+* 24+* 25+ 26* 28
	17 19 20 24+
1400–49	11+ ———————————————— 18+ 19 20 22
	15 18+ 20+ 21 24
	15 ——— 18 20
	16 ———— 20
	18 19+
	19
1450–1520	17+ ——————————— 23+* 24+
	15 17 18 19 20+ 23+* 28
	20

Male servants

1301–49   *13* ————————— *19*   20   22   29
                                        21 ———— 24   25+

1350–99   16+   18   *19+*   20   21 ———— 24   26
                                19+

1400–49   14+ — — — 17+   *19+*   20   21 ———— 24   25+   26
                          18+   *19+*   20   21 ———— 24   27+

1450–1520   17   18+   *19*   20   22   24   25+   27+
                                        20+   24
            8+ — — — — — — — — — — — — — — — 20+

Notes: Figures in regular type represent age of service at deposition, figures in *italic type* represent age at service calculated retrospectively.
* Status as servant uncertain.

Sources: BIHR, CP. E, F, G various; D/C CP various; Appendix III.

described as servants although considerably older than the majority of servants in the sample. In particular may be noted the male
servants of Roger de Morton, a York merchant of substance, two
of whom were stated to be 40 years of age. Their status as servants
is confirmed by the poll tax entry for the previous year (1381).[35]
In contrast no female servant is to be found within the sample
population beyond 28 years of age.[36] The unequal proportion of
servants said to be 20 found in the third time period is probably
only an indication of the approximate nature of the age data. With
this proviso in mind, if the table is regarded as reflecting the age
range of female servants then it appears that relatively few
individuals remained in service beyond their mid-twenties. 28
years can be seen as an upper limit and is perhaps over-represented in the sample.

It might be remarked that the younger age groups are poorly
represented in the later periods, but this can only reflect the age-
specific bias of the sample. Witnesses of extreme youth were not
examined and the youngest deponent was over 14 years of age.
There is some evidence that this preference for older witnesses
became more marked with time, hence the skewed age distribution observed for the final period. Servants in their early teens can
consequently only be observed retrospectively in causes relating
to actions several years or more prior to litigation. Such causes
are significantly more common for the earlier periods. For comparative purposes there are rather fewer male servants within the
sample population. Here, even allowing for the small number of
servants in excess of 30 years, the age distribution suggests that
males remained in service a year or two longer than females, i.e.
to 26 or more as against 24 or more. There is too little evidence to
show whether service commonly commenced at the same early
age as for girls or correspondingly later, although one 13-year-old
male servant can be identified retrospectively.[37] It would be
mistaken, however, to conclude that all girls remained in service
into their early twenties for the deposition population also includes

[35] BIHR, CP. E. 128 (1382); Bartlett (ed.), *Lay Poll Tax Returns for the City of
York*, 65.
[36] Joan Wales, servant to Robert Lee, was 28 when she testified in 1509 and
another woman servant of Moor Monkton was of like age in 1398: BIHR, CP. E.
238; CP. G. 40.
[37] BIHR, CP. E. 221 (1396).

a small, but not insignificant group of unmarried women of that age apparently not in service. These last are considered in the next chapter, but they accord with the picture of work opportunities for single females described in the preceding chapter.

In general, servants, according to the cause paper evidence, appear to have served for a year at a time, often from Martinmas one year to Martinmas following, although this is made explicit in one cause only.[38] The point at entry into or departure from service is known in twenty-five instances. Nine servants, five female and four male, entered service at Martinmas and eight, four female and four male, left at the same date.[39] Two servants commenced at Christmas and one at the Nativity of St John the Baptist (24 June), both these being English quarter days. One further servant ended her term at Easter.[40] This pattern suggests that the Martinmas hirings traditional to this region from early modern times were already well established in the later fourteenth century.[41] It is probable that the Martinmas hiring fair 'for hiring all sorts of household servants, both men and women' held in the Pavement, York, as observed by Francis Drake in 1736, was likewise much older.[42] Henry Best described such fairs, or 'sittings', in the rural East Riding of the seventeenth century, and it is likely that the needs of the larger agricultural sector determined customary hiring dates even within the urban sector.[43] Other sources confirm this regional pattern and suggest the importance of Pentecost as a regular counterpart to Martinmas for hiring purposes. A Yorkshire peace session cites a ploughman hired from Pentecost to Martinmas of 1361, and a York testator provided for a female servant (not named) of his to remain in service until the following Pentecost.[44] One woman servant within the cause paper sample

---

[38] BIHR, CP. E. 241p (1363).

[39] BIHR, CP. E. 89 (1366); CP. E. 221 (1396); CP. E. 241p (1363); CP. E. 259 (1368); CP. F. 36 (1410); CP. F. 189 (1453); CP. F. 200 (1431); CP. F. 201 (1430).

[40] BIHR, CP. E. 89 (1366); CP. F. 182 (1439); CP. F. 336 (1465).

[41] Martinmas remains a quarter-day north of the border. For the perdurance of Martinmas hirings into the 20th cent. see Kussmaul, *Servants in Husbandry*, 50; F. Kitchen, *Brother to the Ox* (London, 1940); H. Reffold, *Pie for Breakfast* (Cherry Burton, 1984).

[42] F. Drake, *Eboracum* (London, 1736), 218.

[43] C. B. Robinson (ed.), *Rural Economy in Yorkshire in 1641, being the Farming and Accounts Books of Henry Best* (Surtees Soc. 33; 1857), 134–5.

[44] L. R. Poos, 'The Social Context of Statute of Labourers Enforcement', 32; BIHR, Prob. Reg. 4, fo. 130ᵛ (William Nevile, esquire, d. 1469).

was hired at Pentecost and another left at Pentecost.[45] Regional rentals, as for example the York Vicars Choral series dating from the early fourteenth century, follow the same pattern running from Martinmas to Pentecost and from Pentecost to Martinmas.[46] A pattern of biannual hirings has likewise been described for late medieval Munich and Strasbourg.[47]

In southern and midland England other hiring dates, notably Michaelmas, appear, as at later periods, to have been normal. Thus Hammer found that Oxford apprenticeship contracts of the earlier sixteenth century were most frequently dated Michaelmas.[48] Likewise it is difficult not to associate the high October and lesser May peaks in marriage seasonality derived by Razi from the court rolls of Halesowen with traditional hiring practices.[49] The Coventry Leet Book makes specific reference in 1452 to a Good Friday fair 'be which people were lette for service' held within the city.[50] There is further evidence for Easter hirings, and clearly additional research in this area could greatly extend the range of evidence available, although the perdurance of traditional regional hiring customs does appear highly significant.[51]

To examine the length of time a servant stayed within a given position it is again necessary to consider the cause paper evidence. Here it must immediately be acknowledged that male and female experience was more likely to be divergent since few girls were formally apprenticed and thus bound to a single master for a period usually specified at seven years. The Statute of Labourers (1351) stipulated that servants were to be contracted by the year or 'other usual terms' rather than by the day.[52] This was a response

---

[45] BIHR, CP. E. 155; CP. F. 201. The fixed feast of St John the Baptist may also have approximated to Pentecost for hiring purposes: e.g. BIHR, CP. E. 89.

[46] YML, VC 6/2.

[47] Wiesner, *Working Women in Renaissance Germany*, 84. Exactly the same pattern of hirings around 'summer' and 'winter' terms have been described for Norway, Sweden, and Denmark for the late medieval period.

[48] C. I. Hammer, 'The Mobility of Skilled Labour in Late Medieval England: Some Oxford Evidence', *Vierteljahrscrift für Social- und Wirtschaftsgeschichte*, 63 (1976), 200.

[49] Razi, *Life, Marriage and Death*, 152–3.

[50] Harris (ed.), *Coventry Leet Book*, 272.

[51] For Easter hirings see ibid. 673; Thomas (ed.), *Calendar of Plea and Memoranda Rolls, 1364–81*, 145. For Christmas hirings see Thomas (ed.), *Calendar of Plea and Memoranda Rolls, 1413–37*, 53–4.

[52] *Statutes of the Realm*, i. 311.

to, and an attempt to mitigate, the economic consequences of the Black Death. In a period of acute labour shortage wage labour could obtain the best returns from short contracts, but the Statute regulated against this in the interest of the employer. This regulation is similarly reflected in craft gild ordinances, and certainly in the case of servants the annual contract seems to have been the norm from early modern times.[53] The case of Isabella, servant to Thomas de Queldale, is here most instructive. She was contracted for the term of one year and had agreed to serve subsequently Master John de Risheton, rector of St Peter's school in York, for a like term. But in the wake of the 'Grey Death' or plague of 1361 when competition for labour was intense, the unfortunate Isabella was forced to continue in service with her first master and was thus prosecuted for breaking her contract.[54] The circumstances of this case are exceptional, but they are consonant with the impression to be drawn from the cause paper evidence that a year was indeed the regular term of service. Only in four instances can servants be found within the cause paper sample who left service after only some six months.[55] There is good evidence, however, that some servants remained in the same household for several years. Some dozen servants of either sex included within the cause paper sample can be shown to have served for periods of between two and seven years.[56] The will of Thomas Parys, wright, d. 1408, refers uniquely to a five-year contract for service drawn up between himself and the mother of his *famula*.[57]

It is uncertain if this kind of contractual arrangement was exceptional, but the arrangement suggests a form of apprenticeship. Testamentary evidence likewise indicates a small number of female servants still in service with their master's widow three, five, eight, and even fifteen years after the death of the master

---

[53] Swanson, *Medieval Artisans*, 114; Kussmaul, *Servants in Husbandry*.

[54] BIHR, CP. E. 241p.

[55] BIHR, CP. E. 79 (Alice de Harpham; Michaelmas to feast of translation of St Thomas, 1349; this aberrant pattern probably reflects conditions in the plague year); CP. E. 89 (Maud de Herthill and Henry Vaux); CP. F. 201 (Alice Dalton).

[56] e.g. BIHR, CP. E. 89, 121, 155, 221, 259; CP. F. 56, 189, 200, 201, 336.

[57] 'Lego Alicie, famule mee si serviat michi uxori usque ad terminum factum inter me et matrem suam durantem quinque annis ijs': BIHR, Prob. Reg. 3, fo. 282ᵛ.

they first served.[58] Terms of service of only one year are not generally specified within the depositions, but this may only add weight to the idea that a year was the more normal term. Reference to former service was a means of locating in time past events and it would thus only be necessary to state the length of service where this was greater than a single year. Alice Doncastre, d. 1430, a mercer's wife, left money to each of her servants in service for a year at the time of her death.[59] A sixteenth-century observer, James Ryther of Harewood, a southerner by birth, likewise observed that Yorkshire servants 'chaunge their maysters yearly, huntinge after more wages and lesse labor . . .'.[60] This pattern is confirmed from other sources. Oxford Statute of Labourers litigation for the years 1390–2 demonstrates little continuity of servant groups from one year to the next within servant groups associated with particular employers.[61] Kowaleski, using borough court material, has similarly observed that servants in late fourteenth-century Exeter tended to be hired by the year.[62] This may reflect the stronger bargaining position of servants at this period of high wages that prompted them to continually seek better positions. Brodsky, by contrast, writing of female servants in Jacobean London, has described a mean length of service within a single household of four years.[63]

The weight of evidence thus points to hirings taking place annually around a traditional date and indicates servants gathered for this purpose at customary locations such as the Pavement, York's principal market-place. James Ryther refers disparagingly to these 'marketts and faiers in which they ar suffred to go sell themselves, wher men and women servants make appointments to

---

[58] e.g. Alice de Fourneys was servant to a York mercer in 1396 and was still with his widow at her death in 1411: BIHR, Prob. Reg. 1, fo. 99; YML, D/C Reg. 1, fo. 161.

[59] BIHR, Prob. Reg. 2, fo. 628.

[60] W. G. Craig, 'James Ryther of Harewood and His Letters to William Cecil, Lord Burghley', *Yorkshire Archaeological Journal*, 56 (1984), 108.

[61] e.g. servants associated with John Dadyngton, John Hickes, spicer, John Leper, baker, and John Cade, weaver: Salter (ed.), *Medieval Archives of the University of Oxford*, 1–128.

[62] Kowaleski, 'Women's Work in a Market Town', 153.

[63] V. Brodsky (Elliot), 'Single Women in the London Marriage Market: Age, Status and Mobility, 1598–1619', in R. B. Outhwaite (ed.), *Marriage and Society: Studies in the Social History of Marriage* (London, 1981), 92.

place them selves comodyusly the year ensuing . . .'.[64] The Coventry Good Friday fair already noted was specifically described as a servant hiring fair and represents a most valuable early example of this practice. But though the operation of these more or less formalized hiring fairs must for this period remain largely a matter of speculation, it is evident that other mechanisms operated alongside or within the market place by which servants found positions with particular households. These observations are based primarily upon an analysis of 185 named female servants associated with York households headed by male traders and craftsmen making wills before *c*.1500. This sample is supplemented by a further 218 named women servants associated with female-headed, professional, gentry, or otherwise unidentified households. This sample population was analysed against a range of nominative sources and a number of positive and more or less tentative identifications between sources were made. This analysis suggests three areas of possible contact between servant and employer. The first, and best documented, is that of kinship. Kussmaul found kinship links common for the early modern era and it seems further evidence of the essentially classless nature of service.[65] Brodsky has noted much the same phenomenon in Jacobean London and Phythian-Adams in early sixteenth-century Coventry.[66] Kin relationships are sometimes explicitly noted in wills. Thus Agnes Milde is described as the *cognata* of her master Richard Appilgarth, d. 1437, and Isabell de Syggeston is named the *nepota* of her employer, Robert de Harom, d. 1390. Elena Swyne, servant to Richard Hebson, is likewise noticed as a *cognata* in his wife's will.[67] The supplementary sample includes four female servants stated to be kin and ten servants with surnames in common with their employer. Since surname evidence is limited to blood relationships, the true proportion of servants that were kin is necessarily understated. Kin relationships are further demonstrated from the cause paper evidence. One Joan Yarm, for example, a witness in a cause dated 1439, is described as both

---

[64] Craig, 'James Ryther of Harewood', 108.
[65] Kussmaul, *Servants in Husbandry*, 59.
[66] Brodsky, 'Single Women in the London Marriage Market', 93; Phythian-Adams, *Desolation of a City*, 152.
[67] BIHR, Prob. Reg. 1, fo. 48ᵛ; 2, fo. 441; 3, fo. 384ᵛ; 4, fo. 143ᵛ.

servant and *consanguinea* in the fourth degree to William Wright of North Street.[68]

Another possible area of contact was trade. Joan Kyrkby, servant to the dyer John Usburn, d. 1428, was herself the daughter of Usburn's trade associate, John Kyrkby.[69] Likewise Joan Askham, Agnes Monkton, and Isabella Sutton may all have had close relatives in the same trade as their employers, namely merchant, fishmonger, and tanner respectively.[70] It is also possible that Margaret Acclom, servant to the fishmonger William Muston of St Denys's parish, was a migrant from the major fishing town of Scarborough. A number of Accloms of Scarborough had their wills registered at York and St Denys's parish by Fossbridge was the centre of the trade in seawater fish.[71] Clearly, identification by surname alone based exclusively on the testamentary population can only be tentative, but this method seems justified in the absence of alternative sources. Where such identifications exist in significant quantities, moreover, they must constitute real evidence of a particular trend even though individual cases may be uncertain. It is upon such evidence that the third point of contact between servant and employer can be established, though the case is substantiated by several more definite instances. This third is the link of neighbourhood, for the evidence points to servants finding employment in their natal parish through successive placements. This seems all the more significant since York parishes are both small and numerous. Thus Joan Howsom served first a fuller and subsequently a widow between 1428 and 1431 in the parish of St Mary, Bishophill Senior.[72] Likewise, Joan Cotyngham, one-time servant to Robert de London, d. 1406, a capper, may have been the daughter of a tailor listed in the same parish of St Helen, Stonegate, in the poll tax assessment of 1381.[73]

[68] BIHR, CP. F. 181.

[69] BIHR, Prob. Reg. 2, fos. 532, 533ᵛ.

[70] BIHR, Prob. Reg. 2, fos. 357Aᵛ, 573, 610; 3, fo. 602; 5, fo. 169.

[71] BIHR, Prob. Reg. 3, fo. 605ᵛ; *Index of Wills in the York Registry, 1389–1514* (Yorkshire Archaeological Society Record Ser. 6; 1989); Raine, *Mediaeval York*, 70–1.

[72] BIHR, Prob. Reg. 2, fos. 543ᵛ, 658ᵛ.

[73] A John Cotyngham, tailor, is so listed married to a Joan. It was common for daughters to be given their mother's name, hence the plausibility of this identification; Bartlett (ed.), *Lay Poll Tax Returns for the City of York*, 44; BIHR, Prob. Reg. 3, fo. 276.

Of particular interest is the example of Margaret Hall. She can be associated, albeit tentatively, with the parish of St John at Ousebridge end (Micklegate). In 1442 she was in service with the goldsmith John Close of St John's parish and in 1460 with one Richard Hebson, chandler, also of St John's parish. She continued in the service of Hebson's widow, who died in 1468, and cannot be traced thereafter. It is unfortunate that the links in this brief biography cannot be proven and Hall was not such an uncommon surname in late medieval York. Nevertheless it is hard to believe that these supposed links are purely a product of coincidence since the probability of finding two Margaret Halls within the same small parish at about the same date cannot be great.[74] Several further instances of servants engaged within the same, or immediately adjacent parish as that of their birth were observed and it should be noted that ties of neighbourhood might overlap also with trade contacts. Both Agnes Monkton and Isabella Sutton, cited earlier, may have been born within the same parish in which they are subsequently noticed as servants. This last follows from the tendency of particular trades to be located in the same parish or neighbourhood.

One further observation is the tendency for individual servants serving within a particular household to be themselves blood relatives, though the instances of this are perhaps not great. Joan and Margaret Dewe, for example, were both in service to the brewer Richard Bewe, d. 1465, and Alice and Katherine Gybson were similarly servants to John Browne, cordwainer, d. 1451.[75] Joan Amgill, the servant of John Smith, d. 1463, was probably the sister of his apprentice in the pewterer's craft, John Amgill.[76] Brodsky, describing migrants to London in the early modern era, has suggested that brothers in apprenticeship may often have helped secure positions for their sisters and it seems likely that this was also true of the late medieval era.[77] Likewise it is possible that the long-serving Margaret Hall followed her sister Elena into her first recorded position with John Close.[78] It may be seen, by way of conclusion, that a number of informal networks, based on

[74] BIHR, Prob. Reg. 2, fos. 45ᵛ, 143ᵛ, 401, 441.
[75] BIHR, Prob. Reg. 2, fo. 488ᵛ; YML, D/C Reg. 1, fo. 267ᵛ.
[76] BIHR, Prob. Reg. 2, fo. 599ᵛ.
[77] Brodsky, 'Single Women in the London Marriage Market', 94.
[78] BIHR, Prob. Reg. 2, fo. 45ᵛ.

kinship, trade, and the parish or local community, served to place servants that required positions with masters or mistresses that required labour. It is not possible, however, to say how generally these networks operated. In early modern Nuremberg, a city three times the size of late medieval York, the authorities licensed a number of women to act as employment agents for finding positions for rural migrants.[79] In larger French towns a similar role was played by the *recomandresse*.[80] Perhaps this was only a reflection of scale, but there is reference in some Lincolnshire peace sessions to a man who acted as 'a common forestaller of servants and labourers, so that no one in the neighbourhood can hire servants without his help'.[81] London records include the case of one Agnes taken without her father's knowledge or consent by a Buckinghamshire widow, Thomasina March, to serve a wire-drawer of the City in 1410.[82] This is insubstantial evidence, but it does suggest the possibility of individuals operating more or less formally as agents alongside the hiring fair and the networks just described. Women, by exploiting their own 'gossip' networks, would be well adapted to fulfil such a role.

Any analysis of the conditions of service as experienced by young women of the later Middle Ages is problematical due to the slender nature of the evidence. In the larger towns at least it appears that most servants were employed as part of a group and only a minority served by themselves. This can be demonstrated from an analysis of servant-keeping households listed in the York returns of 1377 as shown in Table 4.4. These proportions compare favourably with those suggested for Coventry in 1523.[83] They are also broadly in line with those derived by Richard Wall from Marriage Duty Act material in respect of Southampton, Shrews-bury, and London, although solitary servants were more common at this late date in the two provincial communities.[84] The York poll tax evidence further suggests that the mean size of servant groups was remarkably uniform across the city. Thus the mean size in Bootham (1.7) was only a little smaller than that in St

[79] Wiesner, *Working Women in Renaissance Germany*, 83.
[80] Shahar, *The Fourth Estate*, 204, citing *Ordinances des Roys de France*, ii. 370.
[81] Poos, 'The Social Context of Statute of Labourers Enforcement', 33.
[82] Thomas (ed.), *Calendar of Plea and Memoranda Rolls, 1413–37*, 53–4.
[83] Phythian-Adams, *Desolation of a City*, table 16, p. 205.
[84] Wall, 'Regional and Temporal Variations', 106, table 4.10, p. 107.

TABLE 4.4.   *Size and distribution of servant groups by households*
from York poll tax returns of 1377

Size of servant group	Number of households	% all households	Number of servants	% all servants
1	134	17.6	134	22.3
2–3	118	15.5	271	45.0
4 and more	39	5.1	197	32.7

Source: Leggett (ed.), '1377 Poll Tax Returns for the City of York'.

Martin, Coney Street (2.2). The highest mean (2.5) was in the parish of St Denys, Walmgate.[85]

It will be shown shortly that the sexual composition (and size) of these servant groups was partly determined by the occupation or status of the household head.[86] Testamentary evidence indicates that there may have been some variation, as might be expected, in the age range within servant groups. Thus, for purposes of bequests, servants having a Christian name in common are sometimes distinguished by the epithets 'big' and 'little'. A York mercer, Thomas Aton, d. 1432, left 5s. to his *famula* 'big' Katerina, but only 3s. 4d. 'utrique aliarum duarum parvarum famularum mearum'.[87] It is possible that within these servant groups there was some degree of continuity from one year to the next despite the high annual turnover of servants generally.[88] Certainly, as has been remarked earlier, a small number of servants are noticed in the service of one family over a number of years. Whether the status of individual servants is reflected in the terminology used is, however, a matter of guesswork. Kowaleski has argued that the frequency with which servants are identified by first name only is indicative of their low status.[89] This is more probably an indication not of status, but of youth. Younger children are regularly so named in York wills and, as is sometimes true of daughters or even wives, female servants may be given diminutive

---

[85] This accords with an occupation-specific analysis of servant groups derived from probate evidence. See Table 4.7.
[86] See Table 4.5.
[87] BIHR, Prob. Reg. 2, fo. 623.
[88] Cf. Kussmaul, *Servants in Husbandry*, 55.
[89] Kowaleski, 'Women's Work in a Market Town', 153.

or pet forms of their names, hence Emmota, Magota, Cissota, and so on. This last is again no evidence of status. The term most frequently applied to describe female servants is *famula*, but the term *ancilla* is often used to describe particular servants. It may be that the *ancilla* represented the junior personal servant as opposed to the general household servant indicated by *famula*. Agnes de Kyrketon generously bequeathed ten marks to her *ancilla* 'little' Margaret 'si vivat ad annos discrecionis', whereas Agnes Palmar gave only one half-mark (6s. 8d.) to her *ancilla* Agnes Burnelay, but seventeen marks to her *famula* Joan Howsom.[90]

Bequests of this kind are indicative of a positive relationship between master or mistress and servant for servants were regularly remembered in wills. Money bequests are common, but not usually substantial. Rather bequests, though they did not constitute dowries, were of a practical nature for a young woman saving against the day she might marry and have a home of her own to furnish. Thus legacies of clothing, beds and bedding, chests, pots and pans are all commonplace.[91] Legacies of wool, cards, and spinning-wheels are also found.[92] More rarely, larger sums of money, as already noted, and even property are bequeathed by substantial testators to their servants. Thus Lady Joan Spenser left her *famula*, in addition to pots, a bed and bedding, and five marks in money, shops in Fossgate and 'Murtonlane'.[93] Perhaps this kind of evidence is ultimately a little misleading; the wealthy are obviously over-represented among the testamentary class. More immediately, it must be the case that relatively few servants can have benefited from the death of their employer during their time in service. But the fact that servants and even former servants are remembered in this way is surely a reflection of a master–servant relationship that was not purely exploitative, a

---

[90] YML, D/C Reg. 1, fo. 151; BIHR, Prob. Reg. 2, fo. 543ᵛ.

[91] e.g. YML, D/C Reg. 1, fo. 118ᵛ (de Bevelaco); BIHR, Prob. Reg. 2, fo. 121 (Kirk); 3, fo. 232ᵛ (Catour). Roper, writing of 16th–cent. Augsburg, has observed that household items, and beds in particular, were an essential part of what a woman brought by way of goods to a marriage: Roper, *The Holy Household*, 145.

[92] e.g. YML, D/C Reg. 1, fo. 275 (Overdo); BIHR, Prob. Reg. 2, fo. 91ᵛ (Chaffer).

[93] BIHR, Prob. Reg. 3, fo. 275ᵛ.

point that is emphasized by the frequency with which the two are linked by ties of kinship.

It should be remembered, moreover, that many employers were themselves former servants and as such not altogether unsympathetic to the wants and needs of the young people in their service. In later fourteenth-century Exeter, Kowaleski has found that masters acted as pledges for their servants and notes that they 'aided them in times of distress'.[94] It is in fact possible to detect a paternalistic tone in these relationships. John Bown showed real outrage when he discovered that his servant John Warryngton was having an affair with a fellow servant, Margaret Barker.[95] The welfare of female servants was the especial responsibility of the mistress of the household.[96] A Beverley woman, Agnes Hylyarde, even left money in her will to her mother's former servant Cecily, then resident in the town's Woodlane maison-dieu.[97] Agnes Grantham, whilst temporarily living away from her home, visited it regularly to see that all was well with her *familia*.[98] *Familia* of course included servants. Robert de Scurveton of York left 12*d.* to each servant 'de mea familia' at his death in 1427.[99] This *familia* can be noticed eating in common and servants were equal witnesses in such important household events as the contract of marriage.[100]

The negative side of this paternalism is the harsh and sometimes brutal way in which servants might be treated, especially by way of punishment. A Nottingham master argued in court that his servant Joan 'answered him back, and consequently the said John Lorymer took up a club and struck her on the head and elsewhere as is proper'.[101] London records do suggest that the courts were prepared to dissolve contracts of service where such punishment was considered excessive and Kowaleski, writing of late four-

---

[94] Kowaleski, 'Women's Work in a Market Town', 154.

[95] BIHR, CP. F. 127.

[96] 'How the Good Wijf', ed. Furnivall, ll. 102–4, p. 41; de Pisan, *The Treasure of the City of Ladies*, 167, 170–1; Power (trans.), *The Goodman of Paris*, 209.

[97] BIHR, Prob. Reg. 5, fo. 491.

[98] '. . . ad videndum familiam suam quam ibidem, habuit et bona ne aliquid incomodum seu detrimentum subirent vel paterentur': BIHR, CP. F. 36.

[99] BIHR, Prob. Reg. 2, fo. 521ᵛ.

[100] e.g. BIHR, CP. E. 121, 238.

[101] 'Sibi dedit contrariam responsionem et ideo ipse Johannes Lorymer cepit quendam *elenwand*, et ipsam percussit super capud et ubique, ut justum est': Stevenson (ed.), *Records of the Borough of Nottingham*, ii. 24–5.

teenth-century Exeter, notes that female servants often alleged physical abuse in order to have their contracts legally terminated.[102] This last must be understood in the context of the high demand for servant labour that characterized the labour-starved later fourteenth century. At other periods a girl might have found it harder to find a new place mid-term, as must have been true of servants whose employers died, and so more readily endured an unsatisfactory master. More serious abuses of servants were not unknown. A Southampton cordwainer and his wife were expelled from the town in 1482 for prostituting their *ancilla*.[103] Some masters exploited their servants sexually and even lived with them as their mistresses.[104] This is very occasionally apparent from testamentary provision as, for example, John Stranton's bequest of ten marks and some household goods to his servant Maud More and an additional ten marks 'to the child with which Maud is now pregnant'.[105] A further reflection of the negative side of relations between master and servant were the employers' allegations of theft by servants.[106] To conclude, however, that such relations were essentially antagonistic and exploitative would be to place undue weight on judicial evidence and exceptional cases, ironically the very material that is best documented.

How much time a servant might have free from duties and how that time was passed can only be a matter for surmise. Once again legal records might give the impression that male servants at least spent their time in alehouses or visiting brothels.[107] Certainly there is good evidence that a considerable amount of social drinking was indulged in and there is no reason to suppose that older female servants did not partake. Civic authorities seem, however, to have frowned upon many forms of recreation outside well-defined hours and regularly prosecuted taverns for remaining open after hours.[108] The authorities at Coventry ruled in 1452 that

[102] Kowaleski, 'Women's Work in a Market Town', 154; Thomas (ed.), *Calendar of Plea and Memoranda Rolls, 1364–81*, 107; id. (ed.), *Calendar of Plea and Memoranda Rolls, 1413–37*, 42.
[103] Anderson (ed.), *The Assize of Bread Book*, 16.
[104] Stevenson (ed.), *Records of the Borough of Nottingham*, iii. 375.
[105] 'Proli cum qua ipsa Matilda modo granda est': BIHR, Prob. Reg. 2, fo. 173. Stranton, a York draper, was a widower at the time of his death. Cf. Kussmaul, *Servants in Husbandry*, 44.
[106] Kowaleski, 'Women's Work in a Market Town', 154.
[107] Cf. Stevenson (ed.), *Records of the Borough of Nottingham*, ii. 330.
[108] See Ch. 3 above.

any servant 'ludens ad aliquem iocum illicitum, vel bettyng, diebus festivis' would be fined and sent to prison for three days.[109] More innocent Sunday recreation is indicated by a cause paper account of a 'pilgrimage' (*peregrinacio*) to Doncaster, the site of a Marian shrine, from York in which a merchant's servant, Elena Stokton, participated.[110] Agnes Nevill, servant to a widow of Coney Street in York, visited a neighbour's house one evening and passed the hours between nine and vespers talking and drinking with the neighbour's servants.[111] It is probably in this informal way that servants formed their own friendship networks, and exchanged information about their respective employers, and, in the case of older servants, conducted their courtships.[112]

This last is an important point because, in life-cycle terms, service can be seen in some ways as preparatory to marriage. In 1490 a shoemaker's wife of Lydd is recorded as having delivered her daughter Elizabeth Harman into service with a Romney man 'until such time as she should marry'.[113] The tendency of employers to bequeath household goods to their female servants has already been noted. Some masters left money specifically towards a girl's marriage. Thus James Lounesdale left 40*s.* for the marriage of Margaret, his servant, but there is no reason to believe that such was a common arrangement.[114] The degree to which a servant might save against such an event may have been limited. The primary return for service was bed and board, not dowry provision. Thus Thomas Neleson of York requested in his will that his servants be retained for six months after his death and be maintained as during his lifetime in food, drink, and other necessaries.[115] Thomas Terry, a canon of Wells, made similar provision in his will of 1409. His servants were to have, in addition to their year's wages, meat and drink for the month following his

---

[109] Harris (ed.), *Coventry Leet Book*, 271.

[110] BIHR, CP. F. 135 (1450); R. C. Finucane, *Miracles and Pilgrims: Popular Beliefs in Medieval England* (London, 1977), 196.

[111] BIHR, CP. E. 121 (1372).

[112] This is explored at greater length in Ch. 5.

[113] A. F. Butcher, 'The Origins of Romney Freemen 1433–1523', *Economic History Review*, 2nd ser. 27 (1974), 23.

[114] BIHR, Prob. Reg. 5, fo. 463ᵛ. Thomas Mayhoo of Chew Magna, Somerset, left a sum of money for the support of Joan Wreche, his servant, until she married and stipulated that she be kept in clothing: Weaver (ed.), *Somerset Medieval Wills*, i. 325.

[115] BIHR, Prob. Reg. 5, fo. 212ᵛ.

death 'so that in the meanwhile they may provide themselves with services'.[116] Where wages were given they do not appear to have been generous and the rates for females lagged well behind those paid to male servants. An analysis of 'excessive' annual wages paid to servants in Oxford in the period 1391–2 suggests a mean wage of 4*s*. 10*d*. for females (N = 6) as against 13*s*. 2*d*. for males (N = 24).[117] This may be compared with some Norwich lay subsidy evidence for Trowse, 1512–13, and a group of parishes comprising St Martin at Oak, St Mary and St Michael, Coslany, *c.*1515.[118] Female servants' wages for these two districts demonstrate an annual mean of 9*s*. (N = 12) and 7*s*. 10*d*. (N = 35) respectively. Male wages were about twice the female rate, but these are based on only very small samples since most male servants noted in this source are described as apprentices serving without wage. Only some half of the female servants listed, however, were waged.[119] Kussmaul, describing agricultural servants of the early modern era, has observed that younger female servants were often unpaid, merely maintained, and it is probable that this age-specific pattern was true of earlier periods.[120] Reference to the yearly wages of servants is found sometimes in wills, and an Ipswich man asked that his servant Margaret Coppyng be duly rewarded for her unpaid service during his illness over and above her regular wages.[121] A York cause of 1410 is unusual in distinguishing a couple of older female servants as *mercenaria* and, though it would be unwise to assume too much from this chance reference, it does imply that female servants at this date often worked purely for their food, lodging, and clothes.[122]

URBAN SERVANTHOOD:
OCCUPATIONAL STRUCTURE

The demand for, and the tasks carried out by, servants were to a considerable extent sex-specific. This can be deduced initially

---

[116] Weaver (ed.), *Somerset Medieval Wills*, i. 37.
[117] Salter (ed.), *Medieval Archives of the University of Oxford*, 13–97.
[118] NRO, NCR Case 7, shelf i.
[119] 54.5 and 53.0 per cent respectively.
[120] Kussmaul, *Servants in Husbandry*, 37.
[121] *Royal Commission on Historical Manuscripts, Ninth Report* (London, 1883), 229.
[122] BIHR, CP. F. 36.

from an analysis of the sexual composition of servant groups associated with particular occupations as derived from the later poll tax listings. These are tabulated in Table 4.5 alongside equivalent data for Coventry in 1523.[123] It would be unwise to place much weight on the absolute value of the observed sex ratios. Thus the Oxford ratios are consistently high through the failure to enumerate satisfactorily female servants, and the York figures may reflect a failure to designate male apprentices as servants. Similarly, some individual ratios appear aberrant as, to cite the most conspicuous instance, the very high service sex ratio identified for the mercantile trades at Wakefield. This last is based on only two households, where the recording of large numbers of male servants may have prejudiced the inclusion of females. Despite the limitations of the source material some surprisingly uniform patterns emerge. Female servants are most frequently found in victualling and mercantile trades and least frequently in the metal and leather trades. The demand for women servants in the textile and clothing trades falls somewhere between these extremes. This pattern may be related to the tasks performed by servants, although the evidence available is often slight. It must

TABLE 4.5. *Occupation-specific analysis of servant-keeping by (i) servant groups and (ii) sex ratios*

	1381						1379				1523	
	York		Oxford		Southwark		Pontefract		Lynn		Coventry	
(i)	a	b	a	b	a	b	a	b	a	b	a	b
Victuals	32.4	1.6	46.9	2.1	26.7	1.9	42.5	2.3	43.5	2.2	71.8	2.4
Leather	19.9	1.4	27.2	2.1	15.3	1.7	38.5	1.5	44.4	2.5	56.7	2.4
Textiles	17.3	1.1	26.5	1.9	9.8	*1.3*	20	2	15.8	2.2	60.8	2.9
Clothing	9.3	1.2	33.8	2.2	4.2	*1.3*	33.3	1.5	4.2	7	56.3	2.6
Mercantile	56.6	2.1	58.8	4.2	—	—	50	4	90.5	3.2	90.0	4.0
Metal	19.4	1.3	47.2	1.6	24		1.7		31.8	*1.1*	26.3	*1.8*	54.5	2.0
Building	6.8	*1.3*	21.2	1.8	—	—	—	—	28.6	2	23.7	1.2
Wood	13.8	1.3	15.4	*1*	13.0	2	22.2	2	—	—	47.8	1.5
Others	11.4	1.4	22.5	2.7	10.8	*1.8*	20	*1*	10	*1*	47.4	1.4

[123] The Coventry data are from Phythian-Adams, *Desolation of a City*, tables 18, 19, pp. 208, 210.

TABLE 4.5. (*Continued*)

(ii)	1381						1379				1523	
	York		Oxford		Southwark		Pontefract		Lynn		Coventry	
	c	d	c	d	c	d	c	d	c	d	c	d
Bakers	31	87.5	28	228.6	5	∞	4	*0*	5	*500*	18	72
Brewers	7	*0*	28	180	24	133.3	—	—	6	33.3	2	n.a.
Butchers	29	200	18	425	4	*75*	8	133.3	3	—	37	45.9
Hostillers	20	30	11	*14.3*	22	116.7	12	88	5	*0*	3	n.a.
Victuals	145	76.2	145	148.3	105	133.3	40	85.7	23	61.5	85	42.1
Cordwainers	46	0	41	280	34	150	10	*50*	7	*200*	4	n.a.
Tanners	44	133.3	17	∞	2	—	7	*300*	6	*200*	4	na
Leather	151	141.2	94	571.4	59	150	26	114.3	18	225	60	137.1
Dyers	18	100	6	*500*	3	*50*	5	*75*	2	*50*	26	82.9
Weavers	72	*300*	34	650	3	∞	16	*150*	10	*300*	23	75.0
Textiles	127	130	102	354.5	41	*150*	30	100	38	220	97	72.7
Tailors	73	*250*	50	200	45	∞	18	175	18	—	20	108.3
Clothing	97	266.7	74	194.7	72	*300*	24	140	24	133.3	87	92.3
Drapers	31	28	8	100	—	—	5	150	—	—	28	46.8
Mercers	39	92.6	3	*200*	—	—	1	*0*	†		28	64.6
Merchants	21	95.5	2	260	—	—	4	85.7	†		2	n.a.
Mercantile	113	64.6	17	162.5	1	—	12	100	21	61.3	60	56.1
Metal	139	288.9	36	285.7	25	900	22	*700*	19	*800*	55	50.0
Building	44	*100*	52	100	47	—	5	—	7	33.3	38	57.1
Wood	65	100	26	*50*	23	*500*	9	*300*	7	—	23	30.8
Others	70	57.1	40	150	37	*250*	10	*100*	10	*0*	19	62.5

Notes: a. Percentage of households with servants.

b. Mean size of servant groups.

c. Total households.

d. Service sex ratio.

Figures in *italics* relate to groups of less than ten servants.

An exclusively female servant population is indicated by '0', an exclusively male servant population by '∞'.

n.a. Not available.

† Mercers and merchants cannot be distinguished.

Sources: Phythian-Adams, *Desolation of a City*, tables 18–19, pp. 208–10; as Table II.1 below.

also be acknowledged that just as many female servants were engaged in non-productive households and there performed partly domestic functions, other female servants were not necessarily wholly involved in trade-specific activities, but probably combined these with household tasks to a greater or lesser degree.

TABLE 4.6. *Proportions of female servants engaged in various occupational categories from poll tax sources*

Occupational category	1379	1381	1379	1381	1381
	Lynn (N = 67)	York (N = 182)	Pontefract (N = 56)	Oxford (N = 147)	Southwark (N = 52)
Victuals	19.4	23.1	37.5	39.5	51.9
Leather	6.0	9.3	12.5	4.8	11.5
Textiles	7.5	5.5	10.7	7.5	3.8
Clothing	4.5	1.6	8.9	12.9	1.9
Mercantile	46.3	45	21.4	10.9	—
Metal	1.5	4.9	1.8	4.8	1.9
Building	4.5	1.1	—	6.8	—
Wood	—	3.3	1.8	2.0	1.9
Transport	6.0	0.5	—	0.7	5.8
Armaments	—	1.6	3.6	0.7	—
Chandlers	3.0	—	—	4.8	1.9
Others	1.5	3.8	1.8	5.4	19.2*

* Includes eight servants employed in the stews.
Sources: As Table II.1 below.

It is likewise noteworthy that the pattern of trade and craft activities regularly performed by female servants does not necessarily correspond to that found for independent female traders.[124] In part this follows from the fact that only a minority of female traders engaged servants, but it is also a reflection of the somewhat marginalized nature of independent female economic activity. The actual proportions of female servants employed in various economically active households by occupational category is shown in Table 4.6. The mercantile and victualling trades account for over half of these servants in all the five towns analysed. The textiles and leather categories account for only modest proportions, and for Oxford and Pontefract alone do the proportions associated with the clothing trades appear statistically significant. Proportions in all other categories are consistently very small.

Within the victualling trades female servants are conspicuous in the households associated with inns and hostelries, where they functioned as chambermaids and tapsters. Thus tapsters are

[124] See Table 3.3 above.

specifically noted among the female servants employed by the York brewsters Katherine Lakensnyder and Agnes Grantham.[125] Likewise a London record of 1372 relates to one Emma atte Grene who was engaged as a servant to Robert Bryan to sell barrels of ale for him.[126] Female servants are frequently associated with bakers' households and it is likely that they were active in the preparation of bread in addition to assisting in the shop. A late Beverley record indicates that bakers' servants might also purchase grain in the market for their masters' business.[127] Butchers seem to have employed female servants on a less regular basis. It is unlikely that girls were much involved in butchering as such, but may have assisted in cleaning and preparing carcases and in the manufacture of black puddings and other meat products.[128] The traditional involvement of women in brewing and fishmongering is also reflected in the low sex ratios associated with servant groups in these occupations. In Nottingham in 1360 there is record of an *ancilla* who was employed to make mustard using querns supplied by her master.[129] Female servants are likewise found in number in the households of spicers and grocers, overlapping terms that tend to describe specialist traders dealing mostly in costly imported goods. In these wealthier households numbers of female servants may have been engaged as an outward sign of prosperity and status, but they may have been actively employed as assistants in the shop.

This last observation must equally apply to households of persons engaged in the mercantile trades. It is not possible to fully distinguish between the trades of draper, mercer, and merchant for although the merchant may be primarily associated with overseas trade he was often active also in the retail trade. The mercer and the draper traded principally in cloth, but the merchant might also, and all are found buying and dealing in cloth on a regional basis. Chapmen are likewise often indistinguishable from merchants. Drapers must often have engaged girls as seam-

---

[125] Bartlett (ed.), *Lay Poll Tax Returns for the City of York*, 40; BIHR, CP. F. 36.

[126] Thomas (ed.), *Calendar of Plea and Memoranda Rolls, 1364–81*, 145–6.

[127] Leach (ed.), *Beverley Town Documents*, 39.

[128] Robert Shawe, a York butcher directed that his male servant Thomas 'assist his widow in respect of the animals': BIHR, Prob. Reg. 4, fo. 261.

[129] Stevenson (ed.), *Records of the Borough of Nottingham*, i. 174.

stresses. The ordinances of the drapers at Beverley for 1493 specifically directed that members employing servants engaged in needlecraft should contribute to the tailors' gild.[130] In a particularly informative York cause of the early fifteenth century the actual deposition of one Joan Scharp, servant to the Petergate merchant Robert Lascels, survives.[131] She describes how she was in her master's shop when a purchase of candlewick was made. She assisted (*interfuit*) in weighing the item and relates how a fellow servant, Alice Bawmburgh, helped carry the material to the customer's home. Later Joan was sent by her master to demand payment from the customer. These must have been routine activities for the many servants like Joan, but, as so often with the mundane and everyday, it is purely by chance that it is reported and recorded.

Although many women engaged in the clothing trades as sempsters and shepsters or dressmakers, the numbers of households in this sector employing servants of either sex tended to be few. London records contain reference to a number of girls apprenticed to embroiderers, or 'broudsters', who were usually married women. These girls came from as far away as Northumberland and it must be assumed that this was work of the very highest quality demanding a long apprenticeship, which was in itself unusual for females, and, as a livelihood, potentially lucrative.[132] In York one Isabella Wakefeld is likewise described as apprentice to the sempstress, Christine de Knarisburgh.[133] London similarly attracted girls into apprenticeships with silk-women and silk throwsters.[134] A very few silkwomen are noted in York records and it is possible that some had been apprenticed in London, but it would seem that the English silk industry lagged far behind such continental centres as Cologne, Paris, Lyons, or even Seville

---

[130] Leach (ed.), *Beverley Town Documents*, 100.

[131] Robert Lascels was admitted to the franchise as a chapman in 1417–18: Collins (ed.), *Register of the Freemen of the City of York*, i. 126; BIHR, CP. F. 174 (1430).

[132] Thomas (ed.), *Calendar of Plea and Memoranda Rolls, 1364–81*, 37, 107; id. (ed.), *Calendar of Plea and Memoranda Rolls, 1381–1412*, 240; id. (ed.), *Calendar of Plea and Memoranda Rolls, 1413–37*, 42, 146, 176.

[133] BIHR, CP. F. 22 (1402).

[134] Thomas (ed.), *Calendar of Plea and Memoranda Rolls, 1413–37*, 71, 162, 166, 227; Jones (ed.), *Calendar of Plea and Memoranda Rolls, 1437–57*, 88; Dale, 'The London Silkwomen'.

where the demand for female labour, particularly servant labour, was considerable.[135] With changing fashions, by the later fifteenth century women servants were employed to knit caps, this being another craft in which women found work in their own right. This is implicit, for example, in the very full ordinances of the cappers at Oxford dated 1499.[136]

As with the clothing trades, the very considerable involvement of women in the textiles industry is not reflected in the service sector. Few spinsters, carders, or even women weavers, relatively numerous in the 1379 West Riding returns, employed servants. Weavers generally did sometimes engage girls as assistants to help operate the loom.[137] Female servants are, however, prominent in the households of dyers. Girls were employed to wash and prepare cloth for the dying process and in a York cause dated 1411 the servants of one Usburn, probably John Usburn who employed two female servants at his death in 1428, are described cleaning cloth by the banks of the River Ouse.[138] As a commonly cited Lincoln ordinance indicates, female servants were also engaged by fullers or walkers, but poll tax evidence suggests they were outnumbered by male assistants.[139]

Few female servants are found within the metal trades, although girls were not infrequently engaged by goldsmiths. Women were frequently involved in working gold and on the Continent gold-spinning was exclusively a female occupation.[140] Female assistants can also be found in Oxford as ironmongers and in some of the basic iron-working occupations as in York as marshals. Testamentary evidence suggests that female servants were also engaged by pewterers, whose craft was established in such centres as London and York only from the later fourteenth century and thus hardly features in the poll tax. Davis cites the example of one female

[135] M. Pia, 'The Industrial Position of Women in the Middle Ages', *Catholic History Review*, NS 4 (1925), 559; M. Wensky, 'Women's Guilds in Cologne in the later Middle Ages', *Journal of European Economic History*, 11, (1982), 639–50; E. Dixon, 'Craftswomen of the Livre des Métiers', *Economic Journal*, 5 (1895), 209–28; Davis, 'Women in the Crafts', 56; M. E. Perry, '"Lost Women" in Early Modern Seville: The Politics of Prostitution', *Feminist Studies*, 4 (1978), 196, 202.

[136] Salter (ed.), *Munimenta Civitatis Oxonie*, 235.

[137] Swanson, 'Craftsmen and Industry', 42.

[138] BIHR, CP. F. 61; Prob. Reg. 2, fo. 533ᵛ.

[139] Smith (ed.), *English Gilds*, 182–3.

[140] Wensky, 'Women's Guilds in Cologne', 635.

servant so employed in sixteenth-century Lyons. She helped prepare alloys and also fetched merchandise.[141] There is little reason
to doubt that this was not also true of late medieval England. A
few female servants may also be observed in the armourer's and
potter's or founder's craft. The early fourteenth-century bellfoun-
der's window in the north nave aisle of York Minster is indeed
supposed to depict such female assistants actively engaged in the
production process, but from their appearance they are more
likely to be male.

Very few women appear to have found employment in the
major leather trades and this is especially true of servants. A few
girls were employed by skinners, as in Pontefract, but perhaps
primarily as sempsters to stitch furs together to produce garments.
A London mercer was presented in 1365 with enticing away a
skinner's servant girl and it may be that both desired her labour
as a needlewoman.[142] Cordwainers, so far as servants are found
within their households, often employed female servants and again
it is probable that these girls sewed the shoe-leather as cut by their
masters. Female servants appear more common in woodworking
and building crafts, presumably as general assistants, though there
is some Norwich evidence that women sometimes traded in timber
and it may follow that some servants assisted their masters in the
purchase of materials.[143] Chandlers also, as at Oxford, frequently
employed female servants in a trade that traditionally enjoyed a
high female participation rate.

This brief survey demonstrates that service cannot be dismissed
as a purely domestic and non-economic function, a form of
disguised unemployment. It is true that the range of tasks performed by female servants in trade households tended to centre
around traditionally 'feminine' skills, that is needlecraft, brewing,
baking, and the preparation of foods, washing clothes, and dealing
in the market place or shop, but by her very presence in such
households a girl or young woman might still familiarize herself
with a range of trade and commercial skills.[144] It is, however,

---

[141] Davis, 'Women in the Crafts', 52.

[142] Thomas (ed.), *Calendar of Plea and Memoranda Rolls, 1364–81*, 30; Veale,
The English Fur Trade, 100.

[143] NRO, NCR Case 18, shelf a (book of accounts 1384–1448), fos. 124, 127^v,
128, 164, 210^v.

[144] Cf. Davis, 'Women in the Crafts', 52; Jacobsen, 'Women's Work', 3–4.

likely that most girls were also required to fulfil some domestic functions. This is seen from cause paper evidence. A female servant is observed in a cause of 1410 fetching food and drink for a visitor and also bringing and lighting candles. Another girl was responsible for carrying a jug of water from the River Ouse to her master's house each day.[145] Servants might also accompany their masters outside the house.[146] When in 1330 Robert de Morewode of Nottingham failed to have water delivered by the waterleader he had contracted, he sent his servant Alice to complain.[147] Outside the trade sector, service must have been more exclusively a matter of housekeeping. This is reflected in the generally low sex ratios associated with such households and particularly the households of widows, although it would be unwise to presume that no such households were engaged in trade. Among the servants remembered in the will of Lady Marjory Salvayn, for example, should be noted Elizabeth 'that wates of me' and Elizabeth 'that is my coke'.[148]

CHANGING PATTERNS OF URBAN SERVICE, 1380–1500

The foregoing analysis has drawn heavily upon poll tax data and the picture that emerges is as a consequence rather static. It is thus unfortunate that between the last poll tax of 1381 and the Coventry enumeration of 1523 no comparable detailed nominative listing is known to exist. It becomes necessary to rely instead upon rather less substantial sources that nevertheless allow for some quantitative analysis. Servants are regularly noted in wills either as individuals or as groups and it is often possible to reconstruct from this source servant groups associated with particular households, and so their sexual composition. Servant-keeping households are probably well represented within the testamentary population as a whole and it follows that the non-inclusion of servants in wills is no evidence for their absence from the household. The regularity with which servants are noted must,

---

145 BIHR, CP. E. 159; CP. F. 36.
146 BIHR, CP. F. 155.
147 Stevenson (ed.), *Records of the Borough of Nottingham*, i. 114.
148 BIHR, Prob. Reg. 5, fo. 480.

therefore, be partly a matter of chance. Indeed there is evidence that though servants are sometimes included in wills, they appear only as individual names and are not specifically designated. The relatively high proportion of wills of persons in mercantile trades naming servants is as much a reflection of their greater wealth as of their propensity to maintain servants. A high proportion of female testators also name servants and this accords with a characteristically female pattern of making large numbers of specific bequests to individuals known to the testator.

It is possible that even where servants are noted, not all those actually employed at the time of making the will are mentioned. Certainly some wills refer, in addition to one or more named individuals, to an unspecified number of 'other' servants. The glazier Thomas Sharley, d. 1458, to give but one example, left 3*s*. 4*d*. to each of his two named *famuli* and 2*s*. to each of his other servants.[149] Neither their sex nor their number can be known. An analysis of the size and sexual composition of servant groups associated with particular occupational categories does not, however, indicate any obvious level of underenumeration or bias in the way servants are recorded. It is possible that larger servant groups are disproportionately represented, but this need not detract from the validity of the data. The mean sizes of servant groups derived from wills by occupational category are given in Table 4.7. The equivalent measures derived from the poll tax of 1381 almost certainly understate the true sizes of these groups as comparison with tax data elsewhere would suggest.[150] In part this must be due also to the exclusion of under-age servants from the assessment.

By calculating service sex ratios associated with different occupational categories it is possible to derive from wills some measure of secular change. It must be acknowledged that there are still certain difficulties in this method. The number of wills naming servants within any given occupation or period is often small and sometimes tiny. This analysis is thus necessarily limited to six major occupational categories over four broad, but unequal time periods: 1380–1414, 1415–44, 1445–69, and 1470–1500. The numbers of wills registered after *c.*1500 rises sharply and it would thus

---

[149] BIHR, Prob. Reg. 2, fo. 380ᵛ.
[150] See Table 4.5.

TABLE 4.7. *Analysis of named servants by occupational categories from poll tax (1381) and testamentary sources in respect of (i) servant groups and (ii) service sex ratios (SSR)*

	Poll tax	Wills*			
	1381	1380–1414	1415–44	1445–69	1470–1500
(i) Servant groups					
Victuals	1.6	1.9	2.2	1.3	2
N =	47	11	17	9	13
Leather	1.4	1.8	1.9	1.8	2
N =	30	12	17	8	3
Textiles	1.1	1.9	1.6	2.7	1.4
N =	22	10	6	10	10
Clothing	1.2	1.7	>1**	>1.2**	1.7
N =	9	3	6	5	7
Mercantile	2.1	2.7	2.9	1.5	2.1
N =	64	33	25	11	14
Metal	1.3	1.7	1.2	1.8	2.4
N =	27	10	9	13	9
(ii) SSR					
Victuals	76.2	110	76.2	50	136.4
Leather	141.2	340	255.6	100	500
Textiles	130	375	60	433.3	100
Clothing	266.7	66.7	<133.3**	<133.3**	140
Mercantile	64.6	144.4	84.6	70	30.4
Metal	288.9	183.3	120	187.5	450
All trades	95.1	162.9	<107.1	<161.0	104.4
Total of servants	355	184	203+	107+	139

Note: N represents numbers of households or wills with named servants.

* The Exchequer Court register is deficient for 1409–25, and 1470.

** Small clothing samples for 1415–44 and 1445–69 are augmented by inclusion of one servant group containing an unspecified number of female servants.

Sources: Bartlett (ed.), *Lay Poll Tax Returns for the City of York*; BIHR, Prob. Reg. 1–5; YML, D/C Reg. 1–2.

be a very substantial task to extend this analysis into the sixteenth century. There are some serious breaks in the main Exchequer Court sequence of wills before 1500 due to the ravages of time. No Exchequer wills survive before the end of 1389 and there are long gaps between 1408 and 1426.

The range of occupations represented in the wills demonstrates a certain bias and, in some instances, compares less than favourably with the occupational structure derived from the more substantial 1381 poll tax. This observation does much to explain the more marked differences in sex ratios from the poll tax and from wills drawn from the period 1380–1414 as shown in Table 4.7. Thus the paucity of drapers (poll tax 1381, SSR = 28) within the will sample noting servants by name tends to inflate mercantile sex ratios. Likewise, the victualling trades' ratio reflects the relative absence of hostillers (poll tax 1381, SSR = 30) within the sample. The comparatively low poll tax ratio calculated for the textile trades follows from the large number of servants associated with dyers (poll tax 1381, SSR = 100) that are not similarly represented within the will sample.[151] It may be noted that girdlers and spurriers, both demonstrating high service sex ratios within the poll tax population, are hardly represented among testators associated with the metal trades. Saddlers are also largely absent from those leather-workers naming servants in their wills, but this does not seem to influence the high observed service sex ratio. Poll tax service sex ratios may, moreover, be depressed by a failure to record fully male apprentices as servants.

The pattern of service sex ratios demonstrated in 1381 may, nevertheless, be indicative of real trends. It suggests, allowing for the differences in the occupations observed from the two sources, a pattern more like that noticed nearly a century later, i.e. of relatively feminised mercantile and victualling households, but masculinized artisan households. More worrying is the possibility that the population represented by testators itself varied over time and was not, as a consequence, representative of the servant-keeping population at large. Wills were invariably made within a short time of the testator's death.[152] They can, therefore, only represent the composition of the servant group at the end of the head of household's career. This group, it could be argued, would not be representative of servant groups generally. Equally it may be unsafe to compare periods of high epidemic mortality, when a high proportion of testators would have died mid-career, with

---

[151] Dyers account for 14.2 per cent of individuals engaged in textile trades within the poll tax population, but for 75 per cent of servants within the same category.
[152] Goldberg, 'Mortality and Economic Change', 40 and n. 8.

other periods where the population would be older and perhaps have curtailed their trade activities. Certainly the size of servant groups must have fluctuated during the course of an employer's career, but perhaps the greatest change would have been towards the beginning, not the end of that career.

Only in a couple of instances can the size of the servant group as recorded in a will be compared against the equivalent 1377 poll tax measure. In the case of John de Scheffeld, skinner, the servant group remained at four when he made his will seventeen years later. In the case of the apothecary Constantine del Dame, it had grown from three to more than four by the time of his will in 1398, i.e. more than twenty years later.[153] This does not suggest dramatic changes, especially as very young servants will not be recorded in the poll tax, but clearly little weight can be placed on just two cases. There is, however, much evidence to suggest that testators were still nominally in charge of active economic concerns: apprentices still had terms to run; shops were still full of stock and tools; sons or even widows are ready to take over the business. It would probably be mistaken, therefore, to conclude that it is the supposedly shrunken servant groups of semi-retired householders that are here represented. Each of the four periods analysed contains, moreover, several years of epidemic mortality, so there is little cause to suspect great differences in the ages of testators between periods.[154] On balance, the most serious limitation of the source is the unsatisfactory size of the samples obtained in several instances. With such small numbers it needs only one or two atypical servant groups within a given sample to distort the order and even direction of the resultant sex ratio. It follows that only relatively large variations in sex ratios between periods can be regarded as evidence for secular change and of the direction of that change.

The sex ratios calculated, as shown in Table 4.7, do indeed demonstrate considerable variation. The pattern of variation is not, however, consistent over time between occupational categories. The mercantile trades show a continuous feminization from the late fourteenth century until the end of our period. Since these

[153] Leggett (ed.), 'The 1377 Poll Tax Returns for the City of York', 132, 137; BIHR, Prob. Reg. 1, fo. 87; 3, fo. 4ᵛ.
[154] Goldberg, 'Mortality and Economic Change'.

trades already accounted for 45 per cent of female servants engaged in economic activity according to the 1381 poll tax, this observation seems particularly significant.[155] The victualling and leather trades both see a diminution in service sex ratios up to the final testamentary period, although the poll tax material suggests that these ratios may have been moving upwards prior to the fifteenth century and the leather measure for this final period is not derived from a statistically significant sample. The proportion of leather-workers' wills noting servants declined steadily from over 66 to under 15 per cent over the period. It is difficult to assess the significance of this even allowing for the decline in the industry suggested by a relative fall in the number of such workers admitted to the franchise. Service sex ratios in the metal trades show a fall over the later fourteenth and first few decades of the fifteenth century, but this is followed by a steady rise over the remaining period. This last is perhaps rather more significant than the apparent earlier fall, which is based upon a number of unusually small servant groups.

In these three last occupational categories discussed there thus appears a reaction against the employment of female servants in the later years of the fifteenth century following a period of feminization dating from at least the end of the fourteenth century. It is difficult to reach any conclusion in respect of the clothing trades since neither the poll tax nor the testamentary data suggest that servants were employed in any number within this sector within late medieval York. The considerable fluctuations in recorded service sex ratios for the textile trades are no easier to explain, though they cannot be the simple product of small samples. Sex ratios here appear, after an initial upwards trend, to fall dramatically between 1380–1414 and 1415–44 only to rise again steeply by 1445–69 and again seeming to fall back in the last decades of the century. The observed ratios are complicated by the differing composition of crafts represented in the testamentary sample for each period, but the general trend is upheld until the final period where, so far as the evidence allows, there is a divergent pattern between the weaving crafts (weavers and tapiters), which show a continuing upward trend, and the fullers and dyers, which are highly feminised. Textile manufacture at York

[155] See Table 4.6.

was closely tied to an overseas market and may thus have been the city's most volatile industry.[156] The export trade in woollen cloth does not seem to have been too depressed in the earlier part of the fifteenth century and the employment of female weavers' assistants at this date may be related to a growing scarcity of labour, but perhaps also served to reduce labour costs so as to keep the finished product competitive. But as markets contracted from mid-century, so employment opportunities contracted and female workers appear to have been penalized. The weavers of Coventry ruled against the employment of women servants as early as 1453 and the craft gilds at Bristol, Hull, and Norwich followed suit later the same or early the following century.[157]

The implications of these observations will be more fully discussed in the concluding chapter, but a few general observations are appropriate here. Service sex ratios as generated from testamentary sources do suggest that by the late fifteenth century, and by the mid-fifteenth century in the case of the more vulnerable weavers' craft, female servants were being excluded from all skilled artisan craft activity. This chronology coincides with the considerable body of evidence for economic recession within the city apparent from the earlier fifteenth century, but not acute until the middle of that century. In the earlier stages of that recession, however, testamentary evidence suggests that service sex ratios fell as female servants were increasingly employed in all economic sectors so as to compensate for any shortfall in the supply of male labour and at the same time to minimize labour costs and so offset the first effects of recession. Within the commercial centre as represented by the mercantile trades a different pattern emerges. Here servant sex ratios continued to fall throughout the fifteenth century such that by the end of that century this sector was sufficiently feminised as to influence the modest mean sex ratio derived for the sample as a whole. There was thus a polarization in the gender of service between the highly feminised servant groups of the generally more prosperous mercantile households and the predominantly masculine servant groups associated with

---

[156] See Ch. 2 above.
[157] Phythian-Adams, *Desolation of a City*, 87–8; F. B. Bickley (ed.), *The Little Red Book of Bristol* (2 vols.; Bristol, 1900), i. 127; M. D. Lambert, *Two Thousand Years of Gild Life* (Hull, 1891), 206; Hudson and Tingey (eds.), *Records of the City of Norwich*, ii. 378.

skilled artisan households. In this context female service may have come to be linked with unskilled, non-industrial or domestic functions and the advertisement of wealth and status.

It is unfortunate that our study does not allow us to examine the pattern of service sex ratios into the sixteenth century for it may be that the feminization of service became more general as the status of service was undermined. Wiesner has observed such a process in early modern Nuremberg as wealthy households demanded ever increasing numbers of female servants through the sixteenth century.[158] A relatively low service sex ratio of 77.8 can be associated with the Pooterie quarter of Ypres in 1506 and female servants outnumbered males by nearly two to one in Coventry in 1523 (a service sex ratio of only 53.0). This last may be atypical owing to the state of accelerated recession that afflicted the city in the early sixteenth century.[159] As service became more feminised, the social status of female servants may have been eroded. It appears significant that later fifteenth-century York wills frequently fail to distinguish female servants by name, but refer merely to 'women servants'. Thomas Nelson, d. 1490, to cite one example, left 3*s*. 4*d*. to 'cuilibet mulieri servienti sue'.[160]

It may be unwise to put too much weight on such subjective evidence for the diminished status of female servants, but it accords with other observations. More telling is Brodsky's account of the London marriage market in the period 1598–1619. Using data biased towards higher-status groups she found 73 per cent of London-born girls marrying by licence were living at home at the time of their marriage. In contrast she found of a group of migrant females who entered service out of economic necessity 'that entry into apparently low status female occupation' led, regardless of social origin, to 'downward social mobility'.[161] This would suggest that by this late period service had become so socially polarized that the daughters of the social élite remained at home until marriage. The limited number of wills associated with York servants would tend to support such a hypothesis for the later fifteenth century. Houlbrooke's study of the early modern family

[158] Wiesner, *Working Women in Renaissance Germany*, 92.
[159] Calculated from Pirenne, 'Les Dénombrements de la population d'Ypres', 15; Phythian-Adams, *Desolation of a City*, 33–67, 204–20; Table 4.4 above.
[160] BIHR, Prob. Reg. 5, fo. 381.
[161] Brodsky, 'Single Women in the London Marriage Market', 90–9.

provides some evidence for a progressive feminization of service between the fifteenth and seventeenth centuries, a decline in the status of service, such that servants were increasingly differentiated and segregated from the children of their employers, and a reluctance on the part of the upper classes to send their children into other households as servants.[162] The feminization of service was, however, largely an urban phenomenon and the reverse may have been true of the countryside, especially in arable regions. Evidence from parish listings dated between 1599 and 1831 suggests that before the later eighteenth century daughters were more likely to remain at home than were their brothers.[163] Presumably by the latter date towns were beginning to exert such a marked pull on young female domestics that daughters were lost from the natal home more frequently than sons.[164]

---

[162] R. A. Houlbrooke, *The English Family, 1450–1700* (London, 1984), 172–3, 176–7; P. Earle, 'The Female Labour Market in London in the Late Seventeenth and Early Eighteenth Centuries', *Economic History Review*, 2nd ser. 42 (1989), 344.

[163] R. Wall, 'Leaving Home and the Process of Household Formation in Pre-Industrial England', *Continuity and Change*, 2 (1987), 92–7.

[164] Cf. K. D. M. Snell, *Annals of the Labouring Poor: Social Change and Agrarian England, 1660–1900* (Cambridge, 1985), 38, 59. Alternatively there may have been a decline in demand for male farm servants: Wall, 'Leaving Home', 94.

5

Marriage in Town and Country

The question that underlies this study is the degree to which women were dependent upon marriage or were able to support themselves outside marriage. The institution itself may be studied from a variety of perspectives, be they social, legal, economic, demographic, dynastic, or even anthropological. But despite this range of approaches the literature concerning matrimony in later medieval England is still comparatively slender and the differences of interpretation remain fundamental. The implications of our initial question, moreover, have gone unconsidered, yet the status of women, their freedom to conduct courtship relationships and to choose marriage partners is clearly central to marriage formation. This present chapter allows such considerations to form the focus of our interpretation, which depends upon sources that have not hitherto been adequately appreciated. The deposition records of the York ecclesiastical court are especially valuable since they allow two independent forms of analysis, providing an insight on the one hand into the social context of marriage and on the other, by exploiting rare statistical data, the demography of marriage. In reality these are two sides of the same coin because the prevailing marriage regime influences and is influenced by wider social attitudes. The evidence also allows urban and rural experiences to be compared, since both rural and urban deposition material survives in some quantity from the early years of the fourteenth century. The analysis' here attempts to identify the marriage regime, to reconstruct patterns of marriage, and to understand these in the context of changes in the economic status of women in both town and country during the later Middle Ages. It is not our purpose to make a definitive assessment; it is unlikely that the evidence will support any such statement, but it is possible here to contribute to the debate concerning marriage in late medieval England and the possible origins of the 'European marriage pattern'.

THE DEBATE ON MARRIAGE:
MEDIEVAL OR NORTH-WESTERN?

Hajnal's pioneering study of the 'European Marriage Pattern' placed medieval England in the non-European fold.[1] His use of Northumberland poll tax data for 1377 to support this thesis has since been questioned, but the implicit conclusion that a late, companionate marriage regime is a feature of modern Western society has persisted.[2] The work of Wrigley and Schofield in their monumental reconstruction of the demographic history of England from parish register evidence has only served to push the *terminus post quem* for a European marriage regime back to 1541.[3] For those who believe that medieval English society was somehow different from the 'early modern' society that emerged out of it, then this finding is significant; the transition from medieval to early modern, for the Marxist historian, the transition from 'feudal' to 'capitalist' modes of production, may be paralleled by a transition from a 'medieval' early and universal marriage regime to a modern 'European' marriage regime. The actual demography of marriage is just one element within this debate, but it is the issue that is addressed at length in the present chapter.

The most substantial discussions of the demography of marriage in the period before 1400 based on English sources are those contained in the published work of Razi and Smith. These scholars have suggested sharply contrasting views.[4] Razi uses court roll data from the manor of Halesowen in Worcestershire, which, though it included the small town of Halesowen itself, was essentially rural in character.[5] Most of his analysis, moreover, is necessarily concerned with bond rather than free tenants. Smith's data are derived from a rather wider range of sources, but these

---

[1] Hajnal, 'European Marriage Patterns in Perspective', in Glass and Eversley (eds.), *Population in History*, 101–43.

[2] For criticism of the Northumberland poll tax see Smith, 'Hypothèses sur la nuptialité', 109–19.

[3] Wrigley and Schofield, *The Population History of England*.

[4] Razi, *Life, Marriage and Death*; Smith, 'Some Reflections on the Evidence for the Origins of the "European Marriage Pattern"', 74–112; id., 'Hypothèses sur la nuptialité'.

[5] The borough of Halesowen had its own court, the records of which also survive but do not form part of Razi's analysis.

are still exclusively rural and are focused on the period before the end of the fourteenth century. The present chapter, by drawing mostly upon sources for the later fourteenth and fifteenth centuries for both rural and urban communities, thus represents a new departure. It also provides a link with the more substantially documented early modern period and especially Phythian-Adams's exemplary reconstruction of early sixteenth-century Coventry.[6] Before considering this new evidence, however, it is useful to review the work just cited, particularly that of Razi, which apparently suggests a pattern dissimilar from that indicated by the evidence to be considered here.

Razi exploits genealogical data from a remarkably complete sequence of manorial court rolls and uses these to generate ages of individuals on the basis of a number of assumptions. He shows that there was no necessary link between the marriage of sons and paternal mortality, but nevertheless ties marriage to acquisition of land by sons which he times with the minimum legal age for holding land at 20 years. This can, however, hardly be demonstrated and unless land transfer were an integral part of a system of marriage formation, itself suggestive of arranged marriages, it seems unlikely that such events should coincide so closely. The sociology of marriage formation is, moreover, outside the scope of Razi's analysis, limited as it is to the 'accidentals' of the demography. Razi in fact appears to argue that marriage and the rearing of a family were essential aspects of landholding.[7] This view takes no account of the possible role of servants, whose position in Halesowen society is largely ignored in Razi's monograph, and of the hired labour of the landless and near landless.[8] Still more questionable is his assertion that since tenants appeared in the rolls on average 'at least once in three years', then a tenant would first be observed as a landholder between the ages of 20 and 23 years. This repeats the unsubstantiated claim that men acquired land as soon as they achieved their majority, but also implies that tenants were recorded with sufficient regularity as to allow dating within a range of only three years.

It is, nevertheless, implicit in Razi's discussion of his material

---

[6] Phythian-Adams, *Desolation of a City*.

[7] Razi, *Life, Marriage and Death*, 54, 60–1.

[8] For Razi's earlier recognition of rural servants see Smith, 'Hypothèses sur la nuptialité', 129 and n. 62.

that some male tenants appeared in court much more frequently than others, there being some correlation between wealth and frequency of appearance. Indeed he admits that some names appear 'only once or twice', but 'some as many as two or three hundred times'.[9] This is surely no basis from which to generate precise assumptions respecting the regularity with which individuals are noted in the court rolls. It further ignores the possibility that numbers of landless villeins, notably the younger sons of poorer tenants, may never have appeared in the court rolls at all. This may be a very significant observation in the light of Razi's own brief acknowledgement that, 'land shortage and low wages forced a certain number of young adults born to middling and especially to poor families to postpone their marriages, and some of them probably never married at all'.[10] Like criticism applies to his attempt to locate age at marriage retrospectively from the subsequent appearance of landholding sons. If seventeen to twenty-three years after the father is first observed holding land a son is similarly noticed for the first time, then the father can, he reasons, be assumed to have married at about 20. Table 5.1 illustrates the actual range of possibilities. The table shows that, even if Razi's method were sound, marriage at age 20 appears not as a norm, but only as the minimum of a range of possibilities extending up to 26 years.

Clearly this analysis makes no allowance for the interval that might be expected between matrimony and any subsequent male first birth. Even were the table opposite to represent the actual balance of possibilities, and Razi gives no indication of the observed distribution, making minimal allowance for the interval between matrimony and first birth, then the mean age at marriage would be still only about 21. But in reality the data base is much less amenable to statistical manipulation. It may be correct that males quite regularly entered into land soon after their majority, though this argument is unsubstantiated, but it is less likely that, save in the instance of the wealthiest and most litigious tenants, this event can be dated as closely as Razi allows. The true distribution of age data in Table 5.1 should, therefore, include a wider range of older male children.

[9] Razi, *Life, Marriage and Death*, 15.
[10] Ibid. 64. Razi would perhaps argue that this group was not very large.

TABLE 5.1. *Calculated age at first marriage from Razi's estimates*

Father's age	Years between first observation of father and of son							Son's age
	17	18	19	20	21	22	23	
20	—	—	—	20	21	22	23	20
	—	—	—	—	20	21	22	21
	—	—	—	—	—	20	21	22
	—	—	—	—	—	—	20	23
21	—	—	20	21	22	23	24	20
	—	—	—	20	21	22	23	21
	—	—	—	—	20	21	22	22
	—	—	—	—	—	20	21	23
22	—	20	21	22	23	24	25	20
	—	—	20	21	22	23	24	21
	—	—	—	20	21	22	23	22
	—	—	—	—	20	21	22	23
23	20	21	22	23	24	25	26	20
	—	20	21	22	23	24	25	21
	—	—	20	21	22	23	24	22
	—	—	—	20	21	22	23	23

Razi's approach is limited, moreover, to those families where a son can be identified some seventeen to twenty-three years after the father's first observation as a landholder, the son being assumed to be a first child.[11] If the eldest observed son is only noticed some twenty-four or more years after the father, then Razi concludes that there were other children born earlier, but dying before they reached maturity. But equally these might represent the first sons of later marrying fathers. Only 32 of some 261 sons observed in the period 1350–1400 can be shown from similar genealogical techniques to have married at about 20 years.[12] Similar criticism must apply to the age data derived in respect of the marriages of daughters. The actual date of marriage can reasonably be known from the enrolled record of merchet payment; the underlying assumption is that the daughter was born

[11] Ibid. 61.
[12] Ibid. 136.

subsequent to, or at least not significantly before the father's first appearance. Razi is able to cite a small number of specific instances suggestive of an early age at marriage for both sexes and even argues that the mean age at first marriage for women actually fell in the years immediately following the Black Death. He notes that, according to his methodology, some 15 of 119 daughters observed (12.6 per cent) married between 12 and 19 years in the period 1350–1400.[13]

It is quite possible that Razi has indeed succeeded in identifying a number of instances of early marriage, but, without evidence that these marriages represent the norm, this in itself is scarcely proof of a non-European or 'medieval' marriage regime. The methods adopted, moreover, seem constructed to identify only such marriages as are apparently, if not always in fact, early. The evidence is at best limited to the marriages of oldest sons of landholding fathers and to daughters who pay a marriage fine. It is thus limited to those very groups who, for reasons of inheritance, may have been most likely to have suffered parental constraint in their choice of marriage partner and would thus, as the Yorkshire deposition evidence will suggest, have married earlier than their younger brothers or less prosperous cousins. Razi indeed admits 'that the age at marriage for the sons and daughters of well-to-do families was probably lower than that of children of poorer families'.[14] In the cases of younger, non-inheriting children of less prosperous families, and where a father's death preceded marriage, wider family interests would weigh less heavily on individuals, who might exercise greater freedom in the choice of marriage partners and so marry later. It is difficult to concur with Razi's unsubstantiated assertion that in these instances the mean age at first marriage was nevertheless not relatively high.[15] It might further be argued that the higher proportion of leyrewite associated with daughters of poorer family reflects this greater individual freedom in respect of marriage, courtship, and thus sexual morality.[16] It is of interest here that,

---

[13] Razi, *Life, Marriage and Death*, 136–7.　　　　[14] Ibid. 60.　　　　[15] Ibid. 70.

[16] Ibid. 66. For a recent discussion of leyrewite that would accord with this view see T. North, 'Legerwite in the Thirteenth and Fourteenth Centuries', *Past and Present*, 111 (1986), 3–16. For the view that fines reflect social manipulation by the jurors of presentment see L. R. Poos and R. M. Smith, '"Legal Windows onto Historical Populations"? Recent Research on Demography and the Manor Court in England', *Law and History Review*, 2 (1984), 149–50.

over the period 1538–1799 at Shepshed, Levine has demonstrated that children whose fathers died before their first marriage tended to marry later than those who had a living father.[17] This population of potentially later marrying (or never marrying) individuals may reasonably have comprised the majority of Halesowen society, but this same population is largely absent from Razi's study. Razi's methodology may thus in practice disguise many later marriages.

Though Razi's work is largely concerned with the period before 1348, he does consider in theoretical and analytical terms how marriage patterns may have changed between the pre- and immediate post-plague eras. Again his hypothesis concerns land transfer and the availability of land. As land became more available and real wages rose as a consequence of plague losses so, he argues, the opportunity for marriage increased even within poorer families and for women at least the mean age at first marriage may have fallen. At the same time Razi notices a marked fall in the numbers of children observed because recorded for each family in the period 1350–1400. He ascribes this paradoxical trend to the marked increase in infant and child mortality due to plague. In a more problematical area, Razi suggests that the incidence of illegitimacy (measured from incidence of leyrewite only) fell over the same period. This he ties to the supposed fall in age at first marriage and the greater opportunity for women to marry. It is implicit in this assertion that Razi assumes that women would marry as early (and as often) as they were able, and that leyrewite was a fine levied not for simple fornication, but for actually giving birth. This last has been questioned by Poos and Smith, but even if the trend described were real, it need not lend support to Razi's interpretation.[18] Illegitimacy can be shown to have been least common at times when mean marriage ages were high and fertility levels low from the early modern era; by analogy, Razi's data

[17] D. Levine, '"For Their Own Reasons": Individual Marriage Decisions and Family Life', *Journal of Family History*, 7 (1982), table 1, p. 258.

[18] Razi, *Life, Marriage and Death*, 138–9; Poos and Smith, '"Legal Windows onto Historical Populations"?', 148–51. North sees this downward trend as part of a more widespread phenomenon and argues that after the plague lords tended to impose fewer fines, but at a substantially higher rate: North, 'Legerwite in the Thirteenth and Fourteenth Centuries', 15.

could support an upward, not a downward trend in marriage ages.[19]

A marked fall in the proportion of widows remarrying, despite a high rate of widower remarriage, Razi likewise concludes must reflect a higher, and therefore earlier incidence of marriage for young women.[20] This would require a more substantial demographic analysis to demonstrate since there is no simple relationship between widow remarriage rates and age at first marriage as Razi would seem to imply. The argument that in the land-hungry pre-plague decades widows holding customary land by right of dower would be especially attractive to men without land as marriage partners, and indeed that pressure might occasionally be put on such women to remarry, is supported by evidence elsewhere, notably on the Crowland manor of Cottenham near Cambridge. Such observations apply, as Smith stresses, only to villein society and may thus be less applicable to rural society after the Black Death.[21] It is not necessary, however, to conclude that subsequent to the plague widows did not remarry because they could not attract husbands when access to land was comparatively open. It may be that many women preferred the comparative independence of widowhood and, given the opportunity to support themselves independently in the more prosperous peasant economy of the later fourteenth century by retaining family or hired labour, preferred not to remarry. Our own thesis is that the sort of economic climate that allowed widows to remain unmarried also allowed unmarried women to delay marriage.

In conclusion it must appear that, in the absence of a much more rigorous analysis of the demographic possibilities and implications of his data, some of Razi's interpretations respecting matrimony are of questionable value. His analysis of female marriage is necessarily limited to villein families who were liable to merchet, but further biased towards the first-born children of the élite of peasant society. The representativeness of this group must be doubted, but equally problems of methodology remain in

---

[19] Cf. P. Laslett, *The World We Have Lost Further Explored* (3rd edn., London, 1983), 159–62, 177–8.

[20] Razi, *Life, Marriage and Death*, 138.

[21] Smith, 'Hypothèses sur la nuptialité', 125–7. Cf. E. Clark, 'The Decision to Marry in Thirteenth- and Early Fourteenth-Century Norfolk', *Medieval Studies*, 49 (1987), 496–516.

respect of even this group. It is perhaps more useful to consider alternative sources of evidence in order to reconstruct prevailing marriage regimes. The fullest such analysis to date is that provided by Smith in an essay that explores a range of evidence bearing upon a variety of aspects of the marriage regime. Smith reviews Hajnal's pioneering article, together with some of the limited literature on marriage patterns in the later medieval West, and presents some new data derived from the rural Rutland poll tax returns for 1377 to suggest that the English experience at this date was unlike the supposedly 'medieval' regime widely found in southern France and northern Italy.[22] This last is further considered in the same author's review essay on Herlihy and Klapisch-Zuber's detailed study of the Florentine *catasto* of 1427.[23] Smith presents evidence that seignorial control over marriage in respect of bond tenants, as reflected in payments of merchet, did not in practice influence marriage formation and that this is demonstrated by a relatively high observed rate of marital exogamy. This observation challenges some older views about the nature of medieval village society in which the 'individualism' of a Western marriage regime might have little place.[24] Finally, Smith suggests analogies between the institution of service as a life-cycle function in the distinctive marriage regime that prevailed in early modern England and the apparently similar, but little considered institution of the later Middle Ages.[25] This is a theme that was explored in the previous chapter. Smith himself avoids any dogmatic statement in the light of the little research published by 1982, but by rejecting the 'medieval' marriage thesis he, by implication, rejects Razi's interpretation of the Halesowen evidence. More recently, in conjunction with Poos, he has engaged in a debate with Razi in the pages of the *Law and History Review* to question the demographic logic of the patterns described by Razi.[26]

---

[22] Smith, 'Hypothèses sur la nuptialité', 109–19.
[23] Smith, 'The People of Tuscany'.
[24] Smith, 'Hypothèses sur la nuptialité', 127–9.
[25] Ibid. 129–31.
[26] Poos and Smith, ' "Legal Windows onto Historical Populations"?'; Z. Razi, 'The Use of Manor Court Rolls in Demographic Analysis: A Reconsideration', *Law and History Review*, 3 (1985), 191–200; Poos and Smith, ' "Shades Still on the Window": A Reply to Zvi Razi', *Law and History Review*, 3 (1986), 409–29; Z. Razi, 'The Demographic Transparency of Manorial Court Rolls', *Law and History Review*, 5 (1987), 523–35.

Some of Smith's findings can be seen to be supported by the work of Bennett. From the record of merchets recorded in the *Liber Gersumarum* of Ramsey Abbey, Bennett has described a neolocal pattern of marital exogamy, most marriages falling within a radius of 15 miles or rather less.[27] This is parallel to the pattern noticed by Smith from the prior of Spalding's serf lists for the Lincolnshire fenland villages of Weston and Moulton in the later thirteenth century, which he likens to that derived from seventeenth- and eighteenth-century sources, and specifically the pattern of servant hirings out of Spalding fair in the later eighteenth century.[28] Bennett has also rightly drawn attention to the numbers of cases where the woman appears responsible for her own merchet payment, something that is clearly stated in the record, but had hitherto been ignored by historians. This may suggest a degree of economic and personal independence on the part of women paying such fines that ill accords with the notion of early or arranged marriage. In some instances services may have provided that independence. Although female servants are not liable to be recorded in manorial sources other than by chance, Bennett has managed to find a few servants among those women purchasing their own merchets.[29] These observations would be consistent, again by analogy with the early modern era, with a social system that embraced service as an aspect of life-cycle, a period of 'secondary socialization' that frequently preceded marriage.[30] Such a system, involving the annual hiring and migration of labour within a given locality around customary hiring dates, could help explain the pattern of exogamous marriage and the individualism suggested for some villein women in marriage formation by their purchase of their own merchets.

This view is further suggested from the coincidence of merchet payments and the timing of the principal annual hirings known to have been already well established by the early modern era. This would accord with the marriage of servants immediately following the completion of their annual contracts. Thus Bennett found that 27 per cent of 'specific' merchets were recorded in October alone,

---

[27] Bennett, 'Medieval Peasant Marriage', 219–21.

[28] Smith, 'Hypothèses sur la nuptialité', 128–30 and n. 68.

[29] Bennett, 'Medieval Peasant Marriage', 197, 208.

[30] Smith, 'Hypothèses sur la nuptialité', 129–31; Kussmaul, *Servants in Husbandry*; Laslett, 'Characteristics of the Western Family', 43; Ch. 4 above.

despite regular sessions of the manor court through the entire year. Razi presents similar evidence for a post-harvest upswing in recorded merchets.[31] The York cause paper evidence likewise suggests that servants are often the subject of marriage litigation, and that, in a region of Martinmas hirings, marriages were often contracted at about this time.[32] In the absence of more substantial evidence, this is an essentially speculative interpretation of Bennett's evidence. Historians of the manor and later medieval rural society must explore further the available evidence for service and servanthood before the nature of the institution and its possible relation to marriage formation can be fully understood. McIntosh has argued for a growth in the institution of life-cycle service during the later fifteenth century, but, as has been shown earlier, the rural poll tax returns suggest that this form of service was already well developed much nearer to the time of the Black Death.[33] It might further be argued that with a shift in some regions from a predominantly arable-based rural economy to a pastoral economy with some scope for rural manufacture, the year-round demand for labour would be enhanced. With a generally upward trend in the cost of wage labour, moreover, it would seem more appropriate to locate the development of the institution of service, where payment was principally in kind, in the later fourteenth rather than the fifteenth century. These are issues that may be developed from the study of the manor court roll.

Work done to date on the problem of late medieval marriage regimes in England has tended to be stronger on theory than on substantial evidence. Perhaps this will always be the case, but Hanawalt's observation that 'further research will be fruitless' seems unduly pessimistic.[34] The surviving evidence has in no sense been exhausted, nor have the possibilities of this evidence been

[31] Bennett, 'Medieval Peasant Marriage', 230; Razi, *Life, Marriage and Death*, 152–3. Cf. also Kussmaul, *Servants in Husbandry*, 83–93.

[32] e.g. BIHR, CP. E. 157, 215; CP. F. 3, 46, 181, 201, 279. A number of other marriages were contracted around Pentecost, e.g. CP. E. 106, 121, 188; CP. F. 262, 273. This Martinmas/Pentecost pattern may have been more marked in York, where life-cycle service was apparently well established in the late Middle Ages, than in the surrounding countryside. See Ch. 4 above.

[33] M. K. McIntosh, 'Local Change and Community Control in England', *Huntingdon Library Quarterly*, 49 (1986), 224. It may be that this represents a regional development rather than a general phenomenon.

[34] Hanawalt, *The Ties that Bound*, 103.

fully realized. This present study exploits primarily ecclesiastical sources in the form of Church court records and probate registers, but also the Exchequer nominative poll tax returns, i.e. those returns listing individual taxpayers by name. Most of this evidence belongs to the century and a half following the Black Death and, with the exception of the poll tax, relates specifically to York and Yorkshire. Only to a limited extent, therefore, does this study overlap in its terms of reference with the writings already reviewed. It does, however, attempt to examine marriage formation and the prevailing marriage regime within a broader social context and, in this respect, takes up a number of points raised in Smith's 1983 essay. Like Sheehan's analysis of the Ely consistory court records for matrimonial litigation in the late fourteenth century, the present analysis of the York cause papers uses this evidence to answer questions respecting the sociology and thus the structure of marriage as practised in the society from which the litigation arises.[35] The value of biographical data relating to deponents in such actions for generating statistical material for life cycle and marriage has not been hitherto appreciated by medievalists, though Souden, for example, has employed similar evidence to analyse migration in the early modern era. Similarly little use has been made to date of probate sources to analyse marital status at death or underlying trends in marriage or remarriage, although Todd provides an interesting examination of widow remarriage in early modern Abingdon using probate evidence for female testators.[36]

In terms of the sources employed and the treatment of evidence, therefore, this study is on new and uncertain ground. It stresses the individualistic and feminine perspective on marriage. Yet marriage is all too frequently treated either in terms of impersonal aggregative analysis or from the seignorial, communal, parental, or male perspective. Thus Levine, writing of the early modern era, has commented that 'historical demographers have rarely treated marriage patterns in the context of familial relationships, but rather have concentrated their attention on the aggregated statistical behaviour of the group', and Bennett, writing on

[35] Sheehan, 'The Formation and Stability of Marriage'.
[36] Souden, 'Migrants and the Population Structure'; B. J. Todd, 'The Remarrying Widow: A Stereotype Reconsidered', in M. Prior (ed.), *Women in English Society, 1500–1800* (London, 1985), 54–92.

TABLE 5.2.   *Proportion of poll tax populations married in 1377*

	Males		Females	
	N	% married	N	% married
Oxford				
St Peter in the East	88	55.7	89	55.1
St Mary the Virgin	146	62.3	149	61.1
Carlisle	312	61.9	348	55.5
Colchester	1419	61.9	1456	60.3
Hull	749	58.9	808	55.0
Rutland (less Oakham)	1872	65.1	1808	67.4

Source: As Table II.1 below.

merchet, has observed that other historians 'have recognized no economic or personal independence on the part of the couple contracting marriage'.[37] Only by shifting the focus to the part played by the prospective bride can this imbalanced approach be redressed.

THE POLL TAX EVIDENCE

The rather insubstantial poll tax evidence can at this point be briefly considered. Smith has already explored some of the surviving rural nominative returns for 1377. To these may be added the equally insubstantial, but no less valuable urban evidence. Only those few 1377 nominative urban returns where servants are identified by name and thus sex are of value here. To measure proportions of the tax population less servants married would be of little value and the later returns of 1379 and 1380–1 are generally too selective to generate useful measures. The proportions of the urban tax population of either sex married, in theory all lay persons over 14 years, are tabulated in Table 5.2. The proportions achieved are surprisingly uniform. The male proportion, at about 60 per cent, is at most five or six percentage points above the female level and this reflects the generally low adult sex

[37] Levine, 'For their own Reasons', 255; Bennett, 'Medieval Peasant Marriages', 194.

ratio observed within the urban poll tax populations. The measures may superficially be compared against similar data derived
from a variety of cultural and chronological contexts, but adjusted
using model life tables so as to be compatible with demographic
conditions as may have been experienced in England at the time
of the poll tax assessment.[38]

Analogy with the later returns, where under-assessment was
generally a more serious problem, suggests that unmarried females
were most likely and married couples least likely to be excluded.
If this applied also, albeit to a more modest extent, to the 1377
returns, then the true proportions should be lower, especially in
the instance of the females. Fenwick has argued that there is a
problem not of exclusion, but of exemption of the poor.[39] If this
were true, it would again seem reasonable to believe that the
unmarried women would be prominent among those so exempted.
The measures are further misleading in that the underlying age
structure of the urban tax populations is not known. In an urban
context the high level of migration, especially female migration,
may have artificially added to the proportion of young unmarried
persons in the population, though this equally would increase the
proportion of the population 'at risk' to be married. These must
remain areas for speculation since, though it may be surmised that
the net pattern of migration was rural–urban, it is still likely that
there was some out-migration from the town, particularly of
former rural migrants returning to claim inheritances or to marry.
Indeed, given the skewed urban sex ratios, this would seem a
logical response for young women wanting a marriage partner if
unsuccessful in finding such during their residence, whilst servants
or otherwise, within the town.[40] Despite these reservations, the
observed proportions do appear more in line with those patterns
representing English parishes after 1599 or Sweden in 1750 than
Tuscany in 1427, Serbia in 1733–4, or the Russian serf population
of Mishino in 1849, the other examples tabulated by Smith.

[38] Such data are presented in Smith, 'Hypothèses sur la nuptialité', table 2, p.
116. These relate to populations aged over 15, whereas the 1377 poll tax data are
for a slightly younger population. It is not, however, possible to assess how far the
tax was in fact evaded and it is likely that young persons around the minimum age
of taxation were frequently missed or given the benefit of the doubt.

[39] C. C. Fenwick, 'The English Poll Taxes of 1377, 1379 and 1381: A Critical
Examination of the Returns', Ph.D. thesis (London, 1983), 196–7.

[40] See Ch. 6 below.

Certainly the proportion of females married is significantly lower than is true of medieval Tuscany, just as the proportion of males married is noticeably less than on the Russian serf estate of Mishino. The Serbian evidence, indicative of a distinctive East European marriage regime, demonstrates markedly higher proportions of both sexes married than is true of the English poll tax sample. The evidence is thus at least compatible with the north-western regime that was subsequently to prevail, but it would be unwise to put too much weight on this evidence by itself.

THE YORK CAUSE PAPER EVIDENCE

A more direct and detailed insight into the structure of marriage may be derived from the descriptive data relating to deponents in York ecclesiastical causes. The Church's jurisdiction in respect of disputes concerning marriage, tithes, defamation, and the probate of wills placed it in the very midst of secular society. Regrettably it is only sometimes that the actual depositions of witnesses in contested actions have survived. The York cause papers regularly include such depositions and nearly six hundred files of such material are preserved for the fourteenth and fifteenth centuries alone. There are additionally a much smaller number of papers surviving from the Dean and Chapter Court.[41] In general, only cases involving deponents of both sexes have been examined here. This immediately removed disputes concerning tithes and church impropriation from consideration since these made frequent recourse to the collective memory of the older males in the community, but appear not to have drawn upon female witnesses, presumably because their testimony was not considered to carry much weight. Only testamentary, defamation, *violacionis fidei* (breach of promise), and, the majority, matrimonial causes were consequently explored here. Files containing actual depositions were preferred, though a small number of others were found to be of interest despite the loss of such evidence. Rural cases were distinguished from those where the majority of litigants and deponents were normally resident in a town, which in the majority

[41] See Appendix I below. For a discussion of the Dean and Chapter Court and the records of litigation there see S. Brown, 'The Peculiar Jurisdiction of York Minster during the Middle Ages', D.Phil. thesis (York, 1980), 180–228.

of cases was York itself. The sample comprises over two hundred files and includes nearly all matrimonial causes for which actual depositions survive dated between 1303 and 1520. The composition of this sample and an indication of the types of causes is shown in Appendix III. From this material as a whole data relating to 469 urban and 625 rural deponents were extracted.

The depositions represent the actual responses of individual witnesses, examined separately and privately, to the set questions contained within the articles and defendant's interrogatories.[42] Before the later fifteenth century these statements were recorded in Latin, but even in the later fourteenth century reported speech is often represented in the vernacular. Thus it is recorded that Emma Erle of Wakefield exclaimed 'Gramercy schyrre' when her hand was asked in marriage by one John Archier.[43] Likewise Roger Awstynmore recalled that Emma Hare had heatedly declared to John Selby's wife, 'I say to the fals harlot Selby wyfe and that strang thefe and mansmortherer thi husband the whilk was ones at the rope ende and yit I trowe to bryng hym agayne thar to when he sall noght skape.'[44] The immediacy of such first-hand testimony, frequently absent from Act book evidence, is exciting and belies the apparent formalism of the records. It was these actual written depositions that were used in court and evaluated by the judge in reaching a verdict. For this reason deponents were regularly identified by name, age, and status and often asked a variety of questions used to check on consistency between witnesses: At what time of day did events occur? Who was present? How were they dressed? Were they standing or sitting? If they had eaten, was the meal of fish or flesh? What was the weather like?

The court's immediate concern was to establish any ties of blood or service between witnesses and the parties in dispute, which clearly might prejudice their testimony. It was a possible defence to allege that witnesses were hiding such connections. In a matrimonial cause of 1449–50 it was variously claimed that witnesses were in fact blood relatives of one party and that a further witness failed to disclose that he was a fellow servant with another

---

[42] Helmholz, *Marriage Litigation*, 19–20.
[43] BIHR, CP. E. 124 (1381).   [44] BIHR, CP. F. 116 (1436).

party.[45] The court was further concerned to establish status and even wealth in as much as this might have a bearing on the action.[46] There does appear to have existed some prejudice against poor witnesses, but probably because they might be considered most vulnerable to bribery. Allegations of false witness are indeed common. In a matrimonial cause of 1430 evidence was brought that witnesses in an earlier divorce action had perjured themselves. One had been struck by a guilty conscience on his deathbed and a female witness, Alice Ness, confessed to having yielded to a bribe of 40*d.*, an indication, surely, of her poverty.[47] Canon law did not permit the testimony of witnesses below the age of puberty and youthful deponents are found only infrequently. The large number of servants observed, especially in urban causes, does tend to augment the lower end of the age range down to about 16. One girl of 14 or more and a female servant of 15 were deponents in later fourteenth-century causes.[48] It is implicit in the deposition evidence that potential witnesses of younger age were not called, but there is little reason to fear that witnesses in their later teens would be liable to be overlooked.[49] Witnesses of servile status were not normally admitted under canon law, though the York evidence provides a number of exceptions to this rule.[50]

The deposition evidence contained within the York cause paper archive is thus both substantial and uniquely comprehensive. Similar evidence has survived from Canterbury, but mostly for the thirteenth and earlier fifteenth centuries, and some London material survives only for the later fifteenth century.[51] Act books tend often to record only routine detail and are frequently devoid of actual depositions. Excellent use of the unusually detailed Ely Consistory Court book for the period 1374–82 has nevertheless been made by Sheehan to study matrimonial litigation as evidence

[45] BIHR, CP. F. 184, 185, and 237. This is a complex multi-party action contained within three related files.
[46] Cf. Helmholz, *Marriage Litigation*, 132–3.
[47] BIHR, CP. F. 99 (1430).
[48] BIHR, CP. E. 89 (1366); CP. E. 121 (1372).
[49] Cf. BIHR, CP. F. 64 (1412), where are noted the presence of young children at an alleged marriage contract, CP. F. 63 (1414) of a girl of about 14, and CP. F. 155 (1425) of a servant girl. None of these appear as deponents.
[50] e.g. BIHR, CP. E. 235 (1397). Cf. Helmholz, *Marriage Litigation*, 155; Adams and Donahue (eds.), *Select Cases*, 50–1.
[51] Dean and Chapter Library, Canterbury, X. 10. 1; Guildhall Library, London, MS 9065; Greater London Record Office, DL/C/205.

for marriage formation and its social context.[52] Helmholz's more broadly based study employs much York material and provides an authoritative introduction to the nature and types of matrimonial litigation, though it makes no specific use of the biographical data relating to individual deponents that the York cause paper material provides.[53] Donahue also draws upon York matrimonial litigation in an interesting and far-reaching discussion that contrasts this English evidence with that derived from equivalent French sources.[54] This last has been criticized in Finch's recent comparative analysis of matrimonial litigation from Cerisy (Normandy), Rochester, and Hereford, but his sources are Act books and not actual depositions.[55] Only Cosgrove for the diocese of Armagh and Owen for the diocese of York have begun to realize the full potential of the depositions themselves.[56]

Biographical data concerning deponents are inconsistently recorded and are particularly incomplete before *c*.1370. When given in full they consist of the deponent's name (including any alias), domicile (indicated by street or parish in the case of York residents), occupation or status, and age. Any relationship by blood, marriage, or service to the parties contesting the cause is also stated. A critical analysis must, however, raise doubts as to the quality of this evidence. The full range of possible data are only sometimes found and rarely so before the later fourteenth century. Ages in particular are often not stated for the earlier period.[57] Some women can be identified by marital status, though this is most true in the case of married women. Thus we find Agnes, the wife of John Camplay, and Marion, the wife of Nicholas Herforth.[58] Unmarried girls may be described as daugh-

---

[52] Sheehan, 'The Formation and Stability of Marriage'.

[53] Helmholz, *Marriage Litigation*.

[54] Donahue, 'The Canon Law on Marriage'.

[55] Finch, 'Crime and Marriage in Three Late Medieval Ecclesiastical Jurisdictions'. See also id., 'Parental Authority and the Problem of Clandestine Marriage in the Later Middle Ages', *Law and History Review*, 8 (1990), 189–204. I am grateful to Dr Finch for allowing me to read this paper in advance of publication and for allowing me to cite his thesis.

[56] A. Cosgrove, 'Marriage in Medieval Ireland', in id. (ed.), *Marriage in Ireland* (Dublin, 1985), 25–50; D. M. Owen, 'White Annays and Others', in D. Baker (ed.), *Medieval Women* (Studies in Church History, subsidia 1; Oxford, 1978), 331–46.

[57] BIHR, CP. E. 89 (1366) is an early example, but even here only a minority of the deponents are also described.

[58] BIHR, CP. F. 63 (1414).

TABLE 5.3.   *Deponents in matrimonial causes by gender, 1303–1499*

Period	Males		Females		Total number	Total causes
	N	%	N	%		
Urban matrimonial causes						
1303–49	22	75.9	7	24.1	29	4
1350–99	86	69.4	38	30.6	124	20
1400–49	155	71.4	62	28.6	217	32
1450–99	16	76.2	5	23.8	21	8
Rural matrimonial causes						
1306–49	27	69.2	12	30.8	39	9
1350–99	152	72.7	57	27.3	209	29
1400–49	126	81.3	29	18.7	155	30
1450–99	129	86.6	20	13.4	149	24

Note: From *c*.1500 an increasing number of matrimonial causes record only male deponents.

Sources: BIHR, CP. E, F various; D/C CP various; Appendix III below.

ters, thus Isabella, the daughter of Alan de Belyngham, or, allowing that they are indeed unmarried, as servants, e.g. Katherine Lorymer and Alice Burton, the servants of Alice Schilbotill.[59] Very few widows are specified, and no marital status at all is assigned to many women. It would be rash to attempt any general conclusion about the status of this latter group as, though some may be single, some at least can otherwise be identified as married or widowed. The Joan Semer of one cause can probably be identified with the Joan, wife of John Semer, of another the same year.[60] Likewise Isabell Spuret can be recognized from her deposition as a widow, but is not so described.[61] It is consequently only possible to draw a partial picture of the marital status of female deponents.

There is also a discernible bias against females making depositions. Females constituted less than one-third of all deponents even though the sample is designed to include as many causes as are liable to contain depositions made by women.[62] This bias is

[59] BIHR, CP. E. 126 (1382); CP. F. 113 (1434).
[60] BIHR, CP. F. 111 (1432); CP. F. 175 (1432).
[61] BIHR, CP. E. 159 (1393).   [62] See Table 5.3.

made explicit in a fifteenth-century cause where one of the parties in a matrimonial dispute sought a male witness to her marriage because her existing witnesses were 'only women'.[63] It is thus apparent that contestants would have had a greater incentive to produce male deponents than female since their evidence was deemed to carry more weight. It is possible that this bias increased with time, there being a much more pronounced gender imbalance in respect of deponents by the fifteenth century within the rural sample and, to a more modest degree and based upon a small number of causes, by the late fifteenth century within the urban sample.

Although age is recorded fairly consistently for witnesses from the late fourteenth century onwards, it is apparent that this data set is similarly flawed. In the case of younger witnesses, as has already been observed in respect of servants, precise ages are indeed frequently given and these may be regarded with some real measure of confidence. But for most older age groups, including the majority of married deponents, ages are frequently rounded to the nearest decennial. Such ages are often qualified as approximate (*circiter*) or a minimum (*et amplius*). Still more disturbing is the finding that in the very small number of instances where witnesses' ages can be compared within or between records they seldom appear to correlate. Thus John de Akom, a York saddler, was said to be 20 'or more' when first he testified early in 1394, but 30 years when he again made his deposition only five months later.[64] If the Joan Semer noted earlier from two different causes is indeed one and the same person, and this cannot be verified, then her age in 1432 is given variously as 30 and more and 40 and more. It is evident from depositions that past events, including births and birthdates were rarely remembered with any precision. It may even be that some deponents were given an age according to their appearance as much as from their testimony.[65] The informed impression here is that an age of 30 'and more' could well imply a true age of close on 40 years. Conversely, an age stated to be 'about' (*circiter*) 30 might represent a true age a couple of years short of that. The older a deponent is stated to be,

---

[63] 'Dixit quod huismodi testes nisi mulieres fuerunt': BIHR, CP. F. 104 (1432).

[64] BIHR, CP. E. 159 (1393).

[65] See for example the arguments used to define the age of Alice de Rouclif in BIHR, CP. E. 89.

the greater the probable margin of error. One John Wyman of Holy Trinity parish, Goodramgate, was stated to be 50 'and more' in 1431, but if his testimony that he married thirty-nine years earlier were true, he would have wed at little over 11 years of age.[66] Conversely, the ages of younger deponents, which are invariably given with more precision, are probably to be treated with rather greater confidence.

Although ages of adults as recorded amongst the deposition material must be treated with considerable circumspection, some indication of the compatibility of ages at marriage may still be obtained. Since the ages given for young adults tend to be much more precise and, as seems likely, more reliable, it may thus be possible to derive some measure of age at first marriage. Much valuable information has already been described for the servant population and it has been observed that females are frequently to be found as servants into their mid-twenties.[67] In total, using only the biographical data relating to individual deponents, it is possible to identify by age some twenty-four male and twenty-three female servants, thirteen other male and eleven other female single persons, and forty-seven married couples. All but three of these last are drawn from causes dated 1372–1474 and some half from within the narrower period 1416–35. Only thirteen widows are represented, seven of these from the period after 1462. This small sample does not include married persons where the age of their spouse is not also known. The ages of a number of such individuals, mostly female, are known. The actual depositions allow this sample to be further extended to include twenty-nine additional former servants (sixteen male and thirteen female), four further women thought to be servants or former servants, and another four young unmarried women.

The depositions provide clues as to the actual age at marriage in twenty-one instances. In seven causes, all but one rural, these relate to alleged under-age marriages.[68] Two further instances may be cited from a York capitular court book for 1372. These from their context relate to the sons and daughters of the rural gentry. Thus Philip, the son of Richard de Lunde of Beswick, was

[66] BIHR, CP. F. 101 (1431).
[67] See Table 4.3 above.
[68] BIHR, CP. E. 23 (1333); CP. E. 76 (1357); CP. E. 89 (1366); CP. E. 259 (1368); CP. F. 119 (1436); CP. G. 32 (1508); CP. G. 112 (1516).

contracted to Elena, the daughter of Thomas de Nesfeld when they would have been only 10 and 8 years respectively. On achieving their canonical majorities they appeared in the consistory court to ratify their consent. Thomas's son William appeared ten years after he was first contracted to Margaret, daughter to John Grayne, a young woman nearly ten years his senior.[69] A similar pattern appears to be true of those examples for which actual depositions survive. At least three concern children of knights and another, to judge by the dowry arrangements, the daughter of the bailiff of Catton and a man of some landed wealth.[70] It is striking that only one such cause is dated between the time of the Peasants' Revolt and the accession of Henry VIII. Such evidence suggests that child marriages were not usual, and indeed rare by the late fourteenth century, and were primarily confined to the landed aristocracy.

In addition to the age data already described for servants it is possible to describe similar age data for the eleven other unmarried women. Where these women appear as deponents they may be described either as someone's daughter, presumably implying that they were neither married, widowed, nor in service, or more specifically as *soluta*, i.e. unmarried. That such women appear among the sample of deponents is in accord with the poll tax evidence for a relatively high proportion of unmarried adult females, particularly within urban communities. Some of these last may have been widows. Others, as has been described earlier, were daughters living at home and assisting in their fathers' trades.[71] Yet others must have been young women supporting themselves independently. In some instances, as that of the pinner Marjory Kyrkeby, these may themselves have been former servants, but others may have been rural migrants attracted by the prospect of urban employment. In this respect it is perhaps not coincidence that the majority of such single female deponents are found in the latter part of the fourteenth century, a period that may have seen an especially high level of immigration into towns.[72] Their age distribution is set out in Table 5.4. It would be unwise to place too much weight of interpretation on so limited a sample,

---

[69] YML, M2/1c, fos. 11^{r-v}.
[70] BIHR, CP. E. 89, 259; CP. F. 119; CP. G. 112.
[71] See Table 3.4 above. [72] See Ch. 6 below.

TABLE 5.4. *Age distribution of single females, other than servants*

Period	Age observed					
1303–49†		20+	22*			30*
1350–99	14+	20	21+	24	26	
		20	22			
1400–49		20+				30+*
						30+*
1450–1520		20+				30

† Earliest case dated 1338.
* Status uncertain.
Sources: BIHR, CP. E, F, G various; D/C CP various; Appendix III below.

but this evidence does suggest that at least before the mid-fifteenth century there was nothing unusual about women remaining unmarried in their twenties, despite not being engaged as servants. Much the same appears to be true of single males as is shown in Table 5.5.

AGE AT MARRIAGE

The York cause paper deposition material thus provides some substantive evidence for the sorts of age at which young women were liable to remain single. The same source can likewise be

TABLE 5.5. *Age distribution of single males, other than servants*

Period	Age observed					
1303–49						
1350–99	15+	20	21	22		
1400–49		20+			24+	
	18	20			24+	
1450–1520				23+		26+
				24+		
				23+		

Sources: BIHR, CP. E, F, G various; D/C CP various; Appendix III below.

TABLE 5.6. *Age differences between spouses from cause paper sample*

Age difference (years)	Urban couples	Rural couples	All couples
Wife senior			
10	1	—	1
6–9	—	—	—
1–5	5	—	5
Husband and wife same age	8	3	11
Husband senior			
1–5	7	3	10
6–9	4	1	5
10	6	2	8
More than 10	6	1	7

Sources: BIHR, CP. E, F, G various; D/C CP various; Appendix III below.

employed to provide some tangible indication of the modal age at first marriage. The ages of forty-seven married couples are known, the majority from York and ten from rural communities. In interpreting this evidence a number of difficulties arise. Age data must be treated with circumspection, especially in respect of older persons. The material relates only to established unions, some of which may in fact represent the second or subsequent marriage of one or both parties, and not to marriages at formation. It is further necessary to distinguish rural marriages from urban since these appear to have followed slightly different patterns. Deponents were consequently classified as either urban or rural in terms of their domicile at the time of their deposition or, when data relating for example to service or marriage are recorded retrospectively, at the appropriate moment in the past. These are not insurmountable difficulties, however, and it is still possible to derive some valuable measures in respect of the prevailing marriage regime. Age compatibility at marriage may be determined by calculating the difference in recorded ages of couples. Even if these recorded ages are not in themselves entirely trustworthy, they may nevertheless reflect with some measure of sensitivity the actual difference in ages between spouses. The differences calculated are shown in Table 5.6.[73]

[73] Due to the lack of precision in the age data, age ranges rather than specific age differences have been preferred.

It is apparent that the majority of marriages might be described as companionate. Over half the couples (N = 25) were separated by only five years or less, and five more by only six or seven years. Differences of ten years (N = 9) are the product of differencing ages expressed as decennials and are thus only very approximate. These have been disregarded for statistical purposes, though even if they were to be included as they stand they would not greatly detract from the conclusions drawn here. Only in seven instances are differences in excess of ten years. Significantly these differences are all positive, i.e. the husband was the senior. It thus appears that there are here two contrasting sets of results. In the first set age differences are narrow. For urban couples the mean age difference in favour of the husband is 2.9 years (N = 31). The equivalent mean difference for rural couples is slightly greater at 3.8 years (N = 8). In about a fifth of all instances it is the wife that is the senior. It is likely that these all represent first marriages.[74] The second and much smaller set is composed of couples separated by a considerable difference in years. It seems probable that these represent second marriages or remarriages, particularly of widowers to women marrying for the first time. Although the surviving testamentary sources do not allow this hypothesis to be tested, such a pattern is broadly compatible with that described by Wall from five early modern English parish listings.[75] Here again a significant number of marriages, identified by Wall as second marriages, were characterized by a large age difference between spouses, the husband being the senior. The highest proportion of all marriages, however, were marked by differences of between one and four years only. The similarity of the two samples is striking and may again suggest that the prevailing marriage regime differed only slightly between the two periods.

Because this evidence relates specifically to established unions, it is only possible to present some rather negative, but still valuable observations regarding age at marriage. The data set can,

---

[74] This may be demonstrated in at least four instances from testamentary data: BIHR, CP. F. 36; Prob. Reg. 2, fo. 539 (Laxton); D/C CP. 1417/2; Prob. Reg. 2, fos. 45, 308 (del Close); CP. F. 114; Prob. Reg. 3, fo. 575 (Bolton). According to his will, William Pottow had two wives both named Alice, but since he died some 25 years after making his deposition in 1411 it may be presumed that the deposition of his then wife was indeed that of the first Alice: CP. F. 62; Prob. Reg. 3, fo. 444.

[75] Ealing (1599), Chilvers Coton (1684 and 1781), Ardleigh (1796), and Winwick with Hulme (1801): Wall, 'Leaving Home', 88–9.

however, be substantially enhanced by the addition of some further married individuals whose ages are specified. As previously noted, actual marriage ages are known in twenty-one specific cases, although in seven they relate atypically to causes alleging under-age marriage, that is under 12 for females, as in the case of Alice, daughter of Elena de Rouclif in 1366, and 14 for males, as for example William Gascone in 1502.[76] In twenty-three further cases the age by which an individual had married, where this is under 30 years, is known or may be calculated retrospectively. Thus Tedia Lambhird of Weel, a small village between Hull and Beverley, was said variously to be 24, 26, and between 20 and 30 years by deponents in 1370. As the deposition evidence shows her to have married eight years previously, she would then have been some 16 to 18 years.[77]

Age at marriage is rather better documented in the case of rural deponents and litigants than is true of their urban counterparts. Actual age at marriage is known in the case of only two townspeople: Alice de Stodlay of St Saviourgate in York, married to Richard Surteys, may be observed retrospectively to have been already married and pregnant at 18 'or more'; William Gascone, also of York, was married at 14.[78] The latter example is atypical, but the former also appears unrepresentative, as will be seen, when considered in the light of other evidence. Only two other urban married deponents, one male and one female, were said to be under 20 at the time of their giving evidence, i.e. 19 years in both instances.[79] Two women were said to be 20 or more, and one 24. One urban male deponent was married by age 26. All the remaining married urban deponents for whom ages are known were aged 30 years or more. The extreme paucity of young married urban deponents appears significant. Had marriage in town society regularly occurred in the late teens or early twenties, then rather more young married deponents, such as is true of rural deponents, might reasonably have been expected.

This slightly negative evidence accords with the more substantial data previously discussed in respect of the ages of urban servants and other unmarried deponents. Of thirty female servants

---

[76] BIHR, CP. E. 89; CP. G. 32.
[77] BIHR, CP. E. 105 (1370).
[78] BIHR, CP. E. 198 (1394); CP. G. 32 (1508).
[79] Agnes Den, BIHR, CP. F. 75 (1418); Roger Awstynmore, CP. F. 116 (1436).

observed working in urban households, half were aged 20 or more. Of these one was still in service at 23 or more, four at 24 or more, one at 25 or more, and one at 28 years. Similarly, of twenty male servants aged below 30 engaged in urban households, thirteen were aged 20 or more. Of these, three were still servants at age 24, one at 25 or more, two at 26, one at 27 or more, and one at 29. Nine further unmarried townswomen are recorded, all of whom were aged 20 or more, and one unmarried man of 20 years. It thus appears that whereas in the context of Yorkshire towns in the century and a half after the Black Death married folk are rarely found much before their mid-twenties, unmarried women and men in their early to mid-twenties are commonly observed. The evidence consequently indicates a pattern of late marriage, i.e. in the mid-twenties, with a relatively narrow age difference between spouses, husbands being on average some three years older than their partners. This suggested pattern differs from that which emerges from the equivalent rural evidence.

The actual age at marriage is known or may be calculated for twenty individuals noted in rural causes. Eight of these are parties to litigation alleging marriage under canonical age, a phenomenon, as noted before, much more common among the rural aristocracy than was true of peasant society.[80] Such cases appear, moreover, to have been rare between the later fourteenth and early sixteenth centuries. It is unlikely that they have much to say about the modal age at first marriage that may more generally have been found in rural society. Nine of the remaining twelve instances relate to males. Discounting one doubtful case of a man calculated to have married at 37 years, the mean male age at first marriage is in excess of 22 years (N = 8). It should be noted that this rests on age data that are not beyond reproach and makes no allowance for six instances where the age recorded is stated to be a minimum. The true mean may thus be nearer 23 years.[81] For rural women, discounting five cases associated with marriages below canonical age, the ages at first marriage are known in only three instances: at 14 years, between 16 and 18 years, and at 18 years.[82] The first is

---

[80] BIHR, CP. E. 259 is an impotence action, but likewise relates to the youthful marriage of a knight's daughter.

[81] This sample is almost entirely dependent on causes dating between 1430 and 1466.

[82] These are derived from causes dated 1499, 1370, and 1430 respectively.

atypical since it represents an allegedly forced marriage, and the last depends upon a witness, then aged 36, remembering that she had married eighteen years earlier. This slight evidence may be augmented from a further sixteen individuals known to have married by a certain age below 30 years. Two males were married by age 20 or more, a further four by age 24, four more by age 26 or more, and one by age 28. This is again suggestive of an age at first marriage in the early rather than the mid-twenties. Of five females known to have been married before 30 years, one was married by 19 or more, one by 20 or more, two by 26, and one by 29. Again this appears consistent with a pattern of marriage in the late teens or early twenties, but this cannot be more than a hypothesis for the sample is in itself too small to inspire real confidence.

These findings appear more credible when set against similar data pertaining to the ages of the unmarried shown in Tables 5.4 and 5.5. The ages of six unmarried rural females and ten equivalent males other than servants are known from the sample. Five of the women were aged 20 or more, of which two were aged 30. The representativeness of this tiny sample must, however, be doubted; none of these women are drawn from causes dating to the fifteenth century and only two, aged 14 or more and 24, are drawn from later fourteenth-century causes. The male sample is more satisfactory. It is enhanced by five men drawn from a single cause dated 1450 concerning events at the Summer Game in Wistow, near Selby, which, as is apparent from the depositions, only the unmarried were eligible to attend.[83] Although all the men in the sample were aged 20 or more, only one, aged 26 or more, was older than 24 or more. Such a pattern seems in line with the earlier suggestion that the modal male age at first marriage was two or three years short of 25. The ages of rural servants, at deposition or calculated retrospectively, are known in twenty-four cases (eleven female and thirteen male). Unfortunately the female sample is deficient for the fifteenth century. With the exception of one woman servant aged 28 found in a cause dated 1398, women are not apparently found in rural service much beyond their early twenties. The marital status of older male servants is ambiguous and it would be unwise to assume that the man of 40 who had been in service with his master for the previous five years was necessarily

[83] BIHR, CP. F. 246.

unmarried. To use somewhat anachronistic terminology his status may have been equivalent to that of the hired labourer rather than that of the farm servant. Most male servants, however, are found in their late teens or early twenties; three men were still in service at 24 years, one at 25 or more, and one at 27 or more. Once again these observations seem not to conflict with the notion that marriage was generally earlier in the countryside than was true of the town, that is in the early twenties for males and slightly younger for females. This seems to accord with the observation made earlier that a slightly greater age difference between spouses, nearer four years in favour of the husband, characterized rural marriages.

The samples suggest that teenage marriage, though certainly a real phenomenon, was probably not the norm in post-plague society below the level of the aristocracy. This last seems particularly true of urban society, though it appears also true of rural males and, to a lesser degree, rural females. The paucity of youthful marriages is indeed striking and it cannot be explained by any bias against younger witnesses. Thrupp produces some highly selective evidence relating to the marriage of orphaned girls of the propertied mercantile élite of the City of London to argue for an early age at marriage for women.[84] Such women would have been very much at the mercy of their guardians in respect of choosing a marriage partner, and it was very much in the guardians' interests to have arranged a marriage prior to their wards' coming of age. It is thus doubtful that such evidence can be applied more widely. Margery Kempe, herself born to one of the ruling families of Lynn, recalled that she was 'xx yer of age or *sumdele mor*' (my emphasis) when she married early in the fifteenth century.[85] The apparent rarity of teenage marriage may be set in the context of servanthood as a life-cycle institution.[86] It has already been observed that service was often a prelude to marriage and certainly a number of York causes concern alleged marriages between servants. William de Stokton promised, according to a cause of 1382, to marry Elena de Leyrmouth once

---

[84] S. L. Thrupp, *The Merchant Class of Medieval London, 1300–1500* (Chicago, 1948), 196.

[85] Meech and Allen (eds.), *The Book of Margery Kempe*, 6. Commentators persistently ignore the force of 'sumdele mor' since it does not accord with traditional notions about marriage in past times.

[86] See Ch. 4 above.

he had completed his apprenticeship.[87] The sempster Christine de Knarisburgh seems to have been well aware of and to have consented to her apprentice Isabella Wakefeld's courtship with one Thomas Fox. The couple regularly slept together and seem frequently to have admitted their intention to marry.[88] Probate evidence similarly demonstrates that masters were often willing to provide for their servants to marry.[89] One Nicholas Myn of York turned to his master for assistance when he wanted to negotiate dowry arrangements in respect of his intended.[90]

In this context the correlation between the three sets of age data relating to servants, single females, and married females respectively is highly suggestive. The evidence demonstrates that women frequently remained single into their early or mid-twenties, though this was more marked in urban society and need not imply that they were necessarily sexually inexperienced prior to their marriage. The ages of married deponents, though representative only of established marriages, do seem compatible with this pattern of delayed matrimony. Marriages, moreover, appear companionate, i.e. only a small age difference existed between spouses, and in a significant proportion of cases it is the wife who was the senior. More generally, however, the evidence indicates that males tended to remain single a couple of years longer than their sisters, though this was slightly more marked in the countryside than the town. Service as a predominantly life-cycle institution underlies this apparently late marrying regime, though the other work opportunities, perhaps again most pronounced in urban society and pastoral regions, that existed for young unmarried women at least before the later fifteenth century must also be acknowledged. Thus, although the sample is less than ideal, it does seem to demonstrate a first marriage regime compatible with the West European model outlined for the post-medieval era by Laslett in 1977, and with the particular 'north-western' pattern suggested by Smith in 1983.[91]

[87] BIHR, CP. E. 128.
[88] BIHR, CP. F. 22.
[89] See Ch. 4 above.
[90] BIHR, CP. G. 115 (1517).
[91] Laslett, 'Characteristics of the Western Family'; Smith, 'Hypothèses sur la nuptialité'.

THE CONTRACT OF MARRIAGE

It has traditionally been argued that under canon law medieval marriages were very unstable institutions due to the supposed ease with which established unions might be dissolved in the face of 'discovered' impediments. Pollock and Maitland write that 'the church, while she treated marriages as a formless contract, multiplied impediments which made the formation of a valid marriage a matter of chance' and point to the 'incalculable damage done by a marriage law which was a maze of flighty fancies and misapplied logic'.[92] Coulton cites contemporary comment to the effect that all too easily bribery and false testimony could be used to obtain annulments from the Church courts, though it is questionable how far Bromyard and Langland can be thought impartial social observers.[93] Particularly it has been thought that in an essentially static society where the individual was subsumed by the family, the community, and the collectivity, incidence of consanguinity or affinity within marriage would be necessarily high so leaving the door open for subsequent annulment in the absence of formal provision for divorce.

This older view has since been challenged by Sheehan in his careful study of a late fourteenth-century Ely court book, and by Helmholz in his invaluable and scholarly survey of matrimonial litigation.[94] It is challenged, to give an example of actions more substantially documented in the Vatican archives relating to the Papal Penitentiary, by two striking cases drawn from the diocese of Coventry and Lichfield in the later fourteenth century.[95] In one, a couple who had contracted a technically clandestine marriage without banns being read, had subsequently discovered that the woman had previously had sexual intercourse with a man related in the third or fourth degree to her supposed husband.

[92] F. Pollock and F. W. Maitland, *The History of English Law* (2nd edn., 2 vols.; Cambridge, 1898), ii. 385–6, 389.

[93] G. C. Coulton, *Medieval Panorama* (Cambridge, 1938), 638.

[94] Sheehan, 'The Formation and Stability of Marriage', 262–3; Helmholz, *Marriage Litigation*, 77–87.

[95] M. Yates, paper given at Winchester colloquium on recent research in 15th-cent. history, 1987; A. R. Wilson (ed.), *The Register or Act Books of the Bishops of Coventry and Lichfield*, v (Collections for a History of Staffordshire, NS 5; 1905), 116, 150.

Rather than cause the scandal of a 'divorce', the couple obtained a papal dispensation to marry afresh and not have their children deemed illegitimate. The second case concerns a woman who by remarrying had married the godfather of a child of her deceased first husband. Again the couple were worried by the threat of scandal and fears for the canonical validity of their union. In both these instances then canon law was seen as a potential threat to established unions rather than an excuse for divorce. The matrimonial litigation relating to both urban and rural society contained within the York cause papers further serves to undermine this traditional view. Disputes may have arisen from the apparently informal nature of the initial contract of marriage, but rarely in respect of an established marriage or from discovered impediments. The informality of some contracts can itself be related to the apparent lack of parental supervision of courtship for perhaps the majority of urban, and probably also many rural, couples.

The most striking observation to be made from the deposition records of matrimonial litigation contained within the sample of urban cause papers is this freedom seemingly permitted to adult individuals, females and males alike, to make their own decisions about whom they should marry. This itself followed from the early emotional independence from parents created by the institution of service, and the possibility of real economic independence outside marriage through service or other employment. 'Marriages', binding under the canon law of Church courts, were entered into without church solemnization throughout the period. Only some of these were intended to initiate lifelong relationships involving sharing bed and board. Many such contracts were highly informal, not properly witnessed, and liable to be broken off due to change of heart. These are perhaps best viewed not as actual marriages, but as spousals or engagements. Only some of these contracts were more formal and openly witnessed; a couple so contracted were said to be 'handfast'. In a cause of 1417 Robert Topclif is reported as having reminded Agnes Bradford that he had 'hanfest the'.[96] In such instances the couple appear to have been giving publicity to their union, a publicity that was sufficient

---

[96] BIHR, D/C CP. 1417/1. Cf. P. Rushton, 'The Broken Marriage in Early Modern England', 191, 193; J. R. Gillis, *For Better, for Worse: British Marriages, 1600 to the Present* (New York, 1985), 17, 44; Sheehan, 'The Formation and Stability of Marriage', 245.

in the eyes of late medieval English society to constitute matrimony. Even here, however, a church service, or 'solemnisation', was not deemed a necessary part of the proceedings.[97] A growing tendency, encouraged by the Church, to solemnize marriage at the church door (*in facie ecclesie*) can perhaps be observed, but this failed to displace the private 'family' contract. Nor can it be certain that the publicity of church solemnization accounts for the decline in matrimonial litigation over the period. It is the argument here that this decline was caused rather by the erosion of the economic independence of young adult women, and thus a corresponding undermining of their ability, in the face of recession over the later fifteenth century, to take the initiative in marriage formation or to contest disputed contracts, and that church solemnization is only a secondary factor.

Under canon law it was not publicity that made a marriage: canonists from the time of Alexander III (1159–81) stressed individual consent.[98] Thus a technically binding, but not necessarily enforceable, marriage could be made privately and even secretly by the couple alone. What was deemed essential was a verbal exchange indicative of consent. This could be either present consent (*per verba de presenti*), which had immediate effect, or future consent (*per verba de futuro*). This last would become immediately effective if the relationship were consummated, for though sexual relations did not of themselves create a binding marriage, in this context they were deemed to signify present consent to a future contract. Neither contract, however, was actually enforceable in the ecclesiastical courts unless supported by two independent witnesses. Hence it was quite possible to contract a canonical marriage which, for want of necessary witnesses, could not be enforced in court. Equally, and where arranged marriages were not the norm this must often have been the case, a couple might voluntarily dissolve such a contract with impunity, though technically any subsequent contract would be bigamous and canonists would argue that the parties would have to answer for this at the Day of Judgement.

If all contracts were properly publicized, as at the church door

---

[97] Helmholz, *Marriage Litigation*, 27; Sheehan, 'The Formation and Stability of Marriage', 244.

[98] See Brundage, *Law, Sex and Christian Society*, 332–6; Helmholz, *Marriage Litigation*, 26–7.

(*in facie ecclesie*) after the calling of banns, then it might be thought that matrimonial disputes would but rarely arise. The English evidence demonstrates that this was not the case.[99] There were disappointed parties who looked to the courts to enforce their contracts. Sometimes the courts were even asked to decide between the conflicting claims of several parties.[100] By analysing the particular matrimonial litigation that arose from such disputed contracts, it is possible to determine something of the circumstances that lay behind individual cases. It is clear that women especially were subject to more constraints by parents or wider kin groups in rural than was true of urban society, and that women were generally able to exercise the most choice where they enjoyed the greatest emotional and economic independence from their parents. These differences are reflected in the sorts of contract that appear within the litigation evidence.

Marriages appear to have been contracted privately, but not necessarily with any secrecy intended, under a wide variety of circumstances.[101] Often it was in the house of a friend, relative, parent, or, in the case of servants, master of one of the parties, and the contract was there openly witnessed by other household members. So one Katherine was married in her master John Dene's presence and with his consent. Also present were her master's wife and fellow servants and the contract was sealed by sharing a *crater* of wine.[102] Likewise when Robert Tavarner contracted himself to Margaret Goldsmyth in the presence of Robert Stillyngton and his wife, he did so to have witnessed what he had long promised her. Even before this contract the couple had, it was claimed, enjoyed a sexual relationship.[103] Richard Adamson contracted marriage to Beatrix Cuke in the high street in front of his house at Langtoft in the presence of his father, the vicar of Langtoft, and two other witnesses.[104] Many examples of marriages made in more surprising circumstances are regularly to be found—by the Beverley Gate in Hull when milking a cow or at

[99] Cf. Helmholz, *Marriage Litigation*, 27–8.
[100] Ibid. 25–73; Sheehan, 'The Formation and Stability of Marriage', 229–30; Pollock and Maitland, *History of English Law*, ii. 368–74.
[101] Cf. Helmholz, *Marriage Litigation*, 29; Gillis, *For Better, for Worse*, 44–5; Cosgrove, 'Marriage in Medieval Ireland', 38.
[102] BIHR, CP. F. 237 (1449).
[103] BIHR, CP. F. 108 (1433).
[104] BIHR, CP. F. 279 (1449).

St William's tomb in York Minster are but two—but the evidence is by its nature biased towards the atypical.[105] The canonical concept that marriage could be contracted merely by the free exchange of words of consent before witnesses was widely recognized as is shown by a cause of 1402. A young couple are said to have requested a night's lodging at a house in the Fishergate suburb of York. The householder asked the man, 'Is this your wife?' to which he replied, 'She's my fiancée (*est futura*).' The householder responded by warning that 'You'll have no lodging at my house unless you contract marriage in my presence (*nisi contraxeritis in presencia mea*).' The couple therefore promptly made a *de presenti* contract with the householder and his wife for witnesses. 'Et postea', the deposition runs, '. . . manserunt ibi in hospicio et in eodem lecto iacentes soli et nudi per sex dies.'[106] It is pertinent to note here that the Lollard view of marriage may have been more in tune with this essentially individualistic and secular approach to marriage formation than was the contemporary Church; a Lincolnshire source dated 1457 stresses only the need for mutual consent to effect a union, claiming that 'solemnitas per ecclesiam ordinata' was superfluous, the product of clerical avarice.[107]

Several different forms of words were used to indicate consent, but these tend mostly to be based upon a common model. When Richard Adamson and Beatrix Cuke contracted together at Langtoft one Sunday afternoon in 1448, Richard declared conventionally, 'By the feith of my body here I take ye Beatrix to my Wyf', to which Beatrix replied in like fashion and the couple kissed. But Richard had prefaced his declaration by advising Beatrix, 'By the feith of your body and by this hand that ye lay in myn think ye feithfully with your hert as ye sey with your mouth.' Beatrix had replied to this saying, 'Ya by the feith of my body and by this hand that I lay in youres.'[108] A conventional, but unusually full form of words is recorded in respect of a contract made between Thomas Mylner and Joan Northfolk at Wakefield in 1480. The

---

[105] BIHR, CP. F. 46 (1422); CP. F. 63 (1414).
[106] BIHR, CP. F. 22, also printed in Helmholz, *Marriage Litigation*, 228–9.
[107] A. Clark (ed.), *Lincoln Diocese Documents, 1450–1544* (EETS, 149; 1914), 92. See also A. Hudson, *The Premature Reformation: Wycliffite Texts and Lollard History* (Oxford, 1988), 292.
[108] BIHR, CP. F. 247.

couple held hands, i.e. handfast, at the request of one James Huton in whose house they were and repeated after him the following words that follow faithfully the Use of York:

Here I take the Janet to my wedded wife for farer for lather for better for wars in sekenes and in helth and holy kirk wil it ordaynd and therto plight I the my trowth.

Here I take the Thomas to my wedded husband to holde and to have at bed and at burde for fare for lather for better for wars in seknesse and in helth to deth us depart and holy kirk wil it ordaynd and therto plyght I the my trowth.

After the contract the couple went down into the hall to share a customary drink together.[109] A slightly different formula was used by Katherine Augour and Richard Watson in 1489. Richard held Katherine by the right hand and declared, 'Here I take ye Kateryn to my handfest Wif during my [life] and for luf of the to forsake all othre by the faith of my bodie.'[110] The earliest surviving matrimonial cause records, in Latin, another variant: 'I take you Joan to my lawful wife to have and to hold all the days of my life if Holy Church will permit and to this I plight you my troth.'[111] In none of the York causes examined here did the woman promise obedience to her spouse, a clause absent from pre-Reformation service books and that appears to have been added for the first time into the form of service contained in the 1549 Book of Common Prayer.[112]

Tokens were also often exchanged as a more tangible record of a contract. They thus constitute actual marriage tokens rather than more informal love tokens.[113] Such 'gifts in token of contract of wedding', distinct from courtship gifts, are described by Bartho-

---

[109] BIHR, CP. F. 265. Cf. M. Segalen, *Love and Power in the Peasant Family: Rural France in the Nineteenth Century*, trans. S. Matthews (Oxford, 1983), 30; M. Ingram, *Church Courts, Sex and Marriage in England, 1570–1640* (Cambridge, 1987), 196; Gillis, *For Better, for Worse*, 18, 45 concerning the use of an 'orator'. For an almost identical form of words contained within the contemporary Use of York marriage service see *Manuale et Processionale ad Usum Insignis Ecclesiae Eboracensis* (Surtees Society, 63; 1875), 27.

[110] BIHR, CP. F. 273.

[111] BIHR, CP. E. 1. Cf. the words used by Henry Palmer to contract Katherine Boys at Drogheda noted in a cause of 1449: Cosgrove, 'Marriage in Medieval Ireland', 41.

[112] *The Booke of Common Prayer* (London, 1549).

[113] Gillis, *For Better, for Worse*, 31–3, 43; Segalen, *Love and Power*, 18.

lomaeus Anglicus as early as the thirteenth century.[114] When John Wystowe contracted himself in marriage to Elena Couper of Welton in 1490, he gave her a silver-gilt ring by way of 'a trowthplight'.[115] A silver ring was likewise given by William Wykelay to Alice Walton after their contract. Alice in response is said to have tied a ribbon around his arm to remain there until she untied it.[116] The giving of rings was probably the most common token of marriage, but the cause paper evidence would suggest that it had not yet become an essential element in marriages contracted other than at the church door.[117] Gloves seem to have been another common token. Gloves were given to mark an agreement, such as a contract of employment or a property lease, but may have been thought especially appropriate for a contract of marriage involving the joining of hands. Gloves were thus a tangible symbol of handfasting. John Ward gave Margaret Dalton of Burnby a pair of white gloves 'in signum huiusmodi matrimonii' after their contract in 1429.[118] Agnes Ruke of Thorne was similarly presented with a pair of gloves by John Porter after their contract, but rather than welcome the gift Agnes had sighed. John Crubayn, a witness to the contract, rebuked her saying, 'Don't sigh because this agreement is one of the best agreements you have ever made.'[119] Richard Symson gave Alice Tiplady a purse as a token

---

[114] A. Macfarlane, *Marriage and Love in England, 1300–1840* (Oxford, 1986), 307–8. Pope Nicholas I described in a letter to the Bulgarians dated 866 how when a man was contracted to a woman he placed a 'ring of fidelity . . . as a pledge on her finger': quoted in D. Herlihy, *Medieval Households*, 74. See also Klapisch-Zuber, *Women, Family, and Ritual*, 196–7.

[115] BIHR, CP. F. 280.

[116] BIHR, CP. F. 186.

[117] Gillis, *For Better, for Worse*, 62, 203–4. Rings are widely found, e.g. in Siena in the early 13th cent. or in the diocese of Armagh in the later Middle Ages: G. Dolezalek, *Das Imbreviaturbuch des erzbischöflichen Geschichtsnotar Hubaldus aus Pisa, Mai bis August 1230* (Forschungen zur neuersen Privatrechtsgeschichte, 13; Cologne, 1969), 129, 132; Cosgrove, 'Marriage in Medieval Ireland', 40. Rings were used as part of the solemnization of marriage *in facie ecclesie* from an early date. A form of blessing of the ring is, for example, found in the Pontifical of Archbishop Egbert: *Manuale et Processionale*, appendix, 157: L. Roper, *The Holy Household*, 133.

[118] BIHR, CP. F. 20; Gillis, *For Better, for Worse*, 44; Raine (ed.), *Dispositions and other Ecclesiastical Proceedings from the Courts of Durham*, 29; Ingram, *Church Courts, Sex and Marriage*, 199. Gloves were commonly given to acknowledge quit-rents. I am grateful to Dr Rees Jones for this observation.

[119] BIHR, CP. F. 84.

of their contract.[120] More romantically, in 1371 John Beke garlanded Marjory Taliour with flowers and kissed her through the
garland after they had contracted together.[121]

The acceptance of gifts and tokens was regarded as a mark of
consent and evidence of a binding contract, albeit not necessarily
one solemnized at the church door, in a still pre-literate society.
A cause of 1499 records Robert Grene's gift of a mirror to Isabella
Wasse as both evidence of a contract and Isabella's consent to it
in accepting and making use of the present or token. When Joan
Webster of Hambleton was given a gold noble by Nicholas Tup
after their contract, she received it 'as from her husband'.[122] John
Kirkeby of Whitby, contracted to Agnes Barebour of York,
observed that he should wear a ring from her finger which she
promptly gave him. In return he gave her a silver brooch.[123]
Evidence in a cause dated 1436 relating to the giving and acceptance of gifts, including a girdle of silver gilt, two chaplets, and
various purses, given by Robert Thweng to Cecily Fedyrston, was
used to further the case that a valid contract based on mutual
consent had taken place.[124] Conversely, when the contract
between Agnes Cosyn and Robert Chew was repudiated by
Agnes's parents, the ring and other gifts offered as tokens by
Robert were sent back.[125]

To understand more fully social attitudes to matrimony it is thus
necessary to distinguish between those, albeit technically clandestine contracts which were openly and formally witnessed and other
more intimate contracts to which the parties by their very nature
invited no witnesses.[126] Such a contract is that described in a cause

[120] BIHR, CP. G. 26. A purse containing a shilling was likewise given by
Thomas Hokerigge to mark his contract to Godleve Lucas noted in a Canterbury
cause dated 1417: Helmholz, *Marriage Litigation*, 20.
[121] BIHR, CP. E. 121.
[122] BIHR, CP. F. 292; CP. F. 159; W. S. Simpson (ed.), *Visitations of Churches
Belonging to St Paul's Cathedral* (Camden Society, NS 55; 1985), 70. This last
concerns the gift of a noble by the man and of two silver-gilt rings by the woman
at the time of their contract.   [123] BIHR, CP. F. 182.
[124] BIHR, CP. F. 119. For rings as evidence of a contract see Brundage, *Law,
Sex, and Christian Society*, 412, 502. Cf. Ingram, *Church Courts, Sex and Marriage*,
197 for use of tokens as evidence of contracts of marriage in early modern
Wiltshire.   [125] BIHR, CP. F. 189.
[126] Although this is not an approach adopted by Finch, he does caution that
'additional avenues of enquiry should be opened when considering the motives for
clandestine marriages and the ways in which different courts reacted to them':
Finch, 'Crime and Marriage', 271.

of 1418 where a couple in a barn were overheard by people sleeping the other side of the wattle wall in a neighbouring building.[127] The latter might of course, as in this example, be witnessed accidentally and become subsequently the subject of litigation, but it is not the impression formed here that these were immediately intended to constitute binding marriages in the eyes of the local community any more than engagements are today thought to be binding. Thus when Robert Tavarner contracted his marriage to Margaret Goldsmyth he admitted that he had once been espoused to one Marjory Wadyngton, sempster, but that he had no intention of marrying her. He was making a contrast, which neither canon law nor the Church court could uphold, between an openly witnessed plighting of troth and an earlier, but less formal 'engagement' or betrothal. It is apparent that such public contracts were accorded the force of marriage within the community whether or not solemnized and that in manorial society children born subsequent to trothplight, but prior to solemnization were treated as legitimate and able to inherit.[128] It would be mistaken to conclude, therefore, that marriages were readily and informally entered into and equally readily and informally broken off simply on the basis of the numbers of disputed contracts coming before the Church courts. Rather it is that canon law, by recognizing as binding and thus attempting to enforce contracts that may never have in themselves been so intended, was out of step with the needs and sentiments of lay society. Equally, by labelling any contract of marriage made other than in the approved manner at the church door as 'clandestine', the Church blurred the distinction that ordinary lay folk may themselves have perceived between an informal 'engagement' and the binding contract of the 'handfast' or 'trothplight'.

It was to eliminate these acknowledged difficulties inherent in the canonical interpretation of marriage that the Church came to insist on church solemnization. This, together with the publication of banns, served to maximize publicity within the parish community even before a binding contract was entered into. This does seem to have been adopted with increasing regularity during the

---

[127] BIHR, CP. F. 79.
[128] G. C. Homans, *English Villagers of the Thirteenth Century* (Cambridge, Mass., 1941), 164–6.

later Middle Ages, but in practice following and not in place of the private or 'family' contract. Thus witnesses described in 1435 how an alleged marriage between John Skirpenbek and Agnes Miton was contracted first at the house of Hugh Killom and subsequently at St Sampson's church in York.[129] Helmholz has even suggested 'that most people who entered into these private agreements meant to have their unions blessed by a priest at some later time'.[130] This must remain a real possibility since it is uncertain that the large number of unsolemnized contracts apparent within the cause paper sample are representative of prevailing social custom. There is, however, little to suggest that in town society especially, but also in the countryside in respect of the less prosperous peasantry, 'family' contracts were thought incomplete and that solemnization was expected.[131] More informal contracts, on the other hand, may never have been intended to constitute binding marriages and would not have been followed by solemnization of themselves. The differing types of contract may conveniently be listed as follows.

　i. Private, informal, generally unwitnessed contracts which may or may not have been consummated. These would either have been broken off subsequently or have been followed by some more formal contract. Termed 'clandestine' in the Church court, such contracts could only be enforced if a minimum of two witnesses to the same contract could be presented, if there were no lawful impediment, and if the court was satisfied that the words used constituted a canonical *de presenti* or consummated *de futuro* contract.

　ii. Private, formal, witnessed, 'family' contracts or 'handfastings'. Clergy were sometimes present on these occasions and the couple often repeated the words of contract at the direction of an 'orator'.[132] Such contracts may have followed from (i) and often

---

　[129] BIHR, CP. F. 115. Cf. Sheehan, 'The Formation and Stability of Marriage', 239.

　[130] Helmholz, *Marriage Litigation*, 29–30.

　[131] Cf. Cosgrove's comments on Anglo-Irish attitudes to marriage formation in the diocese of Armagh in the 15th cent.: Cosgrove, 'Marriage in Medieval Ireland', 39–40. Brooke likewise concludes that 'a church ceremony was not an essential feature of match-making': C. N. L. Brooke, *The Medieval Idea of Marriage* (Oxford, 1989), 253.

　[132] Brundage, *Law, Sex and Christian Society*, 436; Gillis, *For Better, for Worse*, 18, 45.

involved the giving or exchange of tokens. Consummation frequently followed the contract, often the same night. Likewise termed 'clandestine', they were nevertheless likely to be upheld as canonically binding contracts unless a pre-contract, sometimes of type (i), or other lawful impediment could be proved.[133] Often, but by no means always, followed by solemnization *in facie ecclesie* (iii).

iii. Public, formal, witnessed, contracts at the church door (*in facie ecclesie*) after the reading of banns. In practice, these often followed from (ii). Such contracts were encouraged by the Church and could only be upset if some lawful impediment were subsequently proved.

MARRIAGE IN RURAL SOCIETY

For urban society it is possible to point to the range of economic opportunities open to young women that may have taken young people of both sexes outside the natal home and provided a means of support outside marriage. The institution of life-cycle servanthood seems to have been particularly widespread in towns after the Black Death, if not before, and paid employment was available for women in a variety of trades, notably in victualling, textiles, and clothing trades. This pattern of opportunity for women contrasts with the more constrained picture that emerges for rural communities, though real differences appear to have existed between arable and pastoral regions. Poll tax evidence suggests that in the rural West Riding, a predominantly pastoral region, young persons of both sexes were much more likely to remain with their parents than to live outside the natal home as servants. In respect of non-agricultural employment, rural female adolescents were as likely to work at home as in service, but their male counterparts were more likely to be employed as servants outside the parental home.

In rural Rutland (using more comprehensive data based upon a population aged 14 or more rather than 16 or more as in the case of the West Riding material) the contrast is more sharply defined.

---

[133] The binding nature of such contracts in the popular culture of the early modern era is noted in Gillis, *For Better, for Worse*, 50.

Here craft households drew disproportionately upon male servants and female children. This last is a significant observation since craft households appear to have exercised a particular hold over female children. The child sex ratio for all households in rural Rutland is evenly balanced at 101.0, but in craft households it is only 69.6. Variations in the gender-specific pattern of demand for labour within differing agricultural economies are probably to be found underlying these regional differences. The opportunities for women, whether single or married, appear to have been much greater within the largely pastoral West Riding than may have been true of Rutland, a region that was probably still substantially engaged in arable production at this date. Thus women could find employment carding, spinning, and weaving wool, washing and shearing sheep, milking cows and sheep, making butter and cheese, opportunities not readily available in arable regions.

That in rural society sons and more especially daughters frequently resided with their parents until marriage is also implicit from the deposition evidence. Thus in a cause dated 1333 both parties to a disputed marriage, namely John, son of Ralph de Penesthorp, and Elizabeth, daughter of Walter de Waldegrave, lived with their parents.[134] Matilda, daughter of Robert son of Richard, Joan Thorneton, Agnes, daughter of William Cosyn, and Alice Herkey were likewise all living with their fathers at the time of their contracts according to deposition evidence dated 1373, 1433, 1453, and 1507 respectively.[135] Children were thus more immediately dependant upon their parents in the rural household than was true of most urban households. Parents there were thus in a stronger position to supervise the marriages of their sons and, more especially, their daughters. It is evident that the consent of a parent or guardian was an expected requirement for any woman contemplating matrimony. When early in the fifteenth century Agnes Fraunceys was asked by Robert de Newerk if she intended to marry his brother, she replied, 'I Will have hym in to my Husband if my Fadir will assent.'[136] Alice Herkey is reported to have stated, 'that she would never contract herself to any one . . . unless with her parents present'.[137] The same sentiment

---

[134] BIHR, CP. E. 26.
[135] BIHR, CP. E. 113; CP. F. 177, 189; CP. G. 26.
[136] BIHR, CP. F. 176.
[137] BIHR, CP. G. 26.

was expressed by Isabell Lame in a matrimonial cause of 1445 before the Durham consistory, and the court at Rochester in 1347 similarly heard that Robert, son of Walter Webbe, had promised Juliana atte Wode marriage if his parents would consent.[138] William de Rykall stated in a cause of 1361 that he asked Alice Wright's father if he would give him his daughter in marriage.[139] Agnes Ruke of Thorne promised to marry John Porter on condition that he obtained her uncle's good will.[140] Sometimes the advisability of obtaining the consent of a parent or employer was only remembered after the initial contract. Joan Broke, in a cause of 1442 before the Rochester consistory, added the condition that she needed the consent of her master and her 'friends' only as her intended was walking away after they had exchanged words of present consent.[141] Godleve Lucas tried to add such a condition retrospectively, it may be suspected precisely because her parents opposed the marriage, but the court would not allow this 'remembered' condition.[142]

In practice, parental or familial involvement in the process of marriage often went further. The urban evidence is slight before the end of our period, but among more substantial peasant farmers it appears to have been usual for the families to meet prior to any formal contract being made to discuss arrangements and dowry terms.[143] One such gathering is observed from depositions made in 1466. At nine on the appointed morning there gathered at their own house the parents of Agnes Beleby together with Agnes, her intended, Robert Inkersale, his widowed mother, the vicar of Rotherham, and three other invited witnesses. A discussion of the amount of dowry to be paid followed and the sum of 25 marks proffered by William Beleby was agreed.[144] A similar gathering, also involving a clergyman, whereby a dowry of 20 marks was

[138] Raine (ed.), *Depositions and other Ecclesiastical Proceedings*, 29; C. Johnston (ed.), *Registrum Hamonis Hethe* (2 vols.; Canterbury and York Society, 48–9; 1914–48), ii. 967.

[139] BIHR, CP. F. 84.

[140] BIHR, CP. F. 84; Helmholz, *Marriage Litigation*, 48 n. 85. In this last instance, drawn from a Canterbury cause of 1417, the parties agreed to keep their contract secret until the young man had won the good will of his fiancée's employer.

[141] Ibid. 49.

[142] Ibid. 204, 206.

[143] BIHR, CP. G. 40, 115.

[144] BIHR, CP. F. 242.

arranged, was held prior to the contract between Emma Corry and Thomas del Dale in 1392.[145] As the public ratification of dower provision was an integral part of the ecclesiastical marriage rites, it follows that most contracts involving property or land transfer between families would also have been solemnized *in facie ecclesie*.[146]

Clearly, where families had a material stake in the marriage process the crucial question of choice could not be left solely to the parties contracting. Thus, although canon law insisted on free will as the basis for a valid union, the initiative in bringing young people together often lay with parents. This is apparent in the case of Agnes Beleby and Robert Inkersale; only after the dowry arrangements had been agreed did one Nicholas Keeton advise, 'Lat us now here or we wade any ferther what Robert and Agnes sais in this matier for in thame two lies all.'[147] When Margaret Graunt was asked to contract herself to John Serle she was advised, 'Chese yow now and never say after but that it is your own dede and not oonly your freends [*i.e. family*].' The full force of these words may be appreciated from the subsequent allegation that Margaret had been forced into the marriage by her grandfather. It may also be noted that Margaret was only 14 at the time.[148]

The initiative for making rural marriages may often have lain with parents, but this did not preclude young people in the countryside sometimes taking the initiative in much the same way as their urban cousins. At times, choice may have been exercised by the couple contracting subject only to parental or familial consent. This must have been true, for example, of Alice Wright and William de Rykall noted earlier. When William asked Alice's father if he could marry Alice, he replied, 'If it pleases Alice, I am well satisfied.'[149] At other times individuals may have feared that this consent would be difficult to obtain. When in 1454 Richard Northcroft and Margaret Atkynson of Billingley (near Barnsley) exchanged vows before just two witnesses, Margaret was concerned to keep the contract quiet for a long time as she

---

[145] BIHR, CP. E. 215.
[146] Homans, *English Villagers of the Thirteenth Century*, 170–2.
[147] BIHR, CP. F. 242.
[148] BIHR, CP. F. 308.
[149] BIHR, CP. E. 84.

did not wish certain of her friends (presumably family) or relatives to hear of it.[150] It was, however, only the most determined that were, like Margery Paston, able to withstand the full force of parental opposition in the knowledge that canon law was on their side. The courage of Elena Couper of Welton is conspicuous among the cause papers and was perhaps as rare in her day. One Sunday before Pentecost 1490, we are told, Elena called her young man to a friend's house that she might have witnesses to her contract. She then prompted him with the following words:

John, there is two yonge men abowte me in the town to have me to wiffe. And I have lovyd the thys two yer. And yow knowest wele that yow and I be handfast bitwixt us. And bycause yow shalt not varry nor take an othir and love an othir better then me, We wilbe handfast here afore thies folkes at they may beyr record theropon.

Thus prompted, John Wystowe plighted his troth. Elena's mother responded less favourably to the news declaring: 'thow filth and harlot. Why, art thow handfast with John Wistow? When thy fadre knowys it he wylle dynge the and myschew the.' Elena chose not to await her father's return, but passed the night at the house of a friend. The next morning her father John Couper arrived, but he was only admitted on condition that he would do Elena no harm. He furiously reproached her for contracting herself without his knowledge to the one man he most disliked.

And she fell down upon her knees before her father and said, 'Sir, that at I have doon I will performe if the law will suffre it for I wyll have hym whosoever say nay to it. And I desire no more of your goodes but your blessyng.'

In urban society the institution of life-cycle service was well developed by the mid-fourteenth century and it is likely that relatively few daughters remained with their parents until marriage before the later fifteenth century.[151] Only one urban cause concerns specifically a father's attempt to prevent the marriage of his daughter, who resided with him, to the man of her choice and this dates to 1467.[152]

---

[150] BIHR, CP. F. 194.
[151] See Ch. 4 above.
[152] BIHR, CP. F. 244. A deponent in a York cause dated 1434 claimed that John Preston's father threatened that if he married Joan, daughter of Thomas Lymber, 'he would never have a part of his goods and chattels': CP. F. 114.

Elena Couper sacrificed material advantage for the right to choose her own husband. It follows that daughters of poorer families, who could contribute little in terms of land or wealth, may often have enjoyed greater freedom. This is difficult to demonstrate, however, in as much as the main evidence for the status of parties below the rank of aristocracy is itself derived from reference to dowry provision. Alice Redyng, who successfully brought a suit to enforce a contract of marriage with John Boton, chapman, worked as a servant and could claim little wealth. Significantly she alleged a future contract that had been consummated and there is no evidence of any formal family involvement.[153] Isabella Laurens was drinking with friends at the tavern within Christmas week 1471 when she turned to Thomas Gell with the words, 'Thomas, I luf you wele.' Isabella's status is not apparent, but the circumstances of her alleged contract do not suggest wealth.[154]

For women, however, there was a negative side to any lack of parental supervision of and restraint in courtship. The risks women faced if they entered into a sexual relationship without a properly witnessed contract are well illustrated within the cause paper evidence. Several causes concern attempts by women to enforce dubious contracts against lovers who had abandoned them. In 1423 the court dismissed Beatrix Pulane's claim to have contracted to Thomas Newby before two witnesses in view of the number of young men who testified that Thomas was playing football at the time.[155] The evidence for a contract appears even slighter in the case of Agnes Vasour and William Warthyll of Newton upon Derwent. Agnes had long been William's mistress and was to have a child by him, but when Agnes's stepfather asked him why he would not marry her, he replied that he would either marry her or leave her. In the event he left Agnes and married another woman with her parents for witnesses.[156] In 1354 Maud Schipyn found herself being pressed to have sex with Robert Smyth. She challenged him, 'God forbid that you should have power to know me carnally unless you intend to marry me.' He

[153] BIHR, CP. E. 92.
[154] BIHR, CP. F. 252.
[155] BIHR, CP. F. 137. One of Beatrix's two witnesses believed that the couple had often had intercourse.
[156] BIHR, CP. F. 191.

replied, 'I give you my word that if I take anyone for my wife, I'll take you if you will let me have my will with you', a reply that should have warned Maud, but she responded, 'I give you my word that I will let you have your will with me.'[157] Joan de Brerelay at least had witnesses and was under less immediate threat when Thomas Bakester made a similar request. 'Not unless you marry me', she replied, to which Thomas agreed 'if she would wait for him to finish his apprenticeship'. When Joan's case was heard in 1384, Thomas had failed to honour his promise, although a child that was born to them was then 7½ years old.[158] Still more precarious was the position of Alice de Wellewyk, who likewise consented to intercourse only if she had a promise of marriage. Robert de Midelton replied, 'I do not want to marry you unless I know you are able to conceive and have a child by me.' By the time Alice had had his child, Robert was already looking to marry another.[159]

The dangers young women ran by engaging in sexual relations as part of their courtship might itself be a matter of familial concern. In two instances the woman's brother chose to force a recalcitrant lover to make a binding contract. Perhaps young women found it easier to confide in their brothers than their fathers that they were in trouble. John, son of Ralph of Penisthorpe (near Patrington), was set upon in 1332 by Richard, brother of Elizabeth de Waldegrave, and a handful of armed men whilst he awaited Elizabeth in the bakehouse of her father's home one night and he was forced at the point of a sword to be handfast with Elizabeth.[160] It was alleged in another cause dated 1431 that John Ward was likewise confronted in his master's barn by his lover Alice Skelton, her brother Thomas Holme and his wife, and two other men armed with axes. Thomas threatened John, his hand upon his dagger, that unless he married his sister he would

---

[157] BIHR, CP. E. 70. This exchange and what followed was accidentally witnessed by Margaret Theker, who was lying ill in an adjoining building. Exactly the same formula was used by William Holyngbourne to seduce Agnes Lynch observed in a Canterbury cause of 1374. The court, however, ruled that a canonical marriage had been contracted: Helmholz, *Marriage Litigation*, 198–9.

[158] BIHR, CP. E. 255.

[159] BIHR, CP. E. 79.

[160] BIHR, CP. E. 26. John was wounded and thereafter stayed away.

lose his life, but John refused on the grounds that he was already contracted to another.[161]

Forced marriages were, however, invalid under canon law and the power families had over men who took advantage of their daughters was slight. One can sense the frustration and anger experienced by one Ydonea when she attempted to prevent the marriage of Nigel le Roser to Agnes, the daughter of Beatrix, on the grounds that her own daughter, Alice Godewyn, a close relative of Agnes, was already pregnant by him.[162] Well-to-do families could not have tolerated such a situation and would thus have ensured close supervision of their daughters' courtships. Such a pattern may lie behind the higher incidence of leyrewite levied on daughters of poorer villein families than on those of more substantial families.[163] But women who had no land or wealth to offer may have gambled upon a sexual relationship in the hope that this would lead to a binding contract. By analogy with the early modern era, moreover, the earlier the mean age at first marriage for women, the more likely they would have been to enter into risky relationships. No causes alleging forced marriage or nullity on grounds of marriage within forbidden degrees are to be found, however, within the period 1400–49. This may coincide with a period of greater autonomy for women in the countryside both through access to land and employment.[164] The impression gained from the urban cause paper sample, on the other hand, is that though contracts, which may often have been consummated, were dishonoured from time to time, these were rarely long-standing relationships. Urban women had through paid employment the luxury of exercising more mature decisions about marriage and may not have been so readily frightened into

---

[161] BIHR, CP. F. 200. The men with axes claimed that John did make a contract in the barn and that their axes were merely their tools of trade. John's evidence that he had made an earlier contract seems to have convinced the court since he claimed to have been reaping at the time, yet seven deponents testified that the specified field was fallow at that time.

[162] BIHR, CP. E. 241b.

[163] Razi, *Life, Marriage and Death*, 66; Poos and Smith, 'Legal Windows', 150–1.

[164] Continued demographic recession may have made land more readily available, whereas a shift from arable to pastoral may have ensured demand for female labour. Wages for sheep-shearing, traditionally women's work, seem to have been especially bouyant in the earlier part of the 15th cent. See Ch. 6 below. Several forced marriages are observed in the period from 1450. See Table 5.7.

an unsatisfactory relationship lest that be their only opportunity to secure a partner.

PATTERNS OF LITIGATION

The secular incidence of different types of matrimonial litigation as reflected in urban and rural causes respectively is shown in Table 5.7.[165] The survival of causes over the entire period is seemingly arbitrary. Patently only a fraction of all actions within the consistory have left surviving depositions. The evidence is limited moreover to instance or contested actions as opposed to *ex officio* litigation.[166] The broad secular trends in types of action are, nevertheless, likely to be real given the apparently random nature of the surviving material. There are a number of conspicuous differences between the pattern of matrimonial litigation in the period before 1520 associated with rural causes and that associated with essentially urban causes. No suits for divorce *a mensa et a thoro*, i.e. for legal separation on grounds of excessive cruelty or adultery, are to be found within the rural sample whereas six are found in the equivalent urban sample. Suits for divorce, technically annulment, *a vinculo* are, on the other hand, comparatively common within the rural sample. Eight causes, of which five are located in the period 1450–99, relate to forced marriages and another eight to marriages within forbidden degrees of consanguinity or affinity. This is in contrast to the urban pattern, where only four forced marriages, all located in the first part of the fifteenth century, and no suits alleging either consanguinity or affinity are to be found.[167] Whereas multi-party suits, known as *causae matrimonialis et divorcii*, where the court had to decide between the claims of more than one man alleged to be contracted to the same woman or vice versa, end abruptly *c.*1450 in the urban sample, they are found throughout the period before 1520 within the rural sample.

The reasons for these rather different patterns of matrimonial

---

[165] Causes have been classified as rural or urban according to the place of abode of the principal actors. The actual distribution is shown in Appendix III, though in a few instances where the litigants are from different kinds of location, the allocation is necessarily more arbitrary.

[166] Helmholz, *Marriage Litigation*, 70–2.

[167] Two alleged forced marriages are contained within multi-party actions: BIHR, CP. F. 36, 74, 127.

TABLE 5.7.   *Types of matrimonial cause by period, 1303–1520*

	Suits to enforce marriage contracts	*Causa matrimonialis et divorcii*	Divorce *a vinculo**	Divorce *a mensa et a thoro*	Total
Urban matrimonial causes					
1303–49	—	2	—	2	4
1350–99	7	11	1 (1×c)	1	20
1400–49	9	13	7(2×a;4×b;1×g)	3	32
1450–99	8	—	—	—	8
1500–20	4	—	2 (1×a, d)	—	6
1303–1520	28	26	10	6	70
Rural matrimonial causes					
1306–49	2	3	4 (1×b, d; 2×e)	—	9
1350–99	10	10	10 (2×a, b, d, f; 1×e, g)	—	30
1400–49	12	14	4 (2×a; 1×d, g)	—	30
1450–99	10	6	8(5×b;2×e;1×f)	—	24
1500–20	1	3	1 (1×b/d)	—	5
1306–1520	35	36	27	—	98

* Types of divorce suit are shown in parentheses. They are identified alphanumerically following Helmholz, *Marriage Litigation*, 77–100:

  a Impotence.
  b Force and fear.
  c Impediment of crime (adultery).
  d Under age (*infra annos nubiles*).
  e Affinity.
  f Consanguinity.
  g Error of condition, etc.

Sources: BIHR, CP. E, F, G various; D/C CP various; Appendix III below.

litigation are not immediately apparent. It is to be hoped that the samples are sufficiently large for the patterns generated to be statistically significant, i.e. that the observed differences do relate to real variations between the pattern of rural and urban litigation and are not simply the product of accident. There is little to suggest that radically differing social groups are responsible for the litigation appearing within the cause papers beyond that one group is resident in the larger towns of the region, the other in the country. This can only be a subjective observation, however, since the evidence rarely provides sufficient data from which the social standing of parties may be evaluated. Rather more may in fact be ascertained about the status of the deponents appearing on behalf of the various parties. The conclusion is that the very wealthy are rarely represented and the poor not at all, except as deponents. The moderately well off, skilled artisans and traders or peasants with land to their name, are much better represented. It is thus the argument here that the differing patterns of litigation are to be understood in terms of differences in social structure between town and country as reflected in marriage formation and thus in marriage litigation. But this understanding is no easy matter. The historian must tread warily. The precise circumstances which led to multi-party litigation, for example, cannot be known. The court was primarily concerned to establish which union constituted a canonically binding marriage. The details deponents are asked to recall relate to dates, witnesses, and forms of words used, not to how a couple came to contract marriage in the first place, or how one alleged contract of marriage came to be set aside in favour of another. All too often the depositions survive in incomplete form and it is only possible to know something of one of the disputed contracts. There are, moreover, real uncertainties in attempting to generalize about society from the evidence of a litigious minority whose histories may in any case be atypical. The evidence on a qualitative level is thus suggestive rather than conclusive and the interpretation of this evidence is designed only to show that the patterns observed accord with certain hypotheses regarding the prevailing social system rather than that they demonstrate these.

A decline in both the range and the volume of urban matrimonial litigation by the later fifteenth century is apparent. The data are not ideal since the cause papers seem to have survived by chance and not in quantity before the later fourteenth century, but the trend is sufficiently marked and sufficiently unlike the rural pattern for it not to be accidental. A decline in matrimonial litigation by this date is not a new observation. Houlbrooke has elsewhere suggested that matrimonial cases were being discouraged by the early sixteenth century by canon lawyers keen to pursue more lucrative testamentary and tithe litigation.[168] Helm-

---

[168] R. A. Houlbrooke, *Church Courts and the People during the English Reformation, 1520–1570* (Oxford, 1979), 64–5.

holz argues for a growing acceptance of solemnization *in facie ecclesie*, displacing the private contract, with its scope for subsequent dispute and litigation, to explain a downward trend in matrimonial litigation.[169] As has already been observed, however, there seems little evidence from the York records that the private contract was in fact set aside during the course of the later Middle Ages. Indeed Houlbrooke describes its continuance as an integral part of marriage formation into the early modern era.[170] The continued significance of handfasting as an integral part of marriage formation may likewise be noted in Elizabethan and Jacobean Newcastle. In a case before the Durham court dated 1609 witnesses were clearly unsure whether this form of contract by itself constituted a binding 'marriage', but there is no evidence here that the church ceremony either displaced or yet replaced so important a private ceremony.[171] Ingram suggests that the widespread acceptance of church solemnization had occurred only by the beginning of the seventeenth century, although he notes an increasing reluctance on the part of the Church courts to confirm disputed contracts from before that date.[172] Helmholz's suggestion must thus be open to doubt, but neither his nor Houlbrooke's explanations can account for the apparently divergent trends between urban and rural litigation.

Two factors may be of particular significance in explaining the different observed patterns of litigation. Young urban adults appear to have enjoyed greater economic independence through the range of work opportunities available in urban society, notably after the plague, and appear to have married late. On the other hand, young rural adults, and young women in particular, appear to have enjoyed fewer opportunities outside the home and may have tended to marry slightly earlier than their urban counterparts, but still within the context of a late marriage regime. More youthful couples would probably have been more subject to and compliant with parental wishes and have had less opportunity to become romantic-

---

[169] Helmholz, *Marriage Litigation*, 167–8; B. L. Woodcock, *Medieval Ecclesiastical Courts in the Diocese of Canterbury* (London, 1952), 85.

[170] Houlbrooke, *The English Family*, 78–9.

[171] Rushton, 'The Broken Marriage', 187–96.

[172] Ingram, 'Spousals Litigation', 52–3, 55; id., 'The Reform of Popular Culture? Sex and Marriage in Early Modern England', in B. Reay (ed.), *Popular Culture in Seventeenth-Century England* (London, 1985), 144; id., *Church Courts, Sex and Marriage*, 205–8.

ally involved prior to marriage. Where parents expected to have greater control over the marriages of their children, however, couples may have been more concerned to hide their courtship from their respective parents. When for example Margaret Atkynson of Billingley contracted herself in marriage to Richard Northcroft, she was concerned to keep the news secret for a long time lest her family got to hear of it.[173] Such behaviour would have increased the possibility of canonically valid marriages being repudiated due to parental opposition on learning of the contract. It would also have allowed for formally arranged marriages to be contracted without due regard to any prior, but more informal contract either unknown to or disapproved of by the respective parents. Such subsequent contracts could later be upset, as was true of the example just cited, by means of the *causa matrimonialis et divorcii*.

There are a number of instances within the rural causes of contracts involving parental or familial consent, most of which were actually solemnized, challenged and sometimes upset as a consequence of a pre-contract by one of the parties. Typical is a cause of 1369. John Birkys of Woodhouse contracted one Joan in the presence of her aunt and another witness a week before Michaelmas. The following Sunday banns were read and the couple subsequently had their marriage solemnized in Leeds parish church. This marriage was challenged, however, by Cecily Wright, who claimed that John had promised to marry her some five years earlier and had continued to sleep with her despite being instructed to abjure her by the parish chaplain. The court ruled in Cecily's favour.[174] In a similar cause of 1434 deponents relate how John Maynpurse of Skipsea contracted marriage to Alice Willyamson before a relative and her master, the vicar of Skipsea, who was himself related by blood to both parties. The vicar, however, delayed the reading of banns and an action alleging a pre-contract between John and one Isabella Whitehouse was subsequently begun. Two deponents testified to a contract made just before sunset one Sunday earlier in the year on the road between Skipsea and Ulrome. John is alleged to have said to Isabella on that occasion, 'And by my trowth I sall never wed

---

[173] BIHR, CP. F. 194. Similar motives have been described in respect of some 15th-cent. Anglo-Irish couples: Cosgrove, 'Marriages in Medieval Ireland', 38–9.
[174] BIHR, CP. E. 105.

woman to my wyfe bot ye whylse yu lefes.' The court ruled that John should be bound by this earlier contract.[175] The clearest evidence for parental involvement comes, however, in the several instances where established unions were threatened by remembered, or sometimes invented, pre-contracts.[176] There can be little doubt that in such cases the provisions of canon law were being cynically exploited to obtain what were in effect divorces, something that was not sanctioned by the Church.[177] How far the unhappy unions thus dissolved were a consequence of arranged marriages must remain a matter of speculation, but the formally solemnized contracts that were subject to challenge contrast markedly with the highly informal pre-contracts that on occasion appear to have been genuine love matches.[178]

A cause of 1333 relates to the marriage solemnized between Geoffrey de Brunne and Alice Palmer at Folkton some six years before which was fraudulently annulled after four years on the fabricated testimony of two women for a pre-contract between Alice and one Ralph Fugeler. The marriage had proved acrimonious and Alice had looked to her father for help. Her father had then bribed Ralph to bring an action before the official of the archdeaconry court for the East Riding held at Staxton alleging a pre-contract in order to free Alice from her husband.[179] A cause of 1422 records the church solemnization nine years earlier of the contract of marriage between William Kyng of Bishopthorpe and Alice Cok of Scroby in the porch of the chapel of Scroby. Thirteen years earlier, however, at the time of day that the young men of the village customarily played football, the same William had contracted marriage to Joan Radcliff of Cawood in a house at Wistow before four apparently unrelated witnesses. The court found that the pre-contract was valid and dissolved the later union.[180]

---

[175] BIHR, CP. F. 178.

[176] BIHR, CP. E. 77, 79, 155; CP. F. 3, 133, 158, 201, 262.

[177] Helmholz, *Marriage Litigation*, 64–5; Brundage, *Law, Sex, and Christian Society*, 510; Sheehan, 'The Formation and Stability of Marriage', 252.

[178] Simpson (ed.), *Visitations of Churches Belonging to St Paul's*, 80–2. This seems to be a case of elopement following an arranged marriage.

[179] BIHR, CP. E. 25. Geoffrey subsequently remarried and the action in the consistory was brought in order to restore the original marriage that had been fraudulently dissolved. See Helmholz, *Marriage Litigation*, 65.

[180] BIHR, CP. F. 13. It seems possible that William and Joan were both servants in Wistow as they were then staying in houses of Richard Willowby and Margaret Pyper, both of whom were witnesses to the contract.

The most telling example of this kind of multi-party action is contained in a cause of 1374. Five years before, Joan atte Enges of Patrington had solemnized her marriage to John de Thetilthorp on the feast of St Hugh in the parish church at Kilthorpe. Some eight years before this, however, as a servant in York she had contracted marriage to another servant, Richard, son of Thomas Carter, before three witnesses, one her master, one Richard's master. The court decided that this was a valid contract and so annulled the later marriage. But the court had also received evidence from Richard's brother John that he had last seen Richard three years before and had never heard of him since.[181] By implication Joan was divorced from John because of a pre-contract to a husband she could not live with because his where-abouts were unknown. This case also demonstrates the difficulties that could arise when rural adolescents were for a time granted considerable freedom of courtship whilst engaged as servants away from home, perhaps in the more anonymous atmosphere of the city, but subsequently returned to their natal homes. In 1430, for example, two long-established and solemnized marriages were upset when Joan Ingoly proved to the court's satisfaction her pre-contract with Robert Esyngwald. At the time of their contract Joan was apparently in service in Over Poppleton, Robert, a native of Poppleton, in York. The contract was made at Poppleton before two other servant friends on their Sunday off. Joan's motives for reviving this contract after twenty years cannot, unfortunately, be reconstructed.[182]

The higher profile of rural parents in the process of marriage may thus explain some of the observed differences in the pattern of litigation between town and country. Cosgrove has described much the same pattern of litigation found in York rural causes for the diocese of Armagh in the fifteenth century, and there is much to suggest that there too parents played a prominent role in marriage formation.[183] A higher proportion of rural causes con-cern youthful marriages, though not necessarily under canonical age, and a similarly higher proportion of rural causes concern forced contracts. It was alleged, for example, in a cause dated

---

[181] BIHR, CP. E. 155.
[182] BIHR, CP. F. 201; Helmholz, *Marriage Litigation*, 64–5. Similar circum-stances may lie behind the action contained in BIHR, CP. F. 158.
[183] Cosgrove, 'Marriage in Medieval Ireland', 38–47.

1362 that Alice Bellamy was threatened by her father with being thrown down a well unless she married one Robert Thomson. Alice may have been comparatively youthful as her father threatened to pick her up by the ears, and there is also a reference to her playing with Robert.[184] The rural sample differs also in the presence of suits for nullity of marriage on grounds of consanguinity or affinity. This can reflect parental influence in choice of partners in that parents might look to their own social contacts, including kin, to find suitable candidates. Thus Robert Kyghley was married to Isabella Yonge despite his father's knowledge of their relationship, confessed on his death-bed, and the refusal of the local clergy to solemnize the union.[185] The relationship could then be used to obtain an annulment once the marriage had run into difficulties.

In several instances marriages were challenged on the grounds that an affinity existed as a consequence of a pre-marital liaison (*copula carnalis*). This could again be indicative of parental control of marriage existing alongside more informal patterns of courtship. Sexual relationships arising informally could on occasion be used deliberately to upset more formal contracts where parents may have fallen out over marriage arrangements or the suitability of their choice. Deposition evidence in a cause of 1453 makes it clear that Agnes Cosyn was contracted to Robert Chew at her parents' behest, but that her parents subsequently had a change of heart. A known previous liaison between Robert and an Isabella Alan was used by Agnes's parents on the pretext, rejected by the consistory of York, that Isabella and Agnes were blood relatives in the fourth degree.[186] The marriage of John de Larethorp to Joan de Acclum was similarly challenged by deponents prepared to testify that John had had intercourse sixteen years earlier with one Mariota Lascy, a close relative of Joan. These same deponents suggest that John was forced into his marriage to Joan, presumably by his parents.[187] Such causes represent the negative side of parental influence in the making of marriages. The sample is undoubtedly biased towards the contentious, but this particular pattern is not found generally among equivalent urban causes, where indi-

[184] BIHR, CP. E. 85.   [185] BIHR, CP. F. 202.
[186] BIHR, CP. F. 189.   [187] BIHR, CP. E. 33.

viduals seem to have had greater freedom of choice and their courtship and contracts were not so subject to parental or wider familial intervention.

If the position is adopted that in town society marriage was late and companionate, and that women's dependence on marriage was related to economic status and thus to secular fluctuations in the wider economy and the demand for labour, a greater emphasis is placed upon individual action. At the same time rather less weight is put on changes in social custom in response to Church teaching. Where marriage was in the mid-twenties, the scope for individuals to find of their own free will marriage partners and to discontinue unsatisfying courtship relationships regardless of any sexual involvement is not inconsiderable. This view fits well with the observed urban pattern of multi-party *causa matrimonialis et divorcii* litigation. Alleged pre-contracts appear to represent, in the majority of cases, genuine disputes consequent upon changes of heart or circumstance more often than fictions designed to obtain divorce. In the context of the later fourteenth and, more especially, earlier fifteenth centuries single women would seem to have enjoyed a greater degree of economic independence and, it may be argued, a greater opportunity to meet and to choose between a number of prospective marriage partners. It is out of this relative freedom of choice that multi-party matrimonial litigation might arise; a significant factor is that it was as often the woman that was disputed between rival male lovers as the other way around in the cases observed here. These are, moreover, invariably engagement disputes. Relatively few multi-party actions refer to contracts solemnized *in facie ecclesie* and only one relates to an established marriage.[188]

The urban pattern of multi-party litigation is well illustrated by a cause of 1394. A contract of marriage *per verba de presenti* between Beatrix Gyllyng and Thomas de Hornby, who was servant to his uncle, also Thomas, a saddler, was witnessed by Beatrix's sister Alice Menston, brother-in-law Thomas, and their servant, at their house in York. The validity of this contract was immediately challenged by Margery Spuret, who had been a

---

[188] BIHR, CP. F. 236. John Wollay had contracted Margaret Wright *per verba de presenti* in 1440. Three years later he solemnized a second contract to Beatrix Tarte before a large number of witnesses at St Crux in York. Beatrix is said to have shunned John on learning of this pre-contract.

servant in the same household as Thomas. She claimed that they had contracted in York five years earlier in the presence of her widowed mother and another female relative. Thomas defended himself from this threat to his contract with Beatrix by claiming to have been away in Crayke on the day in question. He also produced a witness who deposed that Margery was herself away from York at the time of the alleged contract. The court believed him, or at least was not satisfied that Margery had proved her case, but the possibility of a romance developing between servants of the opposite sex working together in the same household seems real enough.[189] The circumstances are perhaps not so different from those of John Warryngton's affair with his fellow servant Margaret Barker and subsequent contract to Margaret Foghler.[190] Often the circumstances surrounding multi-party actions defy reconstruction such is their apparent informality. Around 1430 Robert Tavarner contracted himself in marriage to Marjory Wad-yngton at her house before just two witnesses, probably her neighbours. Two years later he made a second contract before three witnesses, a married couple and a priest, this time to Margaret Goldsmyth. The relationship between the couple in whose house they were present and either Robert or Margaret is unknown, but if they were relatives or even employers this should have been acknowledged in their depositions. On this second occasion Robert was said to have been sober.[191]

If the view that the decline in matrimonial litigation in the fifteenth century was consequent upon a greater reliance on church solemnization and an abandonment of the private contract is to be doubted, then some alternative hypothesis is required. It has been seen that the *causa matrimonialis et divorcii*, one component of marriage litigation that appears to decline in frequency, was open to fraud and could be used to upset estab-lished marriages unjustly.[192] It follows that greater resort to church solemnization as part of marriage formation would reduce this possibility, but, unlike some of the rural evidence discussed previously, there is only comparatively little evidence from urban causes that this multi-party action was indeed used fraudulently to

[189] BIHR, CP. E. 159.
[190] BIHR, CP. E. 74, 127.
[191] BIHR, CP. F. 103, 108.
[192] BIHR, Helmholz, *Marriage Litigation*, 64.

manipulate the courts. Examples of such fraud, though real, are uncommon, nor are such actions limited to cases involving marriages not solemnized *in facie ecclesie*. A cause of 1431 concerns an established 'marriage' solemnized in the church of St Gregory in York challenged by an alleged pre-contract that had itself been solemnized at Ripon Minster.[193] The impression here is that in general these multi-party actions concern 'engagement' disputes between rival lovers and do not concern established partnerships in the sense of sharing both bed and board. This is true of the Tavarner case just discussed.[194] It is true of John Warryngton, initially forced against his will by his irate master to marry a fellow servant he had seduced, but subsequently contracting with his master's blessing to another girl.[195] A third example is provided by the case of William de Stockton, brought to court by his rival lovers. In neither instance does there appear to have been a formal 'family' contract and the court is obliged to measure the very informal private contracts of the respective couples against the rigid measure of canon law. In this instance the court upheld the contract between the young apprentice and Elena de Leyrmouth, whom he had known for a number of years, and seems regularly to have visited overnight in her house in Aldwark, York. He had openly promised her marriage on completion of his apprenticeship, but the court was told of a long-standing 'private' contract made before the couple came to York and it is this last that seems to have determined its ruling.[196]

If by the later fifteenth century women's economic status had been eroded, such that marriage became more of an economic necessity for them, and if service became less likely for daughters of good family (and more often in exclusively feminine service groups for the daughters of more humble origin), then both the freedom and the opportunity to form relationships that might or

---

[193] BIHR, CP. F. 101. A case history of bribery and false witness is revealed in CP. F. 99.

[194] BIHR, CP. F. 108.

[195] BIHR, CP. F. 74. This cause is printed in Helmholz, *Marriage Litigation*, 224–8.

[196] BIHR, CP. E. 126, 128. Isabella, daughter of Alan de Belyngham, who lived with Elena in Aldwark and Idonea Bower, who lived nearby in Monkgate, were both able to testify to an earlier contract made at the house of Elena's brother in Newcastle. They also testified to seeing the couple in bed together in either their Monkgate or Aldwark homes in York.

might not lead to marriage would have been eroded. The possibility of pre-contract would thus recede. This hypothesis again satisfies the observed pattern of litigation, for no multi-party actions are found within the sample for the period after 1450. At the same time an increased involvement of parents in marriage formation may be observed from a number of causes. Thus in 1467 William Shirwod, a York merchant, tried to impede the marriage of his daughter, then living at home with him, on the grounds that he had not consented to it.[197] A woman told her fiancé in a London cause of 1489 that, 'I made you promise, but on my fader's good will.'[198] On finding her parents hostile to the match, Alice Cure claimed in a cause of 1509 that she had been forced into making a contract with John Acton whilst she was alone with him in the churchyard of Holy Trinity in Goodramgate, York.[199] By the sixteenth century the view that marriages should not be contracted other than with the consent of parents was common among Protestant divines.[200] More controversially it might be argued that the decline in suits for legal separation *a mensa et a thoro* from cruel and adulterous husbands may have resulted from a greater resignation on the part of women to their lot within marriage when opportunities outside marriage were increasingly closed to them. It may be, however, that most separations were arranged out of court by the families concerned.[201]

In rural districts, where opportunities for women to find employment outside the home, in service or otherwise, tended to be relatively limited, daughters more often than not lived at home. If their parents had land or capital, they also had a vested interest in the marriages of their daughters.[202] In such situations women may have been married at an earlier age than their urban counterparts to men chosen more by their parents than them-

---

[197] BIHR, CP. F. 244; Prob. Reg. 5, fo. 84.

[198] Guildhall Library, London, MS 9065, fo. 52 cited in Helmholz, *Marriage Litigation*, 48 n. 85.

[199] BIHR, CP. G. 30a.

[200] Houlbrooke, *The English Family*, 69; Gillis, *For Better, for Worse*, 86; Macfarlane, *Marriage and Love*, 144–5; Brundage, *Law, Sex, and Christian Society*, 552–3. Wiesner notes that in some early modern German towns children could be disinherited if they wed without parental consent, although in the case of daughters, only if their parents had failed to find partners for them by their early twenties: *Working Women in Renaissance Germany*, 22–3.

[201] Helmholz, *Marriage Litigation*, 101.

[202] Hanawalt, *The Ties that Bound*, 199–200.

selves. This is precisely the position suggested from the age data previously considered. Where women achieved emotional and economic independence from parents through service or other paid employment, as was more often true of urban society, they were enabled to exercise greater personal choice and to delay marriage, even to get by without marrying. Perhaps the point is obliquely illustrated by the case of one Lucy who married William Broun around 1350. William proved an unsatisfactory husband who regularly beat her. Just before autumn 1356 Lucy left William. When she returned at the end of autumn William was living with another woman and refused to be reconciled to the wife that had left him when he had most need of her labour. For William a wife was a valued source of labour. For Lucy labour was a marketable commodity that for a few brief months during the harvest of 1356 freed her from an unloving husband and allowed her control over her own affairs.[203]

The cause paper evidence thus suggests the prevalence of a marriage regime that allowed a considerable degree of freedom to young women and men alike, but most markedly in urban society and in the century following the Black Death. The same source provides some valuable demographic data relating to service and marriage which suggest the existence of a relatively late, companionate marriage regime closely associated with a system of life-cycle servanthood, although this again was more pronounced in the town than the country. These two observations derived from the same material provide telling evidence for a variant of the Western marriage pattern prevailing within Yorkshire society in the later Middle Ages. This was, moreover, a regime closely compatible with that observed in England outside the aristocratic classes from the more substantially documented parish registration period onwards.[204] Hajnal's hypothesis, outlined in his pioneering study, that medieval England was characterized by a radically different 'medieval' marriage regime must now appear fragile. It rests upon an older historiographical tradition that there was a profound cultural transition from medieval to modern which demands re-evaluation. But equally open to question is the

---

[203] BIHR, CP. E. 77.
[204] Phythian-Adams, *Desolation of a City*, 84–7; Wrigley and Schofield, *The Population History of England*.

TABLE 5.8. *Marital status at death for York lay testators from the probate register of the Exchequer Court of York c.1389–1500*

	Single	Married	All married	Remarried	Widowed	All widowed	Widowed after remarriage	Marital status uncertain	Total
1380–1408									
Males	12	202		20	42		2	23	301
%	4	67.1	73.8	6.6	14	14.6	0.7	7.6	
Females	4	67		1	52		8	4	136
%	2.9	49.3	50	0.7	38.2	44.1	5.9	2.9	
1418–44*									
Males	18	358		30	50		4	26	486
%	3.7	73.7	79.8	6.2	10.3	11.1	0.8	5.3	
Females	16	33		2	117		6	8	182
%	8.8	18.1	19.2	1.1	67.6	64.3	3.3	4.4	
1445–69									
Males	5	225		18	22		6	9	285
%	1.8	78.9	85.3	6.3	7.7	9.8	2.1	3.2	

Females	7	1		2	60		10	5	85
%	8.2	1.2	3.5	2.4	70.6	82.4	11.8	5.9	
1470–1500									
Males	4	274		37			8	10	359
%	1.1	76.3	83.6	7.2	10.3	12.5	2.2	2.8	
Females	6	1		1	66		11	4	89
%	6.7	1.1	2.2	1.1	74.2	86.5	12.4	4.5	

* 1419–25 lost from record.

Sources: BIHR, Prob. Reg. 1–5.

assumption of a cultural homogeneity throughout Latin Christendom.[205] Work done by Laslett, Wall, Smith, and others following on from Hajnal demonstrates that with regard to matrimony and family structure, within which context the status of women must be studied, historic Europe shows considerable regional variation.[206] Though the evidence yet collected or even surviving is but slender, there are grounds for believing that some of these differences are deeply rooted and can be traced back at least into the late medieval era. This should not be seen as an argument for absolute secular stability, but it does suggest that real cultural differences underlie the various marriage regimes. By contrasting differing cultural regions and by comparing like, our understanding of the past can only be enhanced. These are issues which are explored more fully in the concluding chapter.

THE URBAN PROBATE EVIDENCE

The third source, probate evidence for marital status at death, may allow some statistical analysis of secular change in the incidence of marriage and remarriage. The source is necessarily limited to the testamentary class and is thus biased towards the more prosperous upper levels of urban society, but it is not without value. The present analysis is primarily limited to data derived from the Exchequer Court wills for persons of both sexes normally resident in York and dying before *c*.1500, and for female testators only before *c*.1520. Data have been tabulated according to five status categories, single, married, remarried, widowed, and widowed following remarriage, and grouped into the four time periods elsewhere adopted.[207] These are shown in Table 5.8. It is unfortunate that there is a marked decline in the proportion of female testators, accounted for by the virtual exclusion of married female testators by the later fifteenth century. Considerable caution must consequently be exercised in determin-

---

[205] Hajnal, 'European Marriage Patterns', 101–43.

[206] Cf. Laslett, 'Characteristics of the Western Family'; R. Wall (ed.), *Family Forms in Historic Europe* (Cambridge, 1983); Smith, 'The People of Tuscany'; id., 'Marriage Processes'; F. Benigno, 'The Southern Italian Family in the Early Modern Period: A Discussion of Co-residence Patterns', *Continuity and Change*, 4 (1989), 165–94.

[207] See Appendix I.

TABLE 5.9. *Rates of remarriage of York widows and widowers from the probate register of the Exchequer Court of York, c.1389–1520*

	Total widowed	% widowed	Total remarried	% remarried
Widows remarrying				
1389–1408	61	45.2	9	14.8
1418–44*	125	68.7	8	6.4
1445–69	72	84.7	12	16.7
1470–1500	78	87.6	12	15.4
1500–20**	73	97.3	10	12.3
Widowers remarrying				
1389–1408	63	20	21	33.3
1418–44*	84	17.3	34	40.5
1445–69	46	16.1	24	52.2
1470–1500	71	19.8	34	47.9

* 1419–25 lost from record.
** From BIHR, Prob. Reg. 6–9, fo. 192ᵛ (More).
Sources: BIHR, Prob. Reg. 1–9.

ing the significance of observed trends since these must reflect differences in convention at least as much as changing attitudes to marriage in response to wider demographic and economic influence, or even changing patterns of mortality. There is an additional problem in that the precise incidence of remarriage or widowhood following remarriage cannot be measured since identification is dependent upon often chance reference to earlier

TABLE 5.10. *Proportion of females and of single women among York lay testators within the Exchequer Court of York, c.1389–1500*

	Females as % of all testators	Single females as % all testators less married females
1389–1408	31.1	18.4
1418–44*	27.2	23.2
1445–69	23.0	22.3
1470–1500	19.9	19.5

* 1419–25 lost from record.
Sources: BIHR, Prob. Reg. 1–5.

marriages within the registered will. There is, however, good reason to believe that the rates observed are at least indicative of the true rates. In a number of instances there is a margin of error in the identification of marital status and this is most true of wills of single and widowed testators where marital status is not stated and no reference is made to a former spouse or to children. Where this margin of error has been deemed very great, no status has been assigned, though the actual status will invariably be single or widowed. It is not thought that these cases detract from the data set as a whole.

There is little indication here of any change in convention in respect of will-making by males, but two significant observations regarding secular change in the profile of marital status at death in response to demographic change and changing attitudes to matrimony. The proportion of males widowed who subsequently married again appears to have increased over the period from about one in three to one in two, though the proportion of males left widowed was never more than 20 per cent of all male testators.[208] At the same time there is a modest secular increase in the proportion of male testators dying married that cannot be explained simply by the increasing proportion of remarriages. Such a trend could be consistent with a growth in the age difference between spouses consequent upon a fall in mean age at first marriage for women. Similar analysis in respect of female testators is complicated by the dramatic fall in the numbers of married women leaving registered wills. This must largely reflect a prejudice over the course of the fifteenth century against married women leaving wills even, as required by canon law, with their husbands' permission.

The sample would suggest that by about the fourth decade of the century hardly any married women were leaving registered wills. This is not a local phenomenon and it may be that custom at York was influenced by conventions elsewhere. At Rochester of fifty wills proved in 1347, twenty were made by women and thirteen by married women. By 1457 only eighteen of 123 proven

---

[208] Males widowed after remarriage are counted as if they had only been widowed once so that the same individual does not contribute disproportionately to the total number of widowers.

wills were made by women, of whom only two were married.[209]
An analysis of the twenty-eight wills recorded for women in the
Great Orphan Book at Bristol for the period 1388–1509 shows
that of those six that died currently married, all but one made
their wills in the years before 1417.[210] It may even be that this
downward trend pre-dates the Black Death; the Dean and Chapter court evidence appears to support this view and it may be
noted that in the early 1340s an attempt by the Church to enforce
the testamentary rights of married women was roundly criticized
by the Commons.[211] In view of the rising trend in males dying
before their spouses, some of this observed decline in the numbers
of wills made by married females, and an equivalent increase in
the numbers of widows leaving wills, is perhaps to be expected.
Equally an increase in fertility consequent upon earlier marriage,
and the increased likelihood of infants surviving to adulthood as
endemic plague waned, would, if true, reduce the probability of
women inheriting in their own right and thus having goods or
property to bequeath before their husbands' decease. These
factors by themselves cannot explain the timing or extent of the
decline in the number of married women's wills; it may, however,
be noticed that the proportion of females to all testators other
than married women leaving wills shows a slight fall from a peak
during the earlier decades of the fifteenth century.

This last may perhaps be explained by the changing proportion
of female testators dying without ever having apparently married.
This phenomenon, which is highly significant in its own right,
reached a comparatively high level in the period 1418–44, and
specifically in the period *c.*1436–42, where at least 13 (16.9 per
cent) of 77 women's testaments pertained to unmarried females.[212]
This period also coincides with a low level of widow remarriages,
less than half the rate calculated for other periods. It is not
possible to explain these observations in terms of high levels of

---

[209] M. M. Sheehan, 'The Influence of Canon Law on the Property Rights of
Married Women in England', *Medieval Studies*, 25 (1963), 109, 122.

[210] Wadley, *Notes or Abstracts*, 22, 31, 39, 80, 97, 177.

[211] Pollock and Maitland, *The History of English Law*, ii. 429; Coulton, *Medieval
Panorama*, 618; *Rotuli Parliamentorum*, ii. 149–50.

[212] A number can be identified as being in trade or in service: BIHR, Prob. Reg.
2, fos. 557ᵛ, 603, 672; Prob. Reg. 3, fos. 456, 459ᵛ, 527ᵛ, 533, 556A, 594ᵛ. Over the
same period may be noted a number of wills of single women proven within the
Capitular Court of York: YML, D/C Reg. 1, fos. 184ᵛ, 205ᵛ, 225ᵛ, 241.

mortality in 1438 forestalling marriages and terminating established marriages since male patterns differ, there is nothing
exceptional about this level of mortality in terms of the testamentary series as a whole, and a rather higher level of remarriage for
both sexes might be expected had marriages indeed been cut
short. Even allowing for the difficulty of identifying second
marriages, this observed pattern can only be a reflection of the
absolute pattern. The same trend is observed from the Dean and
Chapter wills, where 4 of only 24 female wills (16.7 per cent)
pertain to unmarried testators, and the Bristol sample just cited
contains the wills of only two unmarried women dated 1396 and
1420 respectively.[213]

If this high proportion of wills by never-married women from
about the second or third decade to the fifth or sixth decade of the
fifteenth century represents a low marriage rate experienced by
the generation achieving adulthood in the period say *c*.1410–40,
then it would be reasonable to expect a corresponding fall in the
proportion of ever-married women dying. This last may represent
a further minor factor in the decrease of women dying whilst
currently married, but it does not explain the marked upward
trend in the proportion of widows, and particularly widows who
had not subsequently remarried. In part, this may represent a real
increase in the proportion of widows leaving wills, but it is also a
corollary of a depressed marriage rate and the low level of
remarriage. For the period 1445–69 the proportions of female
testators dying without ever having married is rather smaller. This
is also true of the Dean and Chapter series where only two of
fifteen female wills can be ascribed with any certainty to never-
married women. Conversely, the proportion of widows remarrying
is considerably enhanced. The proportions of never-married
female testators (whether measured in relation to all female
testators or all female testators less currently married testators)
continues to decline over the entire period to *c*.1520, whereas the
proportion of female testators known to have remarried remains
stable. This pattern is highly suggestive of an increase in the
female marriage rate, especially in respect of first marriages, over

213 Wadley, *Notes or Abstracts*, 47, 105.

the second half of the fifteenth century and continuing into the early sixteenth century. If this pattern is more widely representative, and it must be acknowledged that this cannot be demonstrated, then it would accord with some wider observations concerning the changing economic status of women.

The unusually high proportion of single female testators observed in the earlier decades of the fifteenth century, a few of whom are described by occupation, would accord with the hypothesis that when work opportunities for women were enhanced many women might have chosen to delay marriage and some women might not have married at all. A pattern of postponed marriage in the earlier fifteenth century would also accord with a supposed subsequent fall in mean age at first marriage over the later fifteenth century as opportunities for women to support themselves outside marriage were eroded. A fall in the mean age at first marriage and an associated rise in the marriage rate is itself suggested by the decline in proportion of never-married female testators from about the middle of the century and the observed high rate of marriage calculated from parish register evidence of the mid-sixteenth century. This pattern may have applied more widely for an examination of the marital status at death of all female testators normally resident within the county of Yorkshire contained within the Exchequer court series suggests a similar secular pattern which cannot be explained solely in terms of the York testators within the sample.[214] Todd, using equivalent sources to study the pattern of widow remarriage at Abingdon during the early modern era, has argued for an inverse relationship between widow remarriage and female economic opportunity.[215] This hypothesis accords well with the fifteenth-century probate evidence; at a period when women do appear to have been particularly active within the urban economy, there is a low level of widow remarriage, yet in the economically harder times of the later fifteenth century, when work for women became scarce, there is an enhanced level of widow remarriage.

The testamentary data may thus be seen to demonstrate certain secular trends that apparently correlate with our evidence for economic and demographic fluctuations and the changing demand for female labour, but are independent of the secular decline in the proportion of married women leaving registered wills. The pattern accords with what can be considered three specific features of the Western marriage regime, namely the greater elasticity of female over male ages at first marriage, the relatively high proportion of women achieving adulthood without ever marrying, and the relative frequency with which widows remarry. These three observations may, for example, be contrasted with the marriage regime prevailing in Tuscany over the same period, where widow remarriage was rare, few women achieving adulthood failed to marry, and male and female marriage ages tended to move in unison.[216] A downturn in female marriage ages and an upward trend in remarriage by the later fifteenth century, following a period characterized by low marriage rates, would help explain why demographic recovery over the fifteenth century may have commenced sometime after the middle of the century, but not before.[217] The equation of delayed marriage with a period that, according to the Phelps Brown and Hopkins Index, was supposedly characterized by high or rising real wages is, however, controversial. This particular thesis will be more fully explored in the concluding chapter.[218]

LATER MEDIEVAL MARRIAGE:
SOME PRELIMINARY CONCLUSIONS

Despite the diversity of the sources used here, the direction of the evidence is surprisingly consistent. There is comparatively little evidence to suggest a distinctive 'medieval' marriage regime. Marriage after the Black Death appears to have been relatively late for both sexes, but particularly in urban society, and to have been companionate. The institution of life-cycle service underlies this regime, though significant work opportunities for women to support themselves independently prior to marriage, or even

---

[216] Herlihy and Klapisch-Zuber, *Tuscans and their Families*, 88, 207–11; Klapisch-Zuber, 'Demographic Decline and Household Structure', in ead., *Women, Family, and Ritual*, 23–35; Smith, 'The People of Tuscany'.
[217] Hatcher, *Plague, Population and the English Economy*, 63.
[218] Cf. ibid. 55–7.

independently of marriage, also existed. Remarriage for males appears, at least within the testamentary classes, to have been relatively common. This accords with other evidence. The ordinances of the Hull gild of the Blessed Virgin Mary, founded in 1357, provided for a widowed brother if 'the said brother afterwards takes another woman to wife as is the normal custom'.[219] The remarriage of widowers may also explain the small number of observed marriages from the deposition evidence in which the husband is considerably the senior of his spouse. Remarriage for widows was not unknown, though perhaps less common. A York cause of 1392 concerns one Elizabeth, the wife of a Beverley draper, who had been married twice before, latterly to a merchant of Wakefield.[220] It was perhaps more substantial widows of this kind who were most likely to remarry, and in this sense the often-cited Wife of Bath is a literary exaggeration for dramatic effect.[221] The remarriage prospects of the poorer widow cannot have been very high. A similar pattern is suggested from the Norwich census of the poor in 1570, which demonstrates that whereas few older men of this class remained as widowers, the majority of older women who had lost their husbands stayed widows.[222] Some men may, however, have remarried in order to provide for young children surviving from an earlier marriage. There is some testamentary evidence for this hypothesis.[223]

The interpretation of the cause paper evidence has stressed what Sheehan has described as 'an astonishingly individualistic attitude to marriage and its problems'.[224] Marriages appear often to have been contracted on the basis of mutual understanding and, it may be assumed, affection. One young man garlanded his sweetheart with flowers and another declared before contracting marriage that he had never seen a woman he was better able to

---

[219] 'Idem frater postmodum aliam mulierem in uxorem ut est moris naturaliter ducat': PRO, C 47/46/451.

[220] BIHR, CP. E. 193.

[221] Cf. Margery Haynes of Castle Combe or Emma Erle of Wakefield: W. D. Robertson, '"And for my land thus hastow mordred me?": Land Tenure, the Cloth Industry, and the Wife of Bath', *Chaucer Review*, 14 (1980), 403–20; BIHR, CP. E. 124.

[222] Houlbrooke, *The English Family*, 213.

[223] This is the impression gained from a reading of York wills, but it would be difficult to demonstrate from this source alone.

[224] Sheehan, 'The Formation and Stability of Marriage', 263.

love.[225] There is also good evidence that many relationships were broken off before marriage. Such is reflected in the *causa matrimonialis et divorcii* litigation and, in the early modern era, by common law actions for breach of promise.[226] Active parental involvement in the initiation of courtship or matrimony seems to have been comparatively rare except among wealthier peasant families and the landed aristocracy. This is supported by the absence of simple *de futuro* contracts and the comparatively socially restricted evidence for anything resembling the *sponsalia* that bear the hallmark of the arranged marriage.[227] Sheehan has described such betrothals for the thirteenth century, but argues that they ceased to be of significance subsequently.[228]

This is not to deny some real degree of parental influence, though urban evidence for this is scarce. Agnes Louth of Hull was unwilling to tell her father of her contract to John Astlott for fear he should not approve, so John promised to bring him a goose and attempt to win the father's consent over dinner. In another rather later instance a young man enlisted his uncle's support to persuade the father of the woman to whom he was contracted to allow the marriage, but the father declared angrily that 'she shall never be maried bot wher me list'.[229] A Hereford woman, Elena Porter, was granted an annulment of her marriage by the sub-dean of the cathedral church there in 1459 because she had been forced by her relatives into a contract against her will.[230] Lastly, in a plea of nullity a Pontefract woman alleged that her father had beaten her with a club to force her to marry against her will.[231] But such actions are comparatively rare, even in respect of rural causes, and the bulk of the evidence points to a remarkable degree of freedom exercised by young people in courtship. Sheehan comments similarly on the lack of evidence for parental or wider

[225] BIHR, CP. E. 121; CP. F. 81.
[226] Houlbrooke, *Church Courts and People*, 66–7; id., *The English Family*, 73, 60.
[227] Cf. Sheehan, 'The Formation and Stability of Marriage', 256; Donahue, 'The Canon Law on Marriage', 149.
[228] M. M. Sheehan, 'Marriage Theory and Practice in the Conciliar Legislation and Diocesan Studies', *Medieval Studies*, 40 (1978), 425–7, 431.
[229] BIHR, CP. F. 46, 244.
[230] *Royal Commission on Historical Manuscripts, Thirteenth Report* (London, 1892), 303.
[231] BIHR, CP. F. 233.

familial pressure on individuals in respect of their choice of marriage partners suggested from his study of an Ely consistory court book for the period 1374–82.[232] The advice of the Goodwife to her daughter was merely that she should consult her friends, probably to be understood as her family, about any proposal of marriage she might receive.[233]

In urban society, as in rural society, pressure may have been more real at upper levels. The conspicuously successful York merchant Thomas Bracebrigg, d. 1437, directed in his will that his son William only marry with his mother's advice and consent, and it has already been suggested that by the later fifteenth century the daughters of the well-to-do were more likely to remain with their parents and may thus have been more compliant with parental wishes.[234] It seems significant that the only urban cause paper references to arrangements regarding dowry both belong to the early sixteenth century.[235] These observations coincide with the thesis that marriage ages fell for women as their opportunities for independent economic activity, more marked in the urban than the rural economy, were eroded during the latter part of the fifteenth century. In this context parental influence over their daughters might be greater and the significance of dowry might loom larger as a young woman's own economic potential declined.

That the age at marriage may indeed have fallen for young urban women is suggested from some Norwich consistory court depositions of the earlier decades of the sixteenth century. Of a small sample, one woman deponent from Norwich was already married at 23 years and another at 24 years. Similarly, a Diss woman can be shown to have married at 23 years.[236] This is slight evidence, but contemporary observers expressed concern at the spate of premature marriages.[237] Crude marriage rates as calculated from parish register data show a sharp fall from a very high level at the beginning of the registration period until the seven-

[232] Sheehan, 'The Formation and Stability of Marriage', 263.
[233] 'How the Good Wijf', ed. Furnivall, ll. 32–8, p. 37.
[234] BIHR, Prob. Reg. 3, fo. 487ᵛ.
[235] BIHR, CP. G. 40, 115.
[236] E. D. Stone and B. Cozens-Hardy, *Norwich Consistory Depositions, 1499–1512 and 1518–30* (Norfolk Record Society, 10; 1938), nos. 85, 141, 390.
[237] Houlbrooke, *The English Family*, 67–8.

teenth century.[238] Despite the uncertain quality of such data at this early period, the pattern is indicative of a relatively early age at first marriage at the time of the Reformation. Ingram and Houlbrooke have both described a greater degree of parental involvement in marriage formation, consistent with a downward trend in marriage ages, dating from this period.[239] These observations do not detract from our main findings concerning the prevailing marriage regime. One of the characteristic features of a north-western regime is indeed the tendency of marriage ages to demonstrate secular fluctuation, and this is especially true of female marriage ages.

It is more difficult to map movements in the proportions of never-marrying persons. Testamentary evidence suggests that the proportion of never-marrying women was at a high level in the earlier decades of the fifteenth century. This would perhaps have been more true of urban populations due to the greater work opportunities available there for women and due to the consequently skewed nature of urban sex ratios. Wall has made a similar observation for the still pre-industrial city of Bruges in 1814.[240] It might be expected that if marriage ages fell later in the century then the proportions never-marrying would follow a similar trend. This is suggested from the testamentary evidence relating to the well-to-do citizens of York, but there may also have been some divergent trends. For very poor women the opportunities for saving against marriage may have diminished and a downward trend in female mean first marriage age, coupled with low sex ratios in towns, would have created a 'surplus' of marriageable females to the detriment of the marital prospects of the dowryless. Some of these women may have found security by remaining in service, others may have been forced into petty retailing, poorly paid piece-rate work, even casual prostitution.

It is against this background that pious bequests of money to 'poor maidens' for their marriages become so relatively numerous during the later fifteenth century. Historically, provision of dowries was an act of piety designed to save girls from falling into prostitution and this may also have been the case in a period when

---

[238] Wrigley and Schofield, *Population History of England*, table 7.26, fig. 10.9, pp. 255, 425.
[239] Ingram, 'Spousals Litigation', 49; Houlbrooke, *The English Family*, 68–9.
[240] Wall, 'The Composition of Households', 433.

civic authorities were increasingly concerned by this apparently growing problem.[241] An increase in prostitution goes hand in hand with the contraction of opportunities for women outside marriage or service. At the same time our evidence has suggested that the status of female service was being undermined. It has been suggested from this that girls from the upper levels of society were less likely to enter service and more likely to remain at home until marriage. This is supported by the paucity of testaments associated with female servants by the last decades of the century, assuming, as seems likely, that such testators were of good family. Only eighteen wills can be associated with women servants in the period c.1389–1520; three fell in the period 1390–1408, eight in the period 1421–40, six in the period 1452–76, and one is dated 1500. For girls of humbler background, for whom service was an economic necessity, failure to secure marriage partners may have led to extended periods of service. Such a pattern has been observed for pre-industrial Reims in 1802.[242] In York Margaret Hall can be observed as a servant between 1442 and 1468, and Margaret Henryson between 1471 and 1493. Henryson was still unmarried in 1499.[243] In early sixteenth-century Norwich, deposition evidence identifies two female servants, of a very small sample, aged 29 and 30 years respectively.[244] Such limited evidence may suggest that the proportions never marrying at the end of the period were rather higher than the postulated trend in age of marriage would indicate. It may have been that there was a socially divisive trend such that the daughters of the social élite married earlier, but the daughters of the lower ranks of society experienced extended courtships.[245] On the other hand, it may be unwise to relate movements in the proportion never-married too closely to the trend in mean age at first marriage, which, it is

[241] J. W. Baldwin, *Master, Princes and Merchants,* i. 137.

[242] A. Fauve-Chamoux, 'The Importance of Women in an Urban Environment: The Example of the Rheims Household at the Beginning of the Industrial Revolution', in R. Wall (ed.), *Family Forms in Historic Europe* (Cambridge, 1983), 490–1. Cf. Brodsky, 'Single Women in the London Marriage Market', 83–91.

[243] BIHR, Prob. Reg. 2, fos. 45ᵛ, 441 (Hall); Prob. Reg. 4, fo. 159; Prob. Reg. 5, fo. 448 (Henryson).

[244] Stone and Cozens-Hardy, *Norwich Consistory Depositions,* no. 125.

[245] Cf. Brodsky, 'Single Women in the London Marriage Market'.

argued, tended to move downwards from the later fifteenth century.

The increasing importance of matrimony for women as job opportunities for the single female diminished is reflected in the changing convention of nomenclature observed in contemporary records. Whereas in the early fifteenth century women are often not distinguished by marital status, but are sometimes described by their trade, by the end of our period females are identified solely in terms of marital status. This is best demonstrated from the record of women intrants (licensed traders) at Canterbury licensed between 1392 and the early sixteenth century. Here there is a marked change from the registration of Christian name and surname of individuals to a record in terms of a husband living or deceased.[246] By the later fifteenth century unmarried women even came to be distinguished by the vernacular term 'singlewoman'. The earliest such usage observed is in a Norwich record dated 1443–4: '*Johanne Semer de Norwico* sengilwoman'.[247] Agnes Kilburn, d. 1477, is described as 'puella' in her will.[248] The term 'singlewoman' itself seems not to appear in the York records before the 1480s when several women admitted to the franchise there are so described.[249] In terms of official documentation, therefore, a woman came to be seen less in respect of her own status as an individual and more in relation to marital status and possible spouse.

A woman's fulfilment came thus to be seen in terms of marriage and family. This may be reflected in the contemporary popularity of images of the Holy Family. The east window of Holy Trinity, Goodramgate in York, dating to the early 1470s strikingly depicts the families of St Anne, St Mary Cleophas, and St Mary Salome.[250] Monumental brasses and other memorials likewise increasingly

---

[246] To cite a few examples: 1392–7, Katherine Orpyngton; 1411–14, Isabel Bertelot, skinner; 1443–4, *Uxor* Thomas Warde, barber; 1479–80, Richard Answorth, 'for his wife's craft'; 1496–1506, the widow of John Smith: Cowper (ed.), *Intrantes*.

[247] NRO, NCR Case 16, shelf a, 1 (mayor's court book, 1425–1510), 133.

[248] BIHR, Prob. Reg. 5, fo. 18.

[249] e.g. Agnes Hall, Isabel Bryniet, Joan Armourer, Alice Philip: Collins (ed.), *Register of the Freemen*, 204, 206, 214–15.

[250] P. E. S. Routh, 'A Gift and its Giver: John Walker and the East Window of Holy Trinity, Goodramgate, York', *Yorkshire Archaeological Journal*, 58 (1986), 109–21.

represented husband and wife together in prayer surrounded by their male and female children respectively.[251] The representation of children in this way coincides with a probable growth of this section of the population consequent upon a falling marriage age and an increase in fertility. It is not evidence for the emergence of the nuclear family, but of a conception of the family as the basic unit of society. The independent female worker, the 'single-woman', fitted only uneasily into that model. The woman's role may thus have been increasingly perceived as that of wife and mother.

[251] M. Clayton, *Catalogue of Rubbings of Brasses and Incised Slabs* (London, 1929).

6

Moving to Town

There survive a number of sources that have been exploited by demographic historians of the pre-industrial era in order to throw light on population movements, but in general the medievalist is less well served than the early modernist. The sort of comprehensive parish listings used by Laslett at Clayworth and Cogenhoe or Schofield at Cardington, or the Marriage Duty Act material worked on by Souden and Wall simply do not exist.[1] Instead the medievalist is forced to rely upon a number of less comprehensive sources which tend to raise almost as many questions as they answer. Patterns of male migration are partially documented, but very few of these sources have much to say about female migration or the destination of migrants. Raftis, Razi, Smith, and others have used manor court rolls to study movements away from the manor recorded either as fines for licence to live outside the manor (chevage) or as notice of illegal exits, but it is predominantly male names that are recorded.[2] The movement of servile women outside the manor to marry may sometimes be recorded as part of the marriage fine (merchet). It must be remembered, however, that the manor court was principally concerned with those who owed suit of court, i.e. villein tenants of the lord and thus predominantly adult males. It is probable that merchets were never demanded of poorer villein women and that many poor and

---

[1] P. Laslett, 'Clayworth and Cogenhoe', in id., *Family Life and Illicit Love in Earlier Generations* (Cambridge, 1977), 50–101; R. S. Schofield, 'Age-Specific Mobility in an Eighteenth-Century Rural English Parish', in P. Clark and D. Souden (eds.), *Migration and Society in Early Modern England* (London, 1987), 253–66; Souden, 'Migrants and the Population Structure of Later Seventeenth-Century Provincial Cities and Market Towns', 133–68; Wall, 'Regional and Temporal Variations in English Household Structure from 1650', 89–113.

[2] J. A. Raftis, *Tenure and Mobility: Studies in the Social History of the Medieval English Village* (Toronto, 1964); Razi, *Life, Marriage and Death*, 117–28; id., 'Rural Mobility and the Family in Late Medieval England', paper given to Social History Society's annual conference, Oxford, 1989; R. M. Smith, 'Seigneurial Reaction to the Scale of Villein Migration in England, 1250–1450', paper given to Social History Society's annual conference, Oxford, 1989.

landless villeins of either sex left the manor to which they were legally bound with impunity and without due record being made within the court rolls.[3]

This last may have been especially true of the late thirteenth and early fourteenth centuries when labour was abundant and land scarce. Poos has utilized some Essex hundredpenny listings to gauge levels of population turnover, but his evidence is by its nature restricted to males over 12 years of age resident within the community for more than a year, but excluding men of substance, who were exempt from tithing.[4] Short-term migrants, such as servants or labourers, are thus likely to be excluded and the number of exits over time due to deaths and the entries of male children achieving 12 years is unknown. Poos has argued that his evidence suggests a high rate of population turnover compatible with that found by Laslett for Clayworth and Cogenhoe, but even if this fragile evidence for continuity within a relatively densely populated region is allowed, it would be unwise to presume that it applied also to the women of Margaret Roding and Chatham Hall. Other sources are no more satisfactory. Wills occasionally note the birthplace of the will-maker, but the evidence is slight and even an exhaustive reading of wills would render little additional material in respect of either sex. Evidence of toponyms drawn from taxation and franchise sources has been used to study the origins of migrants into specific communities, but such studies are heavily biased towards males and are only credible for the period before surnames tended to stabilize.[5] McClure, comparing franchise evidence for York from the period 1312–27 with the period 1360–5, shows that migrants were drawn from a rather wider region after the plague; whereas half the migrants recorded in the earlier period came from within a twenty-mile radius, the same was true of only some third of migrants at the later date. This could suggest an increased rate of migration.[6] It could also suggest, given the bias of the particular source, a stronger pull on skilled labour in the context of labour shortage after the Black Death.

---

[3] Poos and Smith, 'Legal Windows', 145.

[4] L. R. Poos, 'Population Turnover in Medieval Essex: The Evidence of some Early-Fourteenth-Century Tithing Lists', in L. Bonfield, R. M. Smith, and K. Wrightson (eds.), *The World We Have Gained: Histories of Population and Social Structure* (Oxford, 1986), 1–22.

[5] McClure, 'Patterns of Migration in the Late Middle Ages', 168.

[6] Ibid. 180–2.

There remains one source, extensively used by early modernists, but yet to be fully exploited by medievalists, that appears relatively free of many of these problems. These are depositions made within the Church court. Some Canterbury and London material survives for the fifteenth century, but the most substantial of the English sources are the cause papers pertaining to the Court of York from the beginning of the fourteenth century. Migrational details are only very occasionally recorded as part of the biographical data given for each deponent, but further information may readily be reconstructed from the depositions themselves. Information relating to migration can be derived from 33 causes in respect of 63 individuals, that is 32 males and 31 females. These are shown in Table 6.1. Unfortunately the place from which migrants originate is not always known and very few depositions allow age at migration to be calculated very precisely. The evidence does, however, suggest that adolescents and young adults are most conspicuous among those known to have migrated. Most migrants appear to have moved no more than a day's walk, that is between twelve and twenty-four miles, but a few travelled much greater distances, and some, living near large towns, moved much shorter distances into those towns. If the two atypically lengthy journeys are disregarded, the mean distance covered at each move was less than twenty-two miles, but the modal distance would be somewhat smaller.

Before discussing the deposition evidence further, it is appropriate here to reiterate some features of the later medieval economy into which evidence concerning female urban migration must needs be fitted. The late thirteenth and early fourteenth centuries were a period characterized by high population and strained resources. Although it is as yet unclear how far population pressure on limited land resources resulted in an increased level of mortality, or whether the population actually declined following the Agrarian Crisis of the second to third decades of the fourteenth century, it is likely that these adverse economic circumstances would have had some bearing upon migration. Peasants with only small holdings would have found these increasingly uneconomic in runs of poor harvests and would have been forced to sell to peasants with large, viable holdings who were able to make substantial profits from surplus production in years of scarcity. There was thus a growing polarization within peasant society between those with large holdings and those with little or no land. The latter were forced to work as wage labour either on the lord's demesne, where by the later thirteenth century customary services had often been largely commuted, or on the land of those substantial peasants whose holdings were too large to manage using family labour alone.

The probability is that before the Black Death available labour outstripped demand. This is reflected in the low wages commanded by labourers at a period when food was comparatively expensive. Underemployment and unemployment must have been features of rural life. Several of the servile children noted in the thirteenth-century Spalding serf list, for example, were described as vagabond, an epithet that suggests wandering in search of work. Towns, whose growth in the High Middle Ages is inexorably allied to general demographic expansion, probably absorbed some of this surplus labour. For the poor and the destitute towns offered the chimera of work and opportunity. Towns were also more likely to offer welfare to the needy, either in the form of casual almsgiving or in terms of more regular food doles provided by some of the urban hospitals. The deaths by crushing of fifty-five poor men and women awaiting a distribution of alms outside the gates of the house of the Dominicans in London tells its own sad story.[7] It is unclear, however, how far women would have been attracted to towns in a period when a depressed labour market presumably tended to work to the particular disadvantage of women. Hilton has argued that female migrants were particularly conspicuous among the 'flood of recruits' into towns before the Black Death, and has even suggested that in the case of Halesowen 'perhaps three-quarters of the total between 1272 and 1350' were women.[8] This is a remarkable assertion, but the evidence upon which it is based is unclear and perhaps misleading.

It is the case that women feature prominently in the borough court rolls, and Hilton provides a number of illustrations of this. It is probable that women even outnumber men in the frequency of their appearance, perhaps very markedly, but, in the absence of more certain demographic knowledge, this may only be a

---

[7] Sharpe (ed.), *Calendar of Coroners Rolls of the City of London, 1300–1378*, 61.

[8] Hilton, 'Lords, Burgesses and Hucksters', 10.

TABLE 6.1. *Migrants from deposition evidence*

BIHR CP	Date	Sex (m/f)	Moved from/to	Then aged	Current location	Age	Distance moved (miles)
E. 76	1357	m	?Reedness	[8]	'Elsyn'		
E. 89	1366	m	Shipton		?Hutton		3
		m	?		Rawcliffe		1½
		f	Rawcliffe		'Slaykston'		2½
		f	?		Rawcliffe		½
		f	Skelton		Clifton		4
		f	Rawcliffe		Clifton		14
		f	i. Rawcliffe				
			ii. Bootham				
E. 102	1367	f	Aike	[19]	York	23	
E. 111	1372	f	Uncleby	[15+]	Beverley	30+	
		f	?	[14]	York	20	
		m	?	[10+]	York	20+	
		m	?		York	21+	
E. 126	1382	f	Newcastle		York	20	73
		f	Newcastle		York		73
		f	Newcastle		York		73
E. 153	1389	f	?		London		
E. 155	1374	m	?	[15+]	Althorpe	40+	12
E. 159	1394	m	Crayke		York	20+	
E. 193	1392	f	Wakefield		Beverley		46

Ref	Date	Sex	Origin	Age	Destination		
E. 221	1396	m	i. ?	[14]	Ouseburn	20	12
			ii. York	[19]	York		41
E. 248	1346	f	Richmond		York		41
E. 255	1384	m	Skinningrove	[33]	Scarborough	40	28
		f	Skinningrove	[28]	Scarborough	35	28
E. 257	1349	m	nr. ?Leicester		Newcastle		?160+
		m	Benwell		Newcastle		2
F. 46	1422	f	i. Middleton in Teesdale		Newcastle	20+	?30
			ii. Newland, nr. Newcastle				
F. 59	1410	f	?	[18+]	Hull	16+	16
F. 61	1411	m	Bilsdale		York	40	22
		f	Wharram		Bilsdale	40	9
F. 64	1412	f	?		York	30	16
		m	Linton on Ouse	[14+]	York	40	68
		f	Knaresborough		York	40	15
F. 79	1418	f	Preston		York		15
		f	Stockeld	[29]	York	40	20/22
		m	Stockeld	[39]	York	40	
F. 81	1481	f	?Aughton*	[17]	Pontefract		2
F. 113	1434	m	Snape		Well	40	70+
F. 129	early C15	f	Westmorland		Ayton		70+
		f	Westmorland		Ayton		14
F. 177	1433	m	Meltonby		North Burton		14
		f	Meltonby		North Burton		24
			i . Meltonby	[19+]	Barmby	20+	22
			ii. Barton on Humber				
		m	Meltonby	[19+]	Wilberfoss	20+	4

TABLE 6.1 (*Continued*)

BIHR CP	Date	Sex (m/f)	Moved from/to	Then aged	Current location	Age	Distance moved (miles)
F. 179	1438	m	Carnaby		Full Sutton		26
F. 185	1450	m	Kildwick		York	18	38
		m	Marton		York	17	13
		m	Marton		York	20	13
F. 201	1430	m	i. ?Poppleton	[14+]			4
			ii. York	[17+]	Poppleton	36+	4
		f	i. ?Poppleton	[15]			4
			ii. York	[17]			4
			iii. Poppleton	[17½]			4
			iv. York	[18]			4
F. 202	1462	f	Appletreewick		Poppleton	36	4
		m	?	[24]	Denton	80	9
F. 240	1466	m	?	[24+]	Appletreewick	74+	
F. 241	1447	m	?	[24+]	Burn	40+	
		m	?	[10+]	Burton Agnes	30+	
		m	i. Driffield		Driffield	26+	12
			ii. Beverley		Burton Agnes	25+	12
		m	?	[17+]	Beverley	32+	
		m	?	[20+]			
		m	i. Hedon				
			ii. 'Moretown'		Beverley		
F. 257	1477	f	Samlesbury		Ribchester		5

Ref	Year	Sex	Origin	Age	Destination	Distance
F. 284	1494	f	Leconfield	[17+]	London	165
F. 336	1465	f	i. York	[22+]		20
			ii. Methley	23+	York	20
G. 26	1507	m	Pickering		?[the South]	
G. 35†	1409	f	?Rolston		York	?38

Notes: Ages in square brackets have been calculated retrospectively and are thus only approximate. All distances are as the crow flies.

* Identity ambiguous. Two vills similarly distant share the name 'Aughton'. One is to the south, near Rotherham, the other to the north-east, beyond Selby. Text records 'Aghton' or 'Haghton'.

† Cause paper at present wrongly classified. Should be class 'F'.

Sources: BIHR, CP. E, F, G various; Appendix III below.

reflection of the gender-specific incidence of the sorts of transgressions of borough custom most likely to feature in the court rolls. These mostly concern trading offences, such as forestalling and regrating, for which women were frequently presented, though some concern slander, where women again feature prominently, and assault, where women are often the victims.[9] This high profile within the borough court would only serve to strengthen the prejudice that the 'ungoverned' woman was a trouble-maker, hence the particular need for women seeking lodging within the community to find pledges to guarantee their good conduct. It is apparently this high incidence of pledging that Hilton has identified as evidence of a very high rate of female migration into the town of Halesowen from the surrounding countryside, such that women greatly outnumbered men. It is the contention here that this may in fact be an optical illusion. The evidence more readily reflects the marginal economic status of women in towns before the plague, a status that forced many the wrong side of the law simply to survive, rather that any underlying preponderance of females. Analogy with post-plague evidence, or an assertion that low sex ratios, whereby women outnumber men, are characteristic of medieval urban society, are tempting lines of argument, but they do not stand up to critical scrutiny. As will be shown in the following chapter, the low sex ratios found for a number of north European towns of the late fourteenth and fifteenth centuries apply specifically to the post-plague economy and are not, for example, applicable to Tuscan towns for the same period, or to London in the sixteenth century.

If demographic decline did indeed precede the Black Death by some three decades, and Poos's tithingpenny evidence and some wages material would tend to support this supposition, then the foundations for economic renewal were being laid even before the catastrophe of 1348–9.[10] The massive reduction in the population, by perhaps a third or, more likely, nearly a half, caused short-term disruption and acute local labour shortages. The continued impact of epidemic plague, as in the so-called Grey Death of 1361 or the third pestilence of 1368, but extending alongside other

[9] Hilton, 'Small Town Society', 71.
[10] L. R. Poos, 'The Rural Population of Essex in the Later Middle Ages', *Economic History Review*, 2nd ser. 38 (1985), 515–30.

kinds of pestilence far into the fifteenth century served only to further the downward trend.[11] This had a number of economic repercussions. The cost of wage labour rose dramatically as employers were forced to pay high wages to compete for scarce supply. The government responded to this situation with more speed than success by trying to enforce pre-plague wage rates through the Ordinance of Labourers of 1349 and the Statute of Labourers of 1351. The records of indictments under the Statute only confirm that the Statute was regularly violated in all its provisions. Workers demanded and received 'excessive' rates and, significantly, moved about in search of better wages.[12]

The enhanced spending power of labourers generally may have had a beneficial effect on the economy as reflected in both rural and urban market-places, and thus on the demand for non-agricultural labour and the supply of labour. It is apparent from indictments under the Statute of 1351 that women, visible in manorial accounts before the Black Death, became a more conspicuous part of the post-plague labour force, particularly in pastoral regions, partly as a consequence of the shortage of male labour.[13] The level of participation of women in the labour market would, however, have been determined by the demand for labour and the availability of male labour within the local economy, and this last would have varied between town and country, and within different agricultural regions. Demand for labour, moreover, could not grow indefinitely in a climate of demographic attrition. Demand for rural labour would have tended to decline as there was a long-term shift away from arable farming in the face of falling population levels. Similarly, once the decline in population outstripped any growth in spending power on the part of those men and women drawn into the labour market, then demand for goods and services would fall in tandem with demand for urban labour.

Towns, as the principal centres of trade and commerce, following the initial disruption of the Black Death itself, probably

[11] Cf. Goldberg, 'Mortality and Economic Change'.
[12] For regional evidence of this trend see Putnam (ed.), *Yorkshire Sessions of the Peace, 1361–4*.
[13] See Penn, 'Female Wage-Earners', 5–7.

experienced a period of prosperity for several decades from the later fourteenth century.[14] Certainly the poll tax and, more problematically, franchise evidence suggest towns were able to recruit migrants in very considerable numbers despite the greater availability of land and lack of labour in the countryside. But the poll tax evidence also suggests that women came to outnumber men within urban society whereas, to a more modest extent, the reverse was true of rural communities. Thus according to the 1377 nominative poll tax listings, which may if anything tend to under-record women, at towns like Hull, York, and Carlisle there were less than ninety men to every hundred adult women. In view of the high level of immigration generally, this must reflect a dispro-portionately high rate of female migration rather than a net out-migration of males. It is noteworthy that many of the disappoint-ingly small number of female migrants to the city of York identified from cause papers migrated in the half-century or more spanning the last decades of the fourteenth century and the first two decades of the fifteenth.[15] Many youngsters may first have come as servants.

In a period of high and rising wages, but modest food prices, servant labour must have seemed particularly attractive to employ-ers. Poll tax evidence suggests that servants were already compar-atively numerous in both town and country by 1377, but that demand was greatest in towns. In many larger towns a third or more of all households contained servants, and the same source indicates that in the town, unlike the countryside, female servants were as common as male. A cause dated 1430 contains the depositions of a couple from the nearby village of Poppleton who had several years before spent time as servants in York house-holds. Alice Dalton, for example, testified to serving one York man when she would have been about 15 years. She left him at Martinmas to work for a York baker until the following Pentecost, when she returned to Poppleton. She returned again to York in Martinmas for a further year in service.[16] Such detail is recorded by accident, but there is little reason to suspect that it is atypical. Many young women, having spent time in service and acquired modest savings, may have found husbands and settled. This is

---

[14] See Ch. 2 above.   [15] See Table 6.1.   [16] BIHR, CP. F. 201.

certainly the implication of many of the matrimonial causes appearing in the York consistory court. Alice Dalton's case is interesting for she married and settled in Poppleton with a man who had also served in York, but who probably returned to take up a holding of land in his native village.

Patterns of migration must be related to the rural economy and the gender-specific demand for labour. There must be a push side as well as pull side to the high level of migration by women to towns in this post-plague period. In pastoral regions women probably found employment without difficulty since such tasks as shearing sheep, milking, making butter and cheese were traditionally women's work, and women were much involved in the rural clothing trade that seems so vital at this date in woollen districts as spinsters, carders, and weavers. In some arable regions, especially where poorer soils prevailed and production was consequently relatively expensive, there is evidence for a shift away from arable. This shift would have been determined by economic necessity and its timing dictated by relative movements in the price of cereals and of labour. On lands converted to arable farming in years when high population pressure and consequently buoyant prices and depressed wage rates ensured that even comparatively 'marginal' soils were viable, the upturn in wage rates after 1349 may have been sufficient to force a contraction of labour-intensive arable cultivation. On less poor soils pressure to scale down or abandon arable production would have been delayed until the long-term decline in grain prices became apparent in the 1370s and 1380s. There would thus have followed in a number of areas a shift to less labour-intensive pasture farming, for where the land was suitable good profits could be made from sheep and livestock in a period of industrial growth, and, on the poorest lands, the gradual abandonment of some soils. From such areas labour would have been shed, hence the contraction of some settlements and ultimately the abandonment of some communities to create what are now recognized as deserted medieval villages. This was true of parts of midland England and of Northumberland for which last some poll tax evidence survives, but may also have been true of some Wolds and Vale villages that feature within the York deposition evidence.

The chronology of village desertions has tended to suggest that abandonment was often located in the fifteenth or early sixteenth rather than, as would at first sight seem more logical if depopulation was a direct consequence of high plague mortality, the later fourteenth century.[17] But actual abandonment, recorded by the loss of village names from tax records, represents the extreme end-point in a long-term and more widespread process. The sort of process just outlined whereby the twin effects of rising wages and falling grain prices necessitated a retreat from arable farming and the consequent loss of labour accords well with the evidence that the level of migration out of manors was especially high in the later decades of the fourteenth century. Smith notes high levels of illegal migrants from the manors of Codicote in Hertfordshire and Winslow in Buckinghamshire in the two decades following the Black Death.[18] Campbell has described an especially high rate of emigration from the manors of Coltishall and Martham in Norfolk in the decades 1371–81 and 1377–88 respectively.[19] Very high rates of migration from the manors of Ramsey Abbey are described by Raftis from the very beginning of the fifteenth century.[20] Clearly circumstances varied between differing agricultural regions according to the particular interplay of wage rates and labour supply, grain prices, soil fertility, and the viability of pastoral farming, but the trend is clear. A restructuring of the agrarian economy in a time of demographic recession and labour shortage led to an actual contraction in the demand for labour in some localities. It is the contention here that the young and unattached would be the most prominent among those leaving in search of better prospects elsewhere, and that young women would have been especially prominent among these migrants since they would have been most vulnerable in a depressed labour market. This may help explain why females came to outnumber males in those labour-starved urban communities for which nominative poll listings survive from the first poll tax.

---

[17] M. Beresford, *The Lost Villages of England* (Lutterworth, 1954), 162–6.

[18] Smith, 'Seigneurial Reaction to the Scale of Villein Migration'. I am grateful to Dr Smith for allowing me to cite these observations.

[19] B. M. S. Campbell, 'Population Pressure, Inheritance and the Land Market in a Fourteenth-Century Peasant Community', in R. M. Smith (ed.), *Land, Kinship and Life-cycle* (Cambridge, 1984), 100 and n. 37.

[20] Raftis, *Tenure and Mobility*, 153. Dyer observes that rural out-migration must partly be explained by the existence of better opportunities elsewhere: C. Dyer, *Lords and Peasants in a Changing Society: The Estates of the Bishopric of Worcester, 680–1540* (Cambridge, 1980), 261.

There is some slight, but suggestive evidence to indicate that female migrants to York often came from such declining rural communities. Two such migrants from the small Wolds village of Uncleby observed in a matrimonial cause of 1372 settled in York some two decades after the plague. A young woman then living in York had four years earlier been living there. She had then shared her bed with Joan de Suardby. Joan had herself served in York, and was contracted to and subsequently joined her former master in York.[21] A married couple, noticed in a cause of 1418, appear to have abandoned their home at Stockeld near Wetherby on the edge of the Vale of York the previous year. Stockeld subsequently became a deserted village, but the likelihood is that this community was already experiencing economic dislocation as a consequence of a shift away from arable cultivation.[22] Even today evidence of earlier arable cultivation in the form of ridge and furrow is conspicuous in the fields of rough pasture that characterize part of the Vale to the west of York. When after eight years the monks of Meaux caught up with their villein John Helmeslay, who had fled their grange at Wharram and taken a new identity in Bilsdale, his wife chose not to remain, but moved instead to York.[23] The implication is that by *c.*1400 Bilsdale, a region only substantially colonized during the thirteenth century and by this later date probably already in sharp decline, could no longer provide for the single woman and that life within the city was a more attractive prospect.[24]

Any gender-specific pattern of migration would not have been reflected in manor court rolls since in these conditions the loss of female labour would have gone largely unremarked. Thus Campbell notes only two women among the twenty-one migrants noted in the court rolls of Martham between 1377 and 1388. What Campbell's evidence does show is the high rate of urban migration at this date. Seventeen of these rural migrants are recorded as settling in towns.[25] Blanchard, writing of Derbyshire, notes that there was a steady drift of migrants away from non-industrial

[21] BIHR, CP. E. 111.
[22] BIHR, CP. F. 79.
[23] BIHR, CP. F. 59.
[24] Cf. J. McDonnell, 'Medieval Assarting Hamlets in Bilsdale, North-East Yorkshire', *Northern History*, 22 (1986), 278–9.
[25] Campbell, 'Population Pressure', 100.

villages through the late fourteenth and earlier fifteenth centuries seeking wage employment even despite the availability of land within the local community.[26] The effect of such emigration of the young, and especially of young women, away from areas of contracting arable farming would have been to diminish the capacity of some rural communities to reproduce themselves in a period of high mortality. Such communities would have tended to shrink in size, even to disappear altogether as the population literally died away. The point of eventual desertion may, however, have followed the peak period of emigration by a matter of several decades. Poll tax evidence, although focused towards the early stages of this process and indeed probably antedating, as the divergent chronology of illegal exits from manors would suggest, any marked shift away from arable in other than the most vulnerable regions, tends nevertheless to support this hypothesis. Two communities that were abandoned at some point after the Black Death, Lemmington in the Coquetdale ward of Northumberland and Normanton in Rutland, both enjoyed the highest recorded sex ratios, 156.3 and 141.7 respectively, for any of the vills recorded for either of those two regions in 1377. Golder in Oxfordshire, another deserted medieval village, displayed a sex ratio of 144.4 in 1377.[27] Although some other communities identified within the rather small sample of surviving 1377 nominative listings and eventually to be deserted show rather more normal sex ratios, these particular cases still seem highly significant.

THE CIRCUMSTANCES OF MIGRATION

The factors that may have motivated the young, and young women in particular, to migrate from the countryside into the town must be understood in terms both of the particular attractions of urban society, be they economic or social, and the restrictions of rural life. Migration in search of employment, particularly by the young and unmarried, seems to have been a characteristic feature of pre-industrial society. Some of this movement was undoubtedly temporary and often involved only comparatively short distances.

---

[26] I. Blanchard, 'Industrial Employment and the Rural Land Market, 1380–1520', in Smith (ed.), *Land, Kinship and Life-cycle*, 249–50, 253.

[27] Calculated from PRO, E 179/161/41 printed in Beresford, *Lost Villages*, 414.

Thus it is not unusual to find evidence of women seeking employment during the harvest season. Alice Gylot, Margeret Longe, and Emma Shephierd, all of Ashen, were presented before the Justices of the Peace in Essex a few years before the Peasants' Revolt for taking excessive wages and moving from place to place.[28] In Yorkshire numbers of women are found in the Peace Rolls for 1361–4 similarly indicted before the justices. Alice, the wife of Peter Chauntrell, went from Pocklington to Tibthorpe some ten miles across the Wolds for the harvest. Others, such as Emma Ingham, Agnes Skott, and Alice Wassand presented together as hired reapers, were stated simply to have gone outside their own village to find better wages elsewhere.[29] The motives for migration need not, however, always have been primarily economic, but medieval records rarely allow the motives of individuals to be reconstructed. Certainly the York cause papers of the fourteenth and fifteenth centuries are not generally very informative about the circumstances behind migration. Christine Glover of Leconfield near Beverley, in a cause dated 1494, is said to have gone to London to circumvent the court's attempt to enforce a contract of marriage with one John Eshton.[30] It is probable that Lucy Broun left home in the autumn of 1356 because the opportunity of harvest employment took her away from a husband who beat her frequently.[31]

Evidence of merchets suggests that a high rate of marital exogamy was normal in medieval England and many women must have left their native communities to live with their husbands. It may be that some women met their husbands whilst engaged as servants in neighbouring communities. Certainly the cause paper evidence supports this view. Smith has elsewhere noted the similarity in the neo-local pattern of marital exogamy apparent from the Spalding serf lists and the equivalent pattern of servant hirings derived from the Spalding statute sessions of the eighteenth century.[32] There is some correlation between the seasonality of

[28] E. C. Thurber (ed.), *Essex Sessions of the Peace 1351, 1377–1379* (Essex Archaeological Society Occasional Publications, 3; 1953), nos. B. 74–6, pp. 159–60.

[29] Putnam (ed.), *Yorkshire Sessions of the Peace*, nos. 1136/63, 116, pp. 52, 58.

[30] BIHR, CP. F. 284.

[31] BIHR, CP. E. 77.

[32] Smith, 'Hypothèses sur la nuptialité', 127–9.

marriages and the customary dates for servants to enter or leave service, which may suggest young people often married on completing a period of service.[33] As has been previously discussed, towns made particular demands upon servant labour. For younger women migration to the town may have held a number of attractions, most notably in the labour-starved decades of the later fourteenth and earlier fifteenth centuries. Towns then offered the prospect of work. But towns also offered the society of other young people, the chance to meet the opposite sex without the supervision of parents, and the chance to engage in courtship. The freedom of courtship clearly enjoyed by some young women in late medieval York as demonstrated from litigation within the Church court is a world apart from the experience of Isolda Kirby, frequently beaten by her kinsman and guardian John Reeve because she showed too much interest in the company of boys.[34] Older women, on the other hand, may have been cognizant of the greater welfare opportunities within urban society.[35]

Secular changes in the relative demand for female labour in the countryside, and thus the hold over women exercised by some rural economies, is especially difficult to assess in the absence of substantial wage data in respect of women labourers. Some evidence survives, however, in respect of wages paid for washing and shearing sheep, a task that was invariably assigned to women.[36] These seem, using data contained in Thorold Rogers's study, to have risen at some point between the beginning of the fourteenth century and the eve of the Black Death, perhaps due to an expansion of sheep flocks and hence the demand for labour. Wage rates, however, remained stable through the Black Death and only appear to have begun to rise by the 1370s. This is against the trend in male wages, which appear generally to have shown an upward trend immediately following the Black Death. By the early fifteenth century wage rates for washing and shearing sheep had risen sharply, although individual rates appear to have fluc-

[33] See Ch. 5 above.

[34] M. S. Arnold (ed.), *Select Cases of Trespass from the King's Courts, 1307–1399* (Selden Society, 100; 1985), no. 2.25, p. 26.

[35] Joan, formerly wife of John Ireby, apparently moved to York as a widow for she lodged in Goodramgate, York, prior to marrying a York man. Alice Henrison went from Bilsdale to York immediately upon separating from her husband. BIHR, CP. G. 35; CP. F. 59.

[36] Rogers, *A History of Agriculture and Prices in England*, ii.

tuated considerably from year to year, possibly according to whether or not meals were included in the payment. Wages fell back, however, by the fifth decade of the fifteenth century and remained close to or just above the level reached at the time of the Black Death. These again fail to correlate very satisfactorily with the equivalent trends in male wage rates and suggest different gender-specific patterns in the supply and demand for labour.[37]

These wage data would tend to suggest that female labour was relatively abundant in relation to demand for some two decades following the advent of plague, but became particularly difficult to obtain by the early decades of the fifteenth century. These observations coincide with the sort of chronology suggested from other sources. In the immediate aftermath of the plague male labour would have been first to benefit from any shortages of labour and female labour would have been shed first, or at least in greatest numbers, where arable agriculture ceased to be viable in the aftermath of the plague. An expansion of pastoral farming from the later fourteenth century and, as demographic recession continued, an increasingly acute shortage of male labour in towns may have served to stretch the demand for female labour to the point that rural employers had to pay high wages to prevent female workers migrating to the town. It may also be that the Agincourt and Normandy campaigns further served to deplete the supply of male labour at this same period.[38] Once towns began to experience recession, however, women may have been less inclined to seek work outside the countryside, and their wages would as a consequence have fallen back as female labour again became locally more abundant.

Deposition evidence, despite its paucity, does tend to support a chronology that locates the highest levels of female migration in

[37] Wages paid to women working as thatchers, for example, appear to have risen slightly between the late 13th and early 14th cent. (from ½–1*d*. to 1–1¼*d*. per day), but more sharply following the Black Death (to 2*d*. per day). They may have risen again by the later 14th cent. (to 3*d*. per day), but unfortunately Rogers has very little equivalent wage data for the 15th cent. Equivalent male wages were two to three times the female rate before 1348–9, but wage differentials narrow in the decades after the plague. Thus at Oxford in 1393 a woman thatcher was paid 3½*d*. per day whereas her male equivalent was paid 4*d*.

[38] M. M. Postan, 'The Costs of the Hundred Years War', in id., *Essays on Medieval Agriculture and General Problems of the Medieval Economy* (Cambridge, 1973), 65.

the late fourteenth and early years of the fifteenth century. As poll tax sex ratios would suggest, towns may then have exercised their greatest pull over female labour. The unusually detailed 1379 Howdenshire returns even suggest movement of female labour from communities experiencing economic difficulties to other more prosperous 'industrial' villages.[39] Only London, always a magnet for the young migrant, seems to have experienced problems absorbing the influx of labour in the immediate aftermath of the plague as a proclamation of 1359 against vagrants demonstrates.[40] This may perhaps be explained by London's proximity to those arable regions of midland England that experienced the most immediate and severe dislocation in the face of spiralling labour costs and falling demand. The pattern of 'spinster-clustering' in the suburbs and poor tenements may also be related to the migration of women into the town. Deposition evidence again provides a few clues. A cause of 1366 relates to neo-local migration patterns. Two female witnesses, formerly resident in Rawcliffe and Skelton respectively, had moved during the twelve years prior to their testimony further down the main Northallerton–York road into Clifton, virtually a suburb of York. Another, Isabell de Strensall, had moved from Rawcliffe to suburban Bootham, where she had lived for two years, before finally settling in Jubbergate actually within the central area of the city.[41] Three other female migrants to York whose location within the city can be identified all chose districts away from the most central area of the city north-east of the Ouse. Margaret de Burton, aged 30 'or more' in 1372, was said to have been resident in Walmgate for fifteen years.[42] Two further deponents, Alice Spurn and Elena Blakburn, appear to have migrated together along the road into York from the west for they stayed the night at a house near Wetherby two years before their testimony in 1418. Both settled within the same part of suburban York south-west of the Ouse.[43] Isabella, daughter of Alan de Belyngham, and Elena de Leyr-

[39] Goldberg, 'Female Labour, Service and Marriage', 19.
[40] H. T. Riley (ed.), *Memorials of London and London Life in the XIIIth, XIVth and XVth Centuries* (London, 1868), 304.
[41] BIHR, CP. E. 89.
[42] BIHR, CP. E. 111.
[43] BIHR, CP. F. 79.

mouth, who lived together in Aldwark, were recent migrants from Newcastle.[44]

Migrants then would appear to have found accommodation at least initially outside the more prosperous central area of the city, although this would not apply to those who took up positions as servants. The group of cottages constructed by the York Vicars Choral at the corner of St Andrewgate and Aldwark, for example, in 1335 housed significant proportions of female tenants even before the Black Death, but the proportion rose by the last decades of the fourteenth and early decades of the fifteenth century. Between 1399 and 1416 the number of female tenants is consistently greater than the number of male.[45] Among such tenants, however, there is observed a much higher degree of turnover between rentals than is apparent for more expensive properties.[46] Many of these poorer tenants may simply have moved elsewhere within the city, a pattern suggested for example from tracing the names of known prostitutes, but some at least may have moved away from the town either temporarily or permanently. Indeed it is probable that there was a degree of fluidity between rural and urban labour markets in respect of general labourers.

By the mid- to later fifteenth century, however, towns appear to have become less receptive to rural migrants. Gild ordinances attempted to curb the admission of unskilled migrant labour for the first time. They also came to take a more restrictive line on the employment of women, and urban authorities seem to have been increasingly concerned by the problems of disorderly conduct, gaming, crime, and prostitution, regarding single women with downright suspicion, even hostility. The York deposition evidence provides little evidence for female urban immigration at this period, but the samples are too small to regard this as anything more than suggestive of a more general trend. Men do appear, however, to have come to outnumber women in the urban economy as economic opportunities for women were eroded. By the later sixteenth century males appear to have outnumbered females in London, and this was also true of York by the earlier

---

[44] BIHR, CP. E. 126.
[45] YML, VC 6/2/38, 41, 42, 44, 45.
[46] Cf. Rees Jones, 'Property, Tenure and Rents', 243–4.

seventeenth century.[47] The low sex ratio that characterized Coventry in 1523 may thus be atypical, the product of male out-migration in a period of sudden and profound recession.[48]

In several instances it can be demonstrated that women migrated not individually, but with a partner. Two sisters, Alice and Agnes, daughters to Richard Heryng, migrated together from Upwood to Bury St Edmunds early in the fifteenth century. They must have been comparatively youthful at the time since they are reported to have lived in Bury at least forty years.[49] Anabilla Somor and Alice Gelson of Ayton near Scarborough, noted in a stray deposition of the early fifteenth century as having come from Westmorland, were said to be sisters. They were probably single at the time of their migration since both found partners and had children after their arrival in Ayton.[50] Alice Spurn and Elena Blakburn appear likewise to have travelled together to York along the old Roman road from the west early in the fifteenth century. They were said to have originated from Knaresborough and Preston respectively, but are observed lodging together at a house on the manor of Stockeld near Wetherby where they shared the same bed two years before they made their depositions. Since their hosts, Roger and Alice Remyngton, were also resident in York by the same date then it is possible that they all moved together.[51] Three further female migrants, this time from Newcastle upon Tyne, may well have travelled together to York. They are observed in a cause dated 1382 at which date two were living together in Aldwark, and the third nearby in Monkgate. All were single and had journeyed in their late teens or early twenties.[52] This pattern is not perhaps typical of unmarried male migrants, who may have travelled singly, and can probably be explained in terms of the greater sense of security a woman might feel travelling with a companion of her own sex, but also in terms of the social prejudice against the single woman, often associated with loose living and petty crime.[53]

[47] P. Clark and D. Souden, 'Introduction', in eid. (eds.), *Migration and Society in Early Modern England* (London, 1987), 35.

[48] Phythian-Adams, *Desolation of a City*, 189–200.

[49] Raftis, *Tenure and Mobility*, 180.   [50] BIHR, CP. F. 129.

[51] BIHR, CP. F. 79.   [52] BIHR, CP. E. 126.

[53] Dyer, *Lords and Peasants in a Changing Society*, 366. Margery Kempe records her constant fear of sexual assault whilst travelling: Meech and Allen (eds.), *The Book of Margery Kempe*, ch. 30.

Certainly the single woman was vulnerable within medieval society and judicial records frequently contain indictments for assaults on women. The Oxfordshire Peace Roll for 1397–8, for example, contains the indictments of two men for the murder of an unknown woman, a stranger presumably passing through the community.[54] Young, inexperienced female migrants may have been especially vulnerable, though not all female migrants were adolescents or young adults; Elena Blakburn and Alice Spurn were both said to be 40 in a matrimonial cause of 1418.[55] Single females may also have found some difficulty in obtaining accommodation, though this is most likely to have been true of periods of hardship and recession before the Black Death, such as appears to have been the case of Halesowen, or again in the later fifteenth century when towns such as Coventry, concerned by the spread of prostitution and petty crime, started to issue regulations against the lodging of single women.[56]

The means by which migrants were assimilated into urban society cannot easily be reconstructed. Young women who were drawn in as servants may well have depended on having friends or relatives who had migrated earlier finding them positions. It has already been shown that it is common to find servants employed by older relatives.[57] Two of the female servants of Robert Lonesdale and his wife Joan in York early in the fifteenth century were respectively a relative by marriage of Robert and a god-daughter of Joan. The latter may have been a migrant as Joan was herself a recent arrival in York.[58] Isabella Foxhole of Aughton, observed in a cause dated 1418, was employed as a servant in Pontefract, some twenty miles distant, by John Carrow, who was married to her paternal aunt Margaret. It was whilst she was in service there that she contracted marriage to a Pontefract man.[59] Sometimes, as has been seen, it is possible to identify kin relationships between servants. It may be surmised that established servants persuaded their employers to find positions for younger siblings. This is

[54] E. G. Kimball (ed.), *Oxfordshire Sessions of the Peace in the Reign of Richard II* (Oxfordshire Record Society, 53; 1953), no. B. 7, p. 74.
[55] BIHR, CP. F. 79.
[56] Hilton, 'Lords, Burgesses and Hucksters', 10; Goldberg, 'The Public and the Private'; Ch. 3 above.
[57] Ch. 4 above.
[58] BIHR, CP. G. 35.
[59] BIHR, CP. F. 81.

explicit, to take a post-medieval example, in the case of Alice Cutberde of New Romney who came to Cranbrook in 1609 in the expectation that her sister 'would help her to a service'.[60] Much the same may be suggested from the late medieval evidence. Margaret Hall, for example, may have been a sister of one Elena Hall who had earlier served the same York goldsmith.[61] Brodsky, describing female migrants to London at the turn of the seventeenth century, has likewise suggested that male apprentices may have helped secure positions for their younger sisters and the same appears to have been true of later medieval York; Joan Amgill, noted in a will of 1463, was probably a sister to her employer's apprentice in pewtercraft, John Amgill.[62] Such mechanisms may have operated rather more frequently than probate evidence alone would suggest since servants are often not identified by their surnames, and even where surnames are recorded, kin relationships may not be apparent.

Not all women can have enjoyed existing contacts or were successful in establishing themselves within urban society. It is probable that some who migrated without the aid of kith or kin found that any illusions of bright lights and romance, or even, more mundanely, relative security of employment soon evaporated. Migrant women are disproportionately well represented among women indicted for prostitution. Kowaleski notes that females so indicted within the court rolls of late fourteenth-century Exeter were much less likely to have kin within the borough than was true of other working women.[63] For York it has already been observed that women with the surname Scott are conspicuous among the names of women presented for fornication and adultery within the spiritual jurisdiction of the Dean and Chapter.[64] The situation for the female migrant can only have become more difficult by the end of the fifteenth century as work opportunities declined and civic prejudices against the single woman hardened. It is perhaps significant in this context that by

[60] P. Clark, 'Migrants in the City: The Process of Social Adaptation in English Towns, 1500–1800', in id. and D. Souden (eds.), *Migration and Society in Early Modern England* (London, 1987), 272.
[61] BIHR, Prob. Reg. 2, fo. 45ᵛ.
[62] Brodsky, 'Single Women in the London Marriage Market', 94; BIHR, Prob. Reg. 2, fo. 599ᵛ.
[63] Kowaleski, 'Women's Work in a Market Town', 154.
[64] Ch. 3 above.

the very end of the fifteenth century numbers of cheaper rented properties were unable to find tenants; demand for properties at the bottom end of the market was drying up as work for unskilled and semi-skilled migrants, both male and female, itself evaporated.[65]

The degree to which women became permanent residents after their initial migration to the urban community is another problem that cannot readily be resolved in the light of the available evidence. The example of Robert and Alice Dalton, migrant servants from Poppleton, is of especial interest because it is known that they subsequently returned to marry and settle in Poppleton.[66] It is not known, however, how commonly the process of migration from countryside to town was reversed in this way. For towns to grow or even to stand still there must have been a net inflow of migrants, but this may nevertheless disguise a real degree of population turnover. A pattern of mobility and population turnover may, for example, be suggested from the surviving record of intrants or persons licensed by the year to trade in Canterbury. Butcher has calculated that nearly half of all persons licensed in the period *c*.1390–1540 and who were not subsequently admitted to the franchise failed to renew their licences. Conversely, only some 17 per cent were licensed for a period in excess of five years.[67] Female intrants were licensed on average for even shorter periods. Single women who were licensed prior to marriage may explain why some names appear so briefly, but they fail to explain the general pattern. Numbers of traders may only have paid for a licence when discovered to be trading illegally, but this again appears insufficient an explanation. Two further observations are possible: some intrants would have found alternative employment with master artisans and would consequently have been exempt from any licensing requirements; a number of traders may alternatively have constituted temporary migrants who, after trading for a year or two, moved on to find work elsewhere. Hilton paints an apparently analogous picture in respect of pre-plague Halesowen. Male and female migrants are seen to enter the town, some to stay, but others just to pass through. Isabel de Bracton, an

---

[65] Cf. Rees Jones, 'Property, Tenure and Rents', 264, 266–7.
[66] BIHR, CP. F. 201.
[67] Butcher, 'Freemen Admissions and Urban Occupations', table III.

upholder, is observed in the court rolls for 1290 'moving from
lodging to lodging'.[68] It may be that the greater economic security
of the later fourteenth and early fifteenth centuries encouraged a
rather higher proportion of female migrants to settle. The surviving York sources do not allow this hypothesis to be pursued much
further, but, as has been seen, some rental evidence is suggestive.
The cottages built by the Vicars Choral at the corner of St
Andrewgate and Aldwark, for example, were frequently leased to
female tenants even in the earlier fourteenth century, but this
proportion rose over the very period that may have seen the most
acute demand for female labour. Between 1399 and 1416, despite
a very high rate of turnover among tenants between rentals,
women tenants consistently outnumbered men. Thereafter the
sexes tend to be more evenly divided, though males outnumber
females in most years.[69]

[68] Hilton, 'Lords, Burgesses and Hucksters', 11.
[69] YML, VC 6/2/38–78.

7

Patterns of Cohesion and Residence

THE POLL TAX EVIDENCE

Within urban society, some sort of group solidarity among women
may often have been determined by or reinforced by their
concentration within certain areas of the town, a phenomenon
that Hufton has described as 'spinster clustering'.[1] This may be
explored in some detail from some of the 1377 poll tax returns.
For only a handful of towns do nominative listings survive for the
first poll tax of 1377.[2] Although such assessments were compiled
on a street by street or parish by parish basis, as the Shrewsbury
evidence demonstrates, only for the Hull and York returns are
these divisions specifically recorded.[3] From a number of the
returns, however, it is possible to derive a measure of mean
household size (MHS) for the entire community. There are
problems in distinguishing individual households from this material, but these are not sufficient to detract from the derived data. It
is more difficult, however, to allow for persons missing or excluded
from the poll tax. Analysis of the demographic structure of the
tax population does not suggest any bias against particular groups,
though analogy with the later returns would suggest that single
females and servants were vulnerable. To compensate for children
and other excluded dependants a multiplier of 1.65 has been
adopted here, allowing for a proportion of the untaxed population
under 14 years equivalent to more than one-third of the total
population and for a degree of exemption or evasion besides. This
may be on the generous side since the impact of plague and

---

[1] O. Hufton, 'Women without Men: Widows and Spinsters in Britain and France
in the Eighteenth Century', *Journal of Family History*, 9 (1984), 361.
[2] Carlisle, Colchester, Coventry (Bailey Lane), Dartmouth, Hull, Northampton,
Oxford (two parishes), Rochester, York.
[3] W. G. D. Fletcher, 'The Poll-Tax for the Town and Liberties of Shrewsbury,
1380', *Transactions of the Shropshire Archaeological and Natural History Society*,
2nd ser. 2 (1890), 17–28; Leggett (ed.), '1377 Poll Tax Returns for the City of
York'; PRO, E 179/206/45.

TABLE 7.1.   *Mean urban household size from the 1377 poll tax*

	Households	MHS	MHS×1.65
Coventry, Bailey Lane	116	3.77	6.22
Dartmouth	221	2.28	3.76
Hull	691	2.25	3.71
Northampton†	265	2.54	4.18
Oxford			
St Mary the Virgin	123	2.40	3.96
St Peter in the East	72	2.49	4.10
York†	761	2.50	4.12

† Partial return only.
Source: As Table II.1 below.

epidemic disease was probably particularly severe on the young. Any exclusion of solitaries would, moreover, tend to inflate household measures. It must be assumed that most children and other dependants would be distributed evenly between recorded taxation households, but a few may have been associated with exempt or otherwise unrecorded solitaries such as poor widows.[4] The measures achieved must, therefore, be subject to a real margin of error, though it is more likely that derived MHS are too large than too small. Consistent patterns do, moreover, emerge and these assumptions would have to be very wrong to invalidate the observed data.[5]

Household sizes will tend to be higher where wealthier servant-keeping households are well represented. This is conspicuously the case within the Bailey Lane ward of Coventry, but it may be true to a lesser degree of the partial York and Northampton returns.[6] It thus appears that a reconstructed urban mean household size of less than four may have applied fairly generally. Such

[4] It could be argued by analogy with early modern evidence that where a widowed mother lived with her children then that household was more likely to be treated as exempt for tax purposes. On the other hand, wealthier households were perhaps more liable to retain their children longer than was true of less affluent households. (I am most grateful to Dr R. M. Smith for these observations.) The view here is that the level of exclusion was, as the demographic measures suggest, relatively low, and that the institution of life-cycle service was established even within well-to-do urban families.

[5] These are shown in Table 7.1.

[6] Suburban parishes are poorly represented within the York returns.

a mean appears low by comparison with much early modern data, but is more immediately compatible with some urban measures, especially those derived from the Marriage Duty Act at the end of the seventeenth century. MHS for Southampton, Shrewsbury, and some London parishes calculated by Wall for this date are 3.8, 4.0, and 4.4 respectively. The true Shrewsbury measure should perhaps be adjusted downwards as the suburban listing is defective.[7] This correlation appears significant as both periods experienced low or negative demographic growth. Wall has elsewhere observed that an implicit relationship exists between demographic movements and fluctuations in MHS.[8] It might seem that an increase in population consequent upon a rising birth rate would be reflected in MHS, but this general pattern does not satisfy what is known of urban growth and urban households. In both the decades after 1348 and during the later seventeenth century urban growth appears to have been sustained despite sluggish or even negative demographic growth elsewhere. At the same time urban households appear to have been especially small at these same periods. An alternative explanation of the relationship between demographic movements and MHS is consequently needed in the case of towns. A more thorough investigation of urban household structure may help resolve this problem.

Apparently uniform mean global measures can disguise real local variation across urban communities as the high MHS derived from the poll tax fragment for the wealthy Bailey Lane ward of Coventry warns. Such variations can be mapped for Hull and several York parishes in 1377. MHS for individual streets or parishes are tabulated in Table 7.2. Although MHS in Hull tend to be at a lower level than for the sample of York parishes, certain patterns do emerge. The major riverside thoroughfare of Hull Street and the central riverside parish of St Martin, Coney Street, in York were both prosperous mercantile districts with a high proportion of servants. Though neither rivals the Bailey Lane ward of Coventry, each displays a higher than usual MHS. Larger households appear generally to be congregated within more prosperous, central areas of the city. In contrast, marginal and

---

[7] Wall, 'Regional and Temporal Variations', table 4.6, pp. 101–3.
[8] R. Wall, 'Mean Household Size in England from Printed Sources', in P. Laslett (ed.), *Household and Family in Past Time* (Cambridge, 1982), 194.

TABLE 7.2. *Mean household size in Hull and York from the 1377 poll tax*

	Households	MHS	MHS × 1.65
York			
St Martin, Coney Street	93	3.25	5.36
St Crux	120	2.78	4.58
St Mary, Bishophill Senior	45	2.4	3.96
St Helen, Stonegate	82	2.46	4.06
St Sampson	160	2.37	3.91
St Denys, Walmgate	52	2.65	4.38
St Saviour	88	2.24	3.69
All Saints, Pavement	18	2.56	4.22
Bootham	103	1.90	3.14
Hull			
Trippet	16	1.88	3.09
Hull Street	209	2.69	4.44
Blackfriargate	62	1.87	3.09
Marketgate	135	2.21	3.64
Salthouse Lane	21	2.14	3.54
Bishop Lane	43	1.58	2.61
Beverleygate	71	2.16	3.56
Kirk Lane	37	2.19	3.61
Grimsby Lane	17	1.82	3.01
Mytongate	50	1.84	3.04

Sources: Leggett (ed.), '1377 Poll Tax Returns for the City of York'; PRO, E 179/206/45.

suburban areas are characterized by smaller households. Such a pattern can again be described from early modern sources. Phythian-Adams has calculated MHS of only 3.24–3.50 for some of Coventry's poorer wards in 1523.[9] An MHS of 3.4 has likewise been described for some suburban parishes of Canterbury in 1563.[10] Lower than average MHS has been observed in the Cambridge suburban parishes of St Giles and Barnwell early in the seventeenth century.[11] In Romford, Essex, in 1562 household size ranged from a mean of 3.5 in the suburbs to 4.6 in the town

[9] Phythian-Adams, *Desolation of a City*, table 34, p. 301.
[10] Clark and Clark, 'Social Economy', 69.
[11] Goose, 'Household Size', table 5, p. 364.

centre.[12] A similar diversity of household size probably reflected equivalent differences in the towns of late medieval Europe. Dresden demonstrates household sizes over one-quarter of the city in 1453 ranging from a mean of 3.06 in Kundigengasse to 4.28 in Wilische Gasse.[13] Considerable structural variation underlies these crude mean measures and an analysis of this pattern does much to illustrate the social topography of the English medieval town.

Parishes with high MHS within the poll tax sample tended to have relatively high proportions of larger than average servant-keeping households. Indeed there exists a crude correlation between MHS and the proportion of servant-keeping households in a community.[14] Low MHS, on the other hand, is influenced by the number of small and solitary households, many of which are headed by women. Solitary households appear to have been especially common in town society. Thus in Dresden's Kundigengasse 36 per cent of households in 1453 were solitary.[15] Much the same pattern can be observed at Coventry in 1523.[16] It is not strictly possible to identify solitary households from poll tax sources since not all the population was liable to tax. Instead female-headed households have been extracted. Single women, sometimes living in close proximity to one another, are a regular feature of towns. Such households were frequently small and tended to depress MHS. Of all groups in suburban Canterbury in 1563, such households enjoyed the lowest mean size.[17] This observation must be equally true of households at the time of the poll tax. The proportions of female-headed to total households have been tabulated in Tables 7.3 and 7.4 for a number of communities and, for Hull and York, by street and by parish as before.

Two important observations are pertinent here. Considerable

---

[12] McIntosh, 'Servants and the Household', table 1b, p. 8.

[13] Calculated from O. Richter, 'Zur Bevölkerungs- und Vermögensstatistik Dresdens im 15. Jahrhundert', *Neues Archiv für Sächsische Geschichte und Alterthumskunde*, 2 (1881), table IV, p. 281.

[14] Cf. Tables 4.2 and 7.2.

[15] Calculated from Richter, 'Zur Bevölkerungs- und Vermögensstatistik Dresdens', table IV, p. 281.

[16] Phythian-Adams, *Desolation of a City*, 224.

[17] In houses headed by widows, MHS=1.5; in houses headed by other single women, MHS=1.0: Clark and Clark, 'Social Economy', table 7, p. 76.

TABLE 7.3. *Proportion of urban female-headed households from the 1377 poll tax*

	Female-headed households	Total households	% female-headed
Carlisle*	74	309	23.9
Chichester†	8	67	11.9
Colchester**			
Sample (*a*)	73	250	29.2
Sample (*b*)	33	250	13.2
Total***	269	1395	19.3
Coventry, Bailey Lane	10	112	8.9
Dartmouth	34	221	15.4
Hull	162	691	23.4
Northampton†	21	263	8.0
Oxford			
St Peter in the East	12	72	16.7
St Mary the Virgin	11	123	8.9
York†	145	752	19.3

* There are difficulties in identifying households from the Carlisle returns and measures are only approximate.
** Sample (*a*) is calculated from the last 250 households listed, sample (*b*) from 250 households listed between membranes 6–8. These last are conspicuously servant-keeping households.
*** A few households were not identified and so are excluded.
† Partial return only.
Source: As Table II.1 below.

variation may be observed within towns. This is especially conspicuous in Hull where the proportion of female-headed households ranged from only 8.1 per cent in Kirk Lane to 47.1 per cent in Grimsby Lane, although greater uniformity is detectable when the remaining areas of the town are considered.[18] The global mean for the places listed in Table 7.3 is 18.6 per cent (standard deviation = 5.7), though the means for Colchester, York, and, more especially, Hull and Carlisle are rather higher. The York figure should perhaps be adjusted upwards to allow for suburban parishes that are poorly represented within the surviving returns. The regional pattern seems significant and may be related to the

[18] The Hull mean is 23.4%.

TABLE 7.4. *Proportion of female-headed households in Hull and York from the 1377 poll tax*

	Female-headed households	Total households	% female-headed
York			
St Martin, Coney Street	15	93	16.1
St Crux	22	137	16.1
St Mary, Bishophill Senior	8	45	19.3
St Helen, Stonegate	15	82	18.3
St Sampson	30	160	18.8
St Denys, Walmgate	7	43	16.3
St Saviour	32	88	36.4
All Saints, Pavement	2	18	11.1
Bootham	14	86	16.3
Hull			
Trippet	3	16	18.8
Hull Street	28	209	13.4
Blackfriargate	23	62	37.1
Marketgate	37	135	27.4
Salthouse Lane	4	21	19.0
Bishop Lane	16	43	37.2
Beverleygate	20	71	28.2
Kirk Lane	3	37	8.1
Grimsby Lane	8	17	47.1
Mytongate	13	50	26.0

Note: The number of households at York whose head can be identified by sex does not always coincide with the number of households that can be analysed by size.

Sources: Leggett (ed.), '1377 Poll Tax Returns for the City of York'; PRO, E 179/ 206/45.

greater opportunities for female economic activity that may have characterized the North. A similar observation may be true of Colchester, where there was a considerable expansion of the textile industry from the later fourteenth century.[19] These generally high proportions of female-headed households contrast with the generally lower equivalent rural data. In the Rutland villages of Egleton and Hambleton in 1377, for example, 14.7 and 10.7 per cent of households respectively were headed by women. In

[19] Britnell, *Growth and Decline in Colchester*.

the Northumberland villages of Long Framlington and Alwinton the same year 15.6 and 12.5 per cent respectively were female-headed.

Such high urban proportions are somewhat larger than those suggested by Laslett's survey of 70 early modern listings, though this does not distinguish urban from rural settlements.[20] They are, however, more in line with a mean of 18.3 per cent derived by Wall from a sample of listings dated 1650–1749. This Wall contrasts with an equivalent mean measure of only 13.9 per cent for the period 1750–1821. This fall he suggests 'is best seen in the context of the decline in the percentage widowed in the population'. Wall's data likewise fail to distinguish urban from other household samples, but the direction of the trend is clearly demonstrated.[21] Of at least equal significance to any supposed fall in proportions widowed over this period would be the not unrelated phenomenon of an erosion in the employment prospects of urban women. Such would certainly have undermined the ability of the spouseless female to support herself independently and thus have reduced the proportions of female-headed households. Todd, writing of the early modern era, has further suggested that widows were less likely to remarry in periods of economic opportunity for women.[22] The York testamentary data may support this thesis in respect of the later Middle Ages, and these observations may be contrasted with the very high rate (and speed) of widow remarriage described for London at the beginning of the seventeenth century.[23] It is striking that both the late fourteenth and the late seventeenth centuries are apparently characterized by high proportions of urban households headed by widows. This is suggested from the poll tax data, assuming that a significant proportion of female-headed households, as at Sheffield in 1379, represent widows. It is suggested also from the Marriage Duty Act evidence of *c*.1700, which indicates that 24.1 per cent of

---

[20] Laslett found a mean of 12.9% of households headed by widows, 23% by 'unspecified' females, and 1.1% by single females. Laslett, 'Size and Structure of the Household', table 9, p. 216.

[21] Wall, 'Regional and temporal Variations', table 4.3, pp. 93–4.

[22] Todd, 'The Remarrying Widow', 78.

[23] See Ch. 5 above. V. Brodsky, 'Widows in Late Elizabethan London: Remarriage, Economic Opportunity and Family Orientations', in Bonfield, Smith, and Wrightson (eds.), *The World We Have Gained*, 122–54.

households at Southampton and 18.5 per cent at Shrewsbury were headed by widows.[24]

Despite the relatively high proportion of households headed by women over the town as a whole in 1377, the data demonstrate significant concentrations of such households within specific localities. Rental evidence confirms this propensity. Keene has described a concentration of women in Colebrook Street, Winchester, around St Mary's nunnery.[25] Economic necessity rather than spiritual solidarity underlies similar concentrations of women in Aldwark and the poorer suburbs of Barker Hill and Layerthorpe in York. In 1399, eighteen of the twenty-five tenants of one group of properties owned by the Vicars Choral were female.[26] Similar groups of women associated with cottage accommodation in Micklegate, Hamerton Lane, and Rotten Row are conspicuous in the city's Ouse Bridge rentals.[27] Poll tax evidence suggests similar patterns of women living in close proximity. Small clusterings of females are to be observed from the fragmentary 1377 York returns and from the more substantial Hull, Colchester, and Carlisle returns for the same year, but like groupings are also to be found in a rural context. At Anston, for example, a village community in the Strafforth Wapentake of the West Riding, groups of seven and five women are found listed consecutively in 1379. It is in fact possible to detect a crude inverse correlation between prosperity and proportions of female-headed households. This probably reflects the underlying distribution of housing stock since widows and other single females were often of necessity driven to find accommodation in cheap tenements or cottages.

Several Hull streets, St Saviour's parish, York, and the Colchester sample (a), drawn from the last 250 households listed and consequently probably representative of a suburban district, all demonstrate proportions of female-headed households well above the mean. In Hull many such households are concentrated in the underdeveloped south-east part of the walled town.[28] More

[24] Wall, 'Regional and Temporal Variations', table 4.8, p. 105.
[25] Keene, *Survey of Medieval Winchester*, i. 388.
[26] YML, VC 6/2/38.
[27] YCA, C 82–6.
[28] It seems that Grimsby Lane, which contains the highest proportion of female-headed households, was only recently developed at the time of the poll tax: P. Armstrong, 'Grimsby Lane Excavations 1972', *Kingston upon Hull Museums Bulletin*, 10 (1973), 4.

marginal parishes are poorly represented within the surviving York returns and the concentration of female-headed households within St Saviour's parish next to the prosperous parish of St Crux may appear surprising. St Saviour's is, however, also adjacent to a group of apparently impoverished north-eastern parishes, some of which were actually excluded from the 1381 assessment.[29] Closer analysis of the 1377 enumeration indicates groups of single women living separately from the significant number of larger servant-keeping households, probably in the northern part of the parish off St Saviourgate itself. In contrast, areas of substantial, expensive property such as Bailey Lane, Coventry, Hull Street, Hull, and the Colchester sample (b) all display relatively low proportions of female-headed households.[30] But the example of St Saviour's warns that there was no absolute polarity in housing stock between centre and periphery.[31] Substantial housing along the principal thoroughfares was often only yards distant from the cheap housing of the side streets. The York 1377 returns, for example, include within St Saviour's parish one William de Stretford, his wife, and servant. The following entry refers to one Joan 'living in Stretford Lane', presumably a passage running beside Stretford's property.

The concentration of female-headed households in peripheral or suburban districts is further associated with the close congregation of women that has already been remarked upon. This appears a very general phenomenon in pre-industrial town society. Clark and Clark have described widows living side by side in suburban Canterbury's Ivy Lane in 1563.[32] High proportions of widow households have been found in the suburbs of early Stuart Cambridge. In St Giles's parish over 20 per cent of households were headed by widows.[33] Even within a startlingly feminised quarter of Bruges in 1814, Wall has observed 'a huddling together of women in residential groups that were predominantly and sometimes exclusively female'.[34] Such concentrations Hufton has

[29] Goldberg, 'Urban Identity and the Poll Taxes'.
[30] For the quality of housing in Bailey Lane see Phythian-Adams, *Desolation of a City*, 164–6.   [31] Cf. ibid. 166.
[32] Clark and Clark, 'Social Economy', 79.
[33] Goose, 'Household Size', 378.
[34] The Bruges census does not allow strict households to be identified: Wall, 'The Composition of Households in a Population of 6 Men to 10 Women: South-East Bruges in 1814', 426, 454–5.

described, perhaps misleadingly in view of the limited evidence in respect of marital status, as 'spinster clustering'. She is able to cite further examples from fifteenth-century Spain and some early modern French towns.[35] Women also shared households. This is apparent both from poll tax sources, as at Hull, Carlisle, or Chichester in 1377, and from a number of late medieval cause papers. Isabel Henryson and Katherine Burton of Bootham, observed in a cause of 1432, probably lived together. Alice de Bridelyngton of Beverley, similarly noticed in a cause dated 1367, was said to be living 'with her friend' Joan del Hill.[36] It is apparent from a cause dated 1382 that Isabella, daughter of Alan de Belyngham, then aged 21 'or more', shared a house in Aldwark with Elena de Leyrmouth.[37] A tendency for some women to share houses in common has also been noted in Coventry in 1523 and Canterbury in 1563.[38] In Bruges in 1814 Wall has described how women sometimes moved into households already headed by women.[39]

The pattern of 'spinster clustering' in the suburbs and poor tenements may, as indicated in the previous chapter, be related to the migration of women into the town and is apparent from poll tax listings. Migrants would appear to have found accommodation at least initially outside the more prosperous central area of the city, although this would not apply to those who took up positions as servants. Not all women living alone were, however, spinsters in the modern sense and their location within the urban community may have been determined by their wealth rather than the length of their residence within the community. The poll taxes again allow some limited insight into the composition of female-headed households and the marital status of the head. Only a few returns, however, specifically designate widows. At Sheffield (1379) some 21.8 per cent of households were headed by women, but over half of these were widows. In a number of instances the

---

[35] Hufton, 'Women without Men'.

[36] BIHR, CP. E. 102; CP. F. 104.

[37] BIHR, CP. E. 126. Women seem often to have shared beds together. Agnes Kyrkeby testified that 'cum ea [domina Christiana] transivit ipsam nudam in lecto pannis sepius cooperiendo prout consimili modo per vices alie mulieres et servientes eiusdem domus sepius fecerunt . . .': BIHR, CP. F. 36.

[38] Phythian-Adams, *Desolation of a City*, 203; Clark and Clark, 'Social Economy', 79.

[39] Wall, 'The Composition of Households', 454–5.

householder had an adult child, usually a daughter, living with her.[40] It may be noted that 21 per cent of female-headed households at Coventry in 1523 contained children.[41] A number of female householders living with their daughters or, more occasionally, a female servant can likewise be observed at Hull (1377). Here also are found several households shared by women enjoying no obvious kin relationship.[42] The frequency with which more substantial widows employed female servants is illustrated by the surviving York returns for 1381 and from probate sources. The paucity of widows in the York 1381 returns is, however, suggestive of their poverty generally as a group. In St Crux parish, for example, widows are relatively conspicuous because they were subsidized for tax purposes by the large number of wealthy individuals in this prosperous area.[43]

Clark and Clark have suggested that women once widowed often moved to the suburbs to find cheaper accommodation and note the number of widows listed as poor in the suburban Canterbury census for 1563.[44] It may likewise be noted that thirty-nine female as against only six male heads of household were designated poor in the Ghemeene Neringhe quarter of Ypres in 1431.[45] Keene has used taxation evidence to demonstrate a marked decline in the proportion of female taxpayers from the earlier fifteenth into the earlier sixteenth centuries. This he argues 'may reflect the increasing impoverishment of Winchester in which the poorer elements of society, including women, suffered most severely'.[46] There is no evidence that the proportions of women living by themselves increased as economic recession eroded their standing in the labour market. The reverse may indeed have been true as more women were forced to remain in dependent positions as servants or to marry at earlier ages. The growing concern of civic authorities in the later fifteenth century that such younger

[40] Of 61 female householders, 31 were described as widows and four further had adult daughters at home. In total, ten householders retained adult children at home.

[41] Phythian-Adams, *Desolation of a City*, table 24, p. 227.

[42] e.g. Alice Hassel with Isolda de Paule: PRO E 179/206/45.

[43] Goldberg, 'Urban Identity and the Poll Taxes'.

[44] Clark and Clark, 'Social Economy', 71, 79.

[45] Pirenne, 'Les Dénombrements de la population d'Ypres', 30–1. Six further households cannot be identified by sex.

[46] Keene, *Survey of Medieval Winchester*, i. 388 and n. 8.

single women were potential recruits into the world of prostitution has already been observed.[47] This may be said to have culminated in the Coventry ordinances of 1492 that required unmarried women under the age of 50 to enter service rather than live by themselves.[48] The effectiveness of such legislation may be doubted, but the impact of recession on unmarried females in Coventry is demonstrated by the remarkably feminised servant population observed by 1523.[49]

If the evidence relating to the spatial distribution of females within the urban community is compared against the occupational topography from York poll tax and testamentary sources, described in Chapter 2, then certain observations follow. Female servants will tend to be congregated within the central commercial quarter since the households there were the most regular employers of female servant labour.[50] Single and independent females tend, however, to be most conspicuous within the more marginal and less economically developed parishes. In a number of such parishes listed as having a high proportion of female-headed households in 1381 female labourers are to the fore. This is especially true of the North Street parish of All Saints and the parish of St John del Pyke. This last is adjacent to Aldwark, where the clustering of single women in cheap tenements has already been observed. A high proportion of female-headed households in nearby St Saviour's parish has also been noticed from the more satisfactory 1377 return. St Saviour's parish itself adjoined the impoverished Hungate district notorious for the butchers' offal and other waste matter dumped there.[51] It may be that similar poverty and concentrations of female residents would also have characterized a group of south-eastern parishes that, like the Hungate and Aldwark parishes, were excluded from the 1381 assessment.

On one level, single women thus appear in those parishes for which the least evidence for economic activity survives. On another level, neither wills nor even the 1381 poll tax describe

---

[47] See Ch. 3 above.

[48] Harris (ed.), *The Coventry Leet Book*, 542.

[49] A city-wide service sex ratio of 55.0: Phythian-Adams, *Desolation of a City*, table 13, p. 200.

[50] See Table 4.2.

[51] Raine, *Mediaeval York*, 81–3.

independent female traders within such parishes. Alternative sources would indicate, however, that a high proportion of these were employed spinning and carding wool and it seems significant that the dependent textile processes of fulling and weaving appear to have been located within the same marginal areas as females are concentrated. Clark and Clark, writing of a feminised suburb of Canterbury in the mid-seventeenth century, describe the women of Ivy Lane sitting spinning together.[52] These were poorly paid and frequently exploited occupations and the location of such female workers in poorer districts alongside other humbler textile traders seems to make sense of the available evidence. Some women may even have worked themselves as weavers and fullers.[53] Others may have found employment in needlecrafts, small metal trades, or as casual labour in the building trade, itself apparently based in the suburbs. The trade-name surnames of some of the female tenants of the Vicars Choral Aldwark/St Andrewgate group of tenements include both needle and small metal trades.[54] It may finally be noted that the topography of prostitution tends to follow the same peripheral or suburban pattern for the same economic reasons. The occupational by-names of the prostitutes further tend to reinforce the structure just described.[55]

SOCIAL AND SPIRITUAL SOLIDARITY

The spatial clustering of women need not have been determined solely by economic factors. Women frequently turned to their peers for companionship, mutual support, exchange of information, and spiritual and material succour. This was not a specifically urban phenomenon, but it was perhaps both better documented

---

[52] Clark and Clark, 'Social Economy', 80. Cf. the topography of female employment in Bruges in 1814: Wall, 'The Composition of Households', 437–44.

[53] See Ch. 3 above.

[54] The following women may be observed from the rentals for Aldwark/St Andrewgate: 1342, Margaret Scrivaner; 1344–5, Elizabeth Kelleknytter, Isabella Zonaria (girdler); 1389–90, Alice Matrismaker, Alice Koke; 1399, Alice Wympilster, Joan Porter, Ydonia Semster; 1403–4, Isabella Leche; 1409, Agnes Bakster, Agnes Skynner; 1415–16, Christiana Spynner; 1421–2, Alice Locksmyth, Alice Fischer: YML, VC 6/2/13, 33, 38, 42, 44, 45, 49; VC 4/1/7.

[55] See Ch. 3 above.

and more necessary given the greater anonymity of urban society. Urban women appear regularly to have associated together as a social group, but unlike men, only occasionally on a formal basis. Outside Norwich there is no evidence for communities of pious lay women living after the manner of the beguines of the Low Countries and the Rhineland.[56] Unlike Paris in the thirteenth century or Cologne in the fifteenth, little evidence can be found for female craft gilds. There is an ambiguous reference to a 'Brewstergild' in Beverley in 1364, though this probably does not indicate a formal craft gild structure. Women only are referred to in the 1503 ordinances of the Southampton wool-packers.[57] The London silkwomen certainly enjoyed a degree of group solidarity, but no apparent formal gild association.[58] The clearest evidence, albeit the most enigmatic, for a formal association is provided by the existence of groups of 'wives' at various towns. In 1430 Agnes Stanssal, a widow, left 6s. 8d. to 'the wives' of Doncaster where she lived.[59] In practice, the term 'wife' is ambiguous and this bequest could refer to an association of widows.[60] The 1437 record of the order of procession for the feast of Corpus Christi at Winchester includes the wives (*uxores*) bearing a single torch following the various crafts and the gilds of St Thomas and St Anne.[61] At Chester 'the wurshipfull Wyffys' were responsible for the pageant of the Assumption of the Virgin within the annual Corpus Christi play.[62] In view of the traditional devotional relationship between the mercers and the Assumption it may be that the pageant was in fact performed by the wives of the mercers, hence the appropriateness of the epithet 'worshipful'. Much the same social group may lie behind references to the mayoress 'and her sisters' in both Coventry and York sources.[63]

Most associations between females were, however, of a less formal nature. Dillard's work on the women of Reconquest Spain

---

[56] Tanner, *The Church in Late Medieval Norwich*, 64–6.
[57] Leach (ed.), *Beverley Town Documents*, 41; Power, *Medieval Women*, 61.
[58] Dale, 'The London Silkwomen'.
[59] BIHR, Prob. Reg. 2, fo. 633ᵛ.
[60] As was true of the York brewsters' fines: see Ch. 3 above.
[61] Bird (ed.), *The Black Book of Winchester*, 3–4.
[62] P. Happé (ed.), *The English Mystery Plays* (Harmondsworth, 1975), ll. 129–32, p. 46.
[63] Harris (ed.), *The Coventry Leet Book*, 405–6; Phythian-Adams, *Desolation of a City*, 90–1; Raine (ed.), *Testamenta Eboracensia*, v. 87.

indicates that women enjoyed their own society through their regular meeting together at 'bath house, oven, spring, river and at their spinning and weaving'.[64] Clark and Clark have similarly described for early modern Canterbury how women neighbours would sit together to spin and exchange gossip.[65] Throughout the Middle Ages and well into the early modern era women came together to assist and give support during childbirth. As has been shown, medieval women were also much more likely than men to share a house.[66] A York cause of 1410 also suggests that it was common for women to sleep in the same bed. There is much evidence to show that women regularly built up their own friendship networks. This is reflected in the wills of female testators, which are characterized by large numbers of small bequests to females, both kin and non-kin.[67] Thus when Margaret de Knaresburgh, sempster, died unmarried in 1398 she bequeathed items from her wardrobe to, among others, Isabella Barneby of Coppergate, Agnes Dowson of her own parish of All Saints, Pavement, and one Agnes Covyntre living in the churchyard there.[68] This last can probably be identified with the 'poor old woman' remembered in the will of Avice de Pontefract a few years after.[69] Such gifts were tokens by which a woman's friends would be reminded of her after death and pray for her soul. The importance in life of women friends is parodied in the Chester Corpus Christi pageant of Noah's Flood where Noah's wife refuses to join the Ark unless her gossips are also saved from drowning.[70] The natural inclination of women for the company of their friends was indeed often a matter of dispute between married couples.[71] Christine de Pisan, addressing the wives of urban artisans, warns them against leaving

---

[64] H. Dillard, *Daughters of the Reconquest: Women in Castilian Town Society* (Cambridge, 1984), 149–50.

[65] Clark and Clark, 'Social Economy', 80.

[66] Cf. Phythian-Adams, *Desolation of a City*, 90.

[67] This observation is not confined to the medieval era. Cf. R. T. Vann, 'Wills and the Family in an English Town: Banbury, 1550–1800', *Journal of Family History*, 4 (1979), 366–7.

[68] BIHR, Prob. Reg. 2, fo. 14. Cf. the bequest of clothing by Idonea Couper to 'vicine mee' Elena Wright and Cecily: YML, D/C Reg. 1, fo. 132ᵛ.

[69] BIHR, Prob. Reg. 3, fo. 111.

[70] A. C. Crawley (ed.), *Everyman and Medieval Miracle Plays* (London, 1956), 'Noah's Flood', ll. 200–8.

[71] Cf. BIHR, CP. E. 221.

their homes to visit friends and catch up on the latest gossip.[72]
Similar advice is given by the Goodwife to her daughter:

> Go thou not into the toun as it were a gase
> From oon hous to another for to seke the mase . . .[73]

A York woman, Margery Nesfeld, was so savagely beaten by her
husband because she insisted on her right to go outside the home
without his permission that she subsequently sued for a legal
separation.[74] One of the places women might go to enjoy their
own society was the tavern. An ecclesiastical cause of 1341
describes how a group of women assembled at the house of Alice,
wife to Richard de Edern, and a 'common brewster' in order to
taste her ale.[75] The early sixteenth-century satirical poem 'Elynour
Rummynge' describes the exclusively female clientele of an ale-
house where barter prevailed.[76] A later fifteenth-century verse
comments sarcastically of women that:

> To the tavern they will not go,
> Nor to the alehouse never the mo,
> For, God wot, there hartes wold be wo
> To spende ther husboundes money so.[77]

Even the more sympathetic Goodwife warns her daughter 'thei
that tavernes haunten | Her thrifte thei adaunten'.[78]

On another level, women were often active in the life of the
parish church and seem to have been active in the life of the
religious gilds. Isabell de Langwath, in a will that describes her
'sinner's soul' (*animam meam peccatricem*) and 'wretched body'
(*corpus meum miserum*), asked specifically for the prayers of the
brothers and sisters of the York Paternoster gild at their meet-
ings.[79] The ordinances of the gild of St Mary at Beverley allowed
its elder sisters to have a voice in the election of their alderman,
and there is no evidence that women were generally excluded

---

[72] de Pisan, *The Treasure of the City of Ladies*, 168.
[73] 'How the Good Wijf', ed. Furnivall, ll. 68–9, p. 39.
[74] BIHR, CP. E. 221.
[75] BIHR, CP. E. 40.
[76] John Skelton, *The Complete English Poems*, ed. J. Scattergood (Harmondsworth, 1983), 214–30.
[77] R. T. Davies (ed.), *Medieval English Lyrics* (London, 1963), ii. 26–30, p.
222.
[78] 'How the Good Wijf', ll. 71–2, p. 39.
[79] BIHR, Prob. Reg. 2, fo. 604.

from any of the welfare benefits or social activities of these associations.[80] A number of women enjoyed membership of several such gilds. Thus the York skinner's widow Alice Poumfreyt made small money bequests to the gilds of the Paternoster, St Christopher, and the Franciscan gild of St Francis respectively.[81] It is possible that gilds associated with the friaries were especially popular with women and this must reflect the appeal of the mendicant orders to women and widows in particular.[82] A number, like Alice Poumfreyt, preferred to be buried in a friary rather than in their own parish.[83] Lady Marjory Salvayn asked to be buried in the Franciscan friary in York at her death in 1496 and left a relic of St Ninian to the friars there.[84] Another York woman, Margaret Otryngton, not only requested burial within the church of the Dominicans, but named friar John Orr as her executor and left her bed of Norfolk work and quilt to one William Kirkeby, Doctor of Theology.[85]

One final aspect of lay piety that has wider social implications was the provision of alms for the sick and the needy. Though charity was not a female prerogative as the regular death-bed bequests to the poor and to the various maisons-dieu of the will-making classes testify, it was certainly the concern of many better-off women. This may have been a response to the social convention that saw women as the nurturers, the carers in society.[86] One of the attributes of the virtuous woman of Proverbs is that 'she stretcheth out her hand to the poor; yea she reacheth forth her hands to the needy'.[87] At a lower social level, women frequently found employment as sick nurses, and lay women were attached to hospitals.[88] One of the precepts of the Goodwife to her daughter was to remember the poor and bedridden.[89] This was a theme widely propagated during the late medieval era through the

[80] Smith (ed.), *English Gilds*, 149–50; Raine, *Mediaeval York*, 91–2.
[81] BIHR, Prob. Reg. 2, fo. 660ᵛ.
[82] This observation is based on an analysis of gender-specific patterns of post-mortem provisions for gilds as reflected in the will sample.
[83] BIHR, Prob. Reg. 2, fo. 660ᵛ.
[84] BIHR, Prob. Reg. 5, fo. 480.
[85] BIHR, Prob. Reg. 3, fo. 426ᵛ.
[86] Cf. Gold, *The Lady and the Virgin*, 15.
[87] Prov. 31: 20.
[88] See Ch. 3 above.
[89] 'How the Good Wijf', ll. 19, 67–72, pp. 37, 39.

canon of the Seven Corporal Acts of Mercy. This is the message pictured in the early fifteenth-century glass of All Saints, North Street, in York and it was proclaimed each year in the mercers' pageant of Domesday.[90] A York woman possessed a cloth painted with this theme and a York man directed that seven pairs of shoes to symbolize the Seven Corporal Acts be distributed to the poor after his death.[91] A Bristol man bequeathed money in his will to be spent 'in the seven works of mercy'.[92] Thus when Roger Marshall testified to the moral character of a York widow, Agnes Grantham, he drew attention both to her care for her *familia* and her charity to the poor in the form of bringing them wood, fuel, and other necessaries.[93] Turning again to testamentary data it is possible to find numerous other examples of charitable provision by women. Jordan in his study of philanthropy in London observed that female testators 'were particularly concerned with the plight of the poor', a conclusion that is also endorsed by Cullum's findings for later medieval Yorkshire.[94]

[90] Crawley (ed.), *Everyman and Medieval Miracle Plays*, 'Domesday'.
[91] BIHR, Prob. Reg. 5, fo. 154^v; Prob. Reg. 2, fo. 431^v.
[92] Wadley, *Notes or Abstracts*, 109.
[93] BIHR, CP. F. 36.
[94] W. K. Jordan, *The Charities of London, 1480–1660* (London, 1960), 30; P. H. Cullum, '"And Hir Name Was Charite": Charity by and for Women in Late Medieval Yorkshire', in P. J. P. Goldberg (ed.), *Woman is a Worthy Wight: Women in English Society, c.1200–1500* (Stroud, 1992), 182–211.

8

Women, Work, and Life Cycle: A Hypothesis Explored

This book began with a question: was marriage an economic necessity for women in the English later Middle Ages? The corollary of this question is twofold. First, how far were women able to enter into the labour market and allowed access to employment, and secondly, how much choice were women able to exercise in respect of marriage? A quotation from a deposition made before the consistory court of York in a matrimonial cause of 1393 may serve as a useful starting-point. A York saddler testified, 'that Thomas did not surpass the said Margery in wealth, status or ability, either in respect of her standing in society or her craft, for he understood that just as Thomas was able to support himself from his craft so Margery was able as a servant'.[1] This is a partisan statement, but it is no less valuable for that. Such an observation would make little sense in a society that permitted women little or no economic role, that expected women to be dependent upon the support of men (and disparaged those few who were not), and that regarded servants as drudges and social inferiors.

It is the purpose of this final chapter to explore more fully the structure of late medieval English society and to examine the role women like Margery Spuret played in economic life, and then to compare and contrast this with post-medieval English evidence and some continental evidence, notably for Tuscany around the time of the great tax survey or *catasto* of 1427, a society that apparently allowed women little economic or emotional independence.[2] This discussion necessarily confronts two current debates.

---

[1] 'Dicit Thomas non excedit dictam Margeriam divitiis, nobilitate, potencia vel honore vel artificio ut intelligit quod sicut Thomas potest adquirere sustentacionem suam ex artificio suo sic et ipsa Margeria ex servicio suo': BIHR, CP. E. 159.

[2] J. C. Brown, 'A Woman's Place Was in the Home: Women's Work in Renaissance Tuscany', in M. W. Ferguson, M. Quilligan, and N. J. Vickers (eds.), *Rewriting the Renaissance* (Chicago, 1986), 209; ead. and J. Goodman, 'Women and Industry in Florence', *Journal of Economic History*, 40 (1980), 78; Herlihy and Klapisch-Zuber, *Tuscans and Their Families*, 124.

On the one hand is the issue of household and marriage in late medieval England. Age data relating to deponents within the ecclesiastical court and poll tax evidence have been presented which suggest that a distinctively 'European' marriage regime, characterized by late, companionate marriages and a relatively high proportion of individuals who never married, existed in Yorkshire towns, and perhaps more widely, from at least the mid-fourteenth century. Poll tax evidence further suggests that households tended to be small and nuclear. On the other hand is the wider question of the relationship between movements in the economy, measured euphemistically as 'the standard of living', and nuptiality, the propensity of individuals, all too often treated as without gender for purposes of aggregative analysis, to marry. This present analysis questions the assumption, implicit in so much historical and demographic literature, that women in past society played little part in economic life and still less in decisions concerning marriage. Instead a new hypothesis is proposed that links increasing demand for female labour with greater autonomy in deciding, within the context of this late marriage regime, if, when, and whom to marry. This hypothesis suggests an essentially anti-Malthusian relationship between nuptiality and economic opportunity for women. Certain strands of this argument may be drawn out by summarizing the evidence and debates concerning marriage regimes, service, and the economic status of women.

Medievalists lack the vast body of parish register evidence that has proved so rewarding to a whole generation of historical demographers working on the period after 1538.[3] They must rely instead upon a variety of different and often problematical sources scattered in terms of both time and geography. The attempts by Razi to use peasant genealogies derived from the long series of court rolls for the Worcestershire manor of Halesowen before 1400 are well known. Razi's methodology, which links access to land with the need to marry and have children, appears to be biased to detecting early marriages at the expense of others, nor has he been able to convince his critics of the reliability of the assumptions upon which this methodology depends. Similar reasoning in respect of the manor of Thornbury has led Franklin to

---

[3] Notably Wrigley and Schofield, *The Population History of England*.

argue that some males there married as early as 14.[4] Such findings
tend to lend weight to the notion of a 'medieval' marriage regime,
marked by early and relatively universal marriage, that was first
suggested in Hajnal's pioneering study of European marriage
patterns. Implicit in this view is the idea that late marriage is a
characteristic only of modern Western society.[5] Herlihy, viewing
Europe from a Tuscan perspective, would, with the proviso that it
was only women that married early, tend to agree. But Herlihy's
vision, as he readily admits, is geographically limited.[6] Hanawalt
is likewise drawn to this model of early marriage, but has little of
substance to vindicate her preference.[7] Only for the aristocracy
does this view stand up to critical scrutiny, but even this is no
guide to the behaviour of their social inferiors.

Evidence for the view that marriage was located not in the later
teens or early twenties, but more towards the mid-twenties is
contained in Smith's discussion of marriage in England during the
thirteenth and fourteenth centuries.[8] Smith points *inter alia* to the
similarity of the pattern of exogamous marriages observed from
the prior of Spalding's serf lists for the fenland villages of Weston
and Moulton in the later thirteenth century and that observed
from seventeenth- and eighteenth-century sources. A similar
pattern of 'neo-local' exogamous marriages has been described by
Bennett from the *Liber Gersumarum* of Ramsey Abbey.[9] Smith
further remarks the coincidence between this distribution and the
neo-local migration pattern associated with servant hirings at the
Spalding fair during the later eighteenth century.[10] If servanthood
was then already an established function of life cycle, i.e. a stage
of growing up experienced by young persons of both sexes during
their teens and into their twenties, as was true of the early modern
era, then this observation takes on a particular significance.
Exogamous patterns of marriage might then be seen as following
from attachments made during service. This view is supported by
the observed correlation between the incidence of merchet or

---

[4] Razi, *Life, Marriage and Death*. See Ch. 5 above.
[5] Hajnal, 'European Marriage Patterns'.
[6] Herlihy, *Medieval Households*, p. vi.
[7] Hanawalt, *The Ties that Bound*, 96.
[8] Smith, 'Hypothèses sur la nuptialité'.
[9] Bennett, 'Medieval Peasant Marriage'.
[10] Smith, 'Hypothèses sur la nuptialité', 130.

marriage fines and the timing of the principal annual hiring fairs already well established by the early modern period.

The institution of service provides for a high degree of emotional and even economic independence from parents and family at an early age and thus ill accords with a system of early and arranged marriages. Bennett has rightly drawn attention to the frequency with which villein women, and not their fathers, were said to be responsible for their own merchet payments. Such would again be an unlikely occurrence where teenage daughters, still living in the parental home, submitted to marriages arranged on their behalf by their fathers. Such marriages did occur, as the evidence from marriage litigation demonstrates, but they were probably limited to more substantial peasant families where large dowries were at stake. The evidence once more suggests a possible relationship between service, or other employment outside the home, and greater individualism in marriage, a point that has been made independently by Wiesner for servants in early modern German towns; although female servants are unlikely to be recorded with any regularity in manorial sources, Bennett has still been able to identify a few servants among those villein women paying their own merchets.[11]

The evidence for servants as an integral part of the social structure of post-plague England contained within the poll taxes is considerable. Smith has calculated that 15 per cent or more of households in Rutland for which nominative listings for 1377 survive contained servants. The equivalent figure for the city of York is 38.2 per cent, and 31.9 per cent of the adult population there were in service.[12] These observations prompt the question of why such a statistically significant aspect of the social structure should have been largely overlooked by most medievalists, though this may owe something to the generally low regard in which the poll taxes have been held, and also to the ambiguity inherent in the term 'servant'.[13] The poll tax evidence also lends support to the notion that marriage was relatively late since the proportions married recorded in the 1377 returns appear too small to be compatible with a 'medieval' marriage regime. Still more substan-

---

[11] Wiesner, *Working Women in Renaissance Germany*, 92; Bennett, 'Medieval Peasant Marriage', n. 45, pp. 45, 222.

[12] Private communication from Dr R. M. Smith; Ch. 4 above.

[13] Cf. Hilton, *The English Peasantry*, 30–5.

tive evidence for nuptiality and service is contained within the deposition material associated with the consistory court of York in the fourteenth and fifteenth centuries. An analysis of descriptive data relating to 1094 deponents for the period 1303–1520 suggests that in Yorkshire society young people of either sex regularly remained unmarried up until at least their early twenties in rural society and their mid-twenties in the towns. Teenage marriages, by contrast, appear comparatively rare.[14]

The companionate nature of these marriages is demonstrated by the narrowness of the age difference between spouses, although this appears again to have been more marked in urban than rural society; in a significant number of cases it was the wife that was the senior, another observation in line with Laslett's definitions of the Western family.[15] Servanthood can be shown from the same source regularly to have extended from the early teens into the mid-twenties. Servant hirings, moreover, frequently followed an annual cycle centred upon Martinmas (11 November), a pattern that is identical to that described for this region from the sixteenth to the first part of the twentieth century, and a secondary cycle based on Pentecost. A similar pattern of servant hiring has been described by Wiesner for early modern German towns, namely yearly hirings at Nuremberg, but twice yearly at Munich and Strasbourg.[16] This seasonal pattern lends weight to the observations just made concerning the significance of the timing of merchet payments. Marriage litigation itself demonstrates that servants are very frequently the actors in marriage contracts. Indeed servants may often, as they moved every couple of years or so from one household to another, have been brought into contact with future marriage partners.

One of the most striking features of the York matrimonial litigation of the later fourteenth and earlier fifteenth centuries is the remarkable degree of individualism in marriage formation demonstrated, particularly in town society, but also in rural society in respect of less substantial peasant families. The apparent frequency with which the hand of a woman is contested by more than one man (or vice versa) suggests that women were no less

---

[14] See Ch. 5.
[15] Laslett, 'Characteristics of the Western Family', 13, 28.
[16] Wiesner, *Working Women in Renaissance Germany*, 84.

active than men in forging relationships that might, or might not, lead to marriage. Equally, either or both parties may often have terminated unsatisfying courtship relationships regardless of sexual involvement; most disputed contracts had allegedly been consummated whether *de presenti* or *de futuro*. This contrasts radically with the pattern of litigation concerning unconsummated *de futuro* contracts described by Donahue from northern French sources, notably the register of the Officiality of Paris for the period 1384–7, but a similarly high proportion of *de futuro* contracts are described by Finch from the Cerisy register for the early fourteenth century.[17] Donahue attributes this contrasting pattern of litigation to the greater authority exercised by French parents over the marriages of their children. This in itself might be reflected in a pattern of youthful marriage not normal in England.[18] It may finally be noted that testamentary data, also from York, suggest that a significant proportion of women achieving adulthood may never have married. The proportion of female testators dying unmarried reached nearly 17 per cent in the years *c*.1436–42. In Florence at about the same date only some 3 per cent of women remained unmarried after their twenty-fifth birthday.[19] These represent profound cultural differences between the various regions of late medieval Europe. These differences are reflected in the economic status of women as a brief survey of the secondary literature will demonstrate.

[17] Donahue, 'The Canon Law on the Formation of Marriage'. Finch notes that at Cerisy 11 of 21 disputed marriage contracts dated 1322 or before whose nature can be known relate to *de futuro* contracts only one of which was specifically alleged to have been consummated: Finch, 'Crime and Marriage', 35.

[18] Donahue, 'The Canon Law on the Formation of Marriage', 156. The Paris evidence, very much the world of the Ménagier of Paris, may be somewhat atypical in view of the relative prosperity of the litigants there. This deserves further analysis, but see Smith, 'Marriage Processes', 75–7; J.-P. Lévy, 'L'Officialité de Paris et les questions familiales à la fin du XIVᵉ siècle', in *Études d'histoire de droit canonique dédiées à Gabriel le Bras* (Paris, 1965), ii. 1265–94. Donahue also argues that the criminalization of clandestine *de presenti* contracts by the French courts served to discourage such litigation. This has been challenged by Finch, who shows that English courts, as at Rochester on the eve of the plague, could take an equally harsh line with clandestine contracts: Finch, 'Crime and Marriage', 260–76. Finch further argues that the Cerisy evidence is broadly similar to the English pattern, but the evidence he presents suggests both an unusual number of future contracts and a pattern of parental intervention, e.g. Finch, 'Crime and Marriage', 35, 37, 40, 74.

[19] Herlihy and Klapisch-Zuber, *Tuscans and Their Families*, 88.

A number of local studies have emerged of late years that focus more or less specifically on women in the urban economy of the later Middle Ages. Little has yet been achieved for Mediterranean Europe, but the patterns observed are highly suggestive. Brown and Goodman's work on women in the Florentine economy emphasizes the low level of female participation in the years after the Black Death until the later sixteenth century.[20] Herlihy and Klapisch-Zuber virtually ignore this question for lack of evidence in their otherwise comprehensive survey of the Florentine *catasto* for 1427.[21] In Sardinian society women appear only to have engaged in some traditionally feminine tasks and occupations.[22] Vinyoles paints a similarly restricted picture for women in late medieval Barcelona.[23] In all these societies women appear to have married early and female 'honour' seems to have been valued higher than their ability to earn.[24] Perry, writing of early modern Seville, notes specifically the relationship between marriage 'not only as a livelihood, but also as an institution to impose authority over young girls and prevent them from "losing themselves"'.[25]

For parts of Northern Europe a rather different picture emerges, one that suggests a much greater level of female participation within the urban economy, although any implicit relationship between marriage regimes and economic activity has hitherto gone largely unexplored. It is evident that there is no shortage of evidence for the great cities of Flanders and the Low Countries and that the same is true of Germany. Despite this abundance of material, most work to date has been concerned with the early modern rather than the late medieval era. Nicholas produces some useful quantitative evidence for female activity in a range of trades in fourteenth-century Ghent.[26] Here women are

---

[20] Brown and Goodman, 'Women and Industry in Florence', 73–80. See also Brown, 'A Woman's Place', 206–24.

[21] Herlihy and Klapisch-Zuber, *Tuscans and Their Families*.

[22] J. Day, 'On the Status of Women in Medieval Sardinia', in J. Kirshner and S. F. Wemple (eds.), *Women of the Medieval World* (Oxford, 1985), 308, 314.

[23] Vinyoles, *Les Barcelonines*, 33–66.

[24] Day, 'On the Status of Women in Medieval Sardinia', 309–15; Smith, 'The People of Tuscany and their Families', 107–28; E. le Roy Ladurie, *Montaillou: Cathars and Catholics in a French Village, 1294–1324*, trans. B. Bray (Harmondsworth, 1980), 199–200.

[25] Perry, 'Lost Women'.

[26] D. Nicholas, *The Domestic Life of a Medieval City: Women, Children and the Family in Fourteenth-Century Ghent* (Lincoln, Nebr., 1985).

found in all stages of textile manufacture and as cloth traders (*Lakensnider*).[27] Women lent and changed money, and could trade independently of their husbands.[28] The evidence thus points to a high level of female participation in the economic life of the city, and Nicholas's observation that 'women were expected to earn their own keep if single, to contribute materially to the family enterprise if married' appears significant.[29] It is perhaps unfortunate that Nicholas's treatment of servanthood, which he describes on the scantiest evidence as a low status, potentially lifelong occupation, and of marriage formation is so insubstantial.[30]

The importance of women to the textile, and especially the silk industry of post-plague Cologne is demonstrated by their monopoly of the yarn-spinners', gold-spinners', and silk workers' gilds. Wensky also observes the exploitation of female silk-spinners by the late fifteenth century under the putting-out system, and of the gold-spinners from unfair competition of the male gold-beaters.[31] More comprehensive is Wiesner's survey of the activity of women within the economy of early modern German towns.[32] Wiesner stresses the role women were allowed in the distribution of goods and services and their prominence in the market place at a time of apparent economic expansion. Of particular interest are her remarks concerning one group of female traders, the *Keuflinnen* or traders in second-hand goods, who correspond to the upholders noted in English medieval records. Explicit in Wiesner's analysis, however, is the view that economic opportunities for women declined from the later fifteenth century.[33] For the towns of late medieval and early modern Denmark, Jacobsen makes use of gild ordinances to argue for a progressive narrowing of female craft opportunities by the sixteenth century.[34] This is reflected, for example, in the curtailed provision for widows to pursue their late

[27] Ibid. 84–7, 100–3.
[28] Ibid. 85–91, 95–6.
[29] Ibid. 96.
[30] Ibid. 23–32, 104–6.
[31] Wensky, 'Women's Guilds in Cologne'.
[32] Weisner, *Working Women in Renaissance Germany*.
[33] Ibid. 92, 157–8, 171–7, 187.
[34] Jacobsen, 'Women's Work and Women's Role'.

husbands' trades.[35] It is further suggested from the decline of female brewing activity due to mercantile pressures and the consequent erosion of the social standing of brewsters and female innkeepers.[36] Jacobsen prefers, however, to relate these trends to a growth by the early modern period in regulation by patriarchal civic and gild authorities, displacing 'the relatively open economic structures of the medieval city', rather than to wider economic or demographic trends that may themselves have helped shape civic mentalities. This view is also reflected by Howell in her study of Leiden and Cologne in the later fifteenth and sixteenth centuries. Howell argues that the assimilation of gilds into the structure of urban government made the position of female traders within gilds untenable since women were debarred from government.[37]

Perhaps the most sensitive of recent analyses of the working lives of women in the pre-industrial urban community is Davis's study of Lyons in the sixteenth century.[38] Davis uses women's life cycle as her framework and draws together a wide variety of sources to illustrate her discussion. She notices how in a period of recession female apprentices were excluded from the silk industry and the widows of barber-surgeons were discouraged from continuing in trade.[39] But her analysis in general describes a society in which women enjoyed only a relatively circumscribed economic role largely outside the gilds and with little formal training or fixed work identity. Female labour, semi-skilled and poorly paid, could be drawn upon or disbanded according to market forces, but few women occupied economic niches independently or with any degree of security.[40] It is implicit within Davis's discussion of this society that it was common for a woman when widowed to remarry and that the daughters of the more well-to-do, the independent artisan or craft master, stayed in their parental homes until marriage rather than enter service, despite the fact that in early

[35] The Copenhagen gilds of cordwainers, pursers, and glovers permitted widows to trade for an unlimited period in 1460, but curtailed this to a single year in 1514. Jacobsen, 'Women's Work and Women's Role', 14.

[36] Ibid. 17–18.

[37] Howell, *Women, Production, and Patriarchy*, 90–1, 122–37, 161; ead., 'Citizenship and Gender'.

[38] Davies, 'Women in the Crafts'.

[39] Ibid. 68–9.

[40] Ibid. 62–5, 70–1.

modern Lyons, as in Nuremberg at the same period, female domestics were very numerous.[41]

It is these cultural factors that have been too much neglected by most writers, yet they are essential to any understanding of the relationship between movements in the economy, the demand for female labour, and the role of women in marriage formation. It is appropriate here to explore these cultural differences through an examination of how these contrasting systems, Mediterranean, here represented by Tuscany, and north-western, represented by England and, more specifically, Yorkshire, functioned and responded to the profound demographic and economic upheaval precipitated by the Black Death.

SOCIAL STRUCTURE AFTER 1348–9:
TUSCANY AND YORKSHIRE COMPARED

Something of the range of economic activity in which English women engaged at this date in town society has already been discussed. The wives of independent artisans appear regularly to have worked alongside their spouses and may frequently have continued to trade as widows. There is little evidence that before the later fifteenth century there was any actual prejudice against women learning or engaging in particular crafts or trades as unwomanly or beyond their capacity. Only in 1511 did the worsted weavers of Norwich claim that the exclusion of female workers was necessitated by their lack of strength resulting in inferior products, yet only in 1446 had Elizabeth Baret, singlewoman, been admitted to the franchise of the city as a weaver of worsteds.[42] This is not to deny that there were very real restrictions on the sort of work a woman might engage in. For the married woman ties of home and the demands of child-rearing did not permit of full-time, independent employment, although in London many professional embroiderers and silk-workers appear to have been married women.[43] In general, however, when not assisting her husband in the workshop, the married woman turned to a

[41] Ibid. 52, 58; Wiesner, *Working Women in Renaissance Germany*, 92.
[42] Hudson and Tingey (eds.), *Records of the City of Norwich*, ii. 378; NRO, NCR Case 17, shelf c, 1.
[43] Parker, *The Subversive Stitch*, 40–59; Dale, 'The London Silkwomen'.

variety of part-time employments that might usefully augment the familial income without interfering with other responsibilities. Thus married women are found spinning and carding wool, and, in more substantial households, brewing ale. The wives of butchers and skinners made tallow candles. Others may have earned money as child-minders or sick nurses.

For the single woman the most pressing restrictions on employment were financial. Few women can have had access to wealth by inheritance. Service may have allowed young women to accumulate modest savings, but bequests by employers to servants are more often of clothing or household goods than substantial money sums. For most unmarried women, therefore, access to occupations requiring more than incidental outlay on tools or raw materials was severely limited. This explains why so few women are found as tanners, butchers, mercers, or drapers except as widows. To engage in trade independently, furthermore, a woman would have to be admitted to the franchise or be otherwise licensed from year to year. Although a small number of women were admitted to the freedom of York by right of patrimony, and some few women, notably in London, served apprenticeships, redemption or purchase can have been, in theory at least, the only means of entry available to most women. In practice this was beyond the means of all but a handful of women; only four women were admitted to the franchise of Norwich before the sixteenth century, although even these few admissions demonstrate that there was no actual bar against women.[44] Where civic authorities operated a regular and more affordable system of fines or licences to trade, as was true of Hull, Nottingham, Shrewsbury, and Canterbury, then the evidence suggests that women did quite regularly avail themselves of this opportunity.[45] The records of the Canterbury *intrantes* indicate, however, that numbers of women were comparatively small, only a few per cent of all intrants. Very few of these female intrants renewed their licences after more than two or three years, although Butcher has calculated a broadly similar pattern for all intrants.[46]

---

[44] NRO, NCR Case 17, shelf c, 1. It should be remembered that widows of freemen may often have inherited rights to the franchise without being individually registered.

[45] Hutton, 'Women in Fourteenth Century Shrewsbury', 87.

[46] Butcher, 'Freemen Admissions and Urban Occupations'.

It appears that most single women must have found employment outside the formal framework of the franchise or a system of annual fines, and that financial exigence is the principal cause. It is these financial restrictions that explain why so many single women are observed in service occupations, as washerwomen, sick nurses, or even barbers, outside the franchise system, or in crafts organized on a piece-work basis, as for example carding, spinning, sewing, and dressmaking or pin manufacture. Alternatively, women traded in marginal occupations tolerated by civic authorities without enthusiasm. Under this head are found various kinds of petty trader or huckster, and the upholder or second-hand clothes dealer, but in times of necessity the poor female worker might be reduced to prostitution. It is perhaps for this reason that women appear so prominently in borough court records in the depressed years prior to the Black Death.[47]

The evidence as a whole suggests certain gender-specific characteristics of women's work. On one level, women's work identity tended to be rather fluid. Unlike the male apprentice, most female servants would have experience of several different types of household. The example of Margaret Hall of York, servant to first a goldsmith, then a chandler, and lastly his widow, well illustrates the point.[48] A woman might then find work outside service prior to marriage, an observation supported by the York deposition evidence, and on marriage would normally be expected to learn her husband's trade. A woman would in this way build up through life a range of experiences and skills, particularly, it may be surmised, in respect of marketing goods. On another level, women were seldom wholly engaged in a single employment. As servants they probably combined domestic functions associated with house-keeping and craft activity. As wives they ran households, worked alongside their husbands where he had his own shop, and also pursued such by-employments as spinning wool and brewing ale. Even when working independently there is evidence that some women combined occupations. Thus Juliana Bury of Norwich lined the mayor's hat with fur, but also supplied the city with timber, and in York Agnes Barebour traded as both barber and

---

[47] Goldberg, 'The Public and the Private'.
[48] BIHR, Prob. Reg. 2, fos. 45^v, 143^v, 401, 441.

brewster.[49] Women were specifically exempted from the Statute of 1363 that confined workers to a single craft or trade.[50] Lastly it may be observed that women are most frequently occupied in activities associated with traditionally 'feminine' household skills, that is washing, sewing, spinning, and preparing food and drink.

Lacking a well-developed work identity, denied generally the formal training afforded by apprenticeship, circumscribed by economic dependency and the legal limitations on trade that followed from this, women were never able to consolidate their position in the labour market. This position was determined on the one hand by the demand for labour, on the other by the availability of trained male labour.[51] These parameters are themselves related to and dependent on movements in the economy and population levels. The position argued here is that the advent of plague, if indeed it were plague, in 1348–9 marked a profound downturn in demographic levels, but an expansion in the economy. Only slowly did the level of population stabilize and it is unlikely that there was any real trend towards recovery before the later fifteenth century.[52] Recent work on the mortality of monks has even suggested a worsening of adult expectation of life over the course of the later fifteenth century.[53] Declining markets, themselves in part a product of continued demographic attrition, caused economic contraction and even recession in many towns, including York, by this same period. Given these parameters, it is possible to outline three stages in the development of the labour market in respect of females.

The first of these stages saw a steady growth in employment opportunities for women due to an expansion of the economy at a time of perhaps increasing labour scarcity. Women first filled

---

[49] NRO, NCR Case 18, shelf a, book of accounts, 1384–1448, fos. 124, 127^v, 128; YCA, CC 1, pp. 17, 59, 120, 139; CC 1A, fos. 22^v, 35^v, 39, 42^v, 46^v.

[50] *Statutes of the Realm*, i. 379.

[51] See Ch. 3 above.

[52] For a general discussion of demographic trends see Hatcher, *Plague, Population and the English Economy*.

[53] J. Hatcher, 'Mortality in the Fifteenth Century: Some New Evidence', *Economic History Review*, 2nd ser. 39 (1986), 19–38. Hatcher's findings for the monks of Canterbury have recently been supported by Harvey's as yet unpublished findings for the monks of Westminster. See also G. Rosser, *Medieval Westminster, 1200–1540* (Oxford, 1989), 177–80.

those niches where female labour was traditional. The poll taxes of 1379 and 1380–1 represent the mid-point in this process. The feminised nature of the textiles industry in the North at this date is particularly marked.[54] The second stage, extending in the case of York from about the second to the fifth decade of the fifteenth century, represents the high point of female economic activity. Economic expansion itself had probably reached a peak by the last years of the fourteenth century, but continued demographic recession in the face of endemic disease and possibly declining birth rates consequent upon delayed marriage and a growing proportion of women failing to marry, served to further undermine the supply of labour. Women may thus have been drawn into the labour force in yet greater numbers and to have begun to fill some formerly male economic niches. If the employment of women tended to depress wages in those occupations where women were employed, even if it were the case that women were paid the same as men for the same job, employers may have preferred to engage female labour over male labour so as to compensate for the loss of income in a contracting market. In the longer run, a shrinking labour force meant a shrinkage of demand. As economic recession bit deeper into the urban economy, women were gradually excluded from the full range of occupations they had previously enjoyed so as to protect male employment. Women were thus forced increasingly into marginal and poorly paid occupations, and into positions of dependency. This process is most marked and first observed within the woollen textiles sector through the loss of export markets, and it is here that specific gild regulation against the employment of women is observed.[55]

Evidence for this three-phase model is necessarily unsatisfactory due to the paucity of statistical data and observations can only be somewhat impressionistic. Some idea of the debilitating effects of epidemic and even endemic pestilence within the region can be gleaned from probate and chronicle sources. These suggest that levels of mortality may have been especially high in the epidemic years of the later fourteenth century, but probably remained comparatively high into the early fifteenth century reaching a peak in 1438, a year of famine and disease throughout northern

---

[54] See Ch. 3 above.
[55] As at Coventry, Bristol, Hull, and Norwich. See Ch. 3 above.

England. A number of years of pestilence are also recorded between 1459 and 1483–4, and again early in the sixteenth century.[56] If it were indeed the case that marriage rates tended to fall in the century following the Black Death, then there is little here to suggest the possibility of demographic recovery before the last decades of the fifteenth century. How this pattern of demographic recession over more than a century influenced levels of population within York itself is no more easy to assess. The three-phase model does, however, seem to make sense of the, albeit difficult, evidence. In the later fourteenth century York seems to have recruited migrants in number; this is reflected in both the numbers of admissions to the franchise and the toponymic evidence for distances travelled by migrants. By the earlier fifteenth century, and perhaps following the pestilences of 1391, 1429, and 1438, the supply of migrants may have been drying up, but by the later fifteenth century, corresponding to phase three of the model, gild ordinances suggest a hardening of attitudes against the influx of unskilled labour. Rental evidence as analysed by Rees Jones likewise suggests that though the city landlords apparently had little difficulty in finding tenants in the later fourteenth century, cheaper properties, such as might be occupied by labourers, piece-workers, and unskilled rural migrants more generally, became more difficult to let by the earlier fifteenth century. The proportion of female tenants in some areas of the city, moreover, seem to have been especially high early in the fifteenth century. Rental values, especially of cheaper accommodation, seems to have continued to decline into the later fifteenth century.

The pattern of female admissions to the franchise at York also accords well with the second phase of this model. 52, or 45 per cent of all female admissions in the period *c.*1349–1500 are located in the thirty years after 1414. The proportion of female intrants at Canterbury is also at a high level during the earlier decades of the fifteenth century, and most markedly over the third decade of that century. In contrast there are almost no female intrants from the mid-1440s to the early 1470s, when numbers

[56] Goldberg, 'Mortality and Economic Change', 41, 45–50; A. J. Pollard, 'The North-Eastern Economy and the Agrarian Crisis of 1438–1440', *Northern History*, 25 (1989), 88–105.

recover slightly.[57] The pattern of employment of female servants further accords with the trend just outlined. Service sex ratios derived from York wills are observed to fall from the later fourteenth century as servant groups associated with all types of craft or trade household became increasingly feminised. They reached their lowest level in the period 1415–44, precisely the period when female franchise admissions were at their peak. Thereafter there is a divergent trend as female servants were increasingly excluded from households associated with artisan craftsmen. At the same time servant groups associated with mercantile households became increasingly feminised, but the status of these female servants probably fell correspondingly.[58] Service for women became yet another marginal employment and it is probable that the daughters of the well-to-do increasingly remained at home.

Turning to the question of nuptiality the three-phase model can once more be applied. In discussions of marriage historians have often been tempted by the metaphor of the 'marriage market'. This leads to the notion that women were essentially passive commodities to be purchased by men according to their own economic circumstances and social standing. The latter might determine in which part of the market men shopped, the former, the age at which they first entered the market and the age of the commodities they selected. Such an interpretation is not merely sexist, it shows a profound misapprehension of the social implications of a European, late-marriage regime. This present interpretation lays stress on the social consequences of life-cycle service and a pattern of marriage that was both late and companionate (in more than just its demographic sense). During the English later Middle Ages women as well as men could support themselves in work, as servants like the Margery Spuret cited at the beginning of this chapter, or in craft or trade activity. It was this degree of economic independence, and the absence of effective parental control, that allowed women a remarkable degree of freedom in the choice of marriage partner, but also the opportunity to delay marriage or to get by without ever marrying. The way this freedom

---

[57] Collins (ed.), *Register of the Freemen of the City of York*, i; Cowper, *Intrantes*. A similar chronology of female admissions has been observed at Bruges: Howell, 'Citizenship and Gender', 41.
[58] See Ch. 4 and Table 4.7.

is reflected in marriage litigation has already been remarked upon, but the apparent frequency with which multi-party actions are found at York during the later fourteenth and, more especially, earlier fifteenth century is highly suggestive. Conversely, the decline in all types of matrimonial litigation through the later fifteenth century would accord with an erosion of the independent role of females in marriage formation, and thus of scope for matrimonial disputes and litigation.[59]

Trends in nuptiality may be analysed indirectly from testamentary sources by considering marital status at death. Patterns observed may be more generally applicable despite the bias of this source to the more prosperous members of the community, in this case the city of York. Here again the three-phase model seems to fit. The proportion of female testators dying single or, in the case of widows, not having remarried was at its highest level in the period c.1415–44, which coincides with phase two of the model. By the later fifteenth century, however, there is an increase in the proportion of women dying widowed and especially of second-time widows. Parallel to this trend is an equivalent increase in the proportion of men leaving a surviving spouse at their death.[60] Such observations are consistent with a fall in the mean age at first marriage for women since this would tend to increase the probability of their surviving their husbands. Such a pattern would accord with phase three of the model.

This three-phase model may immediately be contrasted with the almost total absence of evidence for the participation of women in craft or trade activity that characterized late medieval Tuscany. To explore the structural implications of these differing traditions it is possible to compare the evidence of the English poll tax of 1377 against data derived from the Florentine *catasto* for 1427 and related sources. Some superficial statistical similarities disguise some very real differences in response to economic and demographic change. Thus mean urban household size (MHS) estimated from the poll tax is perhaps a percentage point or two below four; using the previously adopted multiplier of 1.65 to compensate for evasion and the population of children under 14, MHS in Hull was only 3.71, in Dartmouth 3.76, but in York

---

[59] See Table 5.7.   [60] See Table 5.10.

4.10.[61] In Prato in 1371, MHS was as low as 3.44 and was still only 3.73 in 1427. For the towns of the Florentine region as a whole in 1427 it was only a little higher at 3.91. As the fifteenth century progressed, however, MHS continued to rise. In Florence from 3.80 in 1427 it grew to 4.82 by 1458–9 and 5.20 by 1480. In 1552 it reached 5.66.[62] This was a rate of increase almost entirely independent of demographic growth. Indeed, though the population of Florence may have stabilized by 1427, it certainly did not grow again for a further three decades.

There is little evidence for such a growth in urban MHS over the same period in England. MHS in Coventry in 1523 was only 3.67, though this may be atypically low, and at Romford in 1562 MHS was still only 4.1. It may have been a little higher in early Stuart Cambridge, but it had fallen again by the time of the Marriage Duty Act evidence at the end of the seventeenth century. This last shows MHS in Shrewsbury of 4.0 and Southampton of 3.8.[63] Thus it may be seen that whereas urban mean household sizes grew markedly from a low point after the Black Death in Tuscany, and that much of that growth before the later fifteenth century was independent of general demographic trends, no such dramatic increase is apparent from English urban sources. The evidence further suggests that larger households were rather more common in Tuscany than England. This cannot actually be demonstrated from the poll tax evidence due to the exclusion of children below 14 years, but at Coventry in 1523 only 38 per cent of the population lived in households of six or more persons, whereas in Florence in 1427 the equivalent figure was nearly 46 per cent. In Prato the proportion of households containing six or more persons rose from 18.8 per cent in 1371 to 19.2 per cent in 1427 to 25.6 per cent in 1470.[64]

Turning to the proportion of households headed by women

[61] See Table 7.1.

[62] Klapisch-Zuber, 'Demographic Decline and Household Structure', table 2.1, p. 28; Herlihy and Klapisch-Zuber, *Tuscans and Their Families*, table 3.5, pp. 74, 283.

[63] Phythian-Adams, *Desolation of a City*, table 34, p. 301; McIntosh, 'Servants and the Household', table 1b, p. 8; Goose, 'Household Size', table 5, p. 364; Wall, 'Regional and Temporal Variations', table 4.6, p. 103.

[64] Calculated from Phythian-Adams, *Desolation of a City*, table 37, p. 310; Klapisch-Zuber, 'Demographic Decline and Household Structure', table 2.1, p. 28; Herlihy and Klapisch-Zuber, *Tuscans and Their Families*, fig. 10.11, p. 380.

there is a superficial similarity in the immediate post-plague decades. 19.2 per cent of households in Prato were headed by females in 1371. For Dartmouth in 1377 the proportion is only 15.4 per cent, but for Colchester it was 19.3 per cent and for Hull 23.4 per cent.[65] It may thus be that the English urban proportion slightly exceeded the Tuscan equivalent at this date, but there is little evidence that the English proportion would have fallen substantially before the later fifteenth century. Indeed, if the hypothesis outlined before is correct, then the proportion of women to men can be expected to have followed a fluctuating pattern, to have increased in the earlier decades of the fifteenth century, before falling again from the later fifteenth century, and likewise to have risen in the late seventeenth century, but to have fallen from the mid-eighteenth century. Coventry, with 19.7 per cent of households female-headed in 1523, was perhaps unusually feminised due to the departure of young male workers in the face of swift and profound recession. In Romford in 1562, a period when women may have been especially dependent upon marriage, only 12 per cent of households were female-headed. Wall has calculated a mean of 18.3 per cent from a sample drawn from both urban and rural parishes for the period 1650–1749, but this last coincides with a period of renewed economic opportunity in towns and an equivalent sample for the period 1750–1821 shows a mean of only 13.9 per cent.[66] In Tuscany, by way of contrast, the proportion of households headed by women underwent considerable contraction through the fifteenth century. In Prato the proportion, having slipped to 16.7 per cent in 1427, collapsed to only 10.3 per cent in 1470.[67] This is despite the strong evidence that elderly Tuscan widows often chose to end their days in the city, thus swelling the numbers of widows within the urban population.[68]

The point at which the demographic measures depart most radically is, however, in respect of the sex ratio of the population

[65] Klapisch-Zuber, 'Demographic Decline and Household Structure', table 2.1, p. 28; table 7.3.

[66] Calculated from Phythian-Adams, *Desolation of a City*, 193 and table 15, p. 203; McIntosh, 'Servants and the Household', 9; Wall, 'Regional and Temporal Variations', table 4.3, p. 94.

[67] Klapisch-Zuber, 'Demographic Decline and Household Structure', table 2.1, p. 28.

[68] Herlihy and Klapisch-Zuber, *Tuscans and Their Families*, 157.

(measured here as the number of men to every hundred women). Although later medieval Tuscan sex ratios tend always to be in excess of 100, i.e. males always outnumber females, urban sex ratios are consistently higher than rural sex ratios, i.e. the towns had a greater proportion of males than the countryside. This was most marked in the larger cities of Florence and Pisa, which had sex ratios in 1427 of 117.6 and 112.3. The equivalent ratios for the respective *contadi* were only 108.9 and 106.8.[69] In Prato the sex ratio can be seen to rise progressively from 97.9 in 1371 to 106.6 in 1427 to 107.3 in 1470.[70] It is unlikely that these ratios can be explained by the out-migration of females to the countryside since towns were dependent upon a net inflow of migrants and it is hardly possible to detect any preference for female labour in the countryside. Rather it must be due to the immigration of males seeking work in the city. The reverse appears to be true of post-plague England. Here urban sex ratios (calculated for the adult population only) are consistently below 100. In Hull the ratio was 92.7 and in Carlisle 89.7.[71] In rural Rutland at the same date the equivalent ratio was 103.5.[72] The pattern of migration here was probably also from country into town, but it was female-led. Souden has described a precisely similar pattern for English towns at the end of the seventeenth century, a period of only modest demographic growth following several decades characterized by stagnation and recession, but of urban and economic expansion.[73]

What then do these statistical measures tell about how two different cultures responded to the impact of bubonic plague and the economic changes of the later Middle Ages? In Tuscany it has already been noted that by and large women did not engage in paid employment, nor was service well developed as an institution. The labour shortages created by the plague could, therefore, only be met by males. Town-based industry drew upon a continual influx of male migrants from the surrounding villages, hence the skewed sex ratios. But, as Klapisch-Zuber has convincingly dem-

---

[69] Ibid. table 5.4, p. 157.

[70] Klapisch-Zuber, 'Demographic Decline and Household Structure', table 2.1, p. 28.

[71] See Table II.2.

[72] Table II.2. It is not possible to calculate TSR for Oakham (tenants of the king) since the surviving listing does not identify servants by name. ASR for Oakham is 95.6.

[73] Souden, 'Migrants and the Population Structure'.

onstrated, urban households also responded in a significant number of cases by failing to undergo fission when a son married. As she observes, the profound change from the later fourteenth century 'is the probability that a son who marries will live with his parents and, after the death of the father, with his widowed mother'. But it was by this means that some families were able to ensure 'a minimal manpower . . . in a period of demographic low tide and high salaries'.[74] Hence the fall in the proportion of female-headed urban households, the steady rise in MHS even before the commencement of demographic recovery, and the increase in especially large, multi-generational households.

For England the distinctive social structure outlined earlier allowed for labour shortages to be satisfied from two different sources, neither of which appears in the Tuscan model. On the one hand, there was servant labour, which in an era of rising wage rates was comparatively inexpensive, and on the other, female labour. The thesis here is that the ready availability of these sources of labour was a product of a 'liberal' social structure that did not bind children to the authority of their parents beyond adolescence. It may be that the institution of life-cycle service developed precociously in the larger towns after the Black Death, but there is evidence that the institution was well established even before the advent of plague.[75] There is also evidence that women engaged in a variety of remunerative occupations, particularly in victualling and service trades, before 1348, and Hilton has elsewhere described how migrant women were absorbed into the economy of the nascent borough of Halesowen.[76] There was then no deeply ingrained cultural prejudice against women earning; no father, brother, or husband stood to lose face because they were not the sole means of support for the women in their lives. The combination of early emotional and economic independence from parents, which the institution of service helped foster, and of late marriage offered a springboard from which women could enter the labour market. In Tuscany, however, girls generally remained with their parents until a suitable husband was found for them, often in their late teens. For girls to leave home and seek

[74] Klapisch-Zuber, 'Demographic Decline and Household Structure', 32–3.
[75] See Ch. 4 above.
[76] See Ch. 3 above; Hilton, 'Lords, Burgesses and Hucksters', 10.

employment would have been a threat to their 'virtue' and thus prejudicial to their subsequently marrying, the only 'career' open to women of poor family. In this respect Tuscany of the Quattrocento was more like the England of Victoria than the England of Henry V.

NUPTIALITY AND FEMALE ECONOMIC OPPORTUNITY: AN ANTI-MALTHUSIAN MODEL EXPLORED

In order to illustrate the three-phase model for female employment in English towns outlined earlier, it may be useful to represent the first two phases diagrammatically. This is shown in Fig. 8.1. The focus of this model is the relationship between labour supply and labour demand. After the Black Death the shortage of labour coupled with the relaxation of pressures on agriculture tended to force real wages upwards. The Statute of Labourers might frustrate this process, but it was powerless to reverse it. Rising wages, coupled with the increase in familial incomes through the economic contribution of married women and the fall in the dependency ratio, i.e. the proportion of persons below working age to those of age, notably after the second pestilence of 1361, stimulated demand for manufactured goods and services.[77] There follows from this a benign relationship between demographic recession, wage levels, demand for female labour, and urbanization. These are reflected in the low urban sex ratios observed in 1377 and, given the opportunity now afforded women to support themselves independently, in the concentration of women in the cheap tenements or cottages of the urban periphery.[78] Single women were no longer financially dependent on marriage and may have been more selective of marriage partners. In demographic terms they may have tended to delay getting married or not have married at all. Indeed the skewed nature of urban sex ratios meant that there were insufficient males for all women to find partners. Widows also were more likely to

---

[77] The dependency ratio would be influenced by the particular impact of the plague on children and, it may be argued, by a fall in the birth rate.
[78] Table II.2; Ch. 7 above.

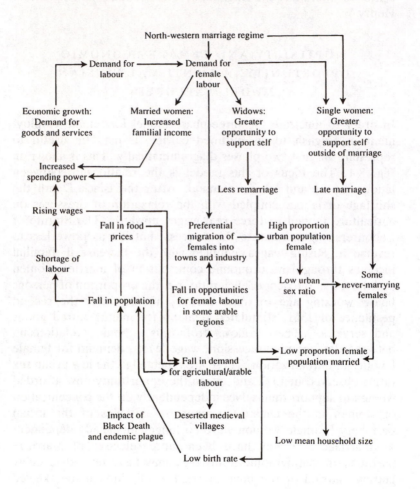

Fig. 8.1.   Stages One and Two of Three-Phase Model

find means of supporting themselves and thus were less liable to remarry. Todd has argued this same thesis in respect of widows in later seventeenth-century Abingdon.[79]

A rising age at first marriage for females, an increase in the proportion of women never-marrying, and a general downturn in marriage rates would result in a falling birth-rate, and hence a postponement in the process of demographic recovery. It would also depress MHS by increasing the numbers of solitary households and reducing the population of dependent children. It is this trend that may be reflected in the low urban poll tax mean household measures and in the high proportions of female-headed households. A parallel pattern has been described for English towns in the later seventeenth century, a period of labour shortage and only modest growth following an immediately preceding period of demographic retrenchment, but also of urban growth and rising wages.[80] Here too urban sex ratios were low, urban households small, and marriage rates depressed; the female age at first marriage reached, according to reconstitution studies, its highest point since 1538.[81] The implications for the later fourteenth and earlier fifteenth centuries, when there is so much more evidence for working women, are to be taken seriously.

The third phase of the model sees the mechanisms just described go sharply into reverse as contracting overseas markets and the receding impact of plague, endemic by the fifteenth century, tended to invert the relationship between labour supply and demand. Women may be seen to have been the primary victims since their always precarious hold on the labour market was thrust aside by males determined upon protecting their share of a contracting job market, hence the Bristol weavers' complaint of 1461 that 'likely men to do the king service in his wars' were threatened by female competition.[82] Women were increasingly forced into dependent positions within service or marriage as their economic status was eroded. Age at marriage probably fell, the marriage rate probably increased, and with it the birth rate. From this followed the demographic recovery of the sixteenth century.

[79] Todd, 'The Remarrying Widow'.
[80] Souden, 'Migrants and the Population Structure'.
[81] See Chs. 6 and 7 above; Wrigley and Schofield, *The Population History of England*, table 7.26, p. 255; Souden, 'Migrants and the Population Structure', 160.
[82] Power, *Medieval Women*, 60.

Such conclusions would accord with Wrigley and Schofield's analysis of the earliest parish register evidence.[83] The declining demand for female labour within the urban economy by the sixteenth century is reflected in evidence for the growth in urban sex ratios. Males appear to have outnumbered females by the late sixteenth century in London and by the early seventeenth century in York. As just observed, this pattern was reversed in the later seventeenth century, but it is again possible to see an analogy between these demographic processes operating from the later fifteenth century to the earlier seventeenth century and the position over the eighteenth century. Here an erosion of female labour is characterized by a fall in age at first marriage, a declining proportion of female-headed households, an increase in MHS, and a feminization of service.[84]

It remains to consider the vexed question of the relationship between 'standard of living' and nuptiality. In their analysis of English parish register evidence Wrigley and Schofield have argued that over the period 1541–1871 changing levels of fertility influenced demographic trends in England much more strongly than mortality. They have argued further that the major influence on changing levels of fertility is the age at which women marry and that this itself is highly responsive to changes in the standard of living as measured by a modified version of the Phelps Brown and Hopkins (PBH) series. Their thesis is essentially that decisions regarding marriage formation were influenced by the relative ability of the couple to acquire sufficient resources to enable them to set up house together and start a family, and by their assessment of their future prospects. In periods of high 'real wages' this would be achieved more quickly than when 'real wages' were depressed. Thus when the PBH index moved upwards through the seventeenth and into the mid-eighteenth century the marriage rate tended to rise and, according to reconstitution studies, age at first marriage tended to fall. Conversely, the downward trends in the PBH series through the later sixteenth century and again through

[83] Wrigley and Schofield, *The Population History of England*, table 7.26, figs. 7.1, 7.2, 10.6, 10.9.

[84] Snell, *Annals of the Labouring Poor*; Wrigley and Schofield, *The Population History of England*, table 7.26, p. 255; Wall, 'Regional and Temporal Variations', tables 4.3, 4.5, pp. 94, 98; Wall, 'Mean Household Size in England from Printed Sources', table 5.2, p. 192.

the later eighteenth century is marked by a subsequent fall in marriage rates and rise in age at first marriage.[85] The demographic system Wrigley and Schofield describe breaks down in their own terms in the later nineteenth century when:

Neither improving standards of living nor the possibility of limiting fertility within marriage persuaded late-Victorian men and women to embark on marriage younger or more generally. They turned away from marriage patterns of earlier generations.[86]

This thesis has since been questioned by Weir, and Schofield has responded to this by revising his original arguments.[87] Weir draws attention to the demographic significance of the wide secular fluctuation in the proportions of the population never-marrying. This he suggests may have moved independently of trends in marriage ages. The observed decline in fertility for the seventeenth century he suggests owed much more to the high level of celibacy than the modest movement in age at marriage, whereas for the period after 1750 the 'proportions married approached their upper limit'.[88] Weir further suggests that the mechanism determining celibacy rates is the tendency of differing regional economies to draw disproportionately upon one sex or the other and, through the migration of labour in response to the sex-specific needs of these economies, to skew sex ratios. So in the later seventeenth century, for example, towns tended to draw on female labour, rural agriculture upon male labour. By following work some young people were thus liable to be disappointed in matrimony.[89] Schofield concedes the effect on fertility of the high proportion of persons never-marrying from the late sixteenth and through the seventeenth century, but reasserts the demographic importance of falling marriage ages through the eighteenth century.[90] On the relationship between nuptiality and 'real wages', however, Schofield allows for a more substantial revision of the

[85] Wrigley and Schofield, *The Population History of England*, table 7.26, figs. 7.1, 7.2, 10.6, 10.9.

[86] Ibid. 438.

[87] D. R. Weir, 'Rather Never than Late: Celibacy and Age at Marriage in English Cohort Fertility, 1541–1871', *Journal of Family History*, 9 (1984), 340–54; R. S. Schofield, 'English Marriage Patterns Revisited', *Journal of Family History*, 10 (1985), 2–20.

[88] Weir, 'Rather Never than Late', 342.

[89] Ibid. 349. Cf. Souden, 'Migrants and the Population Structure'.

[90] Schofield, 'English Marriage Patterns Revisited', 11–12.

case he first argued with Wrigley. He suggests that the inverse
correlation between movements in real wages and marriage age in
fact only holds up when the former is seen to rise 'unequivocally'.
At other times, as in the late sixteenth century or, less certainly,
in the late eighteenth century, the relationship could be reversed
due to the intervention of 'more powerful countervailing factors'.
Instead he argues that it was the level of celibacy that demonstrates
a simple inverse correlation with movements in real wages.[91] He
also poses the question of the demographic significance of secular
changes in the pattern of service and notes Snell's argument that
the erosion of employment prospects for women at the end of the
eighteenth and beginning of the nineteenth century tended to
depress female ages at first marriage.[92]

Clearly this is still an open debate and it is not the intention
here to resolve the very complex pattern of relationships simply
by introducing evidence from the period before parish registration. This earlier evidence does, however, suggest certain possibilities that have not always received sufficient attention. By
contrasting the English and Tuscan experiences in response to the
Black Death attention has been focused on the significance of the
work opportunities afforded women within a late, European
marriage regime. Yet so much of the debate from the early
modern period, with the notable exception of the work of Snell,
has effectively discounted the demographic implications of the
changing status of women within the labour market. It may be
noted that one of the major limitations of the PBH series is that it
is sex-specific; it makes no allowance for this changing secular
pattern of female employment and earning capacity, nor for
consequent shifts in total familial income. Analyses of nuptiality
have, moreover, often been expressed in terms of the marriage
market and, ultimately, only from a male viewpoint.[93] The man is
assumed the principal wage-earner, to whom the woman will be
wed since she will find economic security in matrimony. But the
underlying presumption is, to borrow from Jane Austen, that 'a
single man in possession of a good fortune must be in want of a
wife'.

---

[91] Schofield, 'English Marriage Patterns Revisited', 16.
[92] Ibid. 18–19; Snell, *Annals of the Labouring Poor*.
[93] See above.

This is to ignore the degree to which at certain periods in the past, and the late fourteenth and earlier fifteenth centuries are illustrative of this, women were able to support themselves outside marriage. It is also to underestimate the extent to which marriage could be a real economic partnership. Indeed at times of illness, physical incapacity, or unemployment, the wife might become the principal breadwinner.[94] The degree of economic security granted a woman through marriage must, therefore, be qualified. In relative terms it was greatest when women were largely excluded from the job market. It may be observed that at such periods, as from the late fifteenth century or during the mid-nineteenth century, the dominant culture tended to stress that a woman's place was in home and family, and to exaggerate the differences between the sexes in a way that was detrimental to the female. There is a further cultural component in that when the economic status of women was eroded and the importance of woman's role as wife and mother was stressed, women might be haunted by the fear of not finding a spouse, of being 'left on the shelf', of becoming an 'old maid'. The development of the romantic novel, so much concerned with the progress to the altar and not the realities of married life, coincides with a long period of falling marriage ages and falling rates of celibacy. At the same time there is observed an upward trend in prenuptial pregnancies and illegitimate births, indicators of an 'intensification' of courtship.[95]

Clearly the risk of not finding a marriage partner was of greater moment to women at some periods than at others. Taking up Weir's argument that differences in regional sex-specific labour demand would distort sex ratios and so lead to an increased level of celibacy, it would appear that in the later seventeenth century women could be said to have valued the present prospect of employment over the future risk of remaining single. By the

---

[94] Leggett, 'The 1377 Poll Tax Returns for the City of York', 131 (Matilda de Shirburn), 135 (Isabell de Pantre), 137 (Agnes de Ripon, Alice de Semester, Juliana de Doncaster), 142 (Katherine de Aberford), 145 (Alice Hukster, Agnes de Belton). These examples are too numerous to be a product of carelessness. For several of these women, moreover, there is evidence that they were actually engaged in remunerative employment. An entry from the Oxford (1381) returns is more explicit, 'De Agnete Multon lotrice et marito eiusdem': J. E. T. Rogers (ed.), *Oxford City Documents, 1285–1665* (Oxford Historical Society, 18; 1891), 42.

[95] Laslett, *The World We Have Lost*, 177.

eighteenth century, however, they allowed the present risk of becoming pregnant to weigh more lightly than the future risk of failing to secure a marriage partner. The argument here pursues this point further. In contemporary culture the bachelor is not regarded with condescending pity, yet the term 'spinster' still has many pejorative undertones. Yet it may be unwise to assume that all women want to marry and that those who do not are consequently 'disappointed' in marriage when the same is not assumed of men. This may be of greater relevance when contraception was, if not unknown, at least very unreliable and married life for a woman would normally involve repeated child-bearing and child-rearing. This last may have been a real incentive for women to wish to delay marriage, not to take on this burden too soon in life, and actually to reduce the burden by marrying after their peak fertility. A further advantage for the woman of delaying decisions regarding matrimony would be that it would allow her to be more selective about her partner. These considerations were, however, only really open to women in the context of a European marriage regime when the labour market favoured female employment and permitted women a degree of economic autonomy. Such may be said to have been true of the late fourteenth and first half of the fifteenth century, of the later seventeenth century, and, to a more limited degree, of the earlier nineteenth century and the late nineteenth and early twentieth centuries.

This alternative thesis focuses not on the relationship between 'real', i.e. male wages and nuptiality, but upon the economic status of women and the bearing this has upon marriage decisions. This status is itself determined by the demand for labour generally, the availability of trained male labour, and cultural prejudices regarding the employment of women. After the Black Death the economy appears to have expanded at a time of acute labour shortage. Women, already present in the labour force, were thus actively drawn into the labour market to compensate for the shortfall in male labour. Until recession reversed this process, women were attracted in ever greater numbers as population levels, and thus the availability of trained male labour, continued to decline through the earlier decades of the fifteenth century. In the later seventeenth and early years of the eighteenth century there is likewise evidence of economic growth, as reflected in urbanization, at a time of demographic recession. The period is further characterized by a high rate of emigration that, it may be argued, reduced the male population disproportionately. The evidence again points to women migrating into the towns to take up work opportunities, but it is a period also marked by high levels of celibacy and a relatively late age at first marriage for women. These patterns are found, for example, in Earle's study of women in London in the period 1665–1725 drawn from deposition evidence.[96] In particular he is able to point to a high level of female participation in the labour market; only 28 per cent of a sample of 851 women between 1695 and 1735 gave no indication of employment, about half the equivalent proportion (57 per cent) of all London women over 20 years listed in the census of 1851.[97]

The same period was marked, according to Todd, by a much lower level of widow remarriage than was true of the later sixteenth or early seventeenth centuries, a phenomenon that she ascribes in part to an expansion of the local economy.[98] A number of towns at the end of the seventeenth century were characterized by high proportions of households headed by widows, 18.5 per cent in Shrewsbury and 24.1 per cent in Southampton. For early modern Oxford, Prior has found that the greatest proportions of widows taking apprentices, and thus actively running businesses, were located around the end of the seventeenth and the earlier part of the eighteenth century. Although she prefers economic contraction as an explanation, it seems significant that Oxford continued to grow through the period of demographic recession in the mid-seventeenth century and that women enjoyed most prominence within the local economy just as the supply of migrant labour was drying up.[99] Earle's study shows that 73.2 per cent of London widows in his sample (N = 183) were 'wholly maintained by employment' and that a further 12.0 per cent were 'partly maintained by employment'.[100]

[96] P. Earle, 'The Female Labour Market in London in the Late Seventeenth and Early Eighteenth Centuries', 328–53.

[97] Ibid. 337.

[98] Todd, 'The Remarrying Widow', table 2.5, pp. 64, 70, 78.

[99] M. Prior, 'Women and the Urban Economy: Oxford, 1500–1800', in ead. (ed.), *Women in English Society, 1500–1800* (London, 1985), 99, 109.

[100] Earle, 'Female Labour Market in London', 337. Relatively few London widows appear to have retained their late husbands' businesses and 'some who did so gave up fairly quickly': ibid. 339.

In some regions during the earlier nineteenth century new work opportunities were created for women in regions that had previously been relatively sparsely populated. This is most conspicuously true of the clothing districts of Lancashire and the West Riding. Laslett has noted that in Lancashire illegitimacy actually declined with industrialization and it again may be possible to relate this to the effect increased economic independence for women had on courtship behaviour.[101] Gittins notes of the same region for the earlier twentieth century a degree of frankness in sexual matters that contrasts with the more usual Victorian 'double standard'.[102] Finally, with the expansion of the tertiary sector from the late nineteenth century new opportunities were opened up for women in clerical and retail trades. By the beginning of the twentieth century it had become normal for young women to follow paid employment whilst still single.[103] This same period saw that upward movement in marriage ages for women that represented for Wrigley and Schofield a radical departure from earlier patterns. The timing generally of these periods of economic opportunity for women were often characterized by rising male real wages since wage rates reflect the balance between labour demand and labour supply as a whole, although women might have been preferentially employed where male wages were higher than could be sustained by the economy.

At those periods when women tended to be excluded from the labour market, as male workers attempted to safeguard their own positions, the relationships just described can be shown to have been reversed. Thus for the late fifteenth century and into the sixteenth century it has been argued here that women became more dependent upon marriage and may have married earlier and in greater numbers. Certainly the crude marriage rates calculated from the first half-century of parish registration are startlingly high.[104] At the same time the population tended to recover rapidly after so many years of negative or nil growth. A slow decline in mean female age at first marriage and corresponding rise in the proportions marrying from the later seventeenth century was

[101] Laslett, *The World We Have Lost*, 168.
[102] D. Gittins, *Fair Sex: Family Size and Structure, 1900–39* (London, 1982), 89–92.
[103] Ibid. 69.
[104] Wrigley and Schofield, *The Population History of England*, fig. 10.9.

followed by a sharp acceleration in these patterns from around the middle of the eighteenth century. This may likewise be linked to a progressive erosion of female work opportunities in a period of sustained demographic expansion, itself related to trends in nuptiality. In the mid-nineteenth century also the labour force seems to have grown faster than the economy and women were forced into early marriages or into service, sweated labour, or even prostitution, the dark side of a culture that sought to protect women from 'unsuitable' employment and sanctified their role as 'angels in the house'. In these instances the sort of relationships set out in Fig. 8.1 were reversed. Women by marrying earlier may unconsciously have put back the time when they might once again enjoy a degree of economic independence.

Clearly the patterns just outlined are in reality more complex. Within the late medieval period it has been suggested that there was real regional variation in the degree to which women were drawn into the labour market. It may be that the high level of economic activity enjoyed by women in northern England, and probably also London, before the mid-fifteenth century was only to a more modest degree true of other regions. Certainly Weir is right to draw attention to differing regional demands for different types of labour. Pastoral agriculture, with its dairy component and opportunity for by-employments, appears to have offered more scope for the employment of women (and servants) than was true of arable husbandry with its more seasonal labour requirements. Indeed by the later decades of the fourteenth century some arable regions were caught between rising labour costs and declining crop values and may actually have shed labour, especially female labour, as they moved towards animal husbandry or even abandoned cultivation altogether. Likewise those towns where the textile and clothing trades were well established probably drew upon female labour to a greater degree than other manufacturing towns. The comparatively feminised nature of industry in early sixteenth-century Coventry further warns that low urban sex ratios may not always be explained by economic expansion, though the evidence elsewhere for more masculine urban populations by the later sixteenth century would suggest that this case is perhaps not typical.[105]

[105] Phythian-Adams, *Desolation of a City*, tables 13, 19, pp. 200, 210; Hilton, 'Lords, Burgesses and Hucksters', 10.

Coventry in 1523 may actually have been losing male labour certainly it was failing to attract male migrants in a time of acute
recession.

In periods when urban economic vitality coincided with labour
shortage, such as at Colchester, Hull, or York in 1377, and
Bristol, Lichfield, or Southampton in 1696, there was a positive
pull on rural migrants of either sex seeking employment. Since
agriculture had a greater hold over male labour, even allowing for
a shift away from arable in favour of pastoral agriculture, female
migrants nevertheless outnumbered male.[106] Sustained urban
growth from the late eighteenth century likewise depended upon
high levels of migration from the countryside, but the opportunities created for female migrants in a period also characterized by
growth rates in excess of one per cent per annum were, outside
service, consequently often limited. This was especially true of
those new towns that developed around heavy manufacturing
industry. Lady Bell, writing of Middlesbrough early this century,
observed that:

. . . the only large industry in the town, the iron trade, offers absolutely
no field for women in any part of it. There are not . . . large factories;
there is therefore no organised women's labour. The women have no
independent existence of their own. They mostly marry very young; the
conditions of the town point to their doing so. It is one of the few in the
kingdom in which, from the constant influx of men in search of work, and
not of women, the males outnumbered the females.[107]

Gittins further observes that in such towns there was an actual
movement of girls away to seek positions as domestic servants and
the consequent imbalance in the sex ratio forced female marriage
age down, just as the inverse situation forced it up.[108] On the
other hand, the almost complete feminization of service, which
demanded celibacy, and erosion of other work opportunities for
women may have tended to increase the proportion of women
never marrying.[109]

[106] See Table II.2 and Ch. 6 above; Souden, 'Migrants and the Population
Structure', table 17, p. 150.
[107] F. Bell, *At The Works* (London, 1907), 178.
[108] Gittins, *Fair Sex*, 73–4.
[109] Ibid. 73.

WORK AND MARRIAGE:
SOME CONCLUSIONS

Before this present century it would seem that only when population levels were stagnant or even falling did the economy regularly expand faster than the available male labour force. Indeed, it may even be argued that low or negative demographic growth tended to stimulate manufacture and the development of town-based industry. The hypothesis that there was a benign relationship between female economic status and late marriage thus places greater emphasis on mortality as a dynamic component in demographic change than has perhaps been allowed by Wrigley and Schofield, but then this analysis looks back not to 1541, but to 1348. It is of course tempting to pursue this speculative analysis further. The present thesis has stressed the cultural significance of a European, and more specifically the north-western marriage regime as providing the necessary platform for the participation of servants and women in economic life. Smith has argued that such a regime would not be incompatible with the limited demographic evidence for the decades before 1348.[110] Indeed it would seem proper to assume a degree of cultural continuity over the period of the Black Death despite the profound demographic and economic consequences, particularly as women are known to have engaged in employment outside the home, even perhaps prior to marriage, before 1348.[111]

It has already been shown that the response of two different cultures to the impact of plague was very different; the prevailing social structure was not shaped solely by external factors. The late thirteenth and early years of the fourteenth century were notoriously years of land hunger and population pressure.[112] It may be that in these particular circumstances there was a strong disincentive to marry or rear children unless marriage materially enhanced economic prospects. Smith has drawn attention to the demographic significance in villein society of the strikingly high proportion of marriages between widows holding land as dower and men

[110] Smith, 'Hypothèses sur la nuptialité', 120–4.
[111] Cf. Bennett, *Women in the Medieval English Countryside*; Hilton, 'Lords, Burgesses and Hucksters'; Goldberg, 'The Public and the Private'.
[112] Cf. M. M. Postan, *The Medieval Economy and Society* (London, 1972).

marrying for the first time in these decades. Women without land were thus at a disadvantage had they wanted to marry.[113] In this context the female 'vagabonds' described in the Spalding serf lists are to be found, as are the numbers of women making a living on the margins of the urban economy and thus regularly observed in breach of borough law.[114] It may speculatively be suggested that the demographic response to the conditions encountered in the decades before the Black Death continued to work advantageously after the events of 1348–9. Delayed marriage for women more readily allowed women to participate in the labour market at a time of acute labour shortage. Similarly, the cost of hired labour was an incentive to employ servant labour, paid more in kind than in cash, in its place, especially in regions engaged in or reverting to pastoral agriculture as the pressure to produce grain was relaxed. This may in itself have tended to push up marriage ages for both sexes in both town and country.

The development of servant labour and the expansion of peasant holdings as land again became more plentiful may also have made the 'family farm' enterprise less common and thus have reduced the incentive to have children. This hypothesis can further help explain the greater evidence for female economic activity in the North, a region best suited to pastoral farming and the expansion of cloth manufacture in the period after 1349. It may be that labour shortages following the advent of plague were more acute within this region since the demographic pressures and underemployment that had characterized the early fourteenth century were here not so acute as was true of older settled regions of midland and southern England. It was, moreover, the heavy clay arable regions of midland England that probably faced the greatest economic dislocation after 1349, a process that led to the shedding of labour, to long-term contraction, and in extreme cases to the wholesale abandonment of village settlements.

Despite the tentative nature of this analysis, it is no longer possible to agree that the period following the Black Death saw a simple surplus of women within the population—the so-called 'Frauenfrage' or 'woman question'—and that, to quote Sister

[113] Smith, 'Hypothèses sur la nuptialité', 124–7.
[114] H. E. Hallam, 'Some Thirteenth Century Censuses', *Economic History Review*, 2nd ser. 14 (1957), 352–61; Hilton, 'Lords, Burgesses and Hucksters', 10.

Maria Pia, there existed the 'question chiefly of providing means of support for those women who were prevented from following their natural vocation'.[115] Where the prevailing culture permitted, women appear willingly to have played a much more active role in economic life than this anachronistic view implicitly admits. The skewed urban sex ratios found in England at the time of the first poll tax, but also observed for a number of towns in the Low Countries or the Rhineland during the fifteenth century, are a consequence of this last and not of a general demographic phenomenon. As has been shown, such a pattern was not applicable to Tuscany at a like date, where a different cultural framework prevailed, or to English towns c.1300 or again c.1600. How close the marriage regime prevailing in late medieval Ghent or Cologne was to that of York must, however, remain a matter for further exploration. There is some evidence for a pattern of delayed marriage from a region of Holland at the beginning of the sixteenth century, and Howell cites some slight evidence for a late marriage regime prevailing in mid-sixteenth-century Leiden.[116]

Other indicators are more circumstantial. Fifteenth-century sources for Reims (1422), Ypres (1437), Fribourg (1444), and Dresden (1453) all point to low MHS, i.e. below four, and a high proportion of households with only one to three persons.[117] The same and equivalent sources indicate that for the adult populations urban sex ratios were correspondingly low, i.e. women outnumbered men, at Reims, Ypres, Nuremberg, Zurich, and Basle at various dates from the mid-fourteenth to the early sixteenth century.[118] Women likewise headed about a quarter of households

[115] Pia, 'The Industrial Position of Women', 556.

[116] Smith, 'Hypothèses sur la nuptialité', 110–11, citing H. van Dijk and D. J. Roonda, *Het Patriciaat in Zierekzee Tijdens de Republiek* (Rotterdam, 1979), 75; Howells, *Women, Production and Patriarchy*, 43–4 and n. 22, p. 210.

[117] Phythian-Adams, *Desolation of a City*, table 32, pp. 246–7. These data relate, however, only to partial surveys and these may not be typical of the entire community.

[118] Reims, 1422: St Hilaire = 90.9, St Pierre = 91.7; Ypres, 1502: Poorterie = 82.6; Nuremberg, 1449 = 90.9; Zurich, 1357 = 82.2, 1467 = 72.0; Basle 1454: St Alban and St Leonhad = 93.0. Desportes, 'La Population de Reims', 486; calculated from Pirenne, 'Les Dénombrements de la population d'Ypres', 15; calculated from R. Mols, *Introduction à la démographie historique des vills d'Europe*, ii. 187, 192; calculated from Hajnal, 'European Marriage Patterns', table 9, p. 117; K. Bücher, 'Zur mittelalterlichen Bevölkerungs-statistik mit besonderer Rücksicht auf Frankfurt a. M.', *Zeitschrift für die gesamte Staatswissenschaft*, 37 (1881), 573.

in Trier (1364), Berne (1389), Swäbisch-Hall (1406), and Basle (1429).[119] What is significant here is the corresponding wealth of material for the participation of women and servants within the urban economies of a number of these and other geographically related communities.[120] Seen within this broader north-west European context the patterns observed for urban Yorkshire appear to enjoy a wider cultural significance, namely that there exists a benign relationship between a north-western marriage regime and female economic opportunity. It is tempting to pursue this further. By the seventeenth century, in contrast to the fifteenth, women again appear conspicuous within the Florentine economy.[121] At the same time marriage ages for women appear to have moved upwards. In the period 1650–1700 mean age at marriage for women at Empoli reached 24 years and by 1746 in the rural hinterland of Prato it was 26 years.[122] It may thus be that a similar benign relationship was beginning to operate even within this traditionally 'Mediterranean' region. This also may prove a fruitful area for further research.[123] What is apparent, however, is that the understanding of past society cannot be furthered unless such considerations form part of the framework of analysis. It is no longer appropriate to assume that woman's 'natural' role was always in home, marriage, and family, just as it is inappropriate to presume that women played little part in the economic life of pre-industrial society.

This chapter has argued that cultural, economic, and demographic considerations may all have helped shape woman's role within the labour market and the economy, and her response to matrimony. It has further argued that within the cultural framework of a north-western marriage regime women were less constrained in their ability to respond to changes in the demand for

[119] Wiesner, *Working Women in Renaissance Germany*, 4–5.

[120] e.g. Jacobsen, 'Women's Work'; Wiesner, *Working Women in Renaissance Germany*; Wensky, 'Women's Guilds in Cologne'; Nicholas, *Domestic Life of a Medieval City*; Howell, *Women, Production and Patriarchy*. There is a much fuller literature in German and Dutch.

[121] Brown and Goodman, 'Women and Industry', 78–9.

[122] Smith, 'Some Reflections', 81–2; F. Benigno, 'The Southern Italian Family in the Early Modern Period', 174. A similar marked rise in the mean age of brides between 1650–99 has been noted at Riana, Parma: Hajnal, 'European Marriage Patterns in Perspective', 110–11.

[123] See the discussion in Benigno, 'The Southern Italian Family', 165–94.

labour than was true of, for example, a Mediterranean regime. In the later fourteenth and early fifteenth centuries in Yorkshire, to take the particular case most fully explored here, the demand for labour became sufficiently acute as to draw women into the labour force in strength. The implications of this feminine response to economic opportunity run counter to traditional expectation. Women did not enter into matrimony at the earliest opportunity despite the trend in wage levels. Nor did women play an essentially passive role in marriage formation; economic opportunity allowed them a degree of independence and thus of choice that was otherwise denied them. 'Traditional' female roles and responses thus appear to have been more a product of economic constraint than nature. The value system of a society where economic power is concentrated in male hands tends, however, to stress traditional roles as essentially feminine. These values are reinforced and become self-perpetuating when women are increasingly excluded from the labour market as in the late fifteenth or again during much of the nineteenth century. Two generations on from the Norwich worsted weavers' ordinance of 1511 the view that women were not strong enough to operate the looms may have gone unchallenged. The feminization of service, the more passive response of women to matrimony, itself probably associated with a reduction in mean age at marriage, the possible growth in prostitution, all helped shape and confirm male prejudices concerning the nature and status of women in society.

Appendix I

Probate Evidence

This study has made substantial use of some of the very considerable quantity of testamentary material preserved, usually as registered copies, from the later Middle Ages. Two major wills series survive for York, namely the registers of the peculiar jurisdiction of the Dean and Chapter, which survive in unbroken sequence from 1321, and the more substantial registers of the Exchequer and Prerogative Court dating from 1389. These last are not free from loss and a serious lacuna exists between 1409 and 1425. Comprehensive alphabetical listings for both these early probate series have been published by the Record Series of the Yorkshire Archaeological Society. These print both the date of making the will and the date of probate as recorded in the original registers and are thus invaluable when compiling biographical data.[1] The core of the will sample used here comprises the 2286 wills registered within these two series up to c.1500 relating to lay persons normally resident within a York parish. This encompasses a few individuals who died away from their normal place of residence, but may accidentally fail to eliminate a handful of male religious whose status was not specifically indicated in their wills and does not always exclude the small number of non-city residents whose parish church lay within the city. This last was especially true of the large suburban parish of St Olave in Bootham. To this sample were added the wills of a further 75 York women dating between 1500 and 1520 registered in the Exchequer Court registers. The registered wills of some 350 female testators within the county of Yorkshire as a whole were also read, as were a comparatively small number of other wills separately registered. These include wills proved within the peculiar jurisdiction of St Leonard's hospital and wills proved within the Consistory Court of York and recorded in the archbishops' registers.[2]

The only major series not included here comprises wills registered in the Prerogative Court of Canterbury. These concern usually very wealthy individuals whose property was located in more than one diocese or testamentary jurisdiction. The number of such individuals normally

---

[1] YML, D/C Reg. 1, 2; BIHR, Prob. Reg. 1–8; *Index of Wills, etc. from the Dean and Chapter's Court, 1321–1636* (Yorkshire Archaeological Society Record Ser. 38; 1907); *Index of Wills in the York Registry.*

[2] YML, M2/6e; BIHR, Reg. 5A, 10, 12, 14–16, 18–20, 23.

```
Fol. |   | N              | S C            | M F S M   R   W

p    f                    |      |  / /  |      / /   | E  F

S                                                     |

D                                                     |

Servt.                                                |

                                | P                | 70 |

SP                              | Cog              | 91 |

Fr.                             | Con              | 80 |

Bur Ch Cm  |  | EB WGW | T              | B        | 8- |
```

FIG. I.1.   Will Form

resident within York was probably very small. Some such wills are, however, published in *Testamenta Eboracensia*. Only limited use has been made here of this printed edition, which was published in the last century, since the material is highly selective and indifferently edited, although the volumes for the early years of the sixteenth century have been consulted for comparative purposes.[3] Outside York, the enrolled wills of the Norwich City Court, which relate exclusively to bequests of property, have been read, and Furnivall's edition of the fifty earliest wills in English and Wadley's abstract of wills from the Great Orphan Book of Bristol have likewise been consulted, as also has Weaver's edition of medieval Somerset wills from the Prerogative Court of Canterbury.[4]

To record data from the two main series of wills relating to over two thousand York residents a standard form was devised. This was used to record a range of information, some of it actually superfluous to the needs of this present study. Additional material unsuited to being recorded in so brief a manner was separately noted, but indication of this was given on the will form. It was originally intended to use these forms to compile a machine-readable data file, but in the event the data were analysed without the aid of a computer. The form is illustrated in Fig. I.1. The name (N) and status or occupation (S, where C = citizen) of the testator together with the testator's parish (p) and requested place of burial (Bur), either in the church (Ch) or cemetery (Cm), are all quite

[3] J. Raine (ed.), *Testamenta Eboracensia*, iv–v.
[4] NRO, NCR Case 1, shelf b, 14–19; F. J. Furnivall (ed.), *The Fifty Earliest English Wills*; Wadley, *Notes or Abstracts of the Wills*; Weaver (ed.), *Somerset Medieval Wills*.

regularly recorded. A few testators asked merely that they be buried 'ecclesiastically' (EB) or 'where God wills' (WGW) and the name of the parish is thus not always specified. This can, however, often be reconstructed from bequests to the fabric (f), for tithes 'forgotten', or bequests to the parish clergy, although again the parish need not always be named.

To identify parishes on the will form a parish code was adopted by which all parishes were represented by a two-digit number, the first digit (0–4) representing the district (e.g. 1 = Walmgate, 4 = extra-mural suburbs) and the second the actual parish (e.g. 01 = All Saints, North Street, 35 = St Saviour). Additional two-digit codes were devised to represent the conventual and friary churches (50–5, 05 = Holy Trinity, Micklegate, and 60 = St Clement's nunnery). The Minster church of St Peter was similarly identified (70) as were the various hospitals and more frequently recorded maisons-dieu (80–9, 80 = St Leonard's hospital, 8– = all other hospitals and maisons-dieu). Some types of pious bequest were also codified, including those to the poor, usually on the day of burial by way of a general distribution (91). Most wills were in Latin, but increasingly through the fifteenth century, and especially in the case of female testators, English (E) was used. The use of French (F) was very rare.

Increasing use seems to be made of wills by medievalists to a variety of ends. Moran has used Yorkshire wills to ask questions about education and the provision of schools during the pre-Reformation period, whereas Vale and Cullum employ the same source to approach the problem of piety and charity among Yorkshire gentry families and Yorkshire women respectively.[5] Wills were a major source in Swanson's important study of York craftsmen.[6] Elsewhere Gottfried has employed East Anglian probate evidence to analyse secular patterns of mortality and morbidity.[7] Only one study to date, that by Lorcin in respect of Lyonnais wills for the period *c*.1300–1500, has attempted a more comprehensive range of questions over a long time period. Lorcin's analysis helped to shape the will form just described and increased the present writer's awareness of the possibilities of will data at an early stage.[8] The wills analysed here

[5] J. H. Moran, *The Growth of English Schooling, 1340–1548: Learning, Literacy, and Laicization in Pre-Reformation York Diocese* (Princeton, NJ, 1985); M. G. A. Vale, *Piety, Charity and Literacy among the Yorkshire Gentry* (Borthwick Paper, 50; 1976); Cullum, 'And Hir Name was Charite'; Tanner, *The Church in Late Medieval Norwich*; Heath, 'Urban Piety in the Later Middle Ages'; Thomson, 'Piety and Charity in Late Medieval London'.

[6] Swanson, 'Craftsmen and Industry'; ead., *Medieval Artisans*.

[7] R. S. Gottfried, *Epidemic Disease in Fifteenth Century England* (Leicester, 1978).

[8] M.-T. Lorcin, *Vivre et mourir en Lyonnais à la fin du moyen âge* (Lyons, 1981).

were considered on several levels. Those made by female testators were of obvious interest. A handful related to unmarried women who, significantly, were identified by their occupation, e.g. sempster, silkwoman, but rather more provided evidence for women, especially widows, working since they included bequests of tools (T) or terms in apprenticeships.

Bequests to servants (Servt.) were a very regular feature of the will sample. Sometimes servants are not identified by name, possibly because the testator could not always assume that the servants in the household at the time of making the will would still be in service at the point of death. But most wills were probably made in anticipation of imminent demise and servants are often identified by their first name and sometimes by both Christian name and surname. From this data it was possible to analyse the sexual composition of servant groups as recorded and, in the case of female servants, to attempt to assemble a range of biographical material to further our understanding of service as an institution. Bequests to gilds and confraternities (Fr.) were regularly recorded so as to throw light on their sex-specific popularity. Bequests of books (B) were noted and patterns of female book-ownership were consequently observed. Charitable bequests (80, 8–, 91 etc.) were also noted in the hope that these could be related to economic movements and the changing welfare needs of various groups, and specifically of women.

One further use has been made here of the registered wills, namely to reconstruct the marital status of testators at the time of their making their wills, but in effect at death since this invariably followed the making of the will by less than a year.[9] This novel usage was designed to provide evidence of long-term secular trends in matrimony. The actual marital status of individual will-makers is, however, not always immediately apparent. In the case of female testators identification is uncomplicated where the testator is described in terms of her marital status, thus M the wife of N, or M formerly the wife of N. Unmarried women will bear the same surname as their fathers or brothers, although there is no difference in terminology between brothers and brothers-in-law. (All relatives specified in the will, together with persons of like surname not specified as relatives, were recorded on the will form. Parents were noted after 'P', blood relatives after 'Con', relatives by marriage after 'Cog'. Deceased individuals were represented in parenthesis.) A few unmarried women made bequests to their masters or mistresses, and it is this that suggests that they were servants and thus single. Married persons of both sexes

---

[9] Space was provided on the will form to record both the date of making a will and the date of probate, though in the event the printed index was found sufficient. From this it appeared that the probate date was generally a reasonable guide to the actual date of death since probate might follow the making of the will by only a few days: Goldberg, 'Mortality and Economic Change', 40.

invariably nominate their spouse (recorded on the will form after 'SP') to act as executor. The presence of children among the named beneficiaries (recorded after 'S' for sons and 'D' for daughters) can provide evidence of marriage or even remarriage, but this is again complicated by the common failure to distinguish children from children-in-law, and even children from step-children. In the case of widows and more especially widowers, deceased marriage partners are not necessarily noted, although where provision for memorial masses or prayers is made these are then regularly remembered. It follows that currently married testators are relatively easy to identify, but, in the absence of children, the widowed cannot always be distinguished with certainty from the never-married, and the remarried cannot always be identified as such. Where identification was made this was recorded on the will form as 'S' for single, 'M' for married, 'R' for remarried, 'W' for widowed, 'W×' for widowed after remarriage, and '?' for status uncertain.

Despite the rich possibilities of the source, will evidence suffers certain limitations, not least the class bias of the sample. Whether will-making was confined to the wealthier members of society or was more widespread, as the York sample might suggest, it was clearly only a minority who made and had registered their wills. The poor are not represented at all. It is of interest to note the comment recorded in the first surviving register of the York Exchequer Court against one John Whitteby, barber, that 'quia pauper non condidit testamentum'.[10] To argue from the basis of the will sample to society as a whole is, therefore, fraught with difficulty. The consistency with which certain types of information is recorded in wills also varies and an uncritical acceptance of will data is bound to lead to error. Thus children need not be recorded if otherwise provided for.[11] Servants, if noted, may not be fully represented and it is possible to argue that only older or longer serving servants would be likely to receive bequests and thus be recorded. Such arguments cannot be disproved, but they are not thought to detract seriously from the quality of the servant data generated. It may be noted, however, that servants do appear to be more liable to be remembered in the wills of female testators.[12] Many wills are in fact comparatively brief and uninformative, so much so that they raise questions as to the purpose of the will, and some male testators make no specific bequests, but merely name their wives as executors. Presumably they considered their widows fully competent to administer their estates in accordance with their wishes

---

[10] BIHR, Prob. Reg. 1, fo. 15ᵛ.
[11] This was especially true of married daughters.
[12] Lorcin, *Vivre et mourir*, 109.

without need of formal written directions. The wills of female testators, in contrast, frequently include a range of small bequests to kin, servants, and, very often, female neighbours and friends, a pattern of bequests that may suggest a slightly differing set of concerns on the part of women as against men.

Appendix II

The Poll Taxes of 1377, 1379, and 1380–1

Each of the three assessments for the poll tax differed and individual returns within each assessment vary. The nature of the return determines the quantity and the quality of the recorded data. Only a minority of the 1377 returns are nominative since the flat rate used rendered the recording of individuals by name superfluous, though these lists may have facilitated collection, especially in urban centres. Some nominative material survives for the towns of Hull, Carlisle, Colchester, and Dartmouth, and partial returns from Chichester, Coventry, Oxford, Northampton, Rochester, and York.[1] Returns also survive for a small number of rural areas, most notably Rutland and the Coquetdale ward of Northumberland. The returns for Coventry, Dartmouth, York, some Coquetdale vills, and Oakham in Rutland fail to record servants by name and consequently by sex. The 1379 returns identify individuals by rank for tax purposes and in many instances those designated to be artisans have their particular craft or trade recorded alongside their name. The Howdenshire returns are outstanding in this respect and even record separately the occupations of some married women. Since married couples were assessed together, some returns exclude married women. Occupations are most consistently recorded in the returns for 1380–1, though the nature of the assessment used means that these are often the least satisfactory returns. The listings for 1377, which may be seen to be the most comprehensive, provide some evidence for the demographic structure of the tax population. The sex ratio of the tax community (measured as the number of males per hundred females), the proportions married or single, the proportions of servants, of female-headed households, and of households containing servants can all be measured. From some returns, notably for Hull and York, some of these can be considered on a topographical basis since the individual streets and parishes that form the basis of the returns are specifically recorded.

A number of general measures have been calculated for the bulk of the more substantial surviving urban returns and, less comprehensively, for

---

[1] The Northampton fragment was identified from toponymic evidence and from the presence of one John Geddington, mayor at the time of the poll tax. He is listed alongside his wife and ten servants: PRO E 179/240/308/ [112]. Full references are given in the bibliography of primary source material.

the Rutland and Coquetdale assessments for 1377, for parts of the West Riding in 1379, and for Howdenshire at the same date. These are simple measures of the proportions of the tax population recorded as married, single, or in service and of the sex ratios associated with servants, non-servants and the population as a whole. Single persons are here defined as all unmarried persons not specifically described as servants. All persons described as servant, *garcio*, *famulus* or *famula*, *ancilla*, or apprentice have been counted as servants. Such few servants that appear to have been married are here counted under both the 'married' and 'in service' heads. The adult sex ratio (ASR) is defined as the sex ratio of all non-servants. The service sex ratio (SSR) is the sex ratio in respect of servants. The total sex ratio (TSR) is the ratio for the entire tax population. The populations from which these two sets of data are derived do not always coincide absolutely as defects in or damage to the returns mean that certain individuals cannot be fully identified. The Colchester returns, for example, include some 34 servants whose names are not stated. The results achieved are tabulated in Tables II.1 and II.2.

Analysis of Table II.1 demonstrates a remarkably high degree of uniformity in respect of the two earlier taxes. A more disparate pattern is demonstrated by the returns of 1381, though some, notably the remarkably detailed Southwark returns, show structural similarity with those for 1377. The picture is complicated by the differing age limits operating for each of the three subsidies. It would be expected therefore that the 1379 returns, based on the oldest tax population, would indicate the highest proportions married. The interpretation of data is further complicated by the question of migration. A high rate of teenage and adult in-migration would tend to inflate the proportion of young unmarried to the total population, and the exclusion of particular age groups from the tax population makes comparison between assessments still more uncertain. The data presented here are not sex-specific. Clearly the lower the sex ratio, the further below the mean for both sexes would be the actual female proportion married.

Sex ratios show a generally less uniform pattern, but Table II.2 indicates ASR in the region of 90 in towns, but nearer 100 in rural districts. The lack of uniformity displayed by SSR must in part be due to the small service populations observed in some instances, as at Wakefield. The very high SSR found in some towns in 1381 must, however, be due to a failure satisfactorily to record female servants. In most instances before 1381 TSR is rather less than 100 in towns, but slightly in excess of that in the countryside. This suggests that the adult populations of later medieval English towns were characterized by a preponderance of females, but that the reverse is true of the countryside. It also indicates that the underenumeration of females cannot in itself have been a serious fault of the earlier returns. Only the Oxford returns appear clearly to underenumerate female servants. A comparison of the surviving 1377 returns with the appropriate sections of the 1381 returns shows that male servants are substantially better recorded than female, although, even when allowance is made for the exclusion of the 14–15 age group from the later returns, servants as a whole are underenumerated.

The internal structure of the Lichfield returns also casts useful light on the possible limitations of the 1381 survey. The problem here is of simple

TABLE II.1. *Proportions (%) married, single, and in service derived from the poll tax returns of 1377, 1379, and 1380–1*

	Married	Single	In service	Tax population
1377				
Carlisle	58.4	25.1	17.1	661
Chichester†	63.7	15.6	20.7	331
Colchester	60.3	24.5	15.5	2912
Coventry				
Bailey Lane	38.4	6.0	54.7	437
Dartmouth	67.2	12.3	20.5	512
Hull	57.9	20.6	22.8	1557
Northampton†	59.2	10.6	30.2	672
Oxford				
St Mary the Virgin	61.7	13.9	24.4	295
St Peter in the East	55.4	16.9	27.7	177
Rochester†	59.4	23.4	17.2	128
York†	57.4	10.8	31.9	1934
Northumberland				
Coquetdale Ward	74.8	18.0	7.3	1027
Rutland (less Oakham)	65.5	24.1	10.0	3702
1379				
Canterbury†	65.8	13.4	21.2	471
Howden	64.9	12.8	22.4	407
Lynn*	67.4	12.4	20.2	1154
Pontefract	67.2	15.9	17.4	908
Ripon	64.7	19.7	15.6	482
Rotherham	66.9	21.9	11.8	356
Sheffield	66.8	27.5	5.7	527
Wakefield	72.2	12.5	15.3	313
West Riding				
Strafforth Wap.	65.3	30.2	4.5	3760

TABLE II.1 (*continued*)

	Married	Single	In service	Tax population
1381				
Beverley†	74.7	15.2	10.2	1259
Chichester	60.7	14.3	27.5	244
Lichfield†	76.2	12.8	12	625
Northampton	66.0	19.4	14.7	279
Oxford				
Central	61.8	9.4	28.9	1305
Collegiate	62.9	18.1	19.0	232
Suburban	68.0	17.8	14.2	444
Shrewsbury†	60.6	13.3	26.9	264
Southwark	59.8	22.6	17.6	1047
Worcester†	67.4	6.3	26.3	175
York*	68.2	15.5	16.6	3165

† Partial return only.
* Damaged return. Not all entries can be identified.

Sources: PRO, E 179 various (see bibliography of manuscript sources); 'Assessment Roll of the Poll-Tax for Howdenshire . . . 1379', *Yorkshire Archaeological Journal*, 9 (1886), 129–62; J. N. Bartlett (ed.), *The Lay Poll Tax Returns for the City of York in 1381* (Hull, 1953); W. Boyd (ed.), 'The Poll Tax of 1379–81 for the Hundreds of Offlow and Cuttlestone', *Collections for a History of Staffordshire*, 17 (1896), 155–205; J. L. and A. D. Kirby, 'The Poll-Tax of 1377 for Carlisle', *Transactions of the Cumberland and Westmorland Antiquarian and Archaeological Society*, NS 58 (1959), 110–17; M. Kowaleski, 'The 1377 Dartmouth Poll Tax', *Devon and Cornwall Notes and Queries*, 35 (1985); J. I. Leggett (ed.), 'The 1377 Poll Tax Returns for the City of York', *Yorkshire Archaeological Journal*, 43 (1971), 128–46; E. Lloyd (ed.), 'Poll Tax Returns for the East Riding 4 Ric. II', *Yorkshire Archaeological Journal*, 20 (1909), 318–52; D. M. Owen (ed.), *The Making of King's Lynn* (London, 1984), 221–34; 'Rolls of the Collectors in the West Riding of the Lay-subsidy (Poll Tax) 2 Richard II', *Yorkshire Archaeological Journal*, 5, pp. 1–51, 241–66, 417–32; 6, pp. 1–44, 129–71, 287–342; 7, pp. 6–31, 145–86 (1879–84); J. E. T. Rogers (ed.), *Oxford City Documents, 1268–1665* (Oxford Historical Society, 18; 1891), 8–53.

underenumeration of the unmarried. To the clearly suspect main assessment a separate supplementary assessment, now incomplete, was added. This lists mostly singletons and servants, a number of whom are identified with employers already recorded in the original assessment. In two instances men listed as single in the main return have wives included in the supplementary assessment. The additional persons are all assessed at rates below the shilling mean without any compensatory increase in the assessments of those persons already listed in the first assessment upon whom they were dependent. This must surely be a reflection of the difficulties encountered by the collectors of 1381 whilst attempting to balance the concept of a differential tax assessment against the requirement of a relatively high flat-rate mean.

The Beverley returns of 1381 help further elucidate this matter. As with Lichfield, the Beverley returns appear to understate the true numbers unmarried. For all but two of the Beverley wards servants are separately listed at the end of the return. For two wards, however,

TABLE II.2. *Sex ratios derived from the poll tax returns of 1377, 1379, and 1380–1*

	Adult sex ratio (ASR)	Service sex ratio (SSR)	Total sex ratio (TSR)
1377			
Carlisle	85.4	113.2	89.7
Colchester†	91.9	137.9	100
Coventry			
Bailey Lane*	106.4	—	—
Dartmouth*	87.6	—	—
Hull	86.1	119.1	92.7
Northampton*	93.4	—	—
Oxford			
St Mary the Virgin	100.9	89.5	98.0
St Peter in the East	85.5	145	98.9
Rochester†	—	—	(106.9)
York†*	90.5	—	—
Rutland (less Oakham)	98.9	161.9	103.5
1379			
Bath**	—	175	—
Canterbury†	112	120.5	113.7
Howden	91.3	65.5	84.7
Lynn***	93.4	91	92.9
Marlborough**	—	79.1	—
Pontefract	90.8	102.6	92.8
Ripon	108.2	67.4	100.8
Rotherham	93.8	100	94.5
Sheffield	92.2	200	96.3
Wakefield	100.8	433.3	122.0
West Riding			
Strafforth Wap.	96.5	104.8	99.2

TABLE II.2 (*continued*)

	Adult sex ratio (ASR)	Service sex ratio (SSR)	Total sex ratio (TSR)
1381			
Beverley†	99.1	54.2	93.4
Chichester†	101.1	109.4	103.3
Lichfield†	87.1	108.3	89.4
Northampton†	150.5	115.8	144.7
Oxford			
Central	97.0	185.6	116.4
Collegiate	138.0	173.3	140.6
Suburban	104.8	152	110.4
Shrewsbury†	85.6	69.1	80.8
Southwark	92.2	162.9	101.7
Worcester†	101.6	170.6	116.1
York***	106.1	79.6	101.3

† Partial return only.
* Returns do not name servants.
** Returns exclude married women.
*** Damaged return. Not all entries can be identified.

Sources: As Table II.1 above.

servants are recorded alongside their employers within their appropriate households. Servants seem as a consequence to be much more fully recorded for these wards, which thus display a different, but more plausible structure than is true of the town as a whole. It appears that in other wards sums were collected from the adult population until what was considered a sufficient, possibly predetermined total was achieved. Dependent servants were added subsequently, invariably at the minimum assessment of 4*d.* until the total tax population listed satisfied the sum of shillings collected. Only in the two wards noted was an attempt made to assess the bulk of the population actually liable to tax. It may be that these assessment devices led accidentally to an artificially low SSR as the mean for the two differently assessed wards is significantly higher than is true of Beverley as a whole. The omission of servants may thus be seen as a product of exclusion rather than evasion.

Exclusion of persons liable to tax may also be detected from the York returns for 1381. The number of taxpayers recorded in that year compares unfavourably with that recorded in 1377. Bartlett has argued that at this later date the individual parish assessments were modelled upon the subsidy of 1374.[2] An analysis of the actual sums paid by York taxpayers in 1381 helps explain the circumstances of this 'fraud'. Later medieval York was made up of over thirty parishes. Each of these parishes formed the basic taxation unit for both the poll taxes and the earlier lay subsidies. The effect, therefore, on individual taxpayers of a mean assessment of a shilling would and did vary considerably according to the wealth distribution and general prosperity of individual parishes. In poorer parishes more persons are assessed at the mean and fewer persons (notably servants) are subsidized at lower rates by wealthier parishioners paying tax at substantially higher rates. Poorer individuals do not necessarily appear in proportionately greater or lesser numbers in less prosperous parishes, they merely tend to pay the tax at comparatively higher or less subsidized rates than their counterparts in more affluent parishes. It is within this context that the logic of the assessors in basing the parochial assessments on the 1374 lay subsidy, more sensitive to economic realities and variation between parishes than the poll tax, becomes clear. In poor parishes the poor who paid tax may have done so at higher rates than the equivalent poor of prosperous parishes, but a smaller proportion of the population liable to tax actually paid. Indeed it appears that several impoverished north-eastern and south-eastern parishes not specifically recorded in the 1381 returns were actually excluded since the political and social implications of burdening poor taxpayers, who could not effectively be subsidized, outweighed the fiscal benefits.

A more detailed comparison of the recorded tax populations between 1377 and 1381 for the parishes of St Sampson and of St Martin, Coney Street, in York adds weight to these findings. It appears that for both parishes the 1381 survey tended to exclude households enjoying few or no servants in 1377, and to underestimate more generally the service element. In St Sampson's parish female-headed households were also particularly liable to be excluded and it seems that the wives of some married males were not enrolled in the later returns. More disturbingly, it appears that some individuals classed as children in 1381 may have been listed as servants in 1377. A more general comparison between the two sets of returns indicates a relatively high ASR and low SSR for the 1381 tax which may perhaps be explained by the classification of male journeymen and some apprentices not as servants, but as independent single males. Another striking feature of the analysis is the evidence for a high rate of population turnover even in the four years separating the two assessments. This pattern coincides with that observed from a variety of sources, particularly rentals.[3]

---

[2] Bartlett (ed.), *The Lay Poll Tax Returns for the City of York*, 7, 12.
[3] These points are discussed in more detail in Goldberg, 'Urban Identity and the Poll Taxes'.

On reflection it appears that the 1381 returns do indeed share some common flaws, but equally that they are not without real value. There is certainly a tendency to record preferentially wealthier households which tend to be characterized by the presence of servants. It may follow that female solitaries are consequently under-represented, but the suspicion that wives are not always recorded suggests a more conscious process of exclusion. There are also problems of definition and classification as regards children, servants, and other dependent household members. Simple analysis of the basic demographic measures adopted here highlights some of these problems. More detailed analysis of individual returns suggests that assessors and collectors of the tax in 1381 sacrificed comprehensiveness for a more workable mode of assessment. The problem is ultimately not so much one of evasion, but one of exclusion. This point is especially clearly demonstrated by the Lichfield evidence. The recorded population is thus biased towards more substantial, married, servant-keeping households, but this bias is not absolute. The level of underenumeration at York, by comparison with the 1377 total, is, furthermore, rather greater than is true of Oxford or the majority of other towns for which returns of the third poll tax survive. In conclusion, it would appear that the 1381 urban poll tax returns are not as flawed as may have been thought, and that these flaws can be allowed for since their nature is not unknown. This present analysis would likewise tend to vindicate the earlier returns, which seem free from the sort of problems of evasion by servants and single females that has been noticed of the final poll tax and assumed to apply generally.[4]

[4] See Ch. 7 above.

Appendix III

List of Cause Papers Consulted

The cause papers, so named by Canon Purvis who first indexed them, are housed in the Borthwick Institute of Historical Research, York, and are arranged by file, each file consisting of one or more pieces of parchment or paper. Sometimes these are only indifferently preserved. Nearly six hundred files exist for the fourteenth and fifteenth centuries. They are classed by century, that is E = fourteenth, F = fifteenth, and G = sixteenth century. The files are also numbered, but these numbers do not follow a strict chronological order. Sometimes more than one file refers to the same action. This is especially true of multi-party cases. The files used within this study are tabulated below. The cause papers used have been divided according to whether the action relates principally to an urban or a rural location and the place of residence of the parties and witnesses have been specifically indicated where these are larger towns by the abbreviations listed below. The date of the litigation has also been included after the call number for reference purposes, though this is not an integral part of the call number. Files for which no depositions survive were in general discarded, but occasionally they contained valuable material despite the loss of the actual depositions. Such instances are indicated by a dagger (†).

Bv	Beverley	R	Ripon
D	Doncaster	Sc	Scarborough
K/H	Kingston upon Hull	W	Wakefield
N/T	Newcastle upon Tyne	Wh	Whitby
P	Pontefract	Y	York

URBAN CAUSES

Matrimonial Causes

CP.E.1	(1303) Wh	CP.E.121	(1372) Y	CP.E.159	(1394) Y
CP.E.36	(1338) Y	CP.E.124	(1381) W	CP.E.175	(1390) Y
CP.E.82	(1355) Y	CP.E.126	(1382) Y	CP.E.188	(1391) D
CP.E.102	(1367) Bv	CP.E.138	(1386) Y	CP.E.198	(1394) Y
CP.E.106	(1370) Y	CP.E.150	(1389) Y	CP.E.216	(1395) Y
CP.E.111	(1372) Y	CP.E.157	(1392) Y	CP.E.221	(1396) Y

CP.E.238	(1398) Y	CP.F.101	(1431) Y	CP.F.236	(1448) Y
CP.E.239	(1398) Y	CP.F.103	(1433) Y	CP.F.237	(1449) Y
CP.E.242	(1396) Y	CP.F.104	(1432) Y	CP.F.244	(1467) Y
CP.E.245	(1391) Y	CP.F.108	(1432) Y	CP.F.261	(1486) Y
CP.E.248	(1346) F	CP.F.111	(1432) Y	CP.F.263	(1443) Y
CP.E.257	(1349) N/T	CP.F.113	(1434) Sc, K/H	CP.F.265	(1484) W
CP.F.22	(1402) Y	CP.F.115	(1435) Y	CP.F.269	(1486) Y, K/H
CP.F.33	(1407) Y, P	CP.F.127	(1417) Y	CP.F.336	(1465) Y
CP.F.36	(1410) Y	CP.F.129	(1421) Y	CP.G.8	(1503) Y
CP.F.40	(1410) Y	CP.F.152	(1424) Y	CP.G.32	(1508) Y
CP.F.46	(1422) K/H	CP.F.155	(1425) Y	[CP.G.35]	(1409) Y
CP.F.56	(1410) Y	CP.F.181	(1439) Y	CP.G.40	(1509) YW
CP.F.62	(1411) Y	CP.F.182	(1439) Wh	CP.G.53	(1510) Y
CP.F.63	(1414) Y	CP.F.184	(1449) Y	CP.G.89	(1519) Y
CP.F.64	(1412) Y	CP.F.185	(1450) Y	CP.G.115	(1517) Y
CP.F.65	(1413) Y	CP.F.204	(1464) Y		
CP.F.75	(1418) Y	CP.F.208	(1465) Y	D/C 1417/2	(1418) Y
CP.F.81	(1418) P	CP.F.223	(1442) P		
CP.F.99	(1430) Y	CP.F.235	(1446) Y		

Defamation Causes		*Causa violacionis fidei*		Testamentary Causes	
CP.E.122	(1380) Y	CP.E.217	(1395) Y	CP.E.174	(1390) Y
CP.E.241m†	(1402) Y	CP.E.241p†	(1363) Y	CP.E.193	(1392) W
CP.F.61	(1411) Y	CP.F.23	(1402) Sc		
CP.F.83	(1417) Sc	CP.F.58†	(1410) Y		
CP.F.116	(1436) Y	CP.F.114	(1434) Y		
CP.F. 153	(1422) Y	CP.F.174	(1430) Y		
CP.F.335	(1465) Y				

RURAL CAUSES

Matrimonial Causes

CP.E.18	(1328)	CP.E.181	(1390)	CP.F.137	(1423)
CP.E.23	(1333)	CP.E.186	(1392)	CP.F.158	(1425) Y
CP.E.25	(1333)	CP.E.202	(1394)	CP.F.159	(1425) Y
CP.E.26	(1333)	CP.E.210	(1394)	CP.F.168	(1428) Y
CP.F.28	(1335)	CP.E.211	(1394)	CP.F.169	(1428)
CP.E.33	(1337)	CP.E.212	(1395)	CP.F.175	(1432)
CP.E.37	(1337)	CP.E.213	(1395)	CP.F.176	(1423)
CP.E.40	(1341)	CP.E.215	(1394)	CP.F.177	(1433)
CP.E.70	(1355)	CP.E.235	(1397)	CP.F.178	(1434)
CP.E.71	(1351)	CP.E.236	(1398)	CP.F.179	(1436)
CP.E.76	(1357)	CP.E.241b	(1306)	CP.F.186	(1450)

CP.E.77	(1360)	CP.E.255	(1384) Sc	CP.F.187	(1451)
CP.E.79	(1358)	CP.E.259	(1368)	CP.F.189	(1453)
CP.E.84	(1361)	CP.F.3	(1401) Y	CP.F.191	(1453)
CP.E.85	(1362)	CP.F.15	(1406)	CP.F.194	(1455)
CP.E.87	(1364)	CP.F.28	(1407)	CP.F.200	(1431)
CP.E.89	(1366) Y	CP.F.41	(1411)	CP.F.201	(1430)
CP.E.92	(1366)	CP.F.42	(1411)	CP.F.202	(1462)
CP.E.103	(1369)	CP.F.49	(1433)	CP.F.209	(1465)
CP.E.105	(1370)	CP.F.59	(1410)	CP.F.224	(1441)
CP.E.113	(1373)	CP.F.79	(1418) Y	CP.F.240	(1466)
CP.E.114	(1373) Bv	CP.F.85	(1418)	CP.F.241	(1447) Bv
CP.E.135	(1387)	CP.F.86	(1434)	CP.F.242	(1466)
CP.E.153	(1389)	CP.F.119	(1436)	CP.F.246	(1450)
CP.E.155	(1374) Y	CP.F.120	(1437)	CP.F.247	(1449)
CP.E.179	(1390)	CP.F.133	(1422)	CP.F.252	(1472)
CP.F.253	(1472)	CP.F.284	(1494)	CP.G.30	(1509)
CP.F.256b	(1474)	CP.F.292	(1499)	CP.G.30a	(1509)
CP.F.257	(1477) Y	CP.F.295	(1499)	CP.G.55	(1411)
CP.F.262	(1442) Y	CP.F.300	(1487) R	CP.G.112	(1516)
CP.F.268†	(1484)	CP.F.303	(1491)	CP.G.119	(1519)
CP.F.273	(1489)	CP.F.308	(1499)		
CP.F.279	(1491) P	CP.F.303	(n.d.) K/H	D/C 1417/1	(1416)
CP.F.280	(1491)	CP.G.26	(1507)	D/C 1477/1	(1477)

Defamation Causes

CP.E.72	(1356)
CP.E.171	(1364)
CP.E.181	(1364)
CP.E.227	(1396)
CP.F.124	(1439)
CP.F.256a	(1474)
D/C 1503/1	(1503)

Testamentary Causes

CP.F.87	(n.d.)
CP.F.259	(1479)

Bibliography

Manuscript Sources

Borthwick Institute of Historical Research, St Anthony's Hall, York
  Act books, York Consistory Court: Cons. AB. 1–5
  Act book, Dean and Chapter Court: D/C AB. 1
  Cause papers, York Consistory Court: CP. E, F, G various
  Cause papers, Dean and Chapter: D/C CP. various
  Consistory wills (contained in archiepiscopal registers): Reg. 5A, 10,
    12, 14–16, 18–20, 23
  Parish gild records, St Margaret's, Walmgate: PR Y/Marg. 35, 36
  Probate registers, Exchequer Court: Prob. Reg. 1–9
Lichfield Joint Record Office, Lichfield
  Records of St Leonard's Hospital: QQ 2, 7, 10
  (photographic reproduction held by York City Archives, Acc. 162)
Norfolk Record Office, Norwich city records (classed as NCR)
  Assembly rolls: Case 8, shelf d
  Assessment rolls: Trowse, 1512–13; Coslany, c.1515: Case 7, shelf i
  City court wills (contained in court rolls): Case 1, shelf b, 14–19
  Domesday Book: Case 17, shelf a
  Leet rolls: Case 5, shelf b, 3, 5–8, 17–19
  Market stalls' rent rolls: Case 7, shelf h
  Mayor's court books, 1425–1510, 1510–32: Case 16, shelf a, 1, 2
  Old Free Book: Case 17, shelf c, 1
  Pleas etc. in bailiff's court: Case 8, shelf a
  Quarter sessions' minute book, 1511–41: Case 20, shelf a
  Treasurers' and chamberlains' accounts: Case 18, shelf a
Public Record Office, London
  Court roll, Beverley 2 Edw. II: SC 2/211/11
  Gild returns, 1389: C 47/42, 45, 46 various
  Poll tax returns
  1377:   Carlisle   E 179/158/28
            Chichester   E 179/180/30
            Colchester   E 179/107/54
            Coventry   E 179/240/308 [142]
            Dartmouth   E 179/95/35
            Hull   E 179/206/45
            Northampton   E 179/240/308 [112]
            Northumberland (Coquetdale)   E 179/158/29
            Oxford   E 179/161/36, 37

	Rochester	E 179/123/44
	Rutland	E 179/269/21, 22, 51
	York	E 179/217/13
	Yorkshire, East Riding	E 179/202/58, 59
1379:	Bath	E 179/169/38
	Canterbury	E 179/123/45, 47
	Lynn	E 179/240/308 [156]
	Marlborough	E 179/196/44
1380–1:	Beverley	E 179/202/71
	Chichester	E 179/189/45
	Lichfield	E 179/242/39
		E 179/177/22
	Northampton	E 179/155/41
	Shrewsbury	E 179/166/27
	Southwark	E 179/240/307
	Worcester	E 179/200/27; 146/6

York City Archives, York
  Chamberlains' account books, 1446–50, 1449–54: CC 1, 1A
  Chamberlains' account rolls, 1501–2, 1506–7, 1508–9: C 5: 1–3
  Ouse Bridge rentals: C 82–6 various
  Register of freemen: D 1
  Sheriff's court books, 1478–9, 1497–8: E 25, 25A
  Wardmote court, 1491: CC 1A, fos. 136–9
  Will of Helwise de Wyxstowe, 1320: G 28
York Minster Library, York
  Act book, Dean and Chapter: M2/1f
  Court books, Consistory Court, 1371–5, 1426–7: M2/1c, e
  Court of audience, Spirituality of Bishophill, 1410–29: H2/1, fos. 4–14
  Court leet and sheriff's tourn, Liberty of St Peter, 1445–6: F 1/3/1
  Inventories, Dean and Chapter Court: L 1/17; L 2/5a
  Probate registers, Dean and Chapter Court: D/C Reg. 1–2
  St Leonard's Hospital, accounts, 1343–86, 1409, 1461–2: M2/6b–d
  St Leonard's Hospital, register of wills: M2/6e
  Vicars Choral, Rentals and chamberlains' accounts, *c*.1309–1518: VC 4/1/1–16; VC 6/2/1–78

Printed Primary Sources

Adams, N. and Donahue, J. (eds.), *Select Cases from the Ecclesiastical Courts of the Province of Canterbury* (Selden Society, 95; 1981).

Anderson, R. C. (ed.), *The Assize of Bread Book, 1437–1517* (Southampton Record Society, 23; 1923).

Arnold, M. S. (ed.), *Select Cases of Trespass from the King's Courts, 1307–1399*, i (Selden Society, 100; 1985).

'Assessment Roll of the Poll-Tax for Howdenshire . . . 1379', *Yorkshire Archaeological Journal*, 9 (1886), 129–62.

Baildon, W. P. (ed.), *Court Rolls of the Manor of Wakefield*, i. *1274–97* (Yorkshire Archaeological Society Record Ser. 29; 1901).

'Ballad of a Tyrannical Husband', in T. Wright and J. O. Halliwell (eds.), *Reliquae Antiquae* (London, 1843), ii. 196–9.

Bartlett, J. N. (ed.), *The Lay Poll Tax Returns for the City of York in 1381* (Hull, 1953).

Bateson, M. (ed.), *Records of the Borough of Leicester*, ii. *1327–1509* (London, 1901).

Benham, W. G. (ed.), *Court Rolls of the Borough of Colchester*, i. *(1310–1352)*, trans. I. H. Jeayes (Colchester, 1921).

Bennett, J. H. E. (ed.), *The Rolls of the Freemen of the City of Chester*, i. *1392–1700* (Lancashire and Cheshire Record Ser. 51; 1906).

Bickley, F. B. (ed.), *The Little Red Book of Bristol* (2 vols.; Bristol, 1900).

Bird, W. H. B. (ed.), *The Black Book of Winchester* (Winchester, 1925).

The Booke of Common Prayer (London, 1549).

Boyd, W. (ed.), 'The Poll Tax of 1379–81 for the Hundreds of Offlow and Cuttlestone', *Collections for a History of Staffordshire*, 17 (1896), 155–205.

A Calendar of the Freemen of Lynn, 1292–1836 (Norfolk and Norwich Archaeological Society, 1913).

Calendar of Miscellaneous Inquisitions, vi (London, 1963).

Cawley, A. C. (ed.), *Everyman and Medieval Miracle Plays* (London, 1956).

—— (ed.), *The Wakefield Pageants in the Townley Cycle* (Manchester, 1958).

Childs, W. R. (ed.), *The Customs Accounts of Hull, 1453–1490* (Yorkshire Archaeological Society Record Ser. 144; 1986).

Clark, A. (ed.), *Lincoln Diocese Documents, 1450–1544* (Early English Text Society, 149; 1914).

Collins, F. (ed.), *Register of the Freemen of the City of York*, i. *1272–1588* (Surtees Society, 96; 1896).

Cowper, J. M. (ed.), *Accounts of the Churchwardens of St Dunstan's, Canterbury, 1484–1580* (London, 1885).

—— (ed.), *The Roll of the Freemen of the City of Canterbury, 1392–1800* (Canterbury, 1903).

Cowper, J. M. (ed.), *Intrantes: A List of Persons Admitted to Live and Trade in Canterbury, 1392–1592* (Canterbury, 1904).

Craig, W. G., 'James Ryther of Harewood and His Letters to William Cecil, Lord Burghley', *Yorkshire Archaeological Journal*, 56 (1984), 95–118.

Davies, R. T. (ed.), *Medieval English Lyrics* (London, 1963).

Dobson, R. B. (ed.), *The York Chamberlains' Account Rolls, 1396–1500* (Surtees Society, 192; 1980).

Dolezalek, G., *Das Imbreviaturbuch des erzbischöflichen Geschichtsnotar Hubaldus aus Pisa, Mai bis August 1230* (Forschungen zur neueren Privatrechtsgeschichte, 13; Cologne, 1969).

Fletcher, W. G. D., 'The Poll Tax for the Town and Liberties of Shrewsbury, 1380', *Transactions of the Shropshire Archaeological and Natural History Society*, 2nd ser. 2 (1890), 17–28.

Furnivall, F. J. (ed.), *The Fifty Earliest English Wills* (Early English Text Society, 78; 1882).

Happé, P. (ed.), *The English Mystery Plays* (Harmondsworth, 1975).

Harris, M. D. (ed.), *The Coventry Leet Book* (Early English Text Society, 134–5, 138, 146; 1907–13).

Hartopp, H. (ed.), *Register of the Freemen of Leicester, 1196–1770* (Leicester, 1927).

Hopkins, A. (ed.), *Selected Rolls of the Chester City Courts* (Chetham Society, 3rd ser. 2; 1950).

'How the Good Wijf tauȝte Hir Dauȝtir', in F. J. Furnivall (ed.), *The Babees Book* (Early English Text Society, 32; 1868), 36–47.

Hudson, W. (ed.), *Leet Jurisdiction in the City of Norwich During the Thirteenth and Fourteenth Century* (Selden Society, 5; 1892).

—— and Tingey, J. C. (eds.), *The Records of the City of Norwich* (2 vols.; Norwich, 1906–10).

Jewell, H. M. (ed.), *The Court Rolls of the Manor of Wakefield, 1348–50* (Yorkshire Archaeological Society, Wakefield Court Rolls Ser. 2; 1981).

Johnston, C. (ed.), *Registrum Hamonis Hethe* (2 vols.; Canterbury and York Society, 48–9; 1914–48).

Kimball, E. G. (ed.), *Oxfordshire Sessions of the Peace in the Reign of Richard II* (Oxfordshire Record Society, 53; 1983).

Kirby, J. L. and Kirby, A. D., 'The Poll-Tax of 1377 for Carlisle', *Transactions of the Cumberland and Westmorland Antiquarian and Archaeological Society*, NS 58 (1959), 110–17.

Kowaleski, M., 'The 1377 Dartmouth Poll Tax', *Devon and Cornwall Notes and Queries*, 35 (1985), 286–95.

Leach, A. F., 'The Building of Beverley Bar', *Transactions of the East Riding Antiquarian Society*, 4 (1896), 26–37.

—— (ed.), *Beverley Town Documents* (Selden Society, 14; 1900).

Leggett, J. I. (ed.), 'The 1377 Poll Tax Returns for the City of York', *Yorkshire Archaeological Journal*, 43 (1971), 128–46.

Lister, J. (ed.), *The Early Yorkshire Woollen Trade* (Yorkshire Archaeological Society Record Ser. 64; 1928).

Lloyd, E. (ed.), 'Poll Tax Returns for the East Riding 4 Ric. II', *Yorkshire Archaeological Journal*, 20 (1909), 318–52.

Manuale et Processionale ad Usum Insignis Ecclesiae Eboracensis (Surtees Society, 63; 1875).

Meech, S. B. and Allen, H. E. (eds.), *The Book of Margery Kempe* (Early English Text Society, 212; 1940).

Oschinsky, D. (ed.), *Walter of Henley and other Treatises on Estate Management* (Oxford, 1971).

Owen, D. M. (ed.), *The Making of King's Lynn* (Records of Social and Economic History, ns 9; London, 1984).

Percy, J. W. (ed.), *York Memorandum Book*, iii (Surtees Society, 186; 1973).

Pisan, C. de, *The Treasure of the City of Ladies*, trans. S. Lawson (Harmondsworth, 1985).

Post, J. B., 'A Fifteenth-Century Customary of the Southwark Stews', *Journal of the Society of Archivists*, 5 (1977), 418–28.

Power, E. E., trans., *The Goodman of Paris* (London, 1928).

Prestwich, M. (ed.), *York Civic Ordinances, 1301* (Borthwick Paper, 49; 1976).

Putnam, B. H. (ed.), *Yorkshire Sessions of the Peace, 1361–4* (Yorkshire Archaeological Society Record Ser. 100; 1939).

Raine, J., *Depositions and other Ecclesiastical Proceedings from the Courts of Durham* (Surtees Society, 21; 1845).

—— (ed.), *Testamenta Eboracensia*, iv–v (Surtees Society, 53 and 79; 1869–84).

Riley, H. T. (ed.), *Memorials of London and London Life in the XIIIth, XIVth and XVth Centuries* (London, 1868).

Robinson, C. B. (ed.), *Rural Economy in Yorkshire in 1641, being the Farming and Account Books of Henry Best* (Surtees Society, 33; 1857).

Rogers, J. E. T. (ed.), *Oxford City Documents, 1268–1665* (Oxford Historical Society, 18; 1891).

'Rolls of the Collectors in the West Riding of the Lay-Subsidy (Poll Tax) 2 Richard II', *Yorkshire Archaeological Journal*, 5, pp. 1–51, 241–66, 417–32; 6, pp. 1–44, 129–71, 287–342; 7, pp. 6–31, 145–86 (1879–84).

Rotuli Parliamentorum (6 vols.; London, 1783).

Rowe, M. M. and Jackson, A. M. (eds.), *Exeter Freemen, 1266–1972* (Devon and Cornwall Record Society, extra ser. 1; 1973).

Royal Commission on Historical Manuscripts, Third Report (London, 1872).

Royal Commission on Historical Manuscripts, Fifth Report (London, 1876).

Royal Commission on Historical Manuscripts, Sixth Report (London, 1877).

Royal Commission on Historical Manuscripts, Ninth Report (London, 1883).

Royal Commission on Historical Manuscripts, Thirteenth Report (London, 1892).

Salter, H. E. (ed.), *Munimenta Civitatis Oxonie* (Oxford Historical Society, 71; 1920).

—— (ed.), *Medieval Archives of the University of Oxford* (Oxford Historical Society, 73; 1921).

Sellers, M. (ed.), *York Memorandum Book* (2 vols.; Surtees Society, 120, 125; 1912–15).

—— (ed.), *The York Mercers and Merchant Adventurers, 1356–1917* (Surtees Society, 129; 1918).

Sharpe, R. R. (ed.), *Calendar of Letter-Books . . . of the City of London* (11 vols.; London, 1899–1912).

—— (ed.), *Calendar of Coroners Rolls of the City of London, 1300–1378* (London, 1913).

Shilton, D. O. and Holworthy, R. (eds.), *Wells City Charters* (Somerset Record Society, 46; 1932).

Simpson, W. S. (ed.), *Visitations of Churches Belonging to St Paul's Cathedral* (Camden Society, NS 55; 1985).

Skaife, R. H. (ed.), *The Register of the Guild of Corpus Christi in the City of York* (Surtees Society, 57; 1872).

W. W. Skeat (ed.), *The Vision of William Concerning Piers the Plowman* (Early English Text Society, 38; 1869).

Skelton, John, *The Complete English Poems*, ed. J. Scattergood (Harmondsworth, 1983).

Smith, J. T. (ed.), *English Gilds: Original Ordinances of the Fourteenth and Fifteenth Centuries* (Early English Text Society, 40; 1870).

Sneyd, C. A. (ed.), *A Relation . . . of the Island of England . . . About the Year 1500* (Camden Society, 37; 1847).

Stevenson, W. H. (ed.), *Records of the Borough of Nottingham* (3 vols.; Nottingham, 1882–5).

Stone, E. D. and Cozens-Hardy, B., *Norwich Consistory Depositions, 1499–1512 and 1518–30* (Norfolk Record Society, 10; 1938).

Thomas, A. H. and Jones, P. E. (eds.), *Calendar of Plea and Memoranda Rolls of the City of London* (6 vols.; Cambridge, 1926–61).

Thurber, E. C. (ed.), *Essex Sessions of the Peace 1351, 1377–1379* (Essex Archaeological Society Occasional Publications, 3; 1953).

Tillotson, J. H. (ed.), *Monastery and Society in the Late Middle Ages: Selected Account Rolls from Selby Abbey, Yorkshire, 1398–1537* (Woodbridge, 1988).

Wadley, T. P., *Notes or Abstracts of the Wills Contained in the Volume Entitled the Great Orphan Book and Book of Wills* (Bristol and Gloucester Archaeological Society, 1886).

Weaver, F. W. (ed.), *Somerset Medieval Wills* (3 vols.; Somerset Record Society, 16, 19, 21; 1901–5).

Wilson, A. R. (ed.), *The Register or Act Books of the Bishops of Coventry and Lichfield*, v (Collections for a History of Staffordshire, NS 5; 1905).

Secondary Works

Abram, A., 'Women Traders in Medieval London', *Economic Journal*, 26 (1916), 276–85.

Adams, A., *The History of the Worshipful Company of Blacksmiths* (London, 1951).

Allison, K. J. (ed.), *VCH, York, East Riding*, i. *City of Kingston-upon-Hull* (Oxford, 1969).

Anderson, M. D., *Drama and Imagery in English Medieval Churches* (Cambridge, 1963).

Armstrong, P., 'Grimsby Lane Excavations 1972', *Kingston upon Hull Museums Bulletin*, 10 (1973), special issue.

Baker, D. (ed.), *Medieval Women* (Studies in Church History, Subsidia i; Oxford, 1978).

Baldwin, J. W., *Master, Princes and Merchants* (2 vols.; Princeton, NJ, 1970).

Barron, C. M., 'The "Golden Age" of Women in Medieval London', *Reading Medieval Studies*, 15 (1990), 35–58.

Bartlett, J. N., 'The Expansion and Decline of York in the Later Middle Ages', *Economic History Review*, 2nd ser. 12 (1959), 17–33.

Bell, F., *At The Works* (London, 1907).

Benigno, F., 'The Southern Italian Family in the Early Modern Period: A Discussion of Co-residence Patterns', *Continuity and Change*, 4 (1989), 165–94.

Bennett, J. M., 'Medieval Peasant Marriage: An Examination of Marriage License Fines in the *Liber Gersumarum*', in J. A. Raftis (ed.), *Pathways to Medieval Peasants* (Toronto, 1981), 193–246.

—— 'Spouses, Siblings and Surnames: Reconstructing Families from

Medieval Village Court Rolls', *Journal of British Studies*, 23 (1983), 26–46.

Bennett, J. M., 'The Tie that Binds: Peasant Marriages and Families in Late Medieval England', *Journal of Interdisciplinary History*, 15 (1984), 111–29.

—— *Women in the Medieval Countryside: Gender and Household in Brigstock before the Plague* (New York, 1987).

Beresford, M. W., *The Lost Villages of England* (Lutterworth, 1954).

—— *Lay Subsidies and Poll Taxes* (Canterbury, 1963).

—— and Finberg, H. P. R., *English Medieval Boroughs: A Handlist* (Newton Abbot, 1973).

Beveridge, W., 'Westminster Wages in the Manorial Era', *Economic History Review*, 2nd ser. 8 (1955), 30–5.

Biller, P. P. A., 'Birth-Control in the West in the Thirteenth and Early Fourteenth Centuries', *Past and Present*, 94 (1982), 3–26.

Blanchard, I., 'Reviews', *Economic History Review*, 2nd ser. 37 (1984), 118.

—— 'Industrial Employment and the Rural Land Market, 1380–1520', in R. M. Smith (ed.), *Land, Kinship and Life-Cycle* (Cambridge, 1984), 227–75.

Bossy, J., *Christianity in the West* (Oxford, 1985).

Bridbury, A. R., *Economic Growth: England in the Later Middle Ages* (London, 1962).

—— 'English Provincial Towns in the Later Middle Ages', *Economic History Review*, 2nd ser. 39 (1981), 1–24.

—— *Medieval English Clothmaking* (London, 1982).

Britnell, R. H., *Growth and Decline in Colchester, 1300–1525* (Cambridge, 1986).

Brodsky (Elliot), V., 'Single Women in the London Marriage Market: Age, Status and Mobility, 1598–1619', in R. B. Outhwaite (ed.), *Marriage and Society: Studies in the Social History of Marriage* (London, 1981), 81–100.

—— 'Widows in Late Elizabethan London: Remarriage, Economic Opportunity and Family Orientations', in L. Bonfield, R. M. Smith, and K. Wrightson (eds.), *The World We Have Gained: Histories of Population and Social Structure* (Oxford, 1986), 122–54.

Brooke, C. N. L., *The Medieval Idea of Marriage* (Oxford, 1989).

Brown, J. C., 'A Woman's Place Was in the Home: Women's Work in Renaissance Tuscany', in M. W. Ferguson, M. Quilligan, and N. J. Vickers (eds.), *Rewriting the Renaissance* (Chicago, 1986), 206–24.

—— and Goodman, J., 'Women and Industry in Florence', *Journal of Economic History*, 40 (1980), 73–80.

Brundage, J. A., 'The Problem of Impotence', in V. L. Bullough and

J. A. Brundage, *Sexual Practices and the Medieval Church* (Buffalo, 1982), 135–40.

—— *Law, Sex, and Christian Society in Medieval Europe* (Chicago, 1987).

Bücher, K., 'Zur mittelalterlichen Bevölkerungs-statistik mit besonderer Rücksicht auf Frankfurt a. M.', *Zeitschrift für die gesamte Staatswissenschaft*, 37 (1881), 535–80.

Bunt, C. G. E., *Chaffer's Handbook to Hallmarks on Gold and Silver Plate* (London, 1961).

Burton, J., 'St Mary's Abbey and the City of York', *Annual Report for the Year 1988* (Yorkshire Philosophical Society, 1989), 62–72.

Butcher, A. F., 'The Origins of Romney Freemen, 1433–1523', *Economic History Review*, 2nd ser. 27 (1974), 16–27.

—— 'Rent, Population and Economic Change in Late-Medieval Newcastle', *Northern History*, 14 (1978), 67–77.

Campbell, B. M. S., 'Population Pressure, Inheritance and the Land Market in a Fourteenth-Century Peasant Community', in R. M. Smith (ed.), *Land, Kinship and Life-Cycle* (Cambridge, 1984), 87–134.

Carus-Wilson, E. M., 'The Aulnage Accounts: A Criticism', *Economic History Review*, 2 (1929), 114–23.

—— 'The English Cloth Industry in the Late Twelfth and Early Thirteenth Centuries', *Economic History Review*, 14 (1944), 32–50.

—— 'The Medieval Trade of the Ports of the Wash', *Medieval Archaeology*, 6–7 (1962–3), 182–201.

—— *The Expansion of Exeter at the Close of the Middle Ages* (Exeter, 1963).

—— and Coleman, O., *England's Export Trade, 1275–1547* (Oxford, 1963).

Clark, A., *Working Life of Women in the Seventeenth Century* (2nd edn., London, 1982).

Clark, E., 'The Decision to Marry in Thirteenth- and Early Fourteenth-Century Norfolk', *Medieval Studies*, 49 (1987), 496–516.

Clark, P., 'Migrants in the City: The Process of Social Adaptation in English Towns 1500–1800', in id. and D. Souden (eds.), *Migration and Society in Early Modern England* (London, 1987), 267–91.

—— and Clark, J., 'The Social Economy of the Canterbury Suburbs: The Evidence of the Census of 1563', in A. Detsicas and N. Yates (eds.), *Studies in Modern Kentish History* (Kent Archaeological Society, 1983), 65–86.

—— and Souden, D., 'Introduction', in eid. (eds.), *Migration and Society in Early Modern England* (London, 1987), 11–48.

Clayton, M., *Catalogue of Rubbings of Brasses and Incised Slabs* (London, 1929).

Coleman, O., 'Trade and Prosperity in the Fifteenth Century: Some Aspects of the Trade of Southampton', *Economic History Review*, 2nd ser. 16 (1963), 9–22.

Cosgrove, A., 'Marriage in Medieval Ireland', in id. (ed.), *Marriage in Ireland* (Dublin, 1985), 25–50.

Coulton, G. G., *Medieval Panorama* (Cambridge, 1938).

Crossley, A. (ed.), *VCH, Oxfordshire*, iv. *City of Oxford* (Oxford, 1979).

Cullum, P. H., '"And Hir Name was Charite": Charity by and for Women in Late Medieval Yorkshire', in P. J. P. Goldberg (ed.), *Woman is a Worthy Wight: Women in English Society, c.1200–1500* (Stroud, 1992), 182–211.

Dale, M. K., 'The London Silkwomen of the Fifteenth Century', *Economic History Review*, 4 (1933), 324–35.

Darby, H. C. (ed.), *A New Historical Geography of England* (Cambridge, 1973).

Davis, N. Z., 'Women in the Crafts in Sixteenth-Century Lyon', *Feminist Studies*, 8 (1982), 47–80.

Day, J., 'On the Status of Women in Medieval Sardinia', in J. Kirshner and S. F. Wemple (eds.), *Women of the Medieval World* (Oxford, 1985), 304–16.

Desportes, P., 'La Population de Reims au XVe siècle', *Moyen Âge*, 72 (1966), 463–509.

Diefendorfer, B. B., 'Widowhood and Remarriage in Sixteenth-Century Paris', *Journal of Family History*, 7 (1982), 379–95.

Dillard, H., *Daughters of the Reconquest: Women in Castilian Town Society* (Cambridge, 1984).

Dixon, E., 'Craftswomen of the Livre des Métiers', *Economic Journal*, 5 (1895), 209–28.

Dobson, R. B., 'Admissions to the Freedom of the City of York in the Late Middle Ages', *Economic History Review*, 2nd ser. 23 (1973), 1–22.

—— 'Urban Decline in Late Medieval England', *Transactions of the Royal Historical Society*, 5th ser. 27 (1977), 1–22.

—— 'Cathedral Chapters and Cathedral Cities: York, Durham, and Carlisle in the Fifteenth Century', *Northern History*, 19 (1983), 15–44.

—— 'Mendicant Ideal and Practice in Late Medieval York', in P. V. Addyman and V. E. Black (eds.), *Archaeological Papers from York presented to M. W. Barley* (York, 1984), 109–22.

Donahue, C., 'The Canon Law on the Formation of Marriage and Social Practice in the Later Middle Ages', *Journal of Family History*, 8 (1983), 144–58.

Drake, F., *Eboracum* (London, 1736).

Dyer, A. D., 'Northampton in 1524', *Northamptonshire Past and Present*, 6 (1979), 73–80.

Dyer, C., *Lords and Peasants in a Changing Society: The Estates of the Bishopric of Worcester, 680–1540* (Cambridge, 1980).

—— 'Documentary Evidence: Problems and Enquiries', in G. Astill and A. Grant (eds.), *The Countryside of Medieval England* (Oxford, 1988), 12–35.

—— *Standards of Living in the Later Middle Ages: Social Change in England c.1200–1520* (Cambridge, 1989).

—— 'The Consumer and the Market in the Later Middle Ages', *Economic History Review*, 2nd ser. 42 (1989), 305–27.

Earle, P., 'The Female Labour Market in London in the Late Seventeenth and Early Eighteenth Centuries', *Economic History Review*, 2nd ser. 42 (1989), 328–53.

Faith, R., 'The "Great Rumour" of 1377 and Peasant Ideology', in R. H. Hilton and T. H. Aston (eds.), *The English Rising of 1381* (Cambridge, 1984), 43–73.

Fauve-Chamoux, A., 'The Importance of Women in an Urban Environment: The Example of the Rheims Household at the Beginning of the Industrial Revolution', in R. Wall (ed.), *Family Forms in Historic Europe* (Cambridge, 1983), 475–92.

Finch, A., 'Parental Authority and the Problem of Clandestine Marriage in the Later Middle Ages', *Law and History Review*, 8 (1990), 189–201.

Finnegan, F., *Poverty and Prostitution* (Cambridge, 1979).

Finucane, R. C., *Miracles and Pilgrims: Popular Beliefs in Medieval England* (London, 1977).

Fleming, P. W., 'Charity, Faith, and the Gentry of Kent, 1422–1529', in A. J. Pollard (ed.), *Property and Politics: Essays in Later Medieval English History* (Gloucester, 1984), 36–58.

Franklin, P., 'Peasant Widows' "Liberation" and Remarriage before the Black Death', *Economic History Review*, 2nd ser. 39 (1986), 186–204.

Geremek, B., *The Margins of Society in Late Medieval Paris*, trans. J. Birrell (Cambridge, 1987).

Gillis, J. R., *For Better, for Worse: British Marriages, 1600 to the Present* (New York, 1985).

Gittins, D., *Fair Sex: Family Size and Structure, 1900–39* (London, 1982).

Gold, P. S., *The Lady and the Virgin: Image, Attitude, and Experience in Twelfth-Century France* (Chicago, 1985).

Goldberg, P. J. P., 'Female Labour, Service and Marriage in the Late Medieval Urban North', *Northern History*, 22 (1986), 18–38.

—— 'Mortality and Economic Change in the Diocese of York, 1390–1514', *Northern History*, 24 (1988), 38–55.

Goldberg, P. J. P., 'Urban Identity and the Poll Taxes of 1377, 1379, and 1380–1', *Economic History Review*, 2nd ser. 43 (1990), 194–216.

—— 'The Public and the Private: Women in the Pre-Plague Economy', in P. R. Coss and S. Lloyd (eds.), *Thirteenth-Century England III* (Woodbridge, 1991), 75–89.

Goose, N., 'Household Size and Structure in Early-Stuart Cambridge', *Social History*, 5 (1980), 347–85.

Gottfried, R. S., *Epidemic Disease in Fifteenth Century England* (Leicester, 1978).

Graham, H., '"A Woman's Work . . .": Labour and Gender in the Medieval Countryside', in P. J. P. Goldberg (ed.), *Woman is a Worthy Wight: Women in English Society c.1200–1500* (Stroud, 1992), 126–48.

Green, B. and Young, R. M. R., *Norwich: The Growth of a City* (Norwich, 1981).

Grew, F. and de Neergaard, M., *Shoes and Pattens* (Medieval Finds From Excavations in London, 2; London, 1988).

Hajnal, J., 'European Marriage Patterns in Perspective', in D. V. Glass and D. E. V. Eversley (eds.), *Population in History: Essays in Historical Demography* (London, 1965), 101–43.

—— 'Two Kinds of Pre-Industrial Household Formation System', in R. Wall (ed.), *Family Forms in Historic Europe* (Cambridge, 1983), 65–104.

Hallam, H. E., 'Some Thirteenth Century Censuses', *Economic History Review*, 2nd ser. 14 (1957), 352–61.

Hammer, C. I., 'The Mobility of Skilled Labour in Late Medieval England: Some Oxford Evidence', *Vierteljahrschrift für Social- und Wirtschaftsgeschichte*, 63 (1976), 194–210.

Hanawalt, B. A., 'Peasant Women's Contribution to the Home Economy in Late Medieval England', in ead. (ed.), *Women and Work in Preindustrial Europe* (Bloomington, Ind., 1986), 3–20, also printed as ch. 9 of ead., *The Ties that Bound: Peasant Families in Medieval England* (New York, 1986).

—— 'Seeking the Flesh and Blood of Manorial Families', *Journal of Medieval History*, 14 (1988), 33–45.

Harrison, B., 'Evidence for Main Roads in the Vale of York during the Medieval Period', *Sciant Presentes*, 13 (Yorkshire Archaeological Society, Medieval Section; 1984), 3–8.

Hatcher, J., *English Tin Production and Trade before 1500* (Oxford, 1973).

—— *Plague, Population and the English Economy, 1348–1530* (London, 1977).

—— 'Mortality in the Fifteenth Century: Some New Evidence', *Economic History Review*, 2nd ser. 39 (1986), 19–38.

—— and Barker, T. C., *A History of British Pewter* (London, 1974).

Heath, P., 'North Sea Fishing in the Fifteenth Century: The Scarborough Fleet', *Northern History*, 3 (1968), 53–69.

—— 'Urban Piety in the Later Middle Ages: The Evidence of Hull Wills', in R. B. Dobson (ed.), *The Church, Politics and Patronage in the Fifteenth Century* (Gloucester, 1984), 209–34.

Heaton, H., *The Yorkshire Woollen and Worsted Industries* (Oxford, 1920).

Helmholz, R. H., *Marriage Litigation in Medieval England* (Cambridge, 1974).

Herlihy, D., *Medieval Households* (Cambridge, Mass., 1985).

—— and Klapisch-Zuber, C., *Les Toscans et leurs familles: Une étude du Catasto Florentin de 1427* (Paris, 1978).

—— —— *Tuscans and their families: A Study of the Florentine Catasto of 1427* (New Haven, Conn., 1985).

Hilton, R. H., 'Women in the Village', in id., *The English Peasantry in the Later Middle Ages* (Oxford, 1975), 95–110.

—— 'Lords, Burgesses and Hucksters', *Past and Present*, 97 (1982), 3–15; repr. in his *Class Conflict and the Crisis of Feudalism*, 194–204.

—— 'Small Town Society in England Before the Black Death', *Past and Present*, 105 (1984), 53–78.

—— *Class Conflict and the Crisis of Feudalism* (London, 1985).

Homans, G. C., *English Villagers of the Thirteenth Century* (Cambridge, Mass., 1941).

Hoskins, W. G., 'English Provincial Towns in the Early Sixteenth Century', *Transactions of the Royal Historical Society*, 5th ser. 6 (1956), 1–19.

Houlbrooke, R. A., *Church Courts and the People during the English Reformation, 1520–1570* (Oxford, 1979).

—— *The English Family, 1450–1700* (London, 1984).

—— 'Women's Social Life and Common Action in England from the Fifteenth Century to the Eve of the Civil War', *Continuity and Change*, 1 (1986), 171–89.

Howell, M. C., *Women, Production and Patriarchy in Late Medieval Cities* (Chicago, 1986).

—— 'Citizenship and Gender: Women's Political Status in Northern Medieval Cities', In M. Erler and M. Kowaleski (eds.), *Women and Power in the Middle Ages* (Athens, Ga., 1988), 37–60.

Hudson, A., *The Premature Reformation: Wycliffite Texts and Lollard History* (Oxford, 1988).

Hufton, O., 'Women without Men: Widows and Spinsters in Britain and France in the Eighteenth Century', *Journal of Family History*, 9 (1984), 355–76.

Hutton, D., 'Women in Fourteenth Century Shrewsbury', in L. Charles and L. Duffin (eds.), *Women and Work in Pre-Industrial England* (London, 1985), 83–99.

Index of Wills in the York Registry, 1389–1514 (Yorkshire Archaeological Society Record Ser. 6; 1889).

Index of Wills, etc. from the Dean and Chapter's Court, 1321–1636 (Yorkshire Archaeological Society Record Ser. 38; 1907).

Ingram, M., 'Spousals Litigation in the English Ecclesiastical Courts *c.*1350–*c.*1640', in R. B. Outhwaite (ed.), *Marriage and Society: Studies in the Social History of Marriage* (London, 1981), 35–57.

—— *Church Courts, Sex and Marriage in England, 1570–1640* (Cambridge, 1987).

Jacobsen, G., 'Women's Work and Women's Role: Ideology and Reality in Danish Urban Society, 1300–1550', *Scandinavian Economic History Review*, 31 (1983), 3–20.

Jordan, W. K., *The Charities of London, 1480–1660* (London, 1960).

Karras, R. M., 'The Regulation of Brothels in Late Medieval England', *Signs*, 14 (1989), 399–433.

Keene, D., *Survey of Medieval Winchester* (2 vols.; Winchester Studies, 2; Oxford, 1985).

Kermode, J. I., 'Urban Decline? The Flight from Office in Late Medieval York', *Economic History Review*, 2nd ser. 35 (1982), 179–98.

—— 'The Merchants of Three Northern English Towns', in C. H. Clough (ed.), *Profession, Vocation, and Culture in Later Medieval England* (Liverpool, 1982), 7–50.

—— 'Merchants, Overseas Trade, and Urban Decline: York, Beverley, and Hull, *c.*1380–1500', *Northern History*, 23 (1987), 51–73.

Kettle, A. J., 'City and Close: Lichfield in the Century before the Reformation', in C. M. Barron and C. Harper-Bill (eds.), *The Church in Pre-Reformation Society* (Woodbridge, 1986), 158–69.

Kitchen, F., *Brother to the Ox* (London, 1940).

Klapisch-Zuber, C., 'Demographic Decline and Household Structure', in ead., *Women, Family, and Ritual in Renaissance Florence* (Chicago, 1985), 23–35.

—— 'Female Celibacy and Service in Florence in the Fifteenth Century', in ead., *Women, Family, and Ritual in Renaissance Florence* (Chicago, 1985), 165–77.

—— 'Women Servants in Florence during the Fourteenth and Fifteenth Centuries', in B. A. Hanawalt (ed.), *Women and Work in Preindustrial Europe* (Bloomington, Ind., 1986), 56–80.

Kowaleski, M., 'Women's Work in a Market Town: Exeter in the Late Fourteenth Century', in B. A. Hanawalt (ed.), *Women and Work in Preindustrial Europe* (Bloomington, Ind., 1986), 145–64.

—— and Bennett, J. M., 'Crafts, Gilds, and Women in the Middle Ages', *Signs*, 14 (1989), 474–88.

Kramer, S., *The English Craft Gilds and the Government* (New York, 1905).

Kussmaul, A., *Servants in Husbandry in Early Modern England* (Cambridge, 1981).

Lacey, K. E., 'Women and Work in Fourteenth and Fifteenth Century London', in L. Charles and L. Duffin (eds.), *Women and Work in Pre-Industrial England* (London, 1985), 24–82.

Ladurie, E. le Roy, *Montaillou: Cathars and Catholics in a French Village, 1294–1324*, trans. B. Bray (Harmondsworth, 1980).

Lambert, M. D., *Two Thousand Years of Gild Life* (Hull, 1891).

Laslett, P., 'Size and Structure of the Household in England Over Three Centuries', *Population Studies*, 23 (1969), 199–223.

—— 'Characteristics of the Western Family Considered over Time', in id., *Family Life and Illicit Love in Earlier Generations* (Cambridge, 1977), 12–49.

—— 'Clayworth and Cogenhoe', in id., *Family Life and Illicit Love in Earlier Generations* (Cambridge, 1977), 50–101.

—— *The World We Have Lost Further Explored* (3rd edn., London, 1983).

Levine, D., '"For Their Own Reasons": Individual Marriage Decisions and Family Life', *Journal of Family History*, 7 (1982), 255–64.

Lévy, J.-P., 'L'Officialité de Paris et les questions familiales à la fin du XIVe siècle', in *Études d'histoire du droit canonique dédiées à Gabriel le Bras* (Paris, 1965), ii. 1265–94.

Lobel, M. D. and Johns, W. H. (eds.), *The Atlas of Historic Towns*, ii (London, 1975).

Lorcin, M.-T., *Vivre et mourir en Lyonnais à la fin du moyen âge* (Lyons, 1981).

Lucas, A. M., *Women in the Middle Ages: Religion, Marriage and Letters* (Brighton, 1983).

McClure, P., 'Patterns of Migration in the Late Middle Ages: The Evidence of English Place-Name Surnames', *Economic History Review*, 2nd ser. 32 (1979), 167–82.

McDonnell, J., 'Medieval Assarting Hamlets in Bilsdale, North-East Yorkshire', *Northern History*, 22 (1986), 269–79.

Macfarlane, A., *Marriage and Love in England, 1300–1840* (Oxford, 1986).

McIntosh, M. K., 'Servants and the Household Unit in an Elizabethan English Community', *Journal of Family History*, 9 (1984), 3–23.

—— *Autonomy and Community: The Royal Manor of Havering, 1200–1500* (Cambridge, 1986).

394   *Bibliography*

McIntosh, M. K., 'Local Change and Community Control in England', *Huntingdon Library Quarterly*, 49 (1986), 219–42.

Miller, E., 'Medieval York', in P. M. Tillot (ed.), *VCH, City of York* (Oxford, 1961), 25–116.

—— 'The Fortunes of the English Textile Industry during the Thirteenth Century', *Economic History Review*, 2nd ser. 18 (1965), 64–82.

Miller, K., Robinson, J., English, B., and Hall, I., *Beverley: An Archaeological and Architectural Study* (London, 1982).

Mitterauer, M., 'Servants and Youth', *Continuity and Change*, 5 (1990), 11–38.

Mols, R., *Introduction à la démographie historique des villes d'Europe* (3 vols.; Louvain, 1954–6).

Moran, J. H., *The Growth of English Schooling, 1340–1548: Learning, Literacy, and Laicization in Pre-Reformation York Diocese* (Princeton, NJ, 1985).

Nicholas, D., *The Domestic Life of a Medieval City: Women, Children and the Family in Fourteenth-Century Ghent* (Lincoln, Nebr., 1985).

North, T., 'Legerwite in the Thirteenth and Fourteenth Centuries', *Past and Present*, 111 (1986), 3–16.

Oman, C., *The Great Revolt of 1381* (2nd edn., Oxford, 1969).

Otis, L. L., *Prostitution in Medieval Society: The History of an Urban Institution in Languedoc* (Chicago, 1985).

Owen, D. M., 'White Annays and Others', in D. Baker (ed.), *Medieval Women* (Studies in Church History, Subsidia 1; Oxford, 1978), 331–46.

Page, W. (ed.), *VCH, Somerset*, ii (London, 1911).

Palliser, D. M., 'A Crisis in English Towns? The Case of York, 1460–1640', *Northern History*, 14 (1978), 108–25.

—— *Tudor York* (Oxford, 1979).

—— 'A Regional Capital as Magnet: Immigrants to York, 1477–1566', *Yorkshire Archaeological Journal*, 57 (1985), 111–23.

—— 'Urban Decay Revisited', in J. A. F. Thomson (ed.), *Towns and Townspeople in the Fifteenth Century* (Gloucester, 1988), 1–21.

Palmer, R. C., 'Contexts of Marriage in Medieval England: Evidence from the King's Court circa 1300', *Speculum*, 59 (1984), 42–67.

Pape, T., *Medieval Newcastle-Under-Lyme* (Manchester, 1928).

Parker, R., *The Subversive Stitch: Embroidery and the Making of the Feminine* (London, 1984).

Penn, S. A. C., 'Female Wage-Earners in Late Fourteenth-Century England', *Agricultural History Review*, 35 (1987), 1–14.

Perry, M. E., '"Lost Women" in Early Modern Seville: The Politics of Prostitution', *Feminist Studies*, 4 (1978), 195–214.

Pevsner, N., *The Buildings of England: Yorkshire, The West Riding* (Harmondsworth, 1967).

Phelps Brown, E. H. and Hopkins, S. V., 'Seven Centuries of the Price of Consumables, Compared with Builders' Wage-Rates', *Economica*, NS 23 (1956), 296–314.

Phythian-Adams, C., 'Urban Decay in Late Medieval England', in P. Abrams and E. A. Wrigley (eds.), *Towns in Society* (Cambridge, 1978), 1–32.

—— *Desolation of a City: Coventry and the Urban Crisis of the Late Middle Ages* (Cambridge, 1979).

Pia, M., 'The Industrial Position of Women in the Middle Ages', *Catholic History Review*, NS 4 (1925), 556–60.

Pinchbeck, I., *Women Workers and the Industrial Revolution, 1750–1850* (2nd edn., London, 1981).

Pirenne, H., 'Les Dénombrements de la population d'Ypres au XVe siècle', *Vierteljahrschrift für Social- und Wirtschaftsgeschichte*, 1 (1903), 1–32.

Platt, C., *The English Medieval Town* (London, 1979).

Pollard, A. J., 'The North-Eastern Economy and the Agrarian Crisis of 1438–1440', *Northern History*, 25 (1989), 88–105.

Pollock, F. and Maitland, F. W., *The History of English Law* (2nd edn., 2 vols.; Cambridge, 1898).

Poos, L. R., 'The Social Context of Statute of Labourers Enforcement', *Law and History Review*, 1 (1983), 27–52.

—— 'The Rural Population of Essex in the Later Middle Ages', *Economic History Review*, 2nd ser. 38 (1985), 515–30.

—— 'Population Turnover in Medieval Essex: The Evidence of some Early-Fourteenth-Century Tithing Lists', in L. Bonfield, R. M. Smith, and K. Wrightson (eds.), *The World We Have Gained: Histories of Population and Social Structure* (Oxford, 1986), 1–22.

—— and Smith, R. M., '"Legal Windows onto Historical Populations"? Recent Research on Demography and the Manor Court in England', *Law and History Review*, 2 (1984), 128–52.

—— '"Shades Still on the Window": A Reply to Zvi Razi', *Law and History Review*, 3 (1986), 409–29.

Postan, M. M., *The Medieval Economy and Society* (London, 1972).

—— 'The Costs of the Hundred Years War', in id., *Essays on Medieval Agriculture and General Problems of the Medieval Economy* (Cambridge, 1973), 63–80.

—— *Essays on Medieval Trade and Finance* (Cambridge, 1973).

Postles, D., 'Cleaning the Medieval Arable', *Agricultural History Review*, 37 (1989), 130–43.

Power, E. E., 'The Position of Women', in C. G. Crump and E. F. Jacobs (eds.), *The Legacy of the Middle Ages* (Oxford, 1926).

—— *Medieval Women* (Cambridge, 1975).

Prior, M., 'Women and the Urban Economy: Oxford, 1500–1800', in ead. (ed.), *Women in English Society, 1500–1800* (London, 1985), 93–117.

Raftis, J. A., *Tenure and Mobility: Studies in the Social History of the Medieval English Village* (Toronto, 1964).

Raine, A., *Mediaeval York* (London, 1955).

Raistrick, A., 'A Fourteenth Century Regional Survey', *Sociological Review*, 21 (1929), 241–9.

—— and Jennings, B., *A History of Lead Mining in the Pennines* (Newton Abbot, 1965).

Razi, Z., *Life, Marriage and Death in a Medieval Parish* (Cambridge, 1980).

—— 'The Use of Manor Court Rolls in Demographic Analysis: A Reconsideration', *Law and History Review*, 3 (1985), 191–200.

—— 'The Demographic Transparency of Manorial Court Rolls', *Law and History Review*, 5 (1987), 523–35.

Reffold, H., *Pie for Breakfast* (Cherry Burton, 1984).

Reynolds, S., *An Introduction to the History of English Medieval Towns* (Oxford, 1977).

Richter, O., 'Zur Bevölkerungs- und Vermögensstatistik Dresdens im 15. Jahrhundert', *Neues Archiv für Sächsische Geschichte und Alterthumskune*, 2 (1881), 273–89.

Rigby, S., 'Urban Decline in the Later Middle Ages', *Urban History Yearbook* (1979), 46–79.

Roberts, M., 'Sickles and Scythes: Women's Work and Men's Work at Harvest Time', *History Workshop*, 7 (1979), 3–28.

Robertson, W. D., '"And for my land thus hastow mordred me?" Land Tenure, the Cloth Industry, and the Wife of Bath', *Chaucer Review*, 14 (1980), 403–20.

Rogers, J. E. T., *A History of Agriculture and Prices in England* (8 vols.; Oxford, 1866–1902).

Roper, L., *The Holy Household: Women and Morals in Reformation Augsburg* (Oxford, 1989).

Rosser, G., *Medieval Westminster, 1200–1540* (Oxford, 1989).

Rossiaud, J., *Medieval Prostitution*, trans. L. G. Cochrane (Oxford, 1988).

Routh, P. E. S., 'A Gift and its Giver: John Walker and the East Window of Holy Trinity, Goodramgate, York', *Yorkshire Archaeological Journal*, 58 (1986), 109–21.

Rushton, P., 'The Broken Marriage in Early Modern England: Matrimonial Cases from the Durham Church Courts, 1560–1630', *Archaeologia Aeliana*, 5th ser. 13 (1985), 187–96.

Russell, J. C., *British Medieval Population* (Albuquerque, N.Mex., 1948).

Saul, A., 'English Towns in the Late Middle Ages: The Case of Great Yarmouth', *Journal of Medieval History*, 8 (1982), 75–88.

Schofield, R. S., 'The Geographical Distribution of Wealth in England, 1334–1649', *Economic History Review*, 2nd ser. 18 (1965), 145–64.

—— 'English Marriage Patterns Revisited', *Journal of Family History*, 10 (1985), 2–20.

—— 'Age-Specific Mobility in an Eighteenth-Century Rural English Parish', in P. Clark and D. Souden (eds.), *Migration and Society in Early Modern England* (London, 1987), 253–66.

Segalen, M., *Love and Power in the Peasant Family: Rural France in the Nineteenth Century*, trans. S. Matthews (Oxford, 1983).

Shahar, S., *The Fourth Estate: A History of Women in the Middle Ages* (London, 1983).

Sheehan, M. M., 'The Influence of Canon Law on the Property Rights of Married Women in England', *Medieval Studies*, 25 (1963), 109–24.

—— 'The Formation and Stability of Marriage in Fourteenth-Century England: Evidence of an Ely Register', *Medieval Studies*, 33 (1971), 228–63.

—— 'Marriage Theory and Practice in the Conciliar Legislation and Diocesan Statutes', *Medieval Studies*, 40 (1978), 408–60.

—— 'The Wife of Bath and Her Four Sisters: Reflections on a Woman's Life in the Age of Chaucer', *Medievalia et Humanistica*, NS 13 (1985), 23–42.

Sherborne, J. W., *The Port of Bristol in the Middle Ages* (Historical Association, Bristol Branch, Pamphlet, 43; 1965).

Smith, R. M., 'Some Reflections on the Evidence for the Origins of the "European Marriage Pattern" in England', in C. C. Harris (ed.), *The Sociology of the Family: New Directions for Britain* (Sociological Review Monograph, 28; Keele, 1979), 74–112.

—— 'The People of Tuscany and their Families in the Fifteenth Century: Medieval or Mediterranean?' *Journal of Family History*, 6 (1981), 107–28.

—— 'Hypothèses sur la nuptialité en Angleterre aux XIIIᵉ–XIVᵉ siècles', *Annales: ESC*, 38 (1983), 107–36.

—— 'Marriage Processes in the English Past: Some Continuities', in L. Bonfield, R. M. Smith, and K. Wrightson (eds.), *The World We Have Gained: Histories of Population and Social Structure* (Oxford, 1986), 43–99.

Snell, K. D. M., *Annals of the Labouring Poor: Social Change and Agrarian England, 1660–1900* (Cambridge, 1985).

Souden, D., 'Migrants and the Population Structure of Later Seventeenth-Century Provincial Cities and Market Towns', in P. Clark (ed.),

The Transformation of English Towns, 1600–1800 (London, 1984), 133–68.

Swanson, H. C., *Building Craftsmen in Late Medieval York* (Borthwick Paper, 63; 1983).

—— 'The Illusion of Economic Structure: Craft Guilds in Late Medieval English Towns', *Past and Present*, 121 (1988), 29–48.

—— *Medieval Artisans: An Urban Class in Late Medieval England* (Oxford, 1989).

Tanner, N. P., *The Church in Late Medieval Norwich, 1370–1532* (Toronto, 1984).

Thomson, J. A. F., 'Piety and Charity in Late Medieval London', *Journal of Ecclesiastical History*, 16 (1965), 178–95.

Thrupp, S. L., *The Merchant Class of Medieval London, 1300–1500* (Chicago, 1948).

Tillot, P. M. (ed.), *VCH, City of York* (Oxford, 1961).

Todd, B. J., 'The Remarrying Widow: A Stereotype Reconsidered', in M. Prior (ed.), *Women in English Society, 1500–1800* (London, 1985), 54–92.

Vale, M. G. A., *Piety, Charity and Literacy among the Yorkshire Gentry* (Borthwick Paper, 50; 1976).

Vann, R. T., 'Wills and the Family in an English Town: Banbury, 1550–1800', *Journal of Family History*, 4 (1979), 346–67.

Veale, E. M., *The English Fur Trade in the Later Middle Ages* (Oxford, 1966).

Vinyoles, T. M., *Les Barcelonines a les darreries de l'edat mitjana* (Barcelona, 1976).

Wall, R., 'Mean Household Size in England from Printed Sources', in P. Laslett (ed.), *Household and Family in Past Time* (Cambridge, 1972), 159–203.

—— 'Regional and Temporal Variations in English Household Structure from 1650', in J. Hobcraft and P. Rees (eds.), *Regional Demographic Development* (London, 1980), 89–113.

—— 'The Composition of Households in a Population of 6 Men to 10 Women: South-East Bruges in 1814', in id. (ed.), *Family Forms in Historic Europe* (Cambridge, 1983), 421–74.

—— 'Leaving Home and the Process of Household Formation in Pre-Industrial England', *Continuity and Change*, 2 (1987), 77–101.

Wedermeyer, E., 'Social Groupings at the Fair of St Ives (1275–1302)', *Medieval Studies*, 32 (1970), 27–59.

Weir, D. R., 'Rather Never than Late: Celibacy and Age at Marriage in English Cohort Fertility, 1541–1871', *Journal of Family History*, 9 (1984), 340–54.

Wensky, M., 'Women's Guilds in Cologne in the Later Middle Ages', *Journal of European Economic History*, 11 (1982), 631–50.

Wiesner, M. E., *Working Women in Renaissance Germany* (New Brunswick, NJ, 1986).

Wilson, K. P., 'The Port of Chester in the Fifteenth Century', *Transactions of the Historical Society of Lancashire and Cheshire*, 117 (1965), 1–15.

Woodcock, B. L., *Medieval Ecclesiastical Courts in the Diocese of Canterbury* (London, 1952).

Woodward, D. M., 'Freeman's Rolls', *Local Historian*, 9 (1970), 89–95.

Wright, S., '"Churmaids, Huswyfes and Hucksters": The Employment of Women in Tudor and Stuart Salisbury', in L. Charles and L. Duffin (eds.), *Women and Work in Pre-Industrial England* (London, 1985), 100–21.

Wrigley, E. A. and Schofield, R. S., *The Population History of England, 1541–1871: A Reconstruction* (London, 1981).

Unpublished Theses and Papers

Brown, S., 'The Peculiar Jurisdiction of York Minster during the Middle Ages', D.Phil. thesis (York, 1980).

Butcher, A. F., 'Freemen Admissions and Urban Occupations: Towards a Dynamic Analysis', typescript paper (Urban History Conference, Canterbury; 1983).

Cullum, P. H., 'Hospitals and Charitable Provision in Medieval Yorkshire, 936–1547', D.Phil. thesis (York, 1989).

Fenwick, C. C., 'The English Poll Taxes of 1377, 1379 and 1381: A Critical Examination of the Returns', Ph.D. thesis (London, 1983).

Finch, A. J., 'Crime and Marriage in Three Late Medieval Ecclesiastical Jurisdictions: Cerisy, Rochester and Hereford', D.Phil. thesis (York, 1988).

Kowaleski, M., 'Women and Work in Medieval English Seaports', typescript paper (Berkshire Conference on Women's History, Smith College, 1984).

Rees Jones, S. R., 'Property, Tenure and Rents: Some Aspects of the Topography and Economy of Medieval York', D.Phil. thesis (York, 1987).

Swanson, H. C., 'Craftsmen and Industry in Late Medieval York', D.Phil. thesis (York, 1980).

Index